CANADA

THE NORTHEAST
26–53

THE WEST
128–155

THE MIDWEST
84–113

THE SOUTHEAST
54–83

THE SOUTHWEST
114–127

MEXICO

BAHAMAS

CUBA

NATIONAL GEOGRAPHIC
United States
ATLAS
for **YOUNG EXPLORERS**

From the rugged West (near right) to the rounded mountains of the East (far right), the United States has a landscape as diverse as its people. The varied land and vegetation of the contiguous United States can be seen in the large photograph, which was made by combining satellite images.

NATIONAL GEOGRAPHIC
United States
ATLAS
for YOUNG EXPLORERS

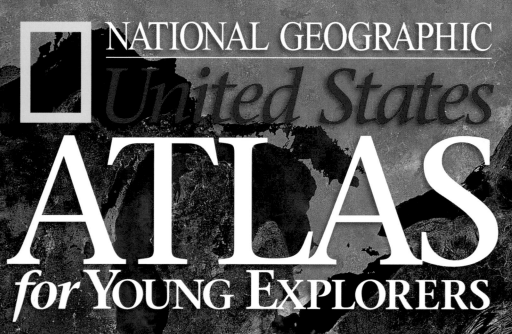

NATIONAL GEOGRAPHIC SOCIETY
WASHINGTON, D.C.

Photographs from Tony Stone Images

Contents

The Physical United States

The Political United States

The Northeast

SAILING, PAGE 31

The Southeast

COTTON, PAGE 59

A rainbow arches over Denali National Park, in Alaska.

The Midwest

84

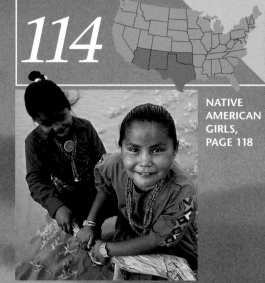

MOUNT RUSHMORE, PAGE 88

The Southwest

114

NATIVE AMERICAN GIRLS, PAGE 118

The West

128

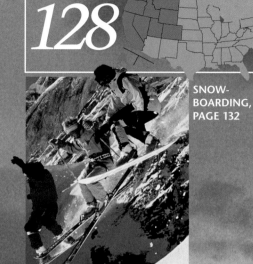

SNOW-BOARDING, PAGE 132

How To Use This Atlas

The maps in this atlas can tell you many things about the United States. Those that immediately follow this section give you information about the whole country, such as its physical features, federal lands, and population.

Then you'll see the states organized into five regions. Each regional section opens with a large photograph showing a landscape in the region and a smaller one that relates to human use of the land. Then a physical map of the region shows mountains, lakes, rivers, deserts, and so forth. After that, a photographic essay lets you "see" the area in words and pictures.

From there, you're ready to meet the states themselves. Each is represented by a political map (like the one of New York, detailed below), a description of the state, and a box with statistics and other useful facts. The back of this atlas has more statistics about the U.S., a glossary, and an index that will help you find any place-name in this atlas.

The Regions of the United States

In this atlas, the 50 states are grouped into five regions: the Northeast, Southeast, Midwest, Southwest, and West. This breakdown is based on what is being taught in most U.S. schools. States within a region have some things in common. Agriculture unites states in the Midwest, for example, where wheat and corn grow in seemingly endless fields. Colors make it easy to identify the states within each region.

Map Icons

The key below names the small pictures, or icons, that tell you where important economic activities take place in each state. It also identifies the symbols that show towns, boundaries, and natural features.

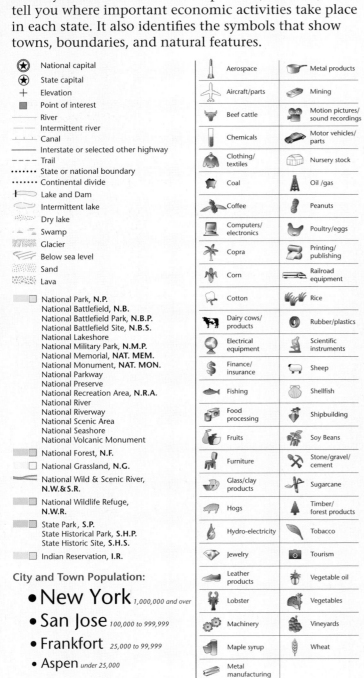

⊛	National capital
⭑	State capital
+	Elevation
■	Point of interest
	River
	Intermittent river
	Canal
	Interstate or selected other highway
	Trail
	State or national boundary
	Continental divide
	Lake and Dam
	Intermittent lake
	Dry lake
	Swamp
	Glacier
	Below sea level
	Sand
	Lava

National Park, N.P.
National Battlefield, N.B.
National Battlefield Park, N.B.P.
National Battlefield Site, N.B.S.
National Lakeshore
National Military Park, N.M.P.
National Memorial, NAT. MEM.
National Monument, NAT. MON.
National Parkway
National Preserve
National Recreation Area, N.R.A.
National River
National Riverway
National Scenic Area
National Seashore
National Volcanic Monument

National Forest, N.F.

National Grassland, N.G.

National Wild & Scenic River, N.W.&S.R.

National Wildlife Refuge, N.W.R.

State Park, S.P.
State Historical Park, S.H.P.
State Historic Site, S.H.S.

Indian Reservation, I.R.

City and Town Population:

● **New York** 1,000,000 and over

● **San Jose** 100,000 to 999,999

● **Frankfort** 25,000 to 99,999

● **Aspen** under 25,000

Aerospace		Metal products	
Aircraft/parts		Mining	
Beef cattle		Motion pictures/ sound recordings	
Chemicals		Motor vehicles/ parts	
Clothing/ textiles		Nursery stock	
Coal		Oil /gas	
Coffee		Peanuts	
Computers/ electronics		Poultry/eggs	
Copra		Printing/ publishing	
Corn		Railroad equipment	
Cotton		Rice	
Dairy cows/ products		Rubber/plastics	
Electrical equipment		Scientific instruments	
Finance/ insurance		Sheep	
Fishing		Shellfish	
Food processing		Shipbuilding	
Fruits		Soy Beans	
Furniture		Stone/gravel/ cement	
Glass/clay products		Sugarcane	
Hogs		Timber/ forest products	
Hydro-electricity		Tobacco	
Jewelry		Tourism	
Leather products		Vegetable oil	
Lobster		Vegetables	
Machinery		Vineyards	
Maple syrup		Wheat	
Metal manufacturing			

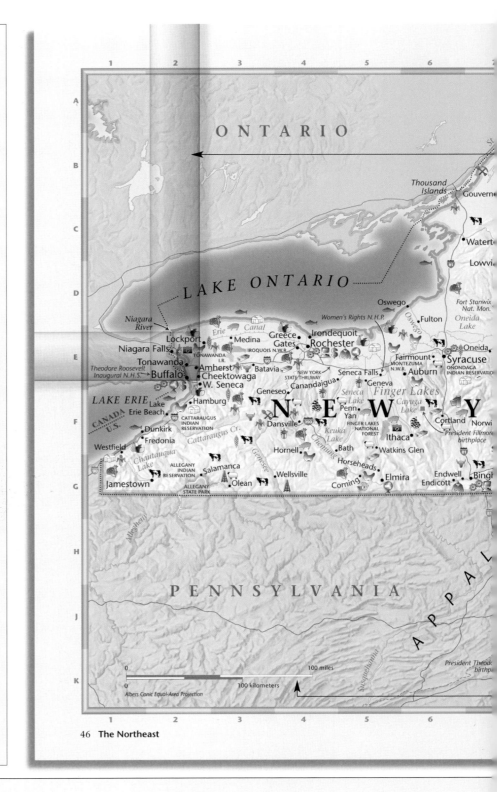

46 The Northeast

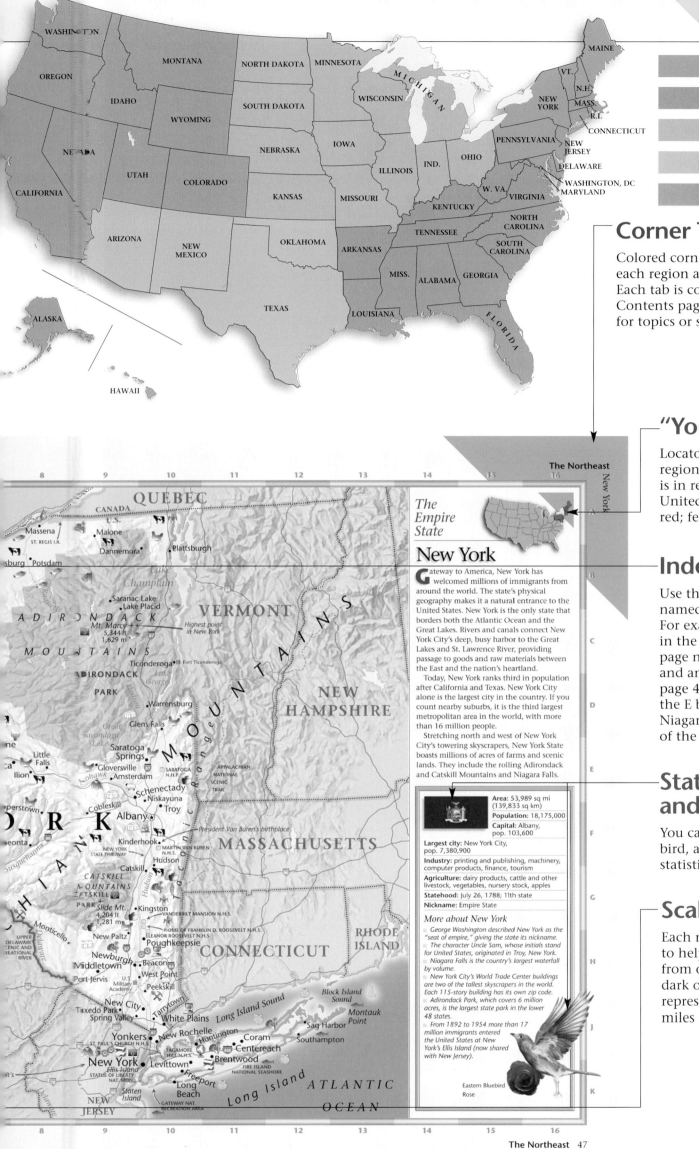

| Northeast |
| Southeast |
| Midwest |
| Southwest |
| West |

Corner Tabs

Colored corner tabs make it easy to find each region as you flip through this atlas. Each tab is color-coded to a heading on the Contents pages. These headings and titles for topics or states appear on each tab.

"You Are Here"

Locator maps show you where each region and state within the region is in relation to the rest of the United States. Regions are shown in red; featured states are in yellow.

Index and Grid

Use the Index to find any place named on the maps in this atlas. For example, look up Niagara Falls in the Index. Next to the name is a page number in bold type, a letter, and another number (**46** E2). Go to page 46. Draw imaginary lines from the E bar and the 2 bar on the grid. Niagara Falls will be within the area of the intersecting lines.

State Flag, Bird, and Flower

You can find the state flag, state bird, and state flower with the statistics box for each state.

Scales

Each map in the atlas has a scale to help you find out how far it is from one place to another. Every dark or light bar on the scale represents a specific number of miles (or kilometers) on the map.

The Empire State

New York

Gateway to America, New York has welcomed millions of immigrants from around the world. The state's physical geography makes it a natural entrance to the United States. New York is the only state that borders both the Atlantic Ocean and the Great Lakes. Rivers and canals connect New York City's deep, busy harbor to the Great Lakes and St. Lawrence River, providing passage to goods and raw materials between the East and the nation's heartland.

Today, New York ranks third in population after California and Texas. New York City alone is the largest city in the country. If you count nearby suburbs, it is the third largest metropolitan area in the world, with more than 16 million people.

Stretching north and west of New York City's towering skyscrapers, New York State boasts millions of acres of farms and scenic lands. They include the rolling Adirondack and Catskill Mountains and Niagara Falls.

Area: 53,989 sq mi (139,833 sq km)
Population: 18,175,000
Capital: Albany, pop. 103,600
Largest city: New York City, pop. 7,380,900
Industry: printing and publishing, machinery, computer products, finance, tourism
Agriculture: dairy products, cattle and other livestock, vegetables, nursery stock, apples
Statehood: July 26, 1788; 11th state
Nickname: Empire State

More about New York

- George Washington described New York as the "seat of empire," giving the state its nickname.
- The character Uncle Sam, whose initials stand for United States, originated in Troy, New York.
- Niagara Falls is the country's largest waterfall by volume.
- New York City's World Trade Center buildings are two of the tallest skyscrapers in the world. Each 115-story building has its own zip code.
- Adirondack Park, which covers 6 million acres, is the largest state park in the lower 48 states.
- From 1892 to 1954 more than 17 million immigrants entered the United States at New York's Ellis Island (now shared with New Jersey).

Eastern Bluebird
Rose

The Physical United States

From sea to shining sea, the United States spans about 3,000 miles (4828 km) from its east to west coasts. On this physical map you will see natural features of the land, including rivers, lakes, mountains, and deserts. Shading shows differences in elevation, or height of the land above sea level. Colors identify vegetation regions. The map shows state boundaries so that you can check out the landscape in each state. At the top of the page, a cross-section of the country from west to east shows the elevation of the land on a line between San Francisco and Washington, D.C.

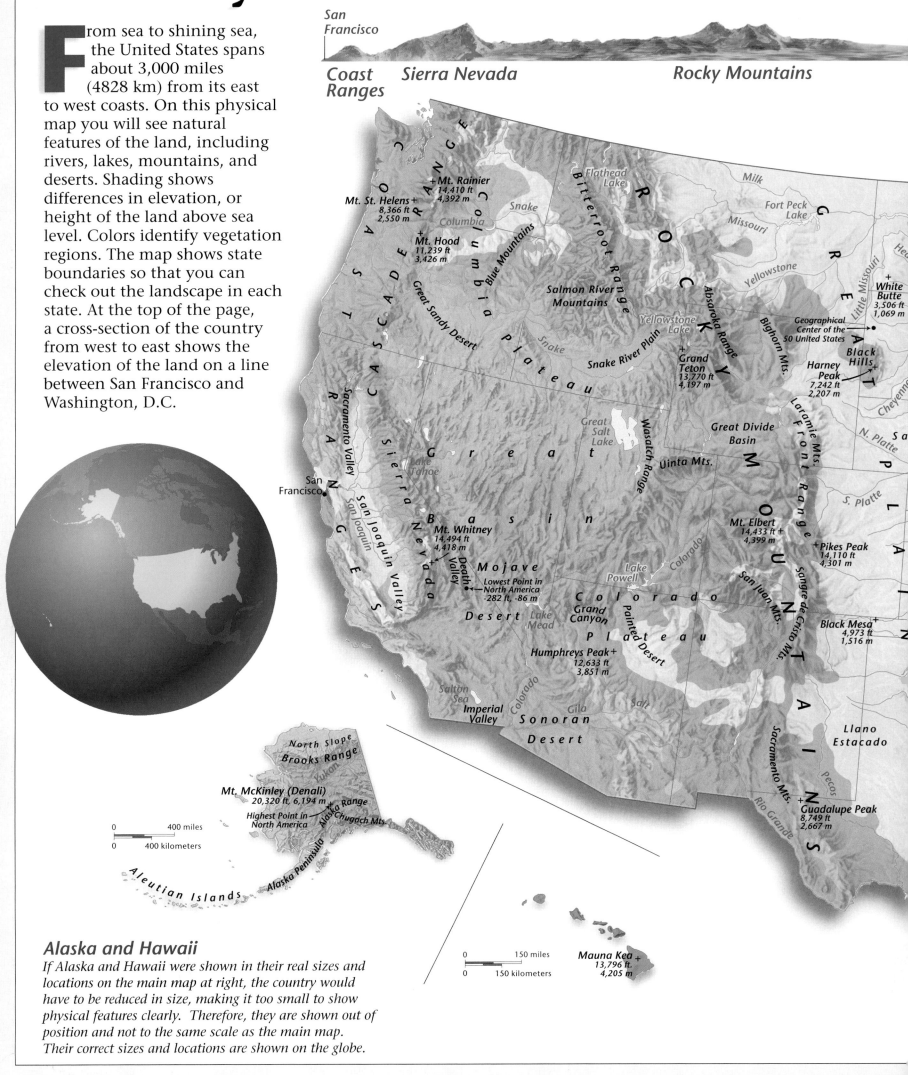

San Francisco

Coast Ranges   Sierra Nevada   Rocky Mountains

Mt. Rainier
14,410 ft
4,392 m

Mt. St. Helens+
8,366 ft
2,550 m

Mt. Hood
11,239 ft
3,426 m

Flathead Lake

Milk

Fort Peck Lake

Missouri

White Butte
3,506 ft
1,069 m

Columbia

Snake

Blue Mountains

Great Sandy Desert

Salmon River Mountains

Yellowstone

Little Missouri

Geographical Center of the 50 United States

Bitterroot Range

Columbia Plateau

Yellowstone Lake

Snake

Snake River Plain

Absaroka Range

Grand Teton
13,770 ft
4,197 m

Bighorn Mts.

Harney Peak
7,242 ft
2,207 m

Black Hills

Cheyenne

Great Salt Lake

Wasatch Range

Great Divide Basin

Uinta Mts.

Laramie Mts.

Front Range

N. Platte

S. Platte

Sacramento Valley

San Joaquin

Lake Tahoe

San Joaquin Valley

Mt. Whitney
14,494 ft
4,418 m

Death Valley

Mojave

Lowest Point in North America
-282 ft, -86 m

Desert

Lake Mead

Grand Canyon

Lake Powell

Colorado

Colorado

Painted Desert

Mt. Elbert
14,433 ft
4,399 m

San Juan Mts.

Pikes Peak
14,110 ft
4,301 m

Black Mesa
4,973 ft
1,516 m

Sangre de Cristo Mts.

Humphreys Peak+
12,633 ft
3,851 m

Plateau

Salton Sea

Imperial Valley

Colorado

Gila

Salt

Sonoran Desert

Llano Estacado

Sacramento Mts.

Pecos

Guadalupe Peak
8,749 ft
2,667 m

Rio Grande

Alaska and Hawaii

If Alaska and Hawaii were shown in their real sizes and locations on the main map at right, the country would have to be reduced in size, making it too small to show physical features clearly. Therefore, they are shown out of position and not to the same scale as the main map. Their correct sizes and locations are shown on the globe.

North Slope

Brooks Range

Yukon

Mt. McKinley (Denali)
20,320 ft, 6,194 m
Highest Point in North America

Alaska Range

Chugach Mts.

Aleutian Islands

Alaska Peninsula

0   400 miles
0   400 kilometers

0   150 miles
0   150 kilometers

Mauna Kea +
13,796 ft.
4,205 m

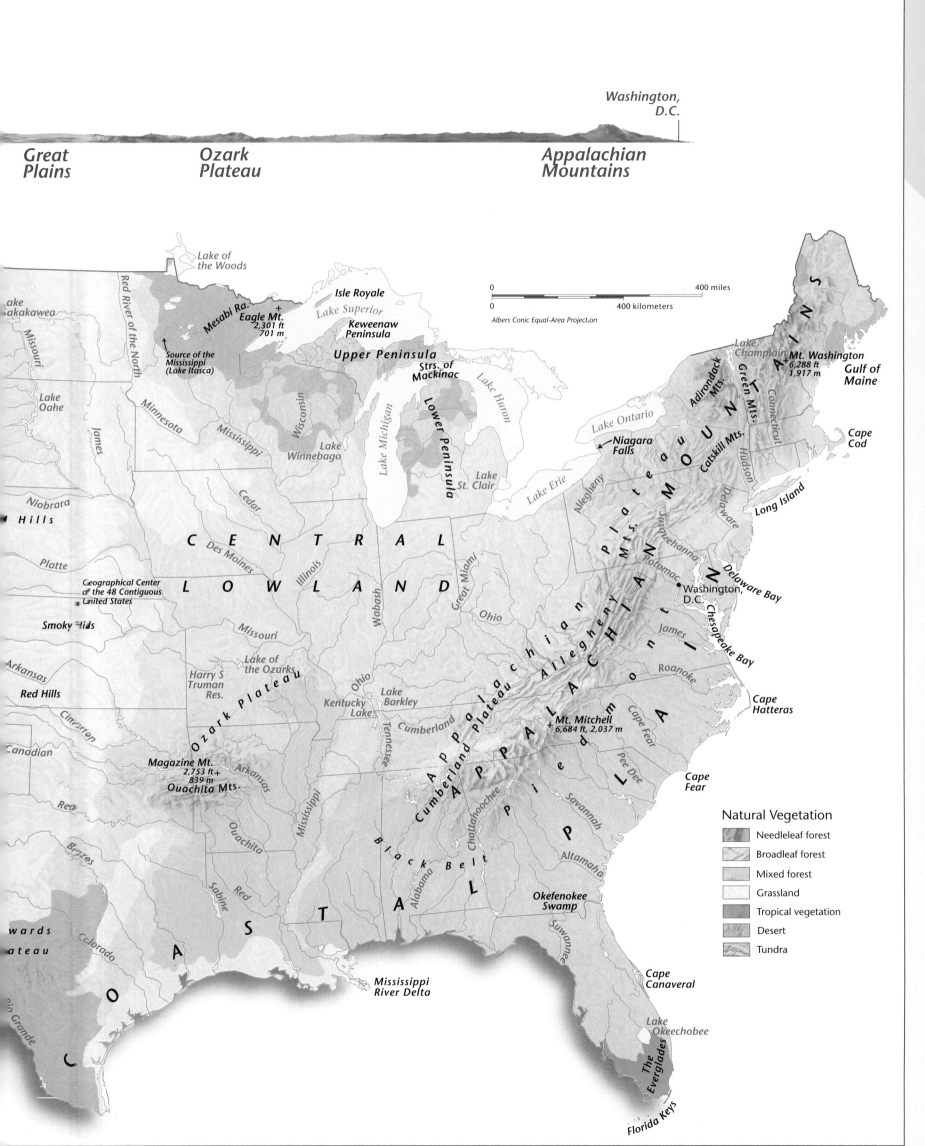

Washington,
D.C.

**Great
Plains**

**Ozark
Plateau**

**Appalachian
Mountains**

Lake of
the Woods

Mesabi Ra.
Eagle Mt.
2,301 ft
701 m

Source of the
Mississippi
(Lake Itasca)

Isle Royale

Lake Superior

Keweenaw
Peninsula

Upper Peninsula

Strs. of
Mackinac

Lake Huron

Lake
Champlain

Adirondack
Mts.

Green Mts.

Mt. Washington
6,288 ft
1,917 m

Gulf of
Maine

0   400 miles

0   400 kilometers

Albers Conic Equal-Area Projection

Lake
Sakakawea

Missouri

Lake
Oahe

James

Red River of the North

Minnesota

Mississippi

Cedar

Lake
Winnebago

Wisconsin

Lake
Michigan

Lower Peninsula

Lake
St. Clair

Lake Ontario

Niagara
Falls

Lake Erie

Allegheny

Catskill Mts.

Hudson

Connecticut

Delaware

Cape
Cod

Long Island

Niobrara

Hills

Platte

Geographical Center
of the 48 Contiguous
United States

Smoky Hills

Arkansas

Red Hills

Cimarron

Canadian

Rea

Edwards
Plateau

Colorado

Rio Grande

C E N T R A L

Des Moines

L O W L A N D

Illinois

Wabash

Great Miami

Ohio

Missouri

Lake of
the Ozarks

Harry S
Truman
Res.

Ozark Plateau

Magazine Mt.
2,753 ft
839 m

Ouachita Mts.

Ohio

Kentucky
Lake

Lake
Barkley

Cumberland

Tennessee

Arkansas

Ouachita

Red

Sabine

Mississippi

Brazos

C   O   A   S   T   A   L

Alabama

Black   Belt

Chattahoochee

Mississippi
River Delta

Appalachian Plateau

Cumberland Plateau

A P P A L A C H I A N

Allegheny

Potomac

Washington,
D.C.

Delaware Bay

Chesapeake Bay

James

Roanoke

Cape Fear

Pee Dee

Mt. Mitchell
6,684 ft, 2,037 m

Savannah

Altamaha

Okefenokee
Swamp

Suwannee

M O U N T A I N S

Piedmont

P L A I N

Cape
Hatteras

Cape
Fear

Cape
Canaveral

Lake
Okeechobee

The Everglades

Florida Keys

Natural Vegetation

Needleleaf forest

Broadleaf forest

Mixed forest

Grassland

Tropical vegetation

Desert

Tundra

Natural Environment

The natural world that surrounds you is called the natural environment. It includes weather and climate plus the geologic forces that shape the Earth.

This map shows the country's many climate regions. Climate is determined by location—in mountains, near oceans, or deep in the continental interior—as well as by prevailing winds and distance from the Equator.

Climate regions have predictable weather patterns, but day-to-day weather can change suddenly, sometimes disastrously. Cool air from the Rockies that meets warm air from the Gulf of Mexico can spawn tornadoes. These are particularly common from Texas to Nebraska in a belt known as Tornado Alley. Without a mountain barrier, cold air from Canada sweeps across the plains and the Great Lakes, causing ice and snow storms. Snowmelt and heavy rains can lead to severe spring flooding. Each summer, the dry, leeward slopes of western mountains are ravaged by wildfires sparked by lightning.

Geology is another source of natural disasters. Earthquakes and volcanoes mark the Pacific coast, where vast geologic plates interact with each other.

Columbia River, 1996 and 1997 Columbia

Snake

Colorado

Gila

Gila River, 1993

ALASKA

0   400 miles
0   400 kilometers

HAWAII

0   150 miles
0   150 kilometers

◄ *Slim and deadly, a tornado touches down in Texas. Some 800 to 1,000 twisters kill 70 to 80 people a year in the United States.*

▶ **Battling** *floodwaters, people try to paddle a canoe through the streets of an Iowa town in the great Midwest flood of 1993.*

◄ **Blinding** *snow forces a farmer to use a guide rope to get from his house to his barn and back. In blizzards people can get lost just a few feet from home.*

▶ **Blazing** *inferno, a forest fire engulfs trees in California. The U.S. spends $1 billion a year fighting wildfires.*

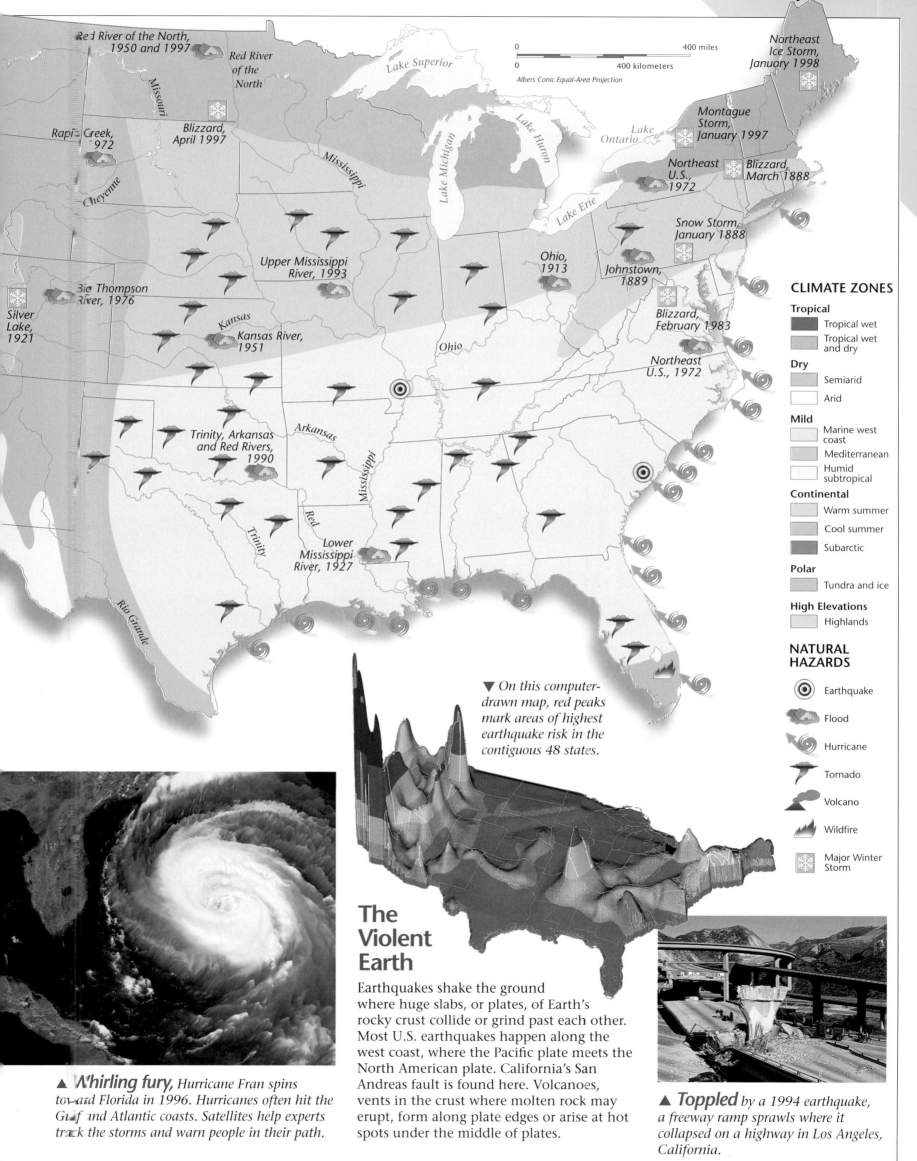

Red River of the North, 1950 and 1997

Red River of the North

Missouri

Lake Superior

0   400 miles
0   400 kilometers
Albers Conic Equal-Area Projection

Northeast Ice Storm, January 1998

Rapid Creek, 1972

Blizzard, April 1997

Lake Michigan

Lake Huron

Lake Ontario

Montague Storm, January 1997

Cheyenne

Mississippi

Lake Erie

Northeast U.S., 1972

Blizzard, March 1888

Big Thompson River, 1976

Upper Mississippi River, 1993

Ohio, 1913

Johnstown, 1889

Snow Storm, January 1888

Silver Lake, 1921

Kansas

Kansas River, 1951

Ohio

Blizzard, February 1983

Northeast U.S., 1972

Trinity, Arkansas and Red Rivers, 1990

Arkansas

Mississippi

Red

Trinity

Lower Mississippi River, 1927

Rio Grande

CLIMATE ZONES

Tropical
- Tropical wet
- Tropical wet and dry

Dry
- Semiarid
- Arid

Mild
- Marine west coast
- Mediterranean
- Humid subtropical

Continental
- Warm summer
- Cool summer
- Subarctic

Polar
- Tundra and ice

High Elevations
- Highlands

NATURAL HAZARDS

- ◉ Earthquake
- Flood
- Hurricane
- Tornado
- Volcano
- Wildfire
- Major Winter Storm

▼ *On this computer-drawn map, red peaks mark areas of highest earthquake risk in the contiguous 48 states.*

The Violent Earth

Earthquakes shake the ground where huge slabs, or plates, of Earth's rocky crust collide or grind past each other. Most U.S. earthquakes happen along the west coast, where the Pacific plate meets the North American plate. California's San Andreas fault is found here. Volcanoes, vents in the crust where molten rock may erupt, form along plate edges or arise at hot spots under the middle of plates.

▲ **Whirling fury,** *Hurricane Fran spins toward Florida in 1996. Hurricanes often hit the Gulf and Atlantic coasts. Satellites help experts track the storms and warn people in their path.*

▲ **Toppled** *by a 1994 earthquake, a freeway ramp sprawls where it collapsed on a highway in Los Angeles, California.*

Federal Lands

ederal lands belong to you. They are public lands, owned by the American people and managed by agencies of the U.S. government. About one-third of the United States is federal land. In some states federal lands take up only a small fraction of the total area. In Idaho, on the other hand, the government owns about two-thirds of the state. Federal lands also include historic buildings, statues such as the Statue of Liberty, parts of some rivers, and even ocean parks.

Of the many kinds of federal lands, the map shows national parks, Indian reservations, national forests, national wildlife refuges,

national wild and scenic rivers, national grasslands, and national marine sanctuaries.

Federal lands are, in part, a legacy of conservationists like John Muir, who convinced President Theodore Roosevelt to take a more active role in protecting America's natural resources. Before the early 1900s, the U.S. government sold or gave away nearly a billion acres to railroad companies, homesteaders, and others. A 1916 NATIONAL GEOGRAPHIC article titled "The Land of the Best" helped convince Congress to establish our National Park Service. The government continues to add protected areas today.

▲ **Giant sequoias** are among the trees protected in national forests. The country's 155 national forests cover nearly 200 million acres (81 million ha).

◄ **Young Blackfeet** girls get dressed for a powwow on their Montana reservation, one of 300 managed as federal lands.

▲ **White water** challenges a kayaker. The U.S. has more than 10,000 miles (16,000 km) of wild and scenic rivers.

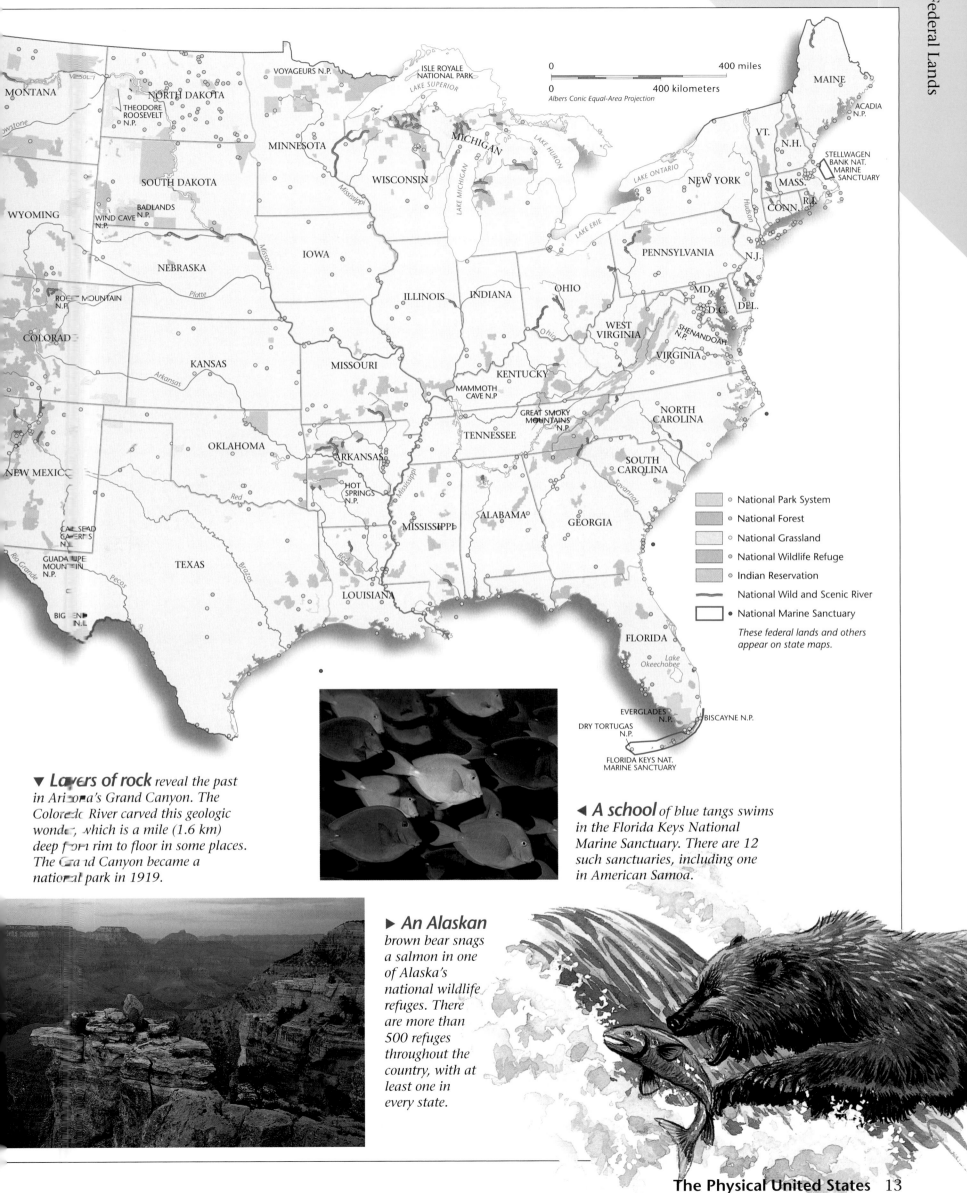

MONTANA

NORTH DAKOTA

VOYAGEURS N.P.

ISLE ROYALE NATIONAL PARK

LAKE SUPERIOR

MAINE

THEODORE ROOSEVELT N.P.

MINNESOTA

WISCONSIN

MICHIGAN

LAKE HURON

VT.

N.H.

ACADIA N.P.

SOUTH DAKOTA

LAKE MICHIGAN

LAKE ONTARIO

NEW YORK

MASS.

STELLWAGEN BANK NAT. MARINE SANCTUARY

WYOMING

BADLANDS N.P.

WIND CAVE N.P.

IOWA

LAKE ERIE

Hudson

CONN.

R.I.

NEBRASKA

Missouri

Platte

ILLINOIS

INDIANA

OHIO

PENNSYLVANIA

N.J.

MD.

D.C.

DEL.

COLORADO

ROCKY MOUNTAIN N.P.

KANSAS

Arkansas

MISSOURI

Ohio

WEST VIRGINIA

SHENANDOAH N.P.

VIRGINIA

KENTUCKY

MAMMOTH CAVE N.P.

GREAT SMOKY MOUNTAINS N.P.

NORTH CAROLINA

NEW MEXICO

OKLAHOMA

ARKANSAS

TENNESSEE

CARLSBAD CAVERNS N.P.

GUADALUPE MOUNTAIN N.P.

HOT SPRINGS N.P.

Red

Mississippi

SOUTH CAROLINA

Savannah

TEXAS

Brazos

MISSISSIPPI

ALABAMA

GEORGIA

Rio Grande

Pecos

Red

LOUISIANA

BIG BEND N.P.

FLORIDA

Lake Okeechobee

0   400 miles

0   400 kilometers

Albers Conic Equal-Area Projection

○ National Park System

● National Forest

○ National Grassland

● National Wildlife Refuge

○ Indian Reservation

National Wild and Scenic River

● National Marine Sanctuary

These federal lands and others appear on state maps.

EVERGLADES N.P.

BISCAYNE N.P.

DRY TORTUGAS N.P.

FLORIDA KEYS NAT. MARINE SANCTUARY

▼ **Layers of rock** *reveal the past in Arizona's Grand Canyon. The Colorado River carved this geologic wonder, which is a mile (1.6 km) deep from rim to floor in some places. The Grand Canyon became a national park in 1919.*

◄ **A school** *of blue tangs swims in the Florida Keys National Marine Sanctuary. There are 12 such sanctuaries, including one in American Samoa.*

▶ **An Alaskan** *brown bear snags a salmon in one of Alaska's national wildlife refuges. There are more than 500 refuges throughout the country, with at least one in every state.*

Endangered Species

From Alaska to Florida and from Hawaii to Maine, hundreds of species of animals and plants that once flourished now struggle to survive.

The greatest threat to wildlife is loss of habitat, or living space. The U.S. population is increasing by 2.4 million people a year. Today about 95 percent of our original forests are gone. Many wetlands, vital to fish, birds, and other animals, have been drained.

Animals have been hunted to near-extinction for food, fur, or blubber to make oil. Wolves and other predators have been killed to protect domestic herds. The bison, which once rumbled across the plains in vast herds, was nearly wiped out by hunters in the 19th century. In addition, people have harmed fish and the animals that eat them by unintentionally poisoning waters with toxic wastes, fertilizers, and pesticides.

In 1973 Congress passed the Endangered Species Act to protect species that were in danger of dying out. The law prohibits killing, collecting, or harming these species. Today, over 300 animals and 500 plant species are listed as endangered in the U.S. The map shows some of these endangered animals and their connection to human use of the land. Fortunately, new laws are helping many species make a comeback.

◀ **Wings spread** wide, a bald eagle dives for a fish. Once extremely endangered, the birds are increasing in numbers.

▼ **A crocodile** native to Florida gives her babies a lift. Hunted for its skin, which was used to make belts, purses, and other items, this species became endangered.

▼ **Biologists examine** a captive-bred red wolf that was introduced into the wild in North Carolina. These endangered wolves are now successfully breeding in their natural habitat.

0 | 400 miles
0 | 400 kilometers
Albers Conic Equal-Area Projection

LAND USE

- Barren land
- Farmland
- Farmland and Forest
- Forest
- Rangeland
- Tundra
- Urban Land
- Wetlands

▼ **The Fender's** blue butterfly was once feared extinct. In 1989 a colony was found in Oregon. Experts are working to preserve its habitat there.

▲ **The black-footed** ferret nearly became extinct when ranchers killed the prairie dogs it depended on for food. To save it, scientists are breeding ferrets in captivity and returning them to the wild.

▲ **Gentle manatees** swim in Florida's Crystal River. Boat propellers kill many of these marine mammals each year. Today only a few thousand survive.

The Political United States

Political maps reflect the way people organize themselves into towns, cities, states, and countries. This map shows state boundaries, state capitals, and large cities as well as some major natural features. Rivers and mountains often serve as boundaries. The 48 states that are connected—called the contiguous or conterminous United States—make up the large map. Alaska and Hawaii are shown as separate insets, each to its own scale. The globe below shows these two states in their real locations.

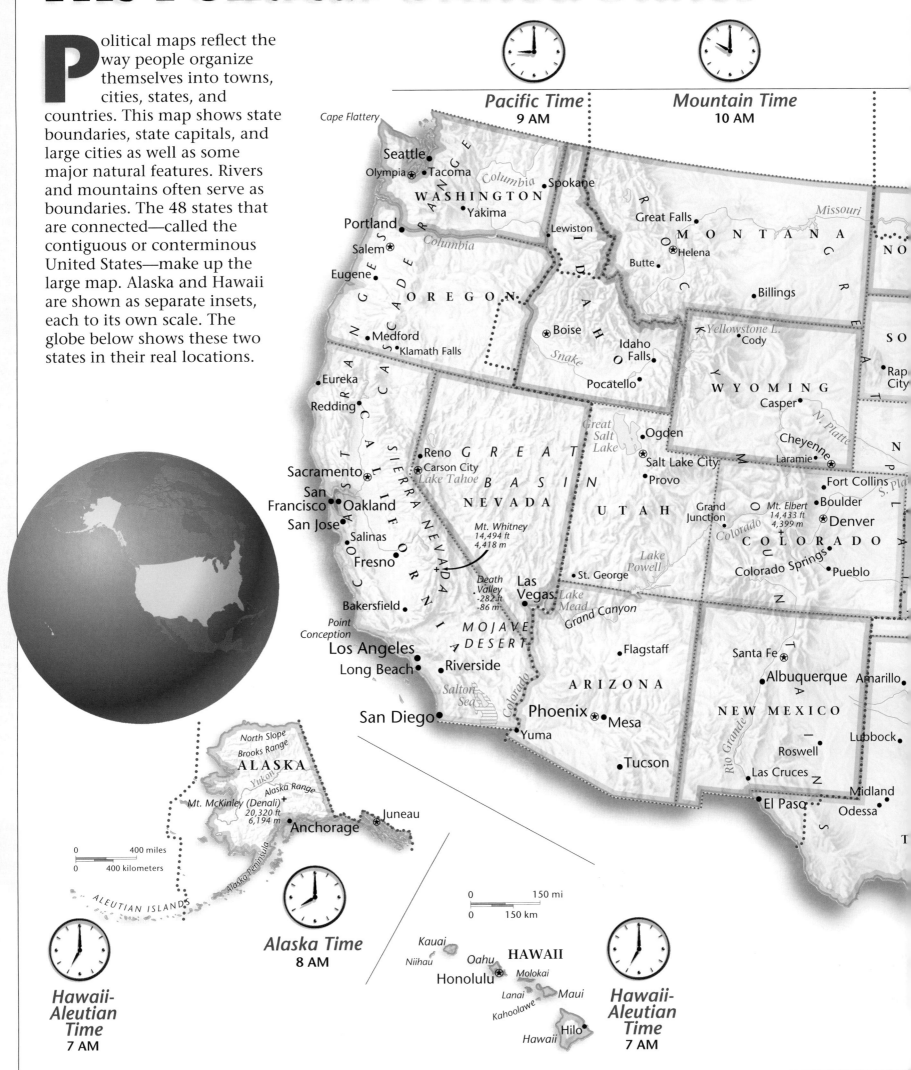

Pacific Time
9 AM

Mountain Time
10 AM

Cape Flattery

Seattle
Olympia · Tacoma
Columbia
Spokane
WASHINGTON
Yakima
Portland
Columbia
Lewiston
Great Falls
MONTANA
Salem
Helena
Butte
Eugene
OREGON
Billings
Boise
Idaho Falls
Yellowstone L.
Cody
Medford
Klamath Falls
Snake
Pocatello
WYOMING
Casper
Eureka
Redding
Great Salt Lake
Ogden
Cheyenne
Laramie
Reno GREAT
Carson City
Lake Tahoe
Salt Lake City
Provo
Fort Collins
Sacramento
BASIN
NEVADA
UTAH
Grand Junction
Mt. Elbert 14,433 ft 4,399 m
Boulder
Denver
San Francisco Oakland
San Jose
Mt. Whitney 14,494 ft 4,418 m
Colorado
COLORADO
Salinas
Lake Powell
Fresno
Death Valley -282 ft -86 m
Las Vegas
St. George
Colorado Springs
Pueblo
Bakersfield
Lake Mead
Grand Canyon
Point Conception
MOJAVE DESERT
Flagstaff
Santa Fe
Los Angeles
Riverside
Long Beach
Salton Sea
Colorado
ARIZONA
Albuquerque
Amarillo
San Diego
Phoenix Mesa
Yuma
NEW MEXICO
Lubbock
Tucson
Rio Grande
Roswell
Las Cruces
El Paso
Midland
Odessa

North Slope
Brooks Range
ALASKA
Yukon
Alaska Range
Mt. McKinley (Denali) 20,320 ft 6,194 m
Anchorage
Juneau

| 0 | 400 miles |
| 0 | 400 kilometers |

ALEUTIAN ISLANDS
Alaska Peninsula

Alaska Time
8 AM

Hawaii-Aleutian Time
7 AM

| 0 | 150 mi |
| 0 | 150 km |

Kauai
Niihau
Oahu
HAWAII
Honolulu
Molokai
Lanai Maui
Kahoolawe
Hilo
Hawaii

Hawaii-Aleutian Time
7 AM

Time Zones

The Earth is divided into 24 time zones, each about 15 degrees of longitude wide. The 50 states span six of these. Most of Alaska lies in one zone, except for the Aleutian Islands, which share a zone with Hawaii.

Central Time
11 AM

Eastern Time
12 NOON

0   300 miles

0   300 kilometers

Albers Conic Equal-Area Projection

Minot
Grand Forks
H DAKOTA
Bismarck   Fargo
Aberdee
H DAKOTA
Pierre
Sio x Falls
RASKA
Grand Island
Omaha
Platte   Lincoln
Topeka
KANSAS
Dodge C ty
rkansas
Wichita
Springfield
OKLAHOMA
Tulsa
Oklahoma City
Lawtor
Fort Smith
ARKANSAS
Little Rock
Wichita Falls
Fort Worth
Abilene   Dallas
Waco
Austin
San Antonio
Laredo
Corpus Christi
Brownsville
Grande

Lake of the Woods
International Falls
Isle Royale
Lake Superior
Duluth   Superior   Marquette
MINNESOTA
Minneapolis
St. Paul
MICHIGAN
WISCONSIN
Green Bay
Madison
Cedar Rapids
Milwaukee
Rockford
IOWA
Des Moines   Davenport
Grand Island
Chicago   Gary
Peoria
Fort Wayne
ILLINOIS   INDIANA
Springfield   Indianapolis
Kansas City
Jefferson City
St. Louis
MISSOURI
Springfield
Paducah
Missouri
Mississippi
Grand Rapids   Lansing
Detroit
Toledo   Cleveland
OHIO
Columbus
Dayton
Cincinnati
Ohio
Louisville
Frankfort
Evansville   Lexington
KENTUCKY
Knoxville
Nashville
TENNESSEE
Chattanooga
Memphis
Huntsville
MISSISSIPPI
Jackson
Birmingham
ALABAMA
Montgomery
Columbus
GEORGIA
Macon
Natchez
LOUISIANA
Red
Shreveport
Baton Rouge
New Orleans
Beaumont   Lafayette
Houston
Biloxi   Mobile
Mobile Bay
Mississippi River Delta
Apalachee Bay

MAINE
Bangor
Augusta
Lake Champlain
VT.   Burlington
Montpelier   N.H.
Concord
Portland
Lake Ontario
Rochester   Syracuse   Albany
NEW YORK   Hartford
Buffalo
MASS.   Boston
Cape Cod
Providence
RHODE ISLAND
CONN.
Erie
Newark   New York
Long Island
PENNSYLVANIA
Trenton   NEW JERSEY
Harrisburg
Pittsburgh   Philadelphia
Baltimore   Dover
Washington   Annapolis   DELAWARE
D.C.   MARYLAND
WEST VIRGINIA
Chesapeake Bay
Richmond
Charleston
VIRGINIA
Roanoke   Norfolk   Virginia Beach
Greensboro
Raleigh
Cape Hatteras
Mt. Mitchell 6,684 ft 2,037 m
NORTH CAROLINA
Charlotte
Greenville
Columbia
SOUTH CAROLINA
Charleston
Savannah
Savannah
Jacksonville
Tallahassee
Gainesville
FLORIDA
Orlando   Cape Canaveral
Tampa
St. Petersburg
Lake Okeechobee
Fort Lauderdale
THE EVERGLADES   Miami
Florida Keys

Territorial Growth

As Europeans began settling America in the 1600s, the 13 British colonies rose along the east coast. After the Revolutionary War ended in 1781, these colonies became the United States. The country grew quickly as Britain gave the new nation land stretching west to the Great Lakes and Mississippi River and south through Georgia.

The United States then expanded by buying land, fighting wars, or negotiating treaties. In 1803 the United States bought a huge parcel of land known as the Louisiana Purchase from France. This land doubled the country's size. The U.S. grew again when Spain agreed to give Florida to the United States in 1819.

Turning west, the United States fought with Mexico. By 1848 it had won most of the land from Texas to California. As settlers flooded the Oregon Country in the 1840s, Britain gave up most of this area to the U.S. As each new territory was settled, it eventually became a state (see big map). Settlers moving West pushed Native Americans off their lands. By 1900 the U.S. government had taken 95 percent of Indian lands.

In 1867 the U.S. bought Alaska from Russia, and in 1898 it annexed the Hawaiian Islands. In 1959 these lands became the 49th and 50th states.

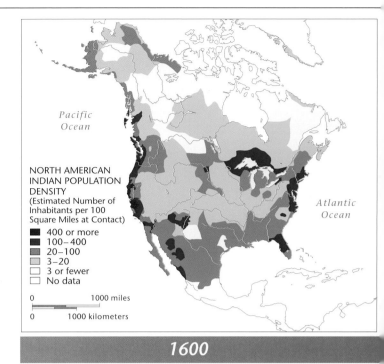

NORTH AMERICAN INDIAN POPULATION DENSITY
(Estimated Number of Inhabitants per 100 Square Miles at Contact)
- ■ 400 or more
- ■ 100–400
- ■ 20–100
- □ 3–20
- □ 3 or fewer
- □ No data

0   1000 miles
0   1000 kilometers

1600

In 1600, before European settlement, America was inhabited by Native Americans. This map shows where the largest numbers of these people lived.

The Westward Expansion

Beginning in the 1820s, thousands of pioneers packed their covered wagons and crossed the Great Plains to the far West. Both Americans and European immigrants wanted land. Some looked for gold or adventure. Others, such as the Mormons, sought religious freedom. The longest of the pioneer trails was the Oregon Trail, winding 2,000 miles (3,220 km) from Missouri to Oregon. It experienced some of its heaviest traffic after gold was discovered in California in 1848.

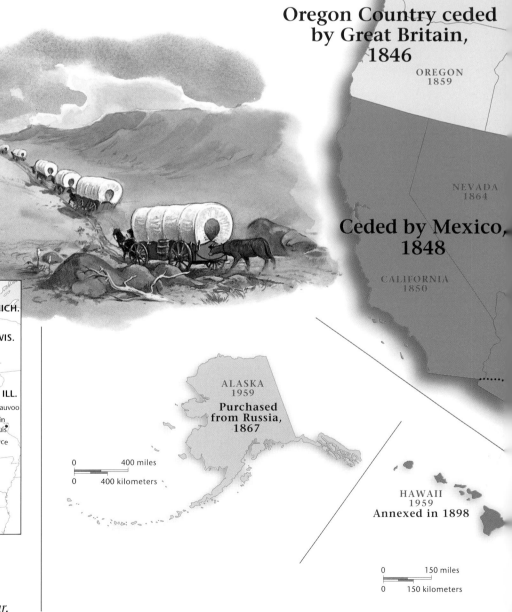

Oregon Country ceded by Great Britain, 1846

Ceded by Mexico, 1848

Purchased from Russia, 1867

HAWAII 1959 Annexed in 1898

Trails West: Routes of the Pioneers

Pioneers followed many trails West in the 1800s. During the height of the westward movement in the 1840s and 1850s, thousands journeyed to Oregon, Utah, and California each year.

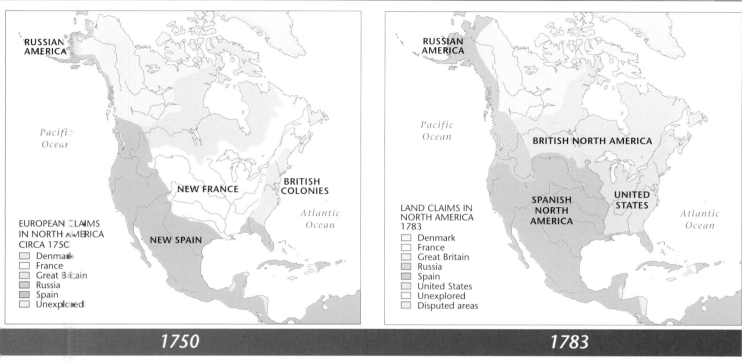

1750

By 1750 Great Britain had 13 colonies in the East. France dominated the interior and Spain the West and Southwest. Russia had settlements in Alaska.

1783

In the Treaty of 1783 Britain recognized the U.S. as a country, granting it land from Canada almost to the Gulf of Mexico and west to the Mississippi.

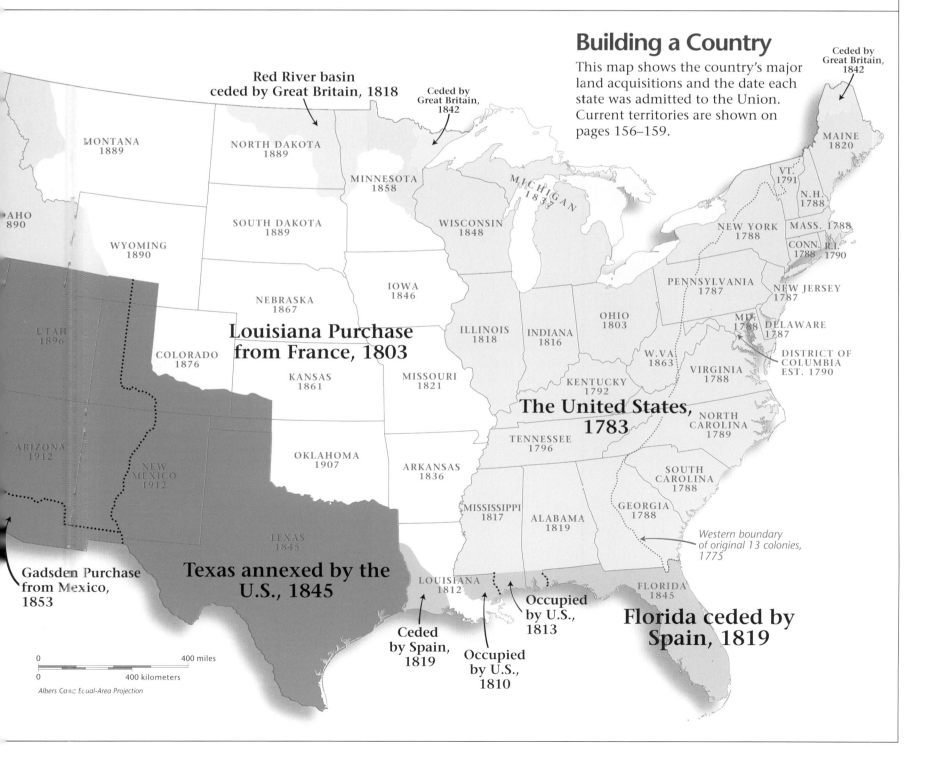

Building a Country

This map shows the country's major land acquisitions and the date each state was admitted to the Union. Current territories are shown on pages 156–159.

Ceded by Great Britain, 1842

Red River basin ceded by Great Britain, 1818

Ceded by Great Britain, 1842

Louisiana Purchase from France, 1803

The United States, 1783

Texas annexed by the U.S., 1845

Gadsden Purchase from Mexico, 1853

Ceded by Spain, 1819

Occupied by U.S., 1810

Occupied by U.S., 1813

Florida ceded by Spain, 1819

Western boundary of original 13 colonies, 1775

MONTANA 1889
NORTH DAKOTA 1889
MINNESOTA 1858
MICHIGAN 1837
MAINE 1820
VT. 1791
N.H. 1788
IDAHO 1890
SOUTH DAKOTA 1889
WISCONSIN 1848
NEW YORK 1788
MASS. 1788
CONN. 1788
R.I. 1790
WYOMING 1890
IOWA 1846
PENNSYLVANIA 1787
NEW JERSEY 1787
UTAH 1896
NEBRASKA 1867
ILLINOIS 1818
INDIANA 1816
OHIO 1803
MD. 1788
DELAWARE 1787
COLORADO 1876
W.VA. 1863
DISTRICT OF COLUMBIA EST. 1790
KANSAS 1861
MISSOURI 1821
KENTUCKY 1792
VIRGINIA 1788
ARIZONA 1912
NEW MEXICO 1912
OKLAHOMA 1907
ARKANSAS 1836
TENNESSEE 1796
NORTH CAROLINA 1789
SOUTH CAROLINA 1788
TEXAS 1845
MISSISSIPPI 1817
ALABAMA 1819
GEORGIA 1788
LOUISIANA 1812
FLORIDA 1845

0   400 miles
0   400 kilometers
Albers Conic Equal-Area Projection

Population

Who are we? Where do we live? How many of us are there? These are basic aspects of population—aspects that are rapidly changing.

Five hundred years ago, the country's population was made up of Native Americans scattered across the land in hundreds of different tribal nations. After colonization began in the 1600s, the population included Europeans and a few Africans clustered in settlements, mainly along the eastern seaboard. By the 19th century, land and the promise of mineral wealth lured adventurous souls all the way to the west coast.

Big industrial areas grew up in the Northeast during the last 200 years, but by the middle of the 20th century these older cities began to decline as people looked for new opportunities. A lower cost of living, jobs, and warmer weather now attract many to the Sun Belt, a region of rapid growth in the South and West.

Metropolitan areas—cities and their suburbs—continue to attract people from less populated areas. Suburbs themselves are growing into "edge cities" where people both live and work. Immigration brings hundreds of thousands of new residents each year—mainly Hispanic and Asian—adding to our growing diversity.

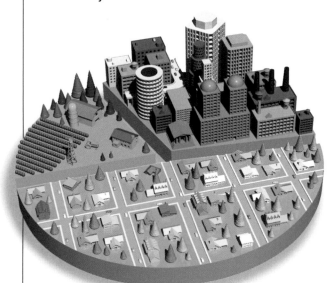

Where We Live

In 1900 about 40 percent of all Americans lived outside of urban areas on farms (green). Four out of five now live in metropolitan areas—in cities (blue) or their suburbs (orange), with the suburbs gaining the most people.

Source (left and below): U.S. Bureau of the Census

How Old Are We?

The median age—meaning the age at which half the population is older, half younger—in the U.S. was once quite young. In 1900 it was only 23 years. In 1960 children under 15 still made up the largest part of the population. But, as people live longer and have smaller families, the median age is rising. By 2040, when the last "baby boomers"(shaded areas) born in the 1960s reach old age, almost one in four Americans will be over 65.

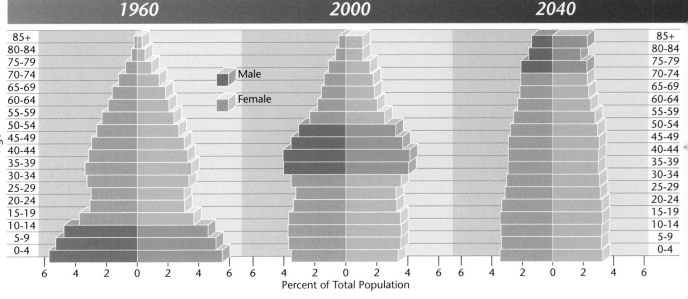

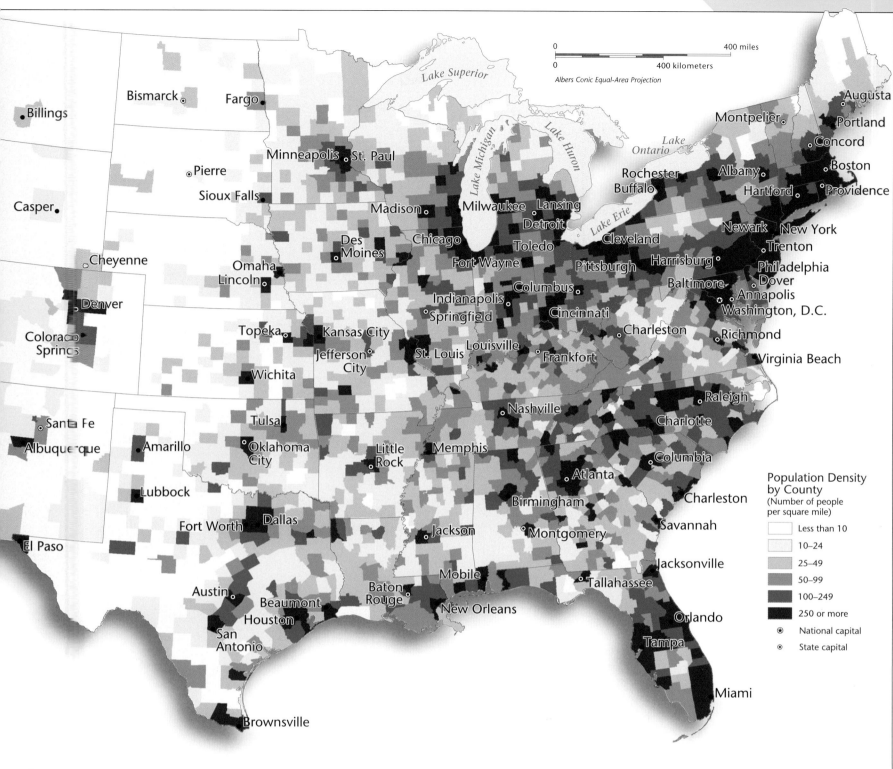

0 | 400 miles
0 | 400 kilometers

Albers Conic Equal-Area Projection

Population Density by County
(Number of people per square mile)

- Less than 10
- 10–24
- 25–49
- 50–99
- 100–249
- 250 or more
- ⊛ National capital
- ⊙ State capital

People of the United States

According to the U.S. Census Bureau, the people of the United States can be divided into five major groups: American Indian (including Eskimos and Aleuts), Asian/Pacific Islander, black, Hispanic, and white non-Hispanic. This map shows where the highest percentage of each group lives, based on state populations. Only the top five states for each group are shown. The percentages can be misleading. For instance, the percentage of Alaskans who are American Indian is double that of Oklahoma. But Oklahoma has three times as many American Indians as Alaska because Oklahoma's total population is larger.

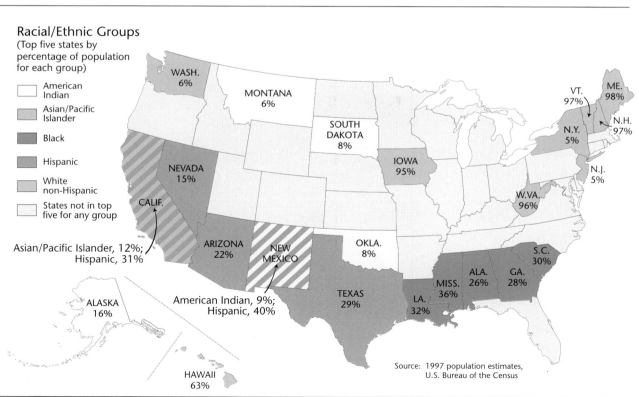

Racial/Ethnic Groups
(Top five states by percentage of population for each group)

- American Indian
- Asian/Pacific Islander
- Black
- Hispanic
- White non-Hispanic
- States not in top five for any group

WASH. 6%
MONTANA 6%
SOUTH DAKOTA 8%
IOWA 95%
VT. 97%
ME. 98%
N.Y. 5%
N.H. 97%
N.J. 5%
NEVADA 15%
W.VA. 96%
CALIF. Asian/Pacific Islander, 12%; Hispanic, 31%
ARIZONA 22%
NEW MEXICO American Indian, 9%; Hispanic, 40%
OKLA. 8%
S.C. 30%
ALA. 26%
GA. 28%
MISS. 36%
TEXAS 29%
LA. 32%
ALASKA 16%
HAWAII 63%

Source: 1997 population estimates, U.S. Bureau of the Census

Transportation

Transportation in the United States has changed dramatically as the country has grown.

In colonial America, travel was slow and difficult. To go between colonies, most people sailed along the coast. Roads were little more than rutted dirt paths through the woods. In the early 1800s, people began moving West. Settlers used rivers as their highways. The steamboat, invented in 1807, helped speed travel along these waterways. When canals, like the Erie Canal, linked eastern cities to rivers, they opened the West even more.

At the same time, railroads began to expand. Steam-powered locomotives pulled trainloads of raw materials and goods to factories and markets. By 1870 railroad lines spanned the continent, and a cross-country trip that used to take months by wagon took just days.

The 20th century transformed travel with automobiles, trucks, buses, and aircraft. Today, a web of interstate highways crisscrosses the nation. Americans drive more than two trillion miles a year. Some 40 million trucks carry goods from fresh foods to gasoline. Barges and ships move cargo to busy seaports. Meanwhile, jets aircraft zip overhead, whisking people coast to coast in hours.

Planes, Trains, and Automobiles

The graph at right shows how American passenger travel between cities has changed since 1940. In the 1940s, during the war years, train travel jumped as gas rationing cut back on the use of cars. After the war, returning G.I.s wanted to get out on the road again. Interstate highways and improvements in automobile reliability and performance have increased intercity auto travel from nearly 300 billion miles in 1940 to 2,000 billion in 1995. The fastest-growing mode of travel has been by airplane. Between 1940 and 1995, while the U.S. population doubled, airplane travel miles jumped by 350 times.

Boston to Philadelphia: Then and Now

The maps at left show roads in 1755 and federal roadways today and compare travel times between Boston and Philadelphia. In 1755 people traveled by horseback or horse-drawn wagon. Rain turned roads to treacherous mud. In 1755 it took a week to make this 320-mile (515-km) trip. An automobile today can cover the same distance in about 7½ hours.

1755
Boston to Philadelphia: At least a week, depending on weather.

1999
Boston to Philadelphia: 7½ hours by car, 7 hours by train, 1½ hours by plane.

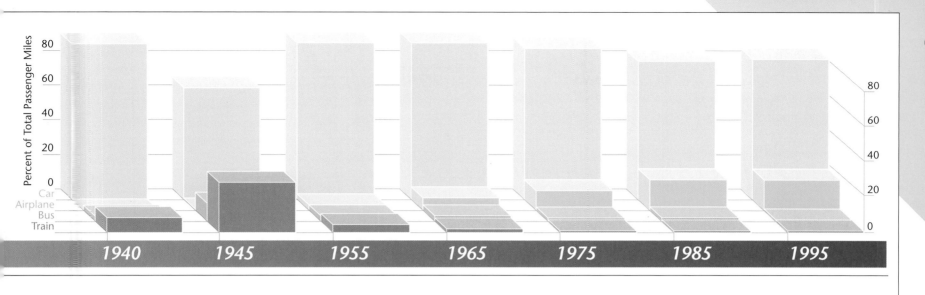

Percent of Total Passenger Miles

Car
Airplane
Bus
Train

1940   1945   1955   1965   1975   1985   1995

0 ___ 400 miles
0 ___ 400 kilometers
Albers Conic Equal-Area Projection

MONTANA
NORTH DAKOTA
Bismarck
Fargo
MINNESOTA
Duluth
Sault Ste. Marie
Lake Superior
MAINE
Augusta
Montpelier VT. N.H. Portland
Concord
SOUTH DAKOTA
Pierre
Minneapolis St. Paul
WISCONSIN
Lake Michigan
Lake Huron
Lake Ontario
Syracuse Albany
MASS.
Boston
Providence
R.I.
WYOMING
Sioux Falls
Madison
Milwaukee
MICHIGAN
Lansing
Port Huron
Buffalo Rochester
NEW YORK
Hartford CONN.
NEW MEXICO
IOWA
Des Moines
Chicago
ILLINOIS
Detroit
Toledo
Cleveland
PENNSYLVANIA
Newark
New York
N.J.
Philadelphia
Cheyenne
NEBRASKA
Omaha
Springfield
Indianapolis
Columbus
OHIO
WEST VIRGINIA
Pittsburgh
Harrisburg
MD. Baltimore
DEL.
Washington, D.C.
Denver
COLORADO
Quincy
MISSOURI
St. Louis
INDIANA
Cincinnati
Charleston
Richmond
VIRGINIA
Norfolk
Topeka
Kansas City
Jefferson City
Louisville
Frankfort
KENTUCKY
KANSAS
Wichita
Nashville
Knoxville
NORTH CAROLINA
Raleigh
Charlotte
Wilmington
Santa Fe
Oklahoma City
Tulsa
ARKANSAS
Memphis
TENNESSEE
Columbia
SOUTH CAROLINA
Charleston
Albuquerque
Amarillo
OKLAHOMA
Little Rock
Birmingham
Atlanta
NEW MEXICO
Lubbock
Wichita Falls
MISSISSIPPI
ALABAMA
GEORGIA
Savannah
Fort Worth
Dallas
Jackson
Montgomery
El Paso
TEXAS
LOUISIANA
Mobile
Tallahassee
FLORIDA
Jacksonville
Austin
Houston
Baton Rouge
Plaquemine
Port of South Louisiana
New Orleans
Orlando
San Antonio
Galveston
Tampa
Laredo
Corpus Christi
Miami

⬡95 Interstate highway
③ State highway
● Major cities
○ Ten busiest ports by tonnage
▲ Top ten airports by passenger traffic
─── Interstate
─── Highway
‑‑‑ Major AMTRAK passenger routes

Our Nation's Capital
The District of Columbia

Not a state, but not merely a city, the District of Columbia is the capital of the United States. Planned in the late 18th century as the seat of the federal government, it is better known as Washington, D.C., in honor of the nation's first President.

Today, nearly a quarter of a million people report to work at government offices in the District. Hundreds of thousands more do work related to government. The U.S. Congress meets here, in the domed Capitol building at the head of the Mall, a grassy promenade surrounded by monuments and the museums of the Smithsonian Institution. More than a collection of monuments, though, the District is also home to more than 500,000 people. Many of them are descendants of black people who settled here after the Civil War.

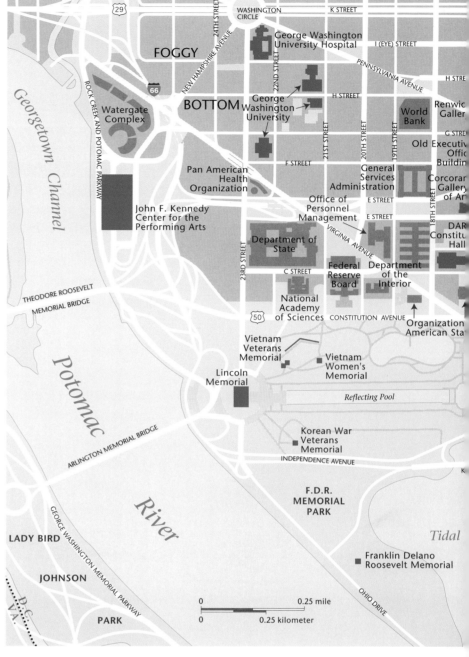

▲ *A visitor touches a name on the granite wall of the Vietnam Veterans Memorial. The wall commemorates those who died in the Vietnam War.*

▼ *Crisp dollar bills from the Bureau of Engraving and Printing represent the millions of dollars in currency that roll off presses there each day.*

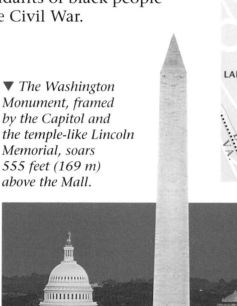

▼ *The Washington Monument, framed by the Capitol and the temple-like Lincoln Memorial, soars 555 feet (169 m) above the Mall.*

▲ *Earth Day draws a gathering of thousands to the Mall. The two-mile-long (3.2 km) Mall has long served as the site of public celebration—and public protest.*

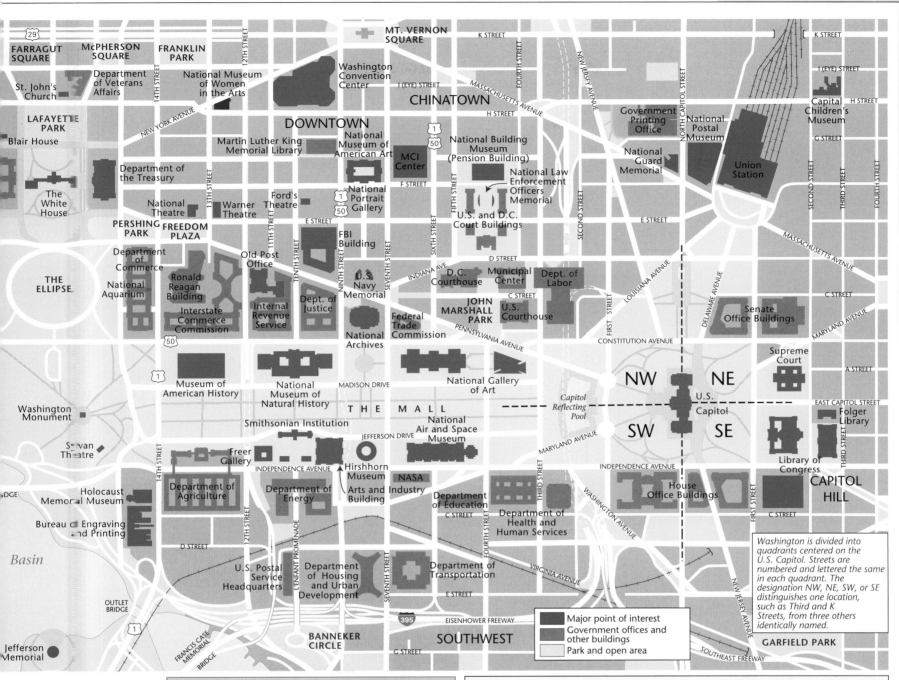

FARRAGUT SQUARE — 29

St. John's Church

McPHERSON SQUARE

Department of Veterans Affairs

FRANKLIN PARK

National Museum of Women in the Arts

MT. VERNON SQUARE

Washington Convention Center

CHINATOWN

DOWNTOWN

LAFAYETTE PARK

Blair House

Department of the Treasury

Martin Luther King Memorial Library

National Museum of American Art

MCI Center

National Building Museum (Pension Building)

National Law Enforcement Officers Memorial

National Guard Memorial

Government Printing Office

National Postal Museum

Capital Children's Museum

Union Station

The White House

National Theatre

Warner Theatre

Ford's Theatre

National Portrait Gallery

U.S. and D.C. Court Buildings

PERSHING PARK

FREEDOM PLAZA

Department of Commerce

Old Post Office

FBI Building

THE ELLIPSE

Ronald Reagan Building

National Aquarium

Interstate Commerce Commission

Internal Revenue Service

Dept. of Justice

U.S. Navy Memorial

D.C. Courthouse

Municipal Center

Dept. of Labor

JOHN MARSHALL PARK

U.S. Courthouse

Federal Trade Commission

National Archives

Senate Office Buildings

Washington Monument

Sylvan Theatre

Museum of American History

National Museum of Natural History

National Gallery of Art

Supreme Court

NW **NE**

U.S. Capitol

SW **SE**

Capitol Reflecting Pool

THE MALL

Smithsonian Institution

National Air and Space Museum

Folger Library

Freer Gallery

Hirshhorn Museum

Arts and Industry Building

NASA

Library of Congress

CAPITOL HILL

Holocaust Memorial Museum

Department of Agriculture

Department of Energy

Department of Education

Department of Health and Human Services

House Office Buildings

Bureau of Engraving and Printing

Basin

U.S. Postal Service Headquarters

Department of Housing and Urban Development

Department of Transportation

OUTLET BRIDGE

Jefferson Memorial

FRANCIS CASE MEMORIAL BRIDGE

BANNEKER CIRCLE

SOUTHWEST

EISENHOWER FREEWAY

GARFIELD PARK

Washington is divided into quadrants centered on the U.S. Capitol. Streets are numbered and lettered the same in each quadrant. The designation NW, NE, SW, or SE distinguishes one location, such as Third and K Streets, from three others identically named.

Major point of interest
Government offices and other buildings
Park and open area

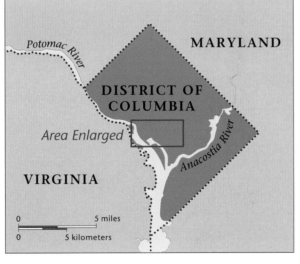

MARYLAND

Potomac River

DISTRICT OF COLUMBIA

Area Enlarged

Anacostia River

VIRGINIA

0 — 5 miles
0 — 5 kilometers

▶ *The White House may be occupied by the President, but it is owned by the people of the United States.*

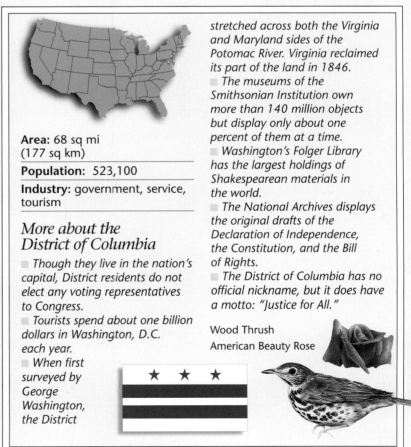

Area: 68 sq mi (177 sq km)

Population: 523,100

Industry: government, service, tourism

More about the District of Columbia

■ *Though they live in the nation's capital, District residents do not elect any voting representatives to Congress.*

■ *Tourists spend about one billion dollars in Washington, D.C. each year.*

■ *When first surveyed by George Washington, the District* stretched across both the Virginia and Maryland sides of the Potomac River. Virginia reclaimed its part of the land in 1846.

■ *The museums of the Smithsonian Institution own more than 140 million objects but display only about one percent of them at a time.*

■ *Washington's Folger Library has the largest holdings of Shakespearean materials in the world.*

■ *The National Archives displays the original drafts of the Declaration of Independence, the Constitution, and the Bill of Rights.*

■ *The District of Columbia has no official nickname, but it does have a motto: "Justice for All."*

Wood Thrush
American Beauty Rose

The North

east

Connecticut
Delaware
Maine
Maryland
Massachusetts
New Hampshire
New Jersey
New York
Pennsylvania
Rhode Island
Vermont

Jostling crowds (above) pack Fifth Avenue in the heart of New York, the largest city in the United States. Not far from its densely populated cities, the Northeast also holds quiet beauty, such as New York's Adirondack Mountains (left), clothed in brilliant fall colors. The view from the Adirondacks takes in three states and one Canadian province.

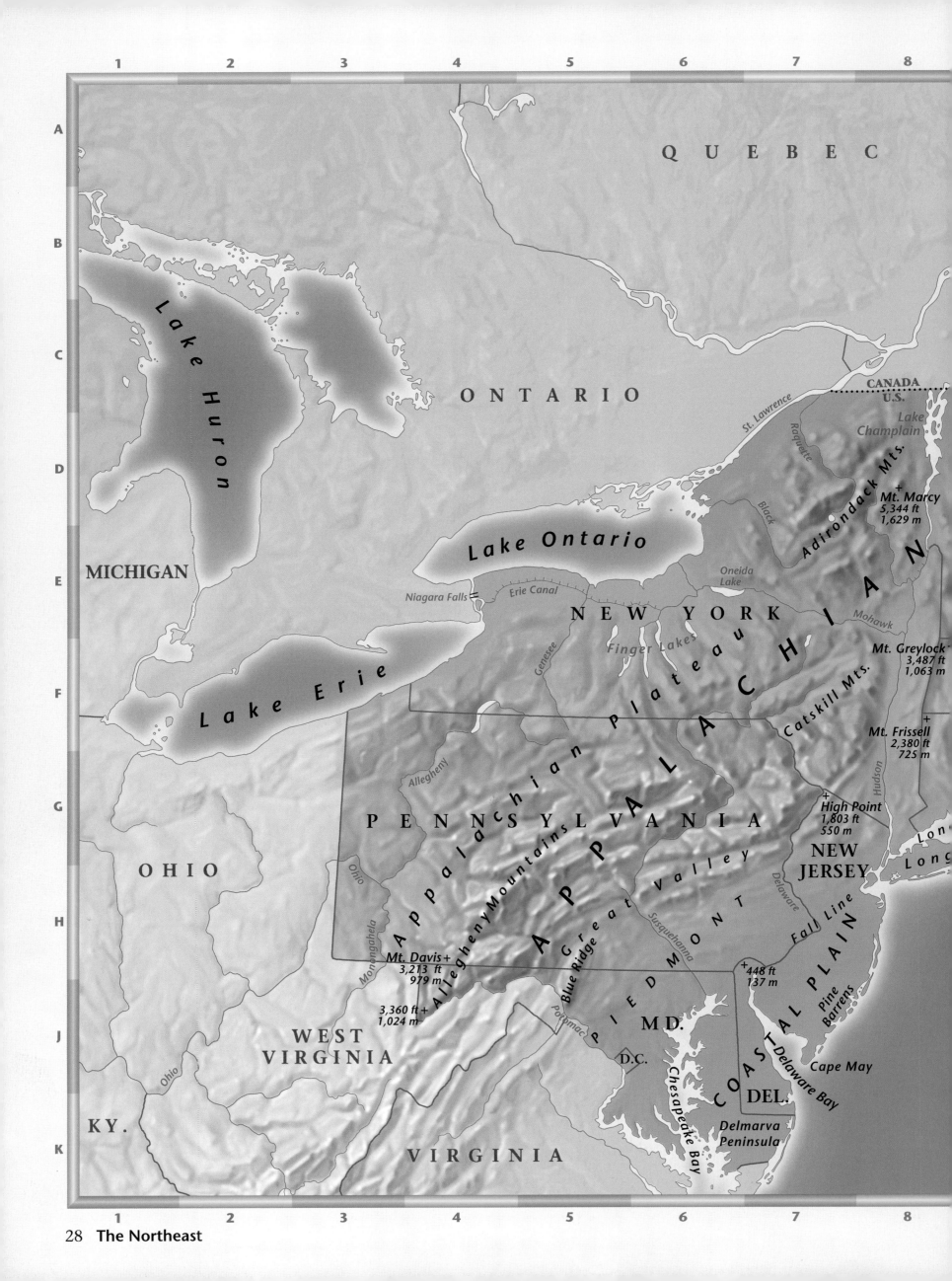

QUEBEC

ONTARIO

CANADA
U.S.

St. Lawrence

Lake Champlain

Raquette

Black

MICHIGAN

Lake Ontario

Adirondack Mts.

+ Mt. Marcy
5,344 ft
1,629 m

Niagara Falls

Erie Canal

Oneida Lake

Mohawk

NEW YORK

Genesee

Finger Lakes

Mt. Greylock +
3,487 ft
1,063 m

Lake Huron

Lake Erie

Appalachian Plateau

Catskill Mts.

Mt. Frissell +
2,380 ft
725 m

Hudson

P E N N s **Y L V A N I A**

Allegheny

High Point +
1,803 ft
550 m

NEW JERSEY

Long

Long

OHIO

Monongahela

Ohio

Allegheny Mountains

A P P A L A

Great Valley

Blue Ridge

Delaware

Susquehanna

P I E D M O N T

Fall Line

Mt. Davis +
3,213 ft
979 m

3,360 ft +
1,024 m

+ 448 ft
137 m

Pine Barrens

WEST VIRGINIA

Potomac

MD.

D.C.

C O A S T A L   P L A I N

Delaware Bay

Cape May

KY.

Chesapeake Bay

Delmarva Peninsula

DEL.

VIRGINIA

9 10 11 12 13 14 15 16

NEW
BRUNSWICK

St. John

Allagash

CANADA
U.S.

St. John

MOUNTAINS

+ Mt. Katahdin
5,267 ft
1,605 m

M A I N E

Kennebec

Penobscot

St. Croix

Bay of Fundy

NOVA
SCOTIA

Mt. Mans'e'd
+ 4,393 ft
1,339 m

Mt. Washington
6,288 ft
+ 1,917 m

Saco

Mt. Desert
Island

Green Mts.

White Mts.

VT.

NEW
HAMPSHIRE

Merrimack

Connecticut

Gulf of Maine

Cape Ann

Massachusetts
Bay

MASSACHUSETTS

Cape Cod

+ Jerimoth Hill
812 ft
247 m

CONN.

R.I.

Island Sound

Island

Martha's
Vineyard

Nantucket
Island

The Northeast
Shaped by Ancient Ice

Ice Age glaciers gave the Northeast its craggy appearance, sculpting coastlines and lakes. The region's forested backbone is formed by the ancient, worn Appalachian Mountains, which run from the tip of Maine through western Maryland and on southward. Rivers spilling from the mountains, as well as deep coastal harbors, provide excellent sites for cities.

About the Region

Highest point: Mount Washington, New Hampshire: 6,288 ft (1,917 m)

Lowest point: sea level, shores of the Atlantic Ocean

Largest lakes: Erie, Ontario, Champlain

Longest rivers: St. Lawrence, Susquehanna, Connecticut

Vegetation: needleleaf, broadleaf, and mixed forest

Climate: Continental to mild, with cool to warm summers, cold winters, and moderate precipitation through the year.

A T L A N T I C

O C E A N

0   150 miles

0   250 kilometers
Albers Conic Equal-Area Projection

9 10 11 12 13 14 15 16

The Northeast
Birthplace of a Nation

Stretching down the Atlantic coast from Maine to Maryland, the Northeast has some of the nation's oldest settlements and most densely populated areas. About a quarter of the country's people live here, many in a string of giant cities—running from Boston through New York to Washington, D.C.—that blend into one huge urban area called a megalopolis.

Excellent harbors first made most of these big cities international trade centers. Then the rise of factories and manufacturing helped them grow into booming metropolises connected by roads, rivers, and railroads.

The Northeast is the birthplace of much of the nation's early history. European settlers came here in 1620, seeking freedom and a new life. Here, the Revolutionary War began, and leaders of the 13 original colonies forged a new nation. Hemmed by mountains and seashores, the Northeast is a place of great variety and beauty. Even near the largest cities, pockets of wilderness remain, including some of the country's most scenic lands.

▲ **SUNLIGHT BATHES** *the skyscrapers of New York's Manhattan Island. The twin towers of the World Trade Center rise at left.*

▶ **WORKERS INSPECT** *chocolate kisses at a Hershey, Pennsylvania, factory. Food processing is a major element of the Northeast's economy.*

▲ **A COVERED** *bridge in Arlington, Vermont, crosses the Batten Kill River. Vermont has more than a hundred of these structures.*

▶ **RACING** *downhill, a skier enjoys a fast run on Olympic slopes near Lake Placid, New York.*

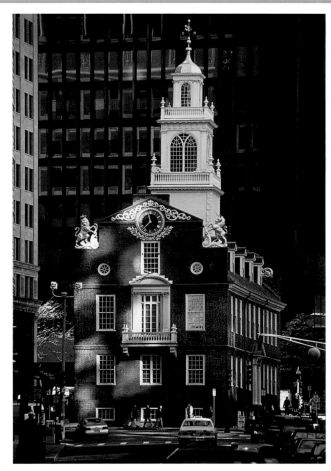

▶ **THE OLD STATE**
House, built in 1713,
is a historic landmark
in Boston, Massachusetts.
It was the center of events,
such as the Boston
"Massacre," that led up to
the American Revolution.

▲ **JUICY RED** *cranberries
grow in peaty bogs.
Massachusetts is the top
grower of the berries,
which are harvested in
September and October.*

▶ **RIDING THE WIND,** *two young boaters enjoy a summer
sail on a breezy river. During warm months, sailing,
motorboating, fishing, and swimming are popular pastimes
along the Northeast's many waterways.*

▼ **BLUE CRABS** *from the
Chesapeake Bay make for tasty
eating. The bay, bordered by
Maryland and Virginia,
is one of the country's richest
sources of seafood. Chesapeake
Bay waterman haul in millions
of pounds of crabs, oysters,
and clams a year.*

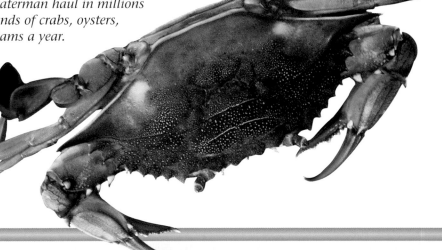

▲ **BASEBALL FANS CROWD** *Camden Yards Stadium in
Baltimore, Maryland. The Northeast is home to many of
the country's oldest ball clubs as well as the Baseball Hall
of Fame in Cooperstown, New York.*

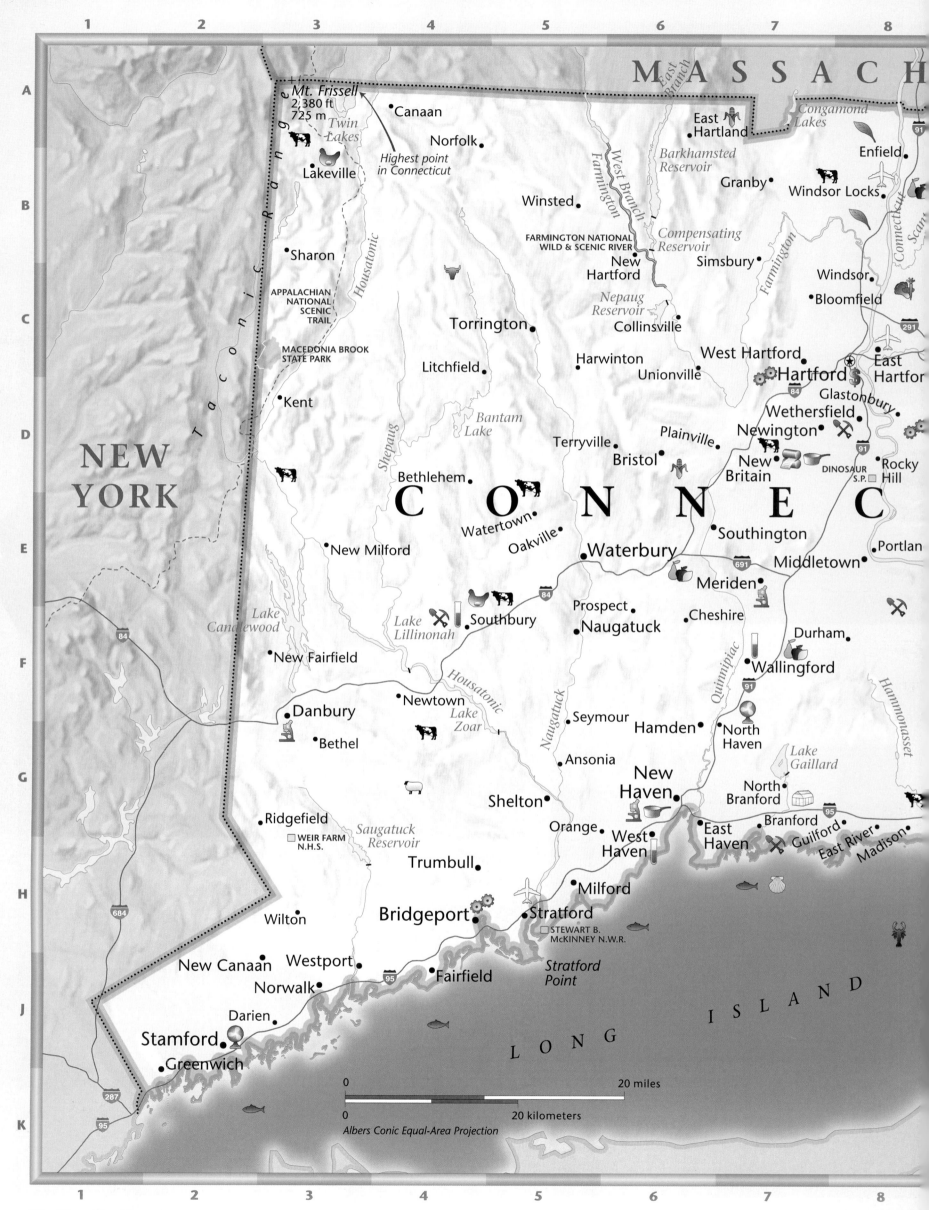

A B C D E F G H J K
1 2 3 4 5 6 7 8

MASSACH

Mt. Frissell +
2,380 ft
725 m
Twin
Lakes
*Highest point
in Connecticut*

Canaan

Norfolk

East
Hartland

*Congamond
Lakes*

Enfield

Lakeville

Winsted

West Branch Farmington

Barkhamsted
Reservoir

Granby

Windsor Locks

Sharon

Housatonic

FARMINGTON NATIONAL
WILD & SCENIC RIVER

*Compensating
Reservoir*

New
Hartford

Simsbury

Windsor

APPALACHIAN
NATIONAL
SCENIC
TRAIL

*Nepaug
Reservoir*

Collinsville

Torrington

Bloomfield

MACEDONIA BROOK
STATE PARK

Litchfield

Harwinton

Unionville

West Hartford

Hartford

East
Hartfor

Kent

*Bantam
Lake*

Terryville

Plainville

Newington

Glastonbury

Bristol

New
Britain

Wethersfield

DINOSAUR
S.P.

Rocky
Hill

Portlan

CONNEC

Bethlehem

Watertown

Southington

New Milford

Oakville

Waterbury

Middletown

*Lake
Candlewood*

Prospect

Meriden

Cheshire

Durham

*Lake
Lillinonah*

Southbury

Naugatuck

New Fairfield

Housatonic

Wallingford

Danbury

Newtown

*Lake
Zoar*

Seymour

Hamden

North
Haven

*Lake
Gaillard*

Bethel

Ansonia

Naugatuck

Quinnipiac

Hammonasset

Ridgefield

*Saugatuck
Reservoir*

Shelton

Orange

New Haven

North
Branford

Branford

WEIR FARM
N.H.S.

Trumbull

East
Haven

Guilford

East River

Madison

Wilton

Milford

Bridgeport

Stratford

STEWART B.
McKINNEY N.W.R.

New Canaan

Westport

Fairfield

*Stratford
Point*

Norwalk

Darien

LONG

ISLAND

Stamford

Greenwich

**NEW
YORK**

Taconic Range

Housatonic

Shepaug

0   20 miles

0   20 kilometers

Albers Conic Equal-Area Projection

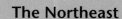

Map labels (New York / Connecticut / Massachusetts / Rhode Island region):

U S E T T S

Hazardville

Staffordville
Reservoir

Broad Brook

Stafford
Springs

North
Grosvenor
Dale

Quaddick
Reservoir

Thompson

Ellington

Shenipsit
Lake

Putnam

Vernon

Manchester

Storrs

Dayville

Danielson

Mansfield
Hollow
Lake

Coventry

Brooklyn

Willimantic
Reservoir

Willimantic

Moosup

Marlborough

Shetucket

Quinebaug

Plainfield

Pocotopaug L.

Baltic

Jewett City

East Hampton

Colchester

Yantic

Pachaug
Pond

Gardner
Lake

Norwich

Moodus

Salmon

Haddam

MASHANTUCKET
PEQUOT I.R.

Connecticut

Chesterfield

Quaker
Hill

Thames

Pawcatuck

Deep River

Essex

New
London

Mystic Seaport

Mystic

Pawcatuck

Niantic

Groton

Poquonock Bridge

Old
Saybrook

Westbrook

Clinton

STEWART B.
McKINNEY N.W.R.

T I C U T

R H O D E   I S L A N D

S O U N D

B L O C K   I S L A N D
S O U N D

NEW YORK

ATLANTIC OCEAN

Constitution State

Connecticut

Connecticut takes its name from the Connecticut River, which winds through the center of the state and empties into Long Island Sound. In fact, the name Connecticut is an Indian word meaning "on the long tidal river."

The nation's third smallest state, Connecticut is a place of surprising contrasts. It has miles of rural countryside with gently rolling hills marked by woodlands, farms, and villages. Yet it also has busy cities that hum with industry.

Since colonial times, Connecticut has been a center of manufacturing and inventing. Connecticut produced America's first copper coins, bicycles, steel fishhooks, friction matches, tin utensils, rubber shoes, and repeating revolvers. Today, the state has moved on to larger things and is a leading manufacturer of helicopters, jet aircraft parts, and submarines.

Connecticut's coast once had busy whaling ports. Today, visitors can explore this heritage at Mystic Seaport.

Area: 5,544 sq mi
(14,358 sq km)

Population: 3,274,000

Capital: Hartford,
pop. 133,100

Largest city: Bridgeport,
pop. 137,990

Industry: transportation equipment, metal products, machinery, electrical equipment, printing and publishing, scientific instruments

Agriculture: nursery stock, dairy products, poultry, eggs, shellfish

Statehood: January 9, 1788; 5th state

Nickname: Constitution State

More About Connecticut

Colonial Connecticut was first governed under the rules of a document called the Fundamental Orders. Often considered the first written constitution, it later served as a model for the U.S. Constitution. Because of this, Connecticut is nicknamed the Constitution State.

Connecticut is famous for its "Yankee ingenuity." In the early 1800s Eli Whitney, inventor of the cotton gin, was one of the first people to develop methods of mass production at a factory in Hamden.

Connecticut's Ella Grasso became the nation's first elected woman governor in 1974.

Robin
Mountain
Laurel

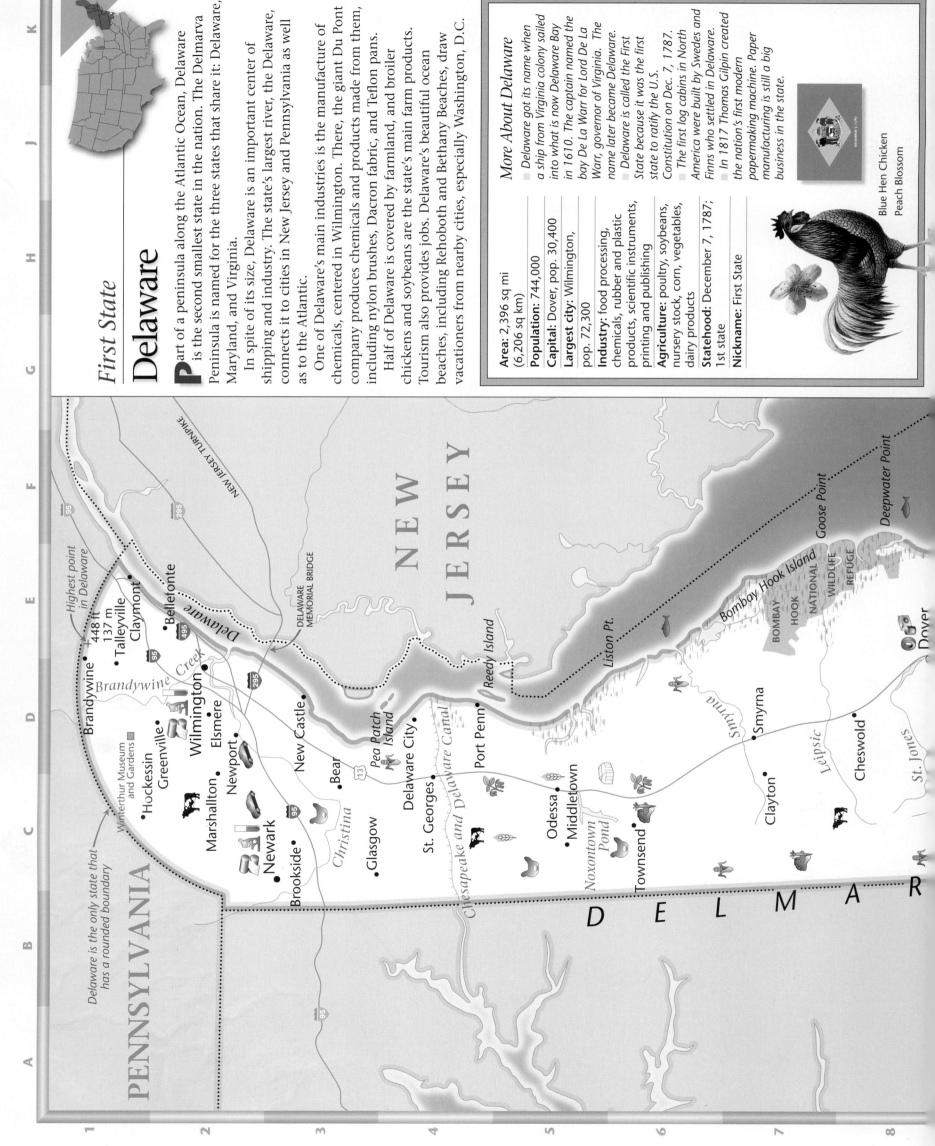

First State

Delaware

Part of a peninsula along the Atlantic Ocean, Delaware is the second smallest state in the nation. The Delmarva Peninsula is named for the three states that share it: Delaware, Maryland, and Virginia.

In spite of its size, Delaware is an important center of shipping and industry. The state's largest river, the Delaware, connects it to cities in New Jersey and Pennsylvania as well as to the Atlantic.

One of Delaware's main industries is the manufacture of chemicals, centered in Wilmington. There, the giant Du Pont company produces chemicals and products made from them, including nylon brushes, Dacron fabric, and Teflon pans. Half of Delaware is covered by farmland, and broiler chickens and soybeans are the state's main farm products. Tourism also provides jobs. Delaware's beautiful ocean beaches, including Rehoboth and Bethany Beaches, draw vacationers from nearby cities, especially Washington, D.C.

Area: 2,396 sq mi (6,206 sq km)

Population: 744,000

Capital: Dover, pop. 30,400

Largest city: Wilmington, pop. 72,300

Industry: food processing, chemicals, rubber and plastic products, scientific instruments, printing and publishing

Agriculture: poultry, soybeans, nursery stock, corn, vegetables, dairy products

Statehood: December 7, 1787; 1st state

Nickname: First State

More About Delaware

- Delaware got its name when a ship from Virginia colony sailed into what is now Delaware Bay in 1610. The captain named the bay De La Warr for Lord De La Warr, governor of Virginia. The name later became Delaware.
- Delaware is called the First State because it was the first state to ratify the U.S. Constitution on Dec. 7, 1787.
- The first log cabins in North America were built by Swedes and Finns who settled in Delaware.
- In 1817 Thomas Gilpin created the nation's first modern papermaking machine. Paper manufacturing is still a big business in the state.

Blue Hen Chicken
Peach Blossom

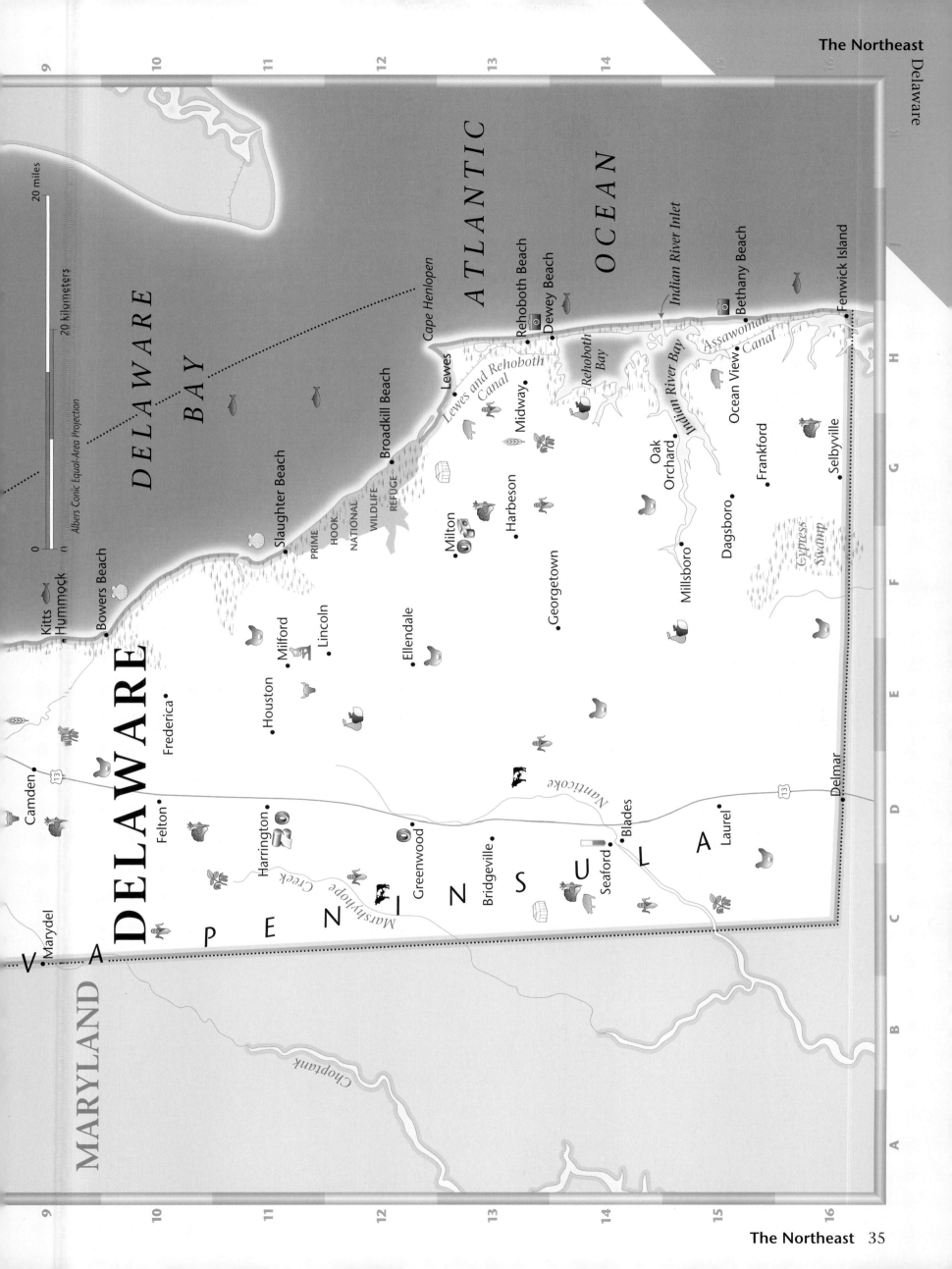

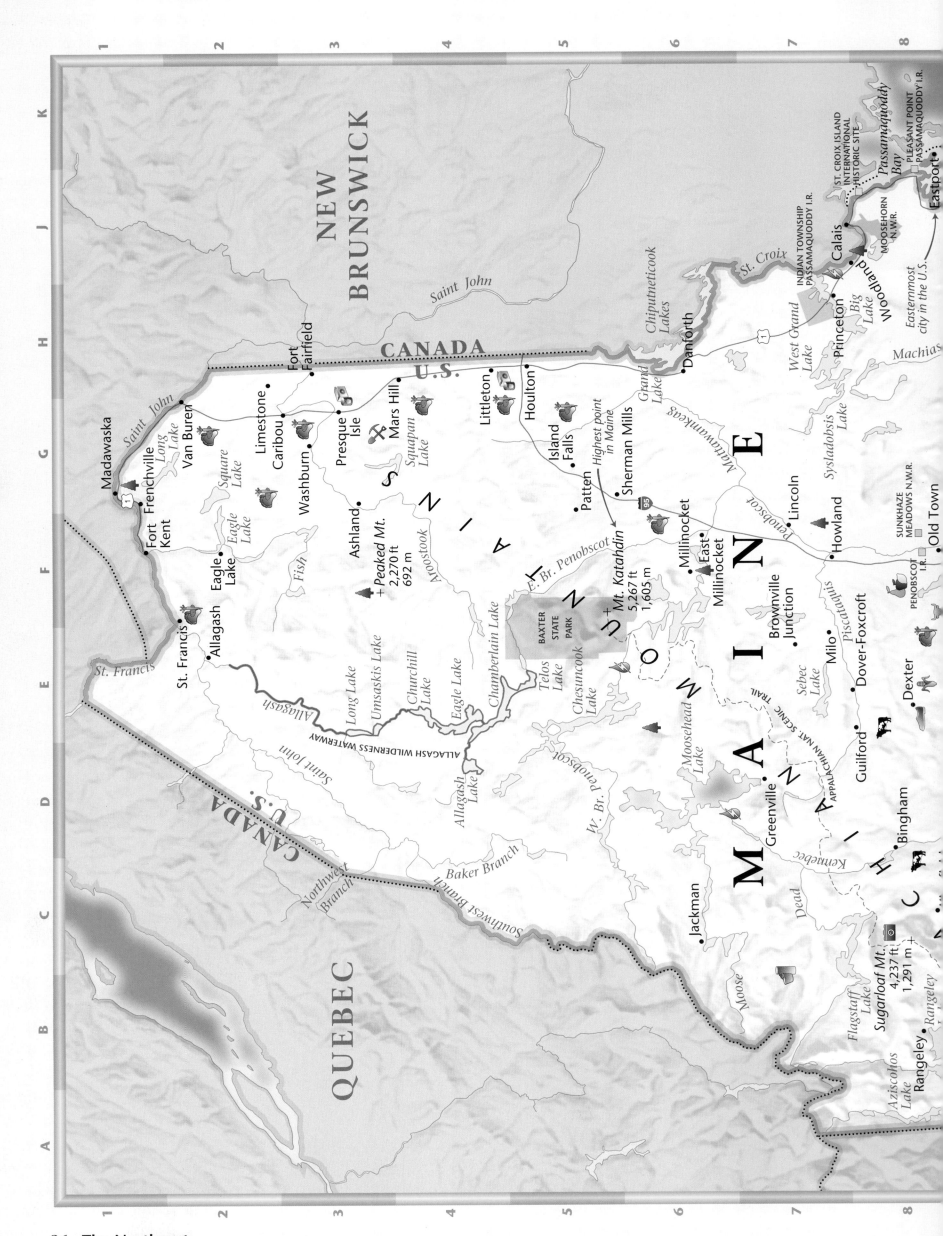

NEW BRUNSWICK

QUEBEC

CANADA
U.S.

Saint John

MAINE

Map labels:

Madawaska
Frenchville
Fort Kent
Van Buren
Limestone
Caribou
Washburn
Presque Isle
Mars Hill
Ashland
Peaked Mt. 2,270 ft 692 m
Eagle Lake
Allagash
St. Francis
St. Francis

Long Lake
Square Lake
Eagle Lake
Fish
Aroostook

Littleton
Houlton
Island Falls
Patten
Sherman Mills
Highest point in Maine
Mt. Katahdin 5,267 ft 1,605 m

CANADA
U.S.

Northwest Branch
Southwest Branch
Baker Branch
Saint John
Allagash Lake
Long Lake
Umsaskis Lake
Churchill Lake
Eagle Lake
Chamberlain Lake
Telos Lake
Chesuncook Lake
ALLAGASH WILDERNESS WATERWAY
Allagash

BAXTER STATE PARK
E. Br. Penobscot
Millinocket
East Millinocket

W. Br. Penobscot

Danforth
Grand Lake
Chiputneticook Lakes
West Grand Lake
Big Lake
Princeton
Woodland
Calais
ST. CROIX ISLAND INTERNATIONAL HISTORIC SITE
INDIAN TOWNSHIP PASSAMAQUODDY I.R.
MOOSEHORN N.W.R.
Passamaquoddy Bay
PLEASANT POINT PASSAMAQUODDY I.R.
Eastport
Easternmost city in the U.S.
Machias
St. Croix

Lincoln
Howland
Old Town
PENOBSCOT
SUNKHAZE MEADOWS N.W.R.
Mattawamkeag
Sysladobsis Lake

Brownville Junction
Milo
Dover-Foxcroft
Dexter
Guilford
Sebec Lake
Piscataquis

Greenville
Moosehead Lake
APPALACHIAN NAT. SCENIC TRAIL
Kennebec

Jackman
Bingham
Dead
Moose

Flagstaff Lake
Sugarloaf Mt. 4,237 ft 1,291 m
Rangeley
Aziscohos Lake

Maine

Pine Tree State

Maine marks the far northeastern corner of the United States. West Quoddy Head, a small peninsula on the Atlantic Ocean, is the point farthest east in the lower 48 states. The state's most famous feature is its coast, known for its rugged beauty and pounding waves. In the cold offshore waters, Maine fishermen catch cod, flounder, and other fish. Maine also harvests more lobster than any other state.

Much of Maine's interior is wilderness, with mountains, woods, sparkling lakes, rivers, and streams. Forests cover 90 percent of Maine's land, more than in any other state. Trees, including evergreens such as pine, fir, and spruce, also supply raw materials for Maine's leading products: lumber, paper, and other forestry goods.

Few people live in Maine's mountainous interior. Most of the state's population is concentrated in cities near its southern coast, where people in Portland, Lewiston, and Bangor benefit from their nearness to the ocean by shipping goods such as paper and leather goods.

Area: 33,741 sq mi (87,388 sq km)

Population: 1,244,000

Capital: Augusta, pop. 20,400

Largest city: Portland, pop. 63,100

Industry: health services, tourism, forest products, leather products, electrical equipment, food processing, textiles

Agriculture: seafood, potatoes, dairy products, poultry and eggs, livestock, apples, blueberries, vegetables

Statehood: March 15, 1820; 23rd state

Nickname: Pine Tree State

More About Maine

■ Mount Katahdin, Maine's highest peak, rises 5,267 feet (1605 m). It marks the beginning of the Appalachian National Scenic Trail, which ends in Georgia.

■ Acadia National Park, on Maine's Mount Desert Island, is the only national park in New England.

■ Maine is the only state that borders just one other state: New Hampshire, on the west.

■ The Maine coast is often called Down East. This is because early sailing ships going from Boston to Maine traveled with the wind at their backs, or "downwind," as they headed east.

■ Maine's official cat is the Maine coon cat, which can grow to 30 pounds (13.6 kg).

Chickadee
White Pine Cone and Tassel

Map Labels

ATLANTIC OCEAN

Gulf of Maine

West Quoddy Head

Grand Manan Channel

MOOSEHORN N.W.R.

Machiasport

Machias

Jonesport

PETIT MANAN N.W.R.

Highest point on the Atlantic coast of North America

Graham Lake

Ellsworth

Bangor

Brewer

Bucksport

Searsport

Belfast

Penobscot

Bar Harbor

Cadillac Mt. 1,530 ft 466 m +

Mt. Desert Island

ACADIA NATIONAL PARK

Southwest Harbor

Castine

Blue Hill Bay

Deer Isle

Stonington

Isle au Haut

ACADIA N.P.

Vinalhaven

Penobscot Bay

Camden

Rockport

Rockland

Thomaston

Waldoboro

Muscongus Bay

Monhegan Island

Newport

Pittsfield

Waterville

Winslow

Augusta

Gardiner

Oakland

Great Pond

Madison

Skowhegan

Wilton

Farmington

Meselookmeguntic Lake

Richardson Lakes

LAKE UMBAGOG N.W.R.

Mexico

Rumford

South Paris

Norway

Bethel

Bridgton

Fryeburg

Sebago Lake

WHITE MOUNTAIN NATIONAL FOREST

Springvale

Salmon Falls

South Berwick

Kittery

Isles of Shoals

York Village

Ogunquit

Wells

Kennebunk

RACHEL CARSON N.W.R.

Biddeford

Saco

Old Orchard Beach

Scarborough

Sanford

Westbrook

Cape Elizabeth

S. Portland

Portland

Casco Bay

Falmouth

Yarmouth

Brunswick

Bath

Kennebec

Wiscasset

Boothbay Harbor

Lisbon Falls

Lewiston

Auburn

Winthrop

Androscoggin

Saco

NEW HAMPSHIRE

MASSACHUSETTS

50 miles

50 kilometers

Albers Conic Equal-Area Projection

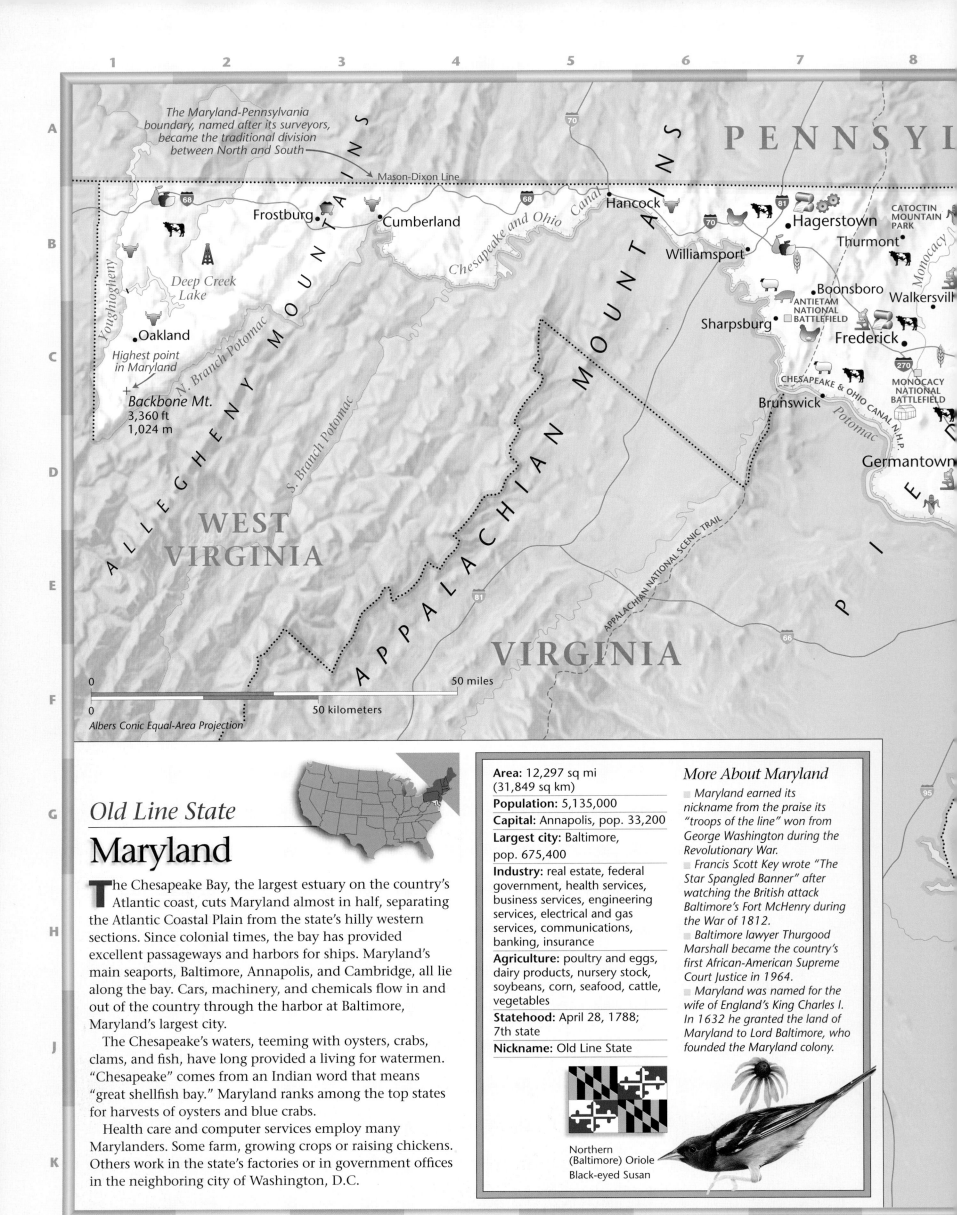

The Maryland-Pennsylvania boundary, named after its surveyors, became the traditional division between North and South

Mason-Dixon Line

PENNSYL

CATOCTIN MOUNTAIN PARK

Frostburg

Cumberland

Hancock

Hagerstown

Thurmont

Williamsport

Boonsboro

Walkersvill

Deep Creek Lake

Youghiogheny

Sharpsburg

ANTIETAM NATIONAL BATTLEFIELD

Frederick

Oakland

N. Branch Potomac

Highest point in Maryland

+ *Backbone Mt.*
3,360 ft
1,024 m

S. Branch Potomac

CHESAPEAKE & OHIO CANAL N.H.P.

MONOCACY NATIONAL BATTLEFIELD

Brunswick

Potomac

WEST VIRGINIA

Germantown

APPALACHIAN NATIONAL SCENIC TRAIL

APPALACHIAN MOUNTAINS

ALLEGHENY MOUNTAINS

VIRGINIA

0   50 miles

0   50 kilometers

Albers Conic Equal-Area Projection

Old Line State

Maryland

The Chesapeake Bay, the largest estuary on the country's Atlantic coast, cuts Maryland almost in half, separating the Atlantic Coastal Plain from the state's hilly western sections. Since colonial times, the bay has provided excellent passageways and harbors for ships. Maryland's main seaports, Baltimore, Annapolis, and Cambridge, all lie along the bay. Cars, machinery, and chemicals flow in and out of the country through the harbor at Baltimore, Maryland's largest city.

The Chesapeake's waters, teeming with oysters, crabs, clams, and fish, have long provided a living for watermen. "Chesapeake" comes from an Indian word that means "great shellfish bay." Maryland ranks among the top states for harvests of oysters and blue crabs.

Health care and computer services employ many Marylanders. Some farm, growing crops or raising chickens. Others work in the state's factories or in government offices in the neighboring city of Washington, D.C.

Area: 12,297 sq mi (31,849 sq km)

Population: 5,135,000

Capital: Annapolis, pop. 33,200

Largest city: Baltimore, pop. 675,400

Industry: real estate, federal government, health services, business services, engineering services, electrical and gas services, communications, banking, insurance

Agriculture: poultry and eggs, dairy products, nursery stock, soybeans, corn, seafood, cattle, vegetables

Statehood: April 28, 1788; 7th state

Nickname: Old Line State

More About Maryland

■ Maryland earned its nickname from the praise its "troops of the line" won from George Washington during the Revolutionary War.

■ Francis Scott Key wrote "The Star Spangled Banner" after watching the British attack Baltimore's Fort McHenry during the War of 1812.

■ Baltimore lawyer Thurgood Marshall became the country's first African-American Supreme Court Justice in 1964.

■ Maryland was named for the wife of England's King Charles I. In 1632 he granted the land of Maryland to Lord Baltimore, who founded the Maryland colony.

Northern (Baltimore) Oriole

Black-eyed Susan

9 10 11 12 13 14 15 16

A

**NEW
JERSEY**

•Taneytown
•Manchester
Westminster•
•Bel Air
Cockeysville•
•Reisterstown
Perry
Hall
Towson•
Parkville•
Essex•
Baltimore
Catonsville•
Ellicott City•
Dundalk•
Montgomery
Village•
Columbia
Gaithersburg•
Rockville•
Potomac•
Silver
Spring
Bethesda•
Severna
Park
Bowie•
Hyattsville•
Annapolis•
Washington
Suitland
Deale•

HAMPTON N.H.S.

U.S. center of
population in 1800

FT. McHENRY NAT. MON.
& HISTORIC SHRINE

PATUXENT
NATIONAL
WILDLIFE REFUGE

GREENBELT
PARK

CLARA
BARTON
N.H.S.

D.C.

FT. WASHINGTON
PARK

PISCATAWAY
PARK

Indian Head•
Waldorf•
•St. Charles

THOMAS STONE
N.H.S.

•La Plata

Golden
Beach•

Prince
Frederick•

Chesapeake
Beach•

Solomons•

Lexington Park•

St. Marys City•

Potomac

Point
Lookout

Susquehanna

•Elkton
Havre de Grace•
•Aberdeen
•Edgewood

Chesapeake and
Delaware Canal

Sassafras

Chestertown•

MARYLAND

WILLIAM PRESTON LANE JR. MEMORIAL BRIDGE
(CHESAPEAKE BAY BRIDGE)

EASTERN NECK N.W.R.

Chester

Kent
Island

•Grasonville

Eastern
Bay

St.
Michaels•

Denton•

Easton•

Choptank

Choptank

Cambridge•

Federalsburg•

Hurlock•

BLACKWATER
NATIONAL
WILDLIFE REFUGE

•Bucktown

Fishing
Bay

Bloodsworth
Island

Smith
Island

Nanticoke

Tangier Sound

Crisfield•

Pocomoke Sound

**D
E
L
M
A
R
V
A
P
E
N
I
N
S
U
L
A**

DELAWARE

Salisbury•
•Fruitland

Ocean Pines•

Berlin•

Ocean
City

Snow
Hill

Pocomoke City•

Pocomoke

Chincoteague Bay

ASSATEAGUE
ISLAND
NATIONAL
SEASHORE

Assateague
Island

**ATLANTIC
OCEAN**

VIRGINIA

Chesapeake Bay

Patuxent

B

C

D

E

F

G

H

J

K

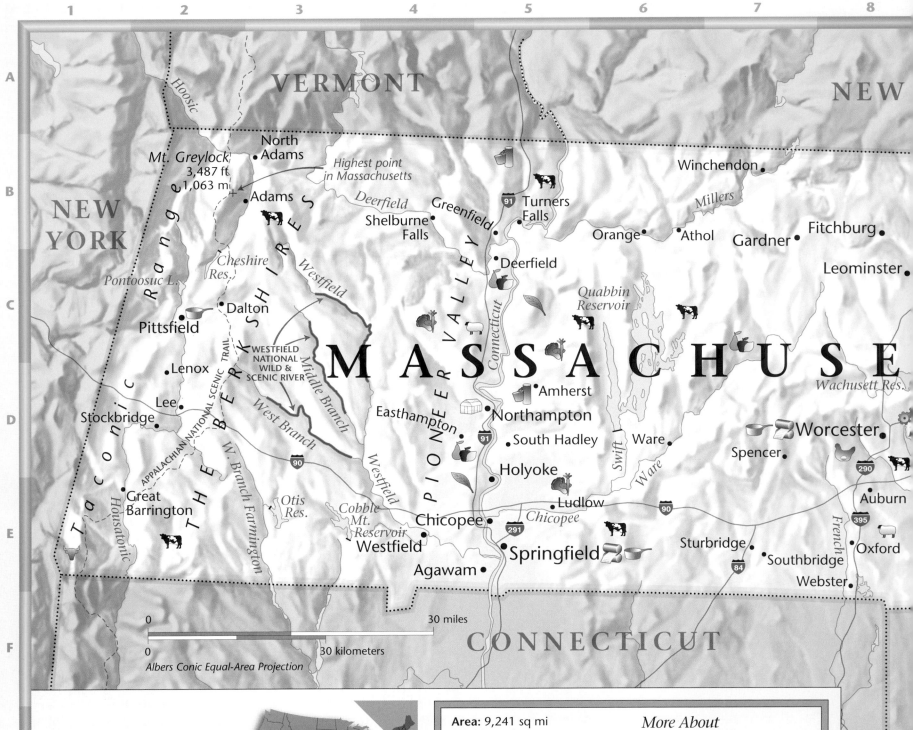

VERMONT

NEW

NEW
YORK

Mt. Greylock
3,487 ft
1,063 m

North
Adams

Highest point
in Massachusetts

Adams

Deerfield

Shelburne
Falls

Greenfield

Turners
Falls

Winchendon

Millers

Orange

Athol

Gardner

Fitchburg

Leominster

Cheshire
Res.

Pontoosuc L.

Westfield

Dalton

Pittsfield

Lenox

Lee

Stockbridge

Deerfield

Quabbin
Reservoir

M A S S A C H U S E

Wachusett Res.

Amherst

Easthampton

Northampton

South Hadley

Worcester

Spencer

Auburn

Great
Barrington

Otis
Res.

Cobble
Mt.
Reservoir

Westfield

Holyoke

Ludlow

Chicopee

Chicopee

Ware

Ware

Sturbridge

Southbridge

Oxford

Springfield

Webster

Agawam

WESTFIELD
NATIONAL
WILD &
SCENIC RIVER

APPALACHIAN NATIONAL SCENIC TRAIL

THE BERKSHIRES

Taconic Range

Housatonic

W. Branch Farmington

West Branch

Middle Branch

Westfield

PIONEER VALLEY

Connecticut

Swift

French

Hoosic

Deerfield

0   30 miles

0   30 kilometers
Albers Conic Equal-Area Projection

CONNECTICUT

Bay State

Massachusetts

Much of America's history began along the Atlantic coast of Massachusetts, which has some of the finest natural harbors in New England. In 1620 the Pilgrims settled at Plymouth. In 1630 Puritans founded the city of Boston on Massachusetts Bay.

In the years since then, and especially in the 19th and 20th centuries, many others have entered Massachusetts through Boston's welcoming harbor. Immigrants from Western Europe came to work in the state's busy factories and mills. They were followed in the 20th century by Asian and Hispanic families. Today, a third of the state's people are either immigrants or are the children of immigrants.

Boston is still a busy seaport. A center of business, culture, and learning, it is one of the largest cities on the East Coast. More than 60 universities and colleges draw students to the Boston area. In turn, the universities supply expert workers to companies in Massachusetts that specialize in computers, electronics, and medical research.

Area: 9,241 sq mi
(23,934 sq km)
Population: 6,147,000
Capital: Boston, pop. 558,400
Largest city: Boston,
pop. 558,400
Industry: electrical equipment, machinery, metal products, scientific instruments, printing and publishing, tourism
Agriculture: fruits, nuts and berries, nursery stock, dairy products, vegetables, tobacco
Statehood: February 6, 1788; 6th state
Nickname: Bay State

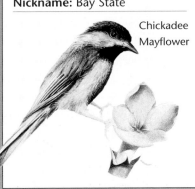

Chickadee
Mayflower

More About Massachusetts

■ *Massachusetts is named for Indians who lived in the area when European colonists arrived.*
■ *Salem was the site of witchcraft trials in the 1690s, when Puritans executed 20 people as witches.*
■ *The game of basketball was invented by Massachusetts teacher James A. Naismith in Springfield. He wanted a game that could be played indoors in winter, so he put up two peach baskets in a gym. His class played the first basketball game in 1891.*
■ *Massachusetts is the birthplace of four Presidents: John Adams, John Quincy Adams, John F. Kennedy, and George Bush.*
■ *Boston opened the country's first subway in 1897.*

AMPSHIRE

9 10 11 12 13 14 15 16

A

B

C

D

E

F

G

H

J

K

Amesbury

Newburyport

Haverhill

Merrimack

495

Methuen

Lawrence

Dracut

Ipswich

PARKER
RIVER
N.W.R.

95

Lowell

93

Lowell N.H.P.

Chelmsford

Cape
Ann

Gloucester

Danvers

Wilmington

Beverly

*Salem Maritime
N.H.S.*

Peabody

Salem

ATLANTIC

OXBOW
N.W.R.

GREAT
MEADOWS
N.W.R.

MINUTE
MAN
N.H.P.

Woburn

SAUGUS IRON
WORKS N.H.S.

Marblehead

*One of the ten most populous
cities in the U.S. in 1790*

STELLWAGEN

OCEAN

BANK

Concord

Concord

Lexington

Lynn

Massachusetts

NATIONAL

SUDBURY, A BET & CONCORD
NATIONAL W D & SCENIC RIVER

GREAT
MEADOWS
N.W.R.

Medford

MARINE

T S

Charles

Cambridge

*Sudbury
Res.*

Boston

Bay

SANCTUARY

orough

90

BOSTON HARBOR
ISLANDS N.R.A.

rewsbur

Wellesley

Brookline

Fram ngham

President Kennedy's birthplace

Milton

igamond

90

President Bush's birthplace

95

Quincy

Weymouth

*Birthplace of Presidents John
and John Quincy Adams*

93

Norwood

Milford

Randolph

Rockland

Provincetown

Stoughton

Franklin

95

Brockton

Whitman

Truro

Bellingham

495

*Silver
Lake*

CAPE
COD

North Attleboro

Plymouth

Plimouth Plantation

Wellfleet

NATIONAL

295

Attleboro

Cape Cod Bay

SEASHORE

Taunton

495

Middleboro

Cape Cod
Canal

Assawompset Pond

Great Quittacus Pond

Buzzards Bay

Sandwhich

Dennis

O

RHO DE ISLAND

Seekonk

195

*Long
Pond*

Taunton

Somerset

Barnstable

Chatham

C

*New Bedford
Whaling N.H.P.*

Fall River

195

New
Bedford

Fairhaven

P

E

C

A

S. Yarmouth

Hyannis

Monomoy Island

MONOMOY N.W.R.

East Falmouth

*Buzzards
Bay*

Woods
Hole

Falmouth

Elizabeth Islands

Vineyard
Haven

Oak Bluffs

Nantucket Sound

Vineyard Sound

NANTUCKET N.W.R.

Edgartown

*Chappaquiddick
Island*

Gay Head

WAMPANOAG
I.R.

*Martha's
Vineyard*

Rhode Island Sound

Nomans Land

Nantucket Island

Nantucket

Granite State

New Hampshire

Lofty mountains, deep woodlands, clear blue lakes—New Hampshire has them all. The variety and spectacular scenery of this state make it a favorite vacation spot. Tourism provides jobs for many New Hampshirites.

Millions of tourists visit the White Mountains, which cover most of the state's north. In summer, hikers can take in views from mountains such as Mount Washington, the highest peak in New England. In winter, skiers come to the snowy slopes for exciting sport. At Lake Winnipesaukee, the state's largest lake, vacationers enjoy fishing for trout or bass, swimming, boating, and camping.

New Hampshire is known for its large deposits of granite. It supplies this rock, along with sand and gravel, for constructing buildings across the nation. But the state's leading products are manufactured goods. In cities such as Manchester, Nashua, and Salem, New Hampshire's workers turn out products such as computers, machine parts, tools, and electrical equipment.

Area: 9,283 sq mi (24,044 sq km)

Population: 1,185,000

Capital: Concord, pop. 37,000

Largest city: Manchester, pop. 100,967

Industry: machinery, electronics, metal products

Agriculture: nursery stock, poultry and eggs, fruits and nuts, vegetables

Statehood: June 21, 1788; 9th state

Nickname: Granite State

More About New Hampshire

■ New Hampshire has the shortest coast of any state on an ocean—18 miles (29 km).

■ About 10 million tourists visit New Hampshire each year, nearly ten times the number of people who live in the state.

■ On April 12, 1934, wind across the top of Mount Washington was measured at an incredible 231 miles an hour (372 kmph). It was the strongest wind ever measured on Earth's surface.

■ New Hampshire is called the Granite State because vast deposits of this hard rock, in gray, red, and other colors, lie under most of the state.

■ New Hampshire has one of the country's largest French-Canadian populations; about a third of the people have French-Canadian roots.

Purple Finch
Purple Lilac

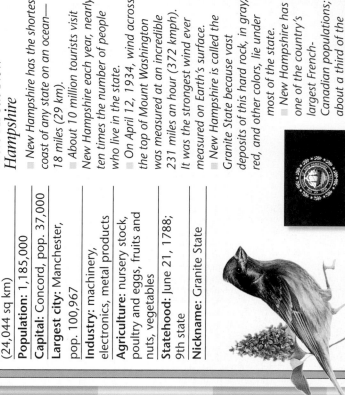

QUEBEC

CANADA
U.S.

MAINE

WHITE MOUNTAINS

APPALACHIAN NATIONAL SCENIC TRAIL

Androscoggin

Third L.
Second Lake
First Connecticut Lake
Lake Francis

Umbagog L.
LAKE UMBAGOG N.W.R.

Colebrook

Blue Mt.
3,723 ft
1,135 m

Connecticut

North Stratford

Groveton

Upper Ammonoosuc

Mt. Cabot
4,160 ft
1,268 m

WHITE MOUNTAIN NATIONAL FOREST

Lancaster

Berlin

Gorham

Mt. Washington
6,288 ft
1,917 m

Highest point in New Hampshire

Presidential Range

WILDCAT BROOK NATIONAL WILD & SCENIC RIVER

Ellis

Saco

North Conway

Whitefield

Whitefield

Moore Reservoir

Littleton

Franconia

Mt. Lafayette
5,249 ft
1,600 m

FRANCONIA NOTCH S.P.

CRAWFORD NOTCH S.P.

Ammonoosuc

WHITE MOUNTAIN NATIONAL FOREST

Oldest covered bridge in the U.S. (1827)

Haverhill
Bath Bridge

Lisbon

Woodsville

93

91

ATLANTIC

OCEAN

NEW HAMPSHIRE

VERMONT

MASSACHUSETTS

Conway
Conway Lake
Saco
Ossipee
Ossipee Lake
Sanbornville
Center Ossipee
Wolfeboro
Merrymeeting Lake
Lake Wentworth
Milton
Salmon Falls
Cocheco
Somersworth
Dover
Portsmouth
Isles of Shoals
Newmarket
Great Bay
Piscataqua
Rye
Hampton
Durham
Rochester
Farmington
Alton Bay
Center Sandwich
Lake Winnipesaukee
Laconia
Pittsfield
Canterbury
Suncook Lakes
Bow Lake
Exeter
Kingston
Raymond
LAMPREY NATIONAL WILD & SCENIC RIVER
Lamprey
Plaistow
Bearcamp
Ossipee Lake
Meredith
Ashland
Squam Lake
Crystal Lake
Northfield
Tilton
Suncook
Suncook
Massabesic Lake
East Derry
Derry
Atkinson
Salem
Winnisquam Lake
Franklin
Concord
Merrimack
Bristol
Pemigewasset
Manchester
Londonderry
Merrimack
Nashua
Warren
Orford
Connecticut
Enfield
Canaan
Newfound Lake
New London
JOHN HAY N.W.R.
Mt. Sunapee 2,743 ft 836 m
MT. SUNAPEE S.P.
Henniker
Hillsboro
President Pierce's birthplace
Contoocook
Contoocook
WAPACK N.W.R.
Peterborough
Wilton
Milford
Greenville
Souhegan
Hanover
Lebanon
Mascoma Lake
Mascoma
Sunapee Lake
Newport
SAINT-GAUDENS N.H.S.
Claremont
Charlestown
North Walpole
Walpole
Antrim
Highland Lake
Nubanusit Lake
Keene
Monadnock Mt. 3,165 ft + 965 m
Troy
Jaffrey
Surry Mt. Lake
Ashuelot
Winchester
PISGAH STATE PARK
Hinsdale
Connecticut
Sugar
Connecticut

20 miles

Albers Conic Equal-Area Projection

APPALACHIAN NAT. SCENIC TRAIL

Garden State

New Jersey

S haped like a short, squat S, New Jersey faces the Atlantic Ocean. The state sits between two giant cities—New York and Philadelphia—and two big rivers, the Hudson and the Delaware. This makes it a key transportation link. The New Jersey Turnpike, part of the highway system that links New York City and Washington, D.C., is the nation's busiest toll road.

New Jersey is the most densely populated state in the country, with most people living in the north around Newark. Finance, services, retail businesses, and manufacturing all provide jobs for New Jersey's residents. Leading products include chemicals, processed food, and machinery.

In contrast to its busy factory cities, New Jersey has a large southern wilderness area of marsh and dwarf pine forests called the Pine Barrens. The state grows many kinds of fruits and vegetables and nursery flowers on its fertile central farmlands. Along the coast are more than 50 resort cities and towns. Most famous is Atlantic City, with its well-known boardwalk.

Area: 8,215 sq mi (21,277 sq km)

Population: 8,115,000

Capital: Trenton, pop. 85,400

Largest city: Newark, pop. 268,500

Industry: chemicals, printing and publishing, food processing, machinery, electronics

Agriculture: nursery stock, vegetables, grain and hay, fruits and berries, dairy products

Statehood: December 18, 1787; 3rd state

Nickname: Garden State

More About New Jersey

- New Jersey's many vegetable farms, flower nurseries, and orchards earned it the nickname Garden State.
- In 1930 Charles Darrow of New Jersey invented the game of Monopoly. He named Boardwalk and other streets in the game after those in Atlantic City.
- In 1838 Samuel F. B. Morse operated the first successful electric telegraph near Morristown.
- New Jersey was the location of more than 100 battles during the American Revolution.
- In 1889 the first electric sewing machine was manufactured by the Singer Company at Elizabeth.

American Goldfinch

Violet

PENNSYLVANIA

MARYLAND

DELAWARE

N E W   "J"   E   R   S   E   Y

Point Pleasant
Seaside Heights
Gilford Park
Barnegat B'y
Toms River
Lakehurst
Crestwood Village
Double Trouble
Browns Mills
Mount Holly
Willingboro
Burlington
Cinnaminson
Pennsauken
Camden
Cherry Hill
Haddonfield
Lindenwold
Woodbury
Pine Hill
Glassboro
Williamstown
Paulsboro
Penns Grove
Woodstown
Pennsville
Salem
Bridgeton
Vineland
Millville
Hammonton
Mays Landing
Egg Harbor City
Mystic Island
Ship Bottom
Surf City
Long Beach
Little Egg Harbor
Beach Haven
Brigantine
Atlantic City
Ventnor City
Somers Point
Ocean City
Absecon
Pleasantville
Sea Isle City
Cape May Court House
North Wildwood
Wildwood
Cape May
Villas
Woodbine

PINE BARRENS

PINELANDS NATIONAL RESERVE BOUNDARY
GARDEN STATE PARKWAY
ATLANTIC CITY EXPRESSWAY

E.B. FORSYTHE N.W.R.
E.B. FORSYTHE N.W.R.
E.B. FORSYTHE N.W.R.

Mullica
Great Egg Harbor
GREAT EGG HARBOR NAT. WILD & SCENIC RIVER
Maurice
MAURICE NAT. WILD & SCENIC RIVER
Cohansey
Tuckahoe
Salem
Delaware

Great Bay

First dinosaur skeleton discovered in North America, 1858

CAPE MAY N.W.R.
CAPE MAY N.W.R.
CAPE MAY

Cape May Canal

DELAWARE BAY

ATLANTIC OCEAN

SUPAWNA MEADOWS N.W.R.
PINELANDS NATIONAL RESERVE BOUNDARY

Toms

Barnegat

20 miles
20 kilometers
Albers Conic Equal-Area Projection

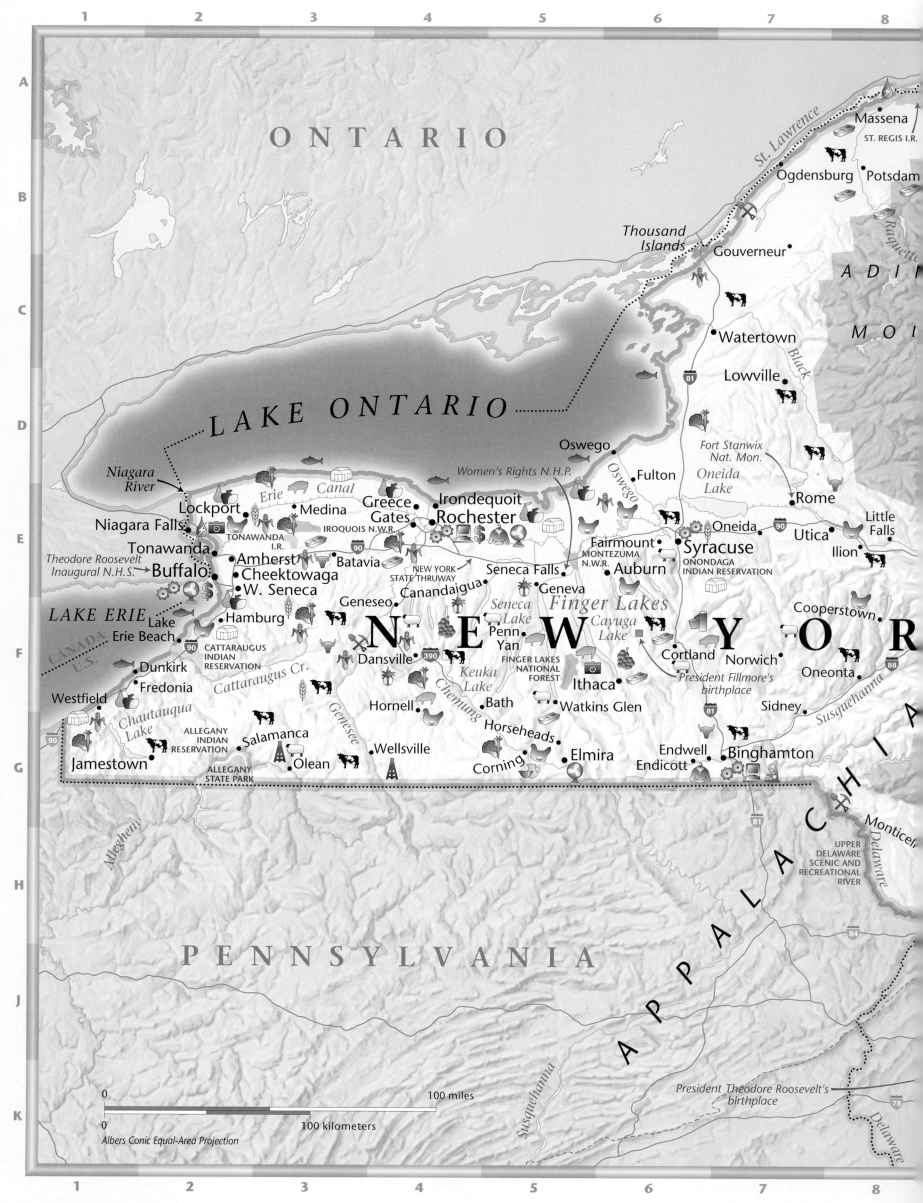

ONTARIO

Massena
ST. REGIS I.R.
Ogdensburg   Potsdam

Thousand
Islands   Gouverneur

LAKE ONTARIO

Watertown

Lowville

Black

Niagara
River   Oswego   Women's Rights N.H.P.   Fort Stanwix
Nat. Mon.

Erie Canal   Greece   Irondequoit   Oswego   Fulton   Oneida
Lockport   Medina   Gates   Rochester   Lake   Rome
Niagara Falls   IROQUOIS N.W.R.   Little
Tonawanda   TONAWANDA I.R.   Fairmount   Oneida   Falls
Theodore Roosevelt   Amherst   Batavia   NEW YORK   Seneca Falls   MONTEZUMA   Syracuse   Utica   Ilion
Inaugural N.H.S.   Buffalo   Cheektowaga   STATE THRUWAY   N.W.R.   ONONDAGA
W. Seneca   Canandaigua   Geneva   Finger Lakes   INDIAN RESERVATION   Cooperstown
LAKE ERIE   Lake   Geneseo   NEW   Penn   Seneca   Cayuga   Auburn   Y   O   R
Erie Beach   Hamburg   Yan   Lake   Lake   Cortland   Norwich
CANADA   CATTARAUGUS   Dansville   FINGER LAKES   President Fillmore's   Oneonta
U.S.   INDIAN RESERVATION   NATIONAL FOREST   birthplace
Dunkirk   Cattaraugus Cr.   Keuka   Chemung   Ithaca   Sidney   Susquehanna
Fredonia   Lake   Hornell   Bath   Watkins Glen
Westfield   Chautauqua   Genesee   Horseheads   Endwell   Binghamton
Lake   ALLEGANY   Wellsville   Endicott
Jamestown   INDIAN   Salamanca   Corning   Elmira
RESERVATION   Olean   APPALACHIA
ALLEGANY
STATE PARK   UPPER
DELAWARE
SCENIC AND
RECREATIONAL
RIVER
Allegheny   Susquehanna

PENNSYLVANIA   APPALACHIA   Monticel

President Theodore Roosevelt's
birthplace   Delaware

0   100 miles
0   100 kilometers
Albers Conic Equal-Area Projection

QUEBEC

CANADA
U.S.

Malone

Dannemora

Plattsburgh

Lake Champlain

VERMONT

Saranac Lake
Lake Placid

N D A C K
Mt. Marcy +
5,344 ft
1,629 m

Highest point in New York

T A I N S

Ticonderoga　Fort Ticonderoga

DIRONDACK

Lake George

PARK

Hudson

Warrensburg

Great Sacandaga Lake

Glens Falls

MOUNTAINS

Saratoga Springs

Gloversville
Amsterdam

SARATOGA N.H.P.

Mohawk

Schenectady
Niskayuna
Troy

APPALACHIAN NATIONAL SCENIC TRAIL

NEW HAMPSHIRE

Cobleskill

K

Albany ★

President Van Buren's birthplace

NEW YORK STATE THRUWAY

Kinderhook

MARTIN VAN BUREN N.H.S.

MASSACHUSETTS

Hudson

Catskill

C A T S K I L L
OUNTAINS
ATSKIL
ARK
Slide Mt.
4,204 ft
1,281 m

Kingston

VANDERBILT MANSION N.H.S.

HOME OF FRANKLIN D. ROOSEVELT N.H.S.
ELEANOR ROOSEVELT N.H.S.

New Paltz

Poughkeepsie

CONNECTICUT

RHODE ISLAND

Newburgh
iddletown
rt Jervis

Beacon

West Point

U.S. Military Academy

Peekskill

New City
uxedo Park
Spring Valley

Tarrytown

White Plains

Long Island Sound

Block Island Sound

Montauk Point

Yonkers

ST. PAUL'S CHURCH N.H.S.

New Rochelle

Huntington

Coram

Centereach

Sag Harbor

Southampton

SAGAMORE HILL N.H.S.

Brentwood

New York

Levittown

Freeport

FIRE ISLAND NATIONAL SEASHORE

Ellis Island
STATUE OF LIBERTY NAT. MON.

Long Beach

Long Island

NEW JERSEY

Staten Island

GATEWAY NAT. RECREATION AREA

ATLANTIC OCEAN

The Empire State

New York

Gateway to America, New York has welcomed millions of immigrants from around the world. The state's physical geography makes it a natural entrance to the United States. New York is the only state that borders both the Atlantic Ocean and the Great Lakes. Rivers and canals connect New York City's deep, busy harbor to the Great Lakes and St. Lawrence River, providing passage to goods and raw materials between the East and the nation's heartland.

Today, New York ranks third in population after California and Texas. New York City alone is the largest city in the country. If you count nearby suburbs, it is the third largest metropolitan area in the world, with more than 16 million people.

Stretching north and west of New York City's towering skyscrapers, New York State boasts millions of acres of farms and scenic lands. They include the rolling Adirondack and Catskill Mountains and Niagara Falls.

Area: 53,989 sq mi (139,833 sq km)

Population: 18,175,000

Capital: Albany, pop. 103,600

Largest city: New York City, pop. 7,380,900

Industry: printing and publishing, machinery, computer products, finance, tourism

Agriculture: dairy products, cattle and other livestock, vegetables, nursery stock, apples

Statehood: July 26, 1788; 11th state

Nickname: Empire State

More about New York

■ George Washington described New York as the "seat of empire," giving the state its nickname.
■ The character Uncle Sam, whose initials stand for United States, originated in Troy, New York.
■ Niagara Falls is the country's largest waterfall by volume.
■ New York City's World Trade Center buildings are two of the tallest skyscrapers in the world. Each 115-story building has its own zip code.
■ Adirondack Park, which covers 6 million acres, is the largest state park in the lower 48 states.
■ From 1892 to 1954 more than 17 million immigrants entered the United States at New York's Ellis Island (now shared with New Jersey).

Eastern Bluebird
Rose

Lake Erie

NEW

OHIO

Erie
Millcreek
Corry
Allegheny Reservoir
Bradford
Warren
Coudersport
Mansfield
Wellsbor
Meadville
ERIE N.W.R.
Titusville
ALLEGHENY
NATIONAL
WILD &
SCENIC
RIVER
ALLEGHENY

ERIE N.W.R.
NATIONAL
Emporium

Pymatuning
Reservoir
FOREST
Greenville
Ridgway
St. Marys
Oil City
Clarion
CLARION NATIONAL
WILD & SCENIC RIVER

Pine Creek

Pine Creek Gorge

Sharon
Clarion
W. Branch Susquehanna
Williamspor
Grove City
Du Bois
Jersey Shore
New Castle
Punxsutawney
Clearfield
Lock Haven

P E N N S Y L V

Butler
Kittanning

Beaver Falls

Aliquippa
Indiana
Tyrone
State
College
Lewistown

McCandless

Plum

Pittsburgh
Penn Hills

Altoona
Huntingdon

McKeesport
ALLEGHENY PORTAGE
RAILROAD N.H.S.
Hollidaysburg

JOHNSTOWN
FLOOD
NAT. MEM.
Raystown
Lake

Jeannette
Johnstown
Greensburg
Windber
President Buchanan's
birthplace
Mechanicsbur
Washington
Monessen

PENNSYLVANIA TURNPIKE
Carlisl

Youghiogheny
Shippensburg
Connellsville
Somerset
Bedford

Waynesburg
Casselman
Highest point
in Pennsylvania
Mercersburg
Chambersburg
Uniontown
FRIENDSHIP HILL
N.H.S.
Mt. Davis
3,213 ft
(979) m
Gettysburg
FT. NECESSITY
NATIONAL
BATTLEFIELD
EISENHOWER N.H.S.
Waynesboro
GETTYSBURG N.M.P.

Monongahela

Cheat

MARYLAND

WEST
VIRGINIA

A P P A L A

Juniata

Tuscarora Mountain

A L L E G H E N Y   M O U N T A I N S

A P P A L A C H I A N

0   100 miles
0   100 kilometers
Albers Conic Equal-Area Projection

VIRGINIA

Keystone State

Pennsylvania

Pennsylvania's location has made it a key state since colonial times. Situated right in the center of the 13 original American Colonies, Pennsylvania won the nickname Keystone State.

Later, the state became a hub of steel-making and a link between the East and the Midwest. Pittsburgh and Philadelphia, both on major rivers, became shipping centers for raw materials and manufactured goods. Pennsylvania mines yielded the coal that fueled power plants and steel factories across much of the country.

Immigrants from all over the world have settled in the Keystone State. Rich farmland and industrial jobs have attracted British, Germans, and Italians as well as Hispanics and Asians to Pennsylvania.

Historic Philadelphia is one of the East's largest cities. There, visitors can see the Liberty Bell, the house of Betsy Ross, and the place where the Declaration of Independence was drafted and signed. To the west is Gettysburg, a famous Civil War site.

Area: 46,058 sq mi (119,291 sq km)

Population: 12,001,000

Capital: Harrisburg, pop. 50,900

Largest city: Philadelphia, pop. 1,478,000

Industry: machinery, printing and publishing, forest products, metal products

Agriculture: dairy products, poultry and eggs, mushrooms, cattle, hogs, grains

Statehood: December 12, 1787; 2nd state

Nickname: Keystone State

More About Pennsylvania

■ Pennsylvania was founded by and named for William Penn, a Quaker. It is sometimes called the Quaker State.

■ Philadelphia, 90 miles (145 km) from the Atlantic on the Delaware River, is the one of the busiest freshwater ports in the world.

■ In 1905 the world's largest chocolate factory opened in Hershey. Today, it produces 33 million candy kisses a day. Even the city's street lamps are shaped like Hershey kisses.

■ Two of the country's first colleges for African-Americans—Cheyney University and Lincoln University—were founded in Pennsylvania in the 1800s.

■ Philadelphia is home to the country's largest mint, where coins are made.

Ruffed Grouse
Mountain Laurel

Map labels

YORK

Chemung

Sayre

Towanda

Susquehanna

Carbondale

Archbald

Scranton
STEAMTOWN N.H.S.

Dunmore

UPPER DELAWARE SCENIC & RECREATIONAL RIVER

Delaware

Lake Wallenpaupack

Kingston

Wilkes-Barre

POCONO MTS.

DELAWARE WATER GAP NATIONAL RECREATION AREA

Lewisburg

Bloomsburg

Hazleton

Lehigh

Stroudsburg

Delaware Water Gap

ANIA

Sunbury

Mt. Carmel

Shamokin

Selinsgrove

Tamaqua

Nazareth

Bangor

Pottsville

Easton

Bethlehem

Allentown

APPALACHIAN NAT. SCENIC TRAIL

Blue Mountain

NEW JERSEY

Quakertown

Harrisburg

Lebanon

Schuylkill

Reading

Doylestown

Hershey

PENNSYLVANIA TURNPIKE

HOPEWELL FURNACE N.H.S.

Pottstown

Levittown

Three Mile Island

Elizabethtown

Ephrata

VALLEY FORGE N.H.P.

Norristown

Lancaster

Upper Darby

Delaware

Columbia

Coatesville

Philadelphia

York

West Chester

Chester

JOHN HEINZ N.W.R.

Red Lion

Kennett Square

Hanover

Mason-Dixon Line

Independence N.H.P. includes Independence Hall, Liberty Bell, Christ Church, Franklin Court; Betsy Ross House; Edgar Allen Poe N.H.S.

Susquehanna

The Pennsylvania-Maryland boundary, named after its surveyors, became the traditional division between North and South

DEL.

Chesapeake Bay

Delaware Bay

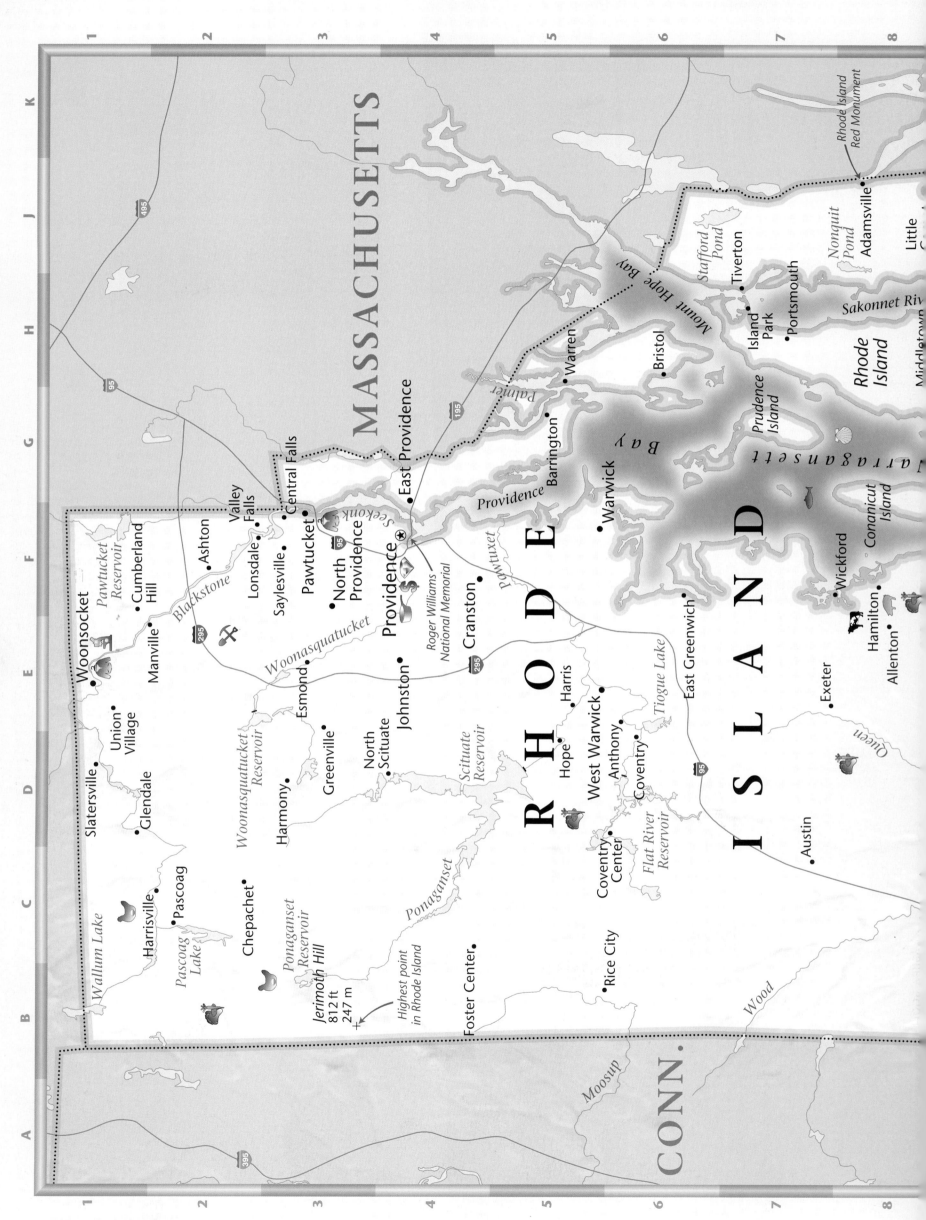

MASSACHUSETTS

RHODE ISLAND

CONN.

Rhode Island
Red Monument

Stafford
Pond

Nonquit
Pond

Adamsville

Little

Tiverton

Island
Park

Portsmouth

Sakonnet Riv

Mount Hope Bay

Warren

Bristol

Rhode
Island

Middletown

Prudence
Island

Palmer

Barrington

Providence

Warwick

Narragansett

Bay

Wickford

Conanicut
Island

Hamilton

Allenton

East Greenwich

East Providence

Central Falls

195

Valley
Falls

Ashton

Cumberland
Hill

Lonsdale

Saylesville

Pawtucket

North
Providence

Seekonk

95

Providence

Roger Williams
National Memorial

Cranston

Pawtuxet

Pawtucket
Reservoir

Woonsocket

Blackstone

295

Manville

Union
Village

Esmond

Johnston

295

Harris

Exeter

Slatersville

Glendale

Harmony

Greenville

North
Scituate

Scituate
Reservoir

Hope

West Warwick

Anthony

Coventry

Tiogue Lake

Queen

Woonasquatucket

Woonasquatucket
Reservoir

Ponaganset

Harrisville

Pascoag

Chepachet

Coventry
Center

Flat River
Reservoir

Austin

Wallum Lake

Pascoag
Lake

Ponaganset
Reservoir

Jerimoth Hill
812 ft
247 m

Highest point
in Rhode Island

Foster Center

Rice City

Wood

Moosup

395

95

495

95

Ocean State

Rhode Island

Measuring just 48 by 32 miles (71 km by 51 km), Rhode Island is the smallest state in the nation. Yet this tiny New England state has a lot of waterfront property. Narragansett Bay, which extends deep into the state from the Atlantic Ocean, has 36 islands, including Rhode Island, for which the state is named. Counting all its ocean, bay, and island shores, Rhode Island's shoreline measures 384 miles (618 km). No wonder it's called the Ocean State!

Lured by jobs in factories, immigrants from Europe, Canada, Southeast Asia, and elsewhere flocked to Rhode Island in the 19th and 20th centuries. The state was founded on the principle of religious tolerance. It has been a haven for Roman Catholics, Quakers, and Jews; Touro Synagogue in Newport, founded in 1763, is the oldest Jewish temple in North America.

Area: 1,231 sq mi (3,189 sq km)

Population: 988,000

Capital: Providence, pop. 152,600

Largest city: Providence, pop. 152,600

Industry: health services, tourism, business services, fashion jewelry, textiles, metal products

Agriculture: nursery stock, vegetables, dairy products, eggs

Statehood: May 29, 1790; 13th state

Nickname: Ocean State

More About Rhode Island

■ More than 500 Rhode Islands could fit into Alaska, the nation's largest state.

■ Although it is the smallest state, Rhode Island has the longest official name: State of Rhode Island and Providence Plantations.

■ According to legend, the pirate Captain Kidd buried treasure on Rhode Island's Conanicut Island in Narragansett Bay.

Rhode Island Red

Violet

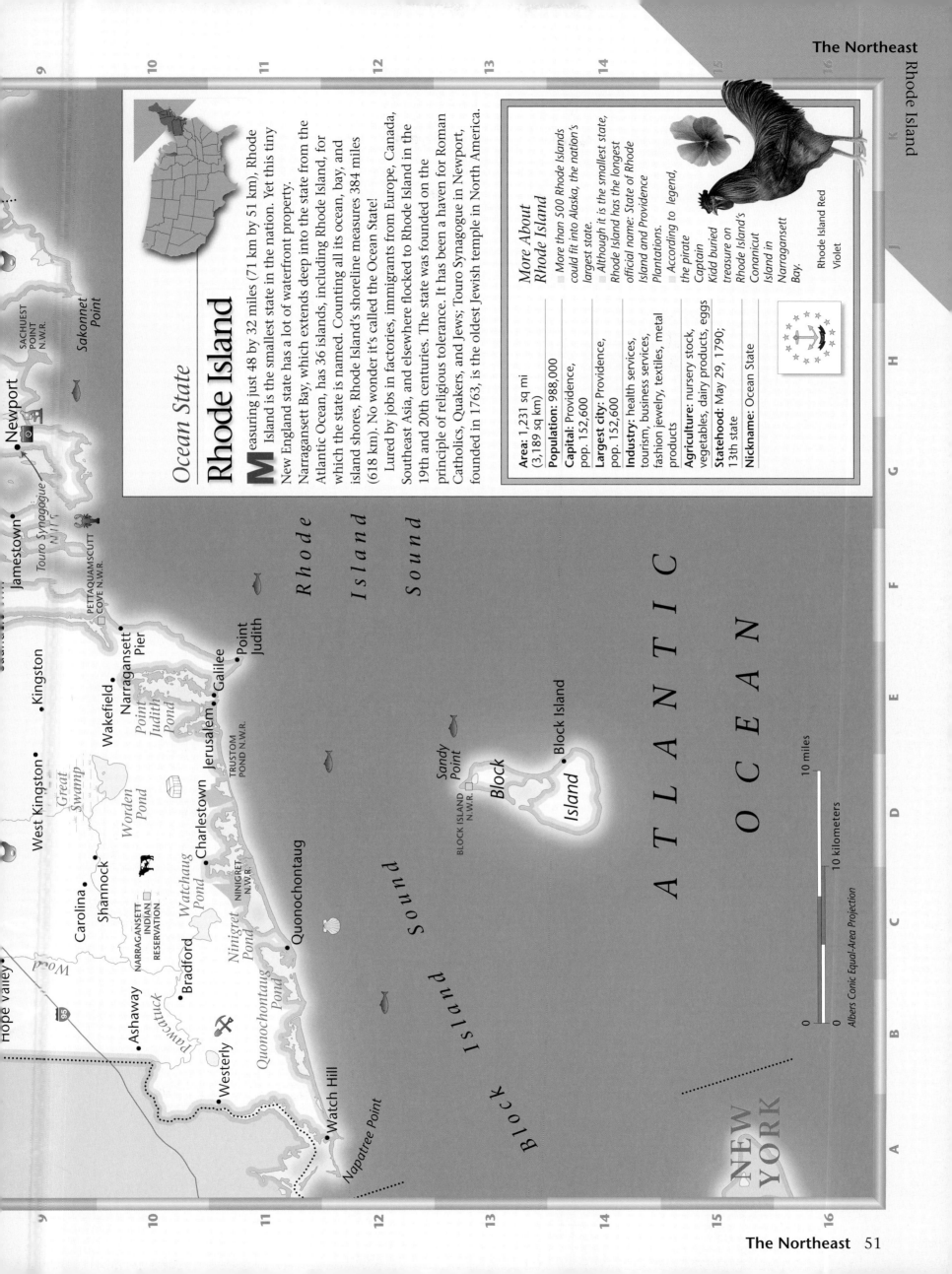

Newport
SACHUEST POINT N.W.R.
Sakonnet Point
Jamestown
Touro Synagogue N.H.L.
PETTAQUAMSCUTT COVE N.W.R.
Point Judith
Galilee
Narragansett Pier
Kingston
Point Judith Pond
Wakefield
Jerusalem
West Kingston
Great Swamp
Worden Pond
TRUSTOM POND N.W.R.
Charlestown
Carolina
Shannock
NARRAGANSETT INDIAN RESERVATION
Watchaug Pond
NINIGRET N.W.R.
Quonochontaug
Ashaway
Bradford
Ninigret Pond
Quonochontaug Pond
Westerly
Watch Hill
Napatree Point
Hope Valley
Pawcatuck
Wood

Rhode Island Sound

Sandy Point
BLOCK ISLAND N.W.R.
Block Island
Block Island

Block Island Sound

ATLANTIC OCEAN

NEW YORK

10 miles
10 kilometers
Albers Conic Equal-Area Projection

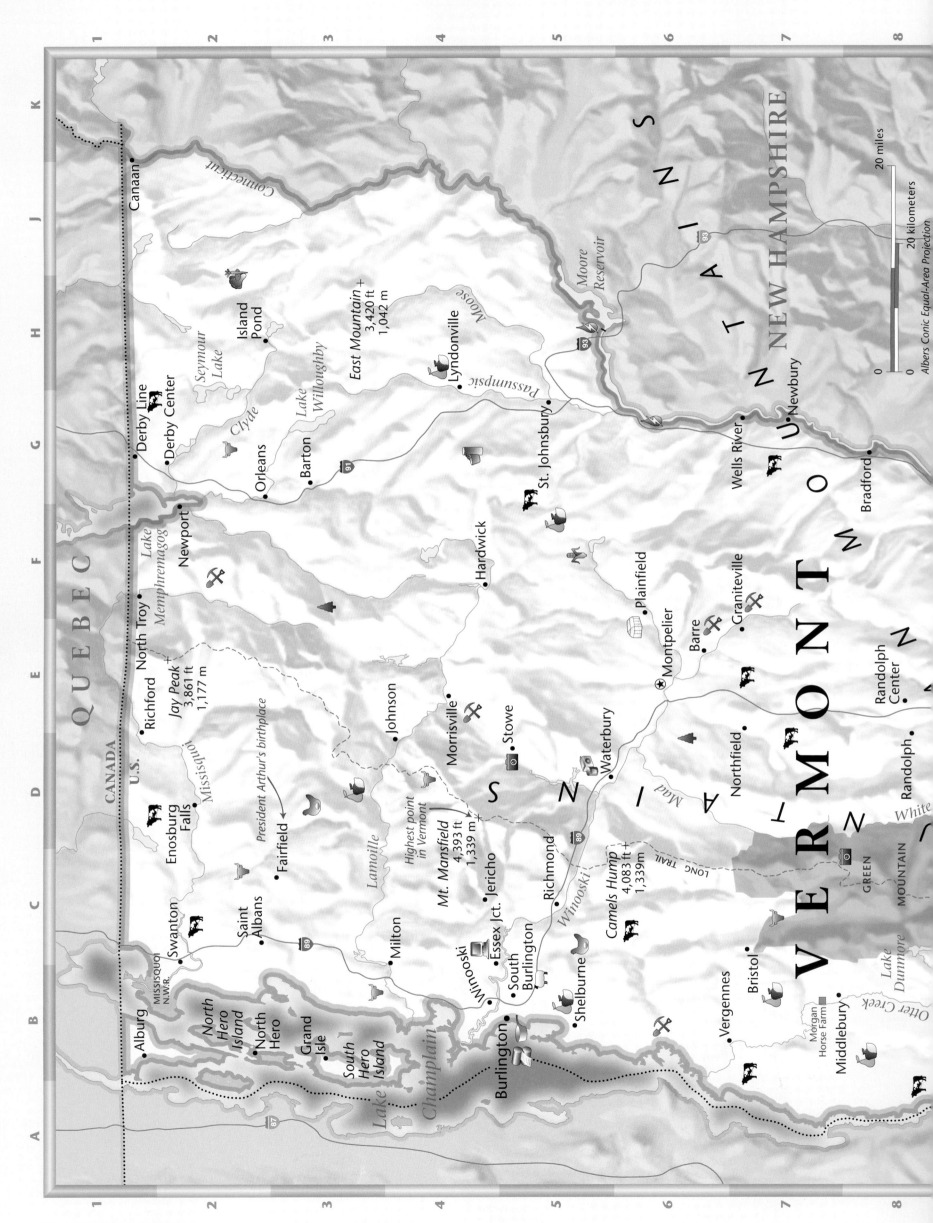

QUEBEC

CANADA
U.S.

NEW HAMPSHIRE

WHITE MOUNTAINS

Connecticut

Canaan

Seymour Lake

Island Pond

Clyde

Lake Willoughby

East Mountain +
3,420 ft
1,042 m

Moose

Lyndonville

Moore Reservoir

93

Derby Line
Derby Center

Orleans

Barton

91

Hardwick

Passumpsic

St. Johnsbury

93

U.

Wells River

Newbury

Lake Memphremagog

Newport

Plainfield

Graniteville

Bradford

North Troy

Richford

Jay Peak +
3,861 ft
1,177 m

President Arthur's birthplace

Fairfield

Johnson

Morrisville

Stowe

Waterbury

Montpelier

Barre

Northfield

Randolph Center

M

O

N

Mississquoi

Enosburg Falls

Mad

Randolph

V E R M O N T

Swanton

Saint Albans

Milton

Lamoille

Highest point in Vermont

Mt. Mansfield +
4,393 ft
1,339 m

Jericho

Essex Jct.

Richmond

89

GREEN MOUNTAINS

Camels Hump +
4,083 ft
1,339m

LONG TRAIL

White

Winooski

S

E

N

I

A

T

N

U

O

MISSISQUOI N.W.R.

Alburg

North Hero Island

North Hero

Grand Isle

South Hero Island

Winooski
South Burlington

Shelburne

Bristol

Vergennes

Morgan Horse Farm

Middlebury

Lake Dunmore

Randolph Center

Burlington

Lake Champlain

Otter Creek

87

89

20 miles

20 kilometers

Albers Conic Equal-Area Projection

Green Mountain State

Vermont

Vermont gets its name from the tree-covered Green Mountains that run down the state's middle. "Vermont" comes from the French words "vert mont," meaning "green mountain." Forests cover three-fourths of the state, and trees such as maples, poplars, and birches blaze with fiery color in the fall, clothing the mountains in red, yellow, and orange. Vermont is the only New England state with no seacoast, yet much of it is bordered by water. The Connecticut River forms the state's eastern boundary. Lake Champlain, New England's largest lake, lies along much of the western edge.

In winter, Vermont's mountains get a whopping 100 inches (254 cm) or more of snow. Ski resorts, such as Stowe and Killington, draw skiers and provide jobs for many Vermonters. Farmers who boil down the sweet sap of sugar maple trees for syrup produce more maple syrup than those in any other state. Vermont is also rich in milk, apples, marble, granite, and manufactured goods ranging from electronic equipment to books.

More About Vermont

Vermont was an independent country from 1777 to 1791. It had its own money and postal service.

Only Wyoming and Alaska have fewer people than Vermont. A Vermont treat is called sugar-on-snow. It is made by pouring maple syrup that has been boiled a long time onto fresh, clean snow. The cold snow hardens the syrup into taffy-like candy.

Some of the nation's most important buildings, including the United States Capitol and the U.S. Supreme Court Building, in Washington, D.C., contain marble and granite from Vermont quarries.

Vermont has 114 covered bridges, built to protect wooden roads from snow and ice.

Area: 9,615 sq mi (24,903 sq km)
Population: 591,000
Capital: Montpelier, pop. 7,900
Largest city: Burlington, pop. 39,000
Industry: electronics, printing and publishing, metal products, forest products, tourism
Agriculture: dairy products, cattle and other livestock, nursery stock
Statehood: March 4, 1791; 14th state
Nickname: Green Mountain State

Hermit Thrush
Red Clover

The South

east

Alabama
Arkansas
Florida
Georgia
Kentucky
Louisiana
Mississippi
North Carolina
South Carolina
Tennessee
Virginia
West Virginia

Ghostly, moss-draped bald cypress trees rise from the quiet waters of Louisiana's Atchafalaya Bay (left). About 600 miles (965 km) east, the Southeast looks to the future as the space shuttle Discovery (above) blasts from its launchpad at Florida's John F. Kennedy Space Center.

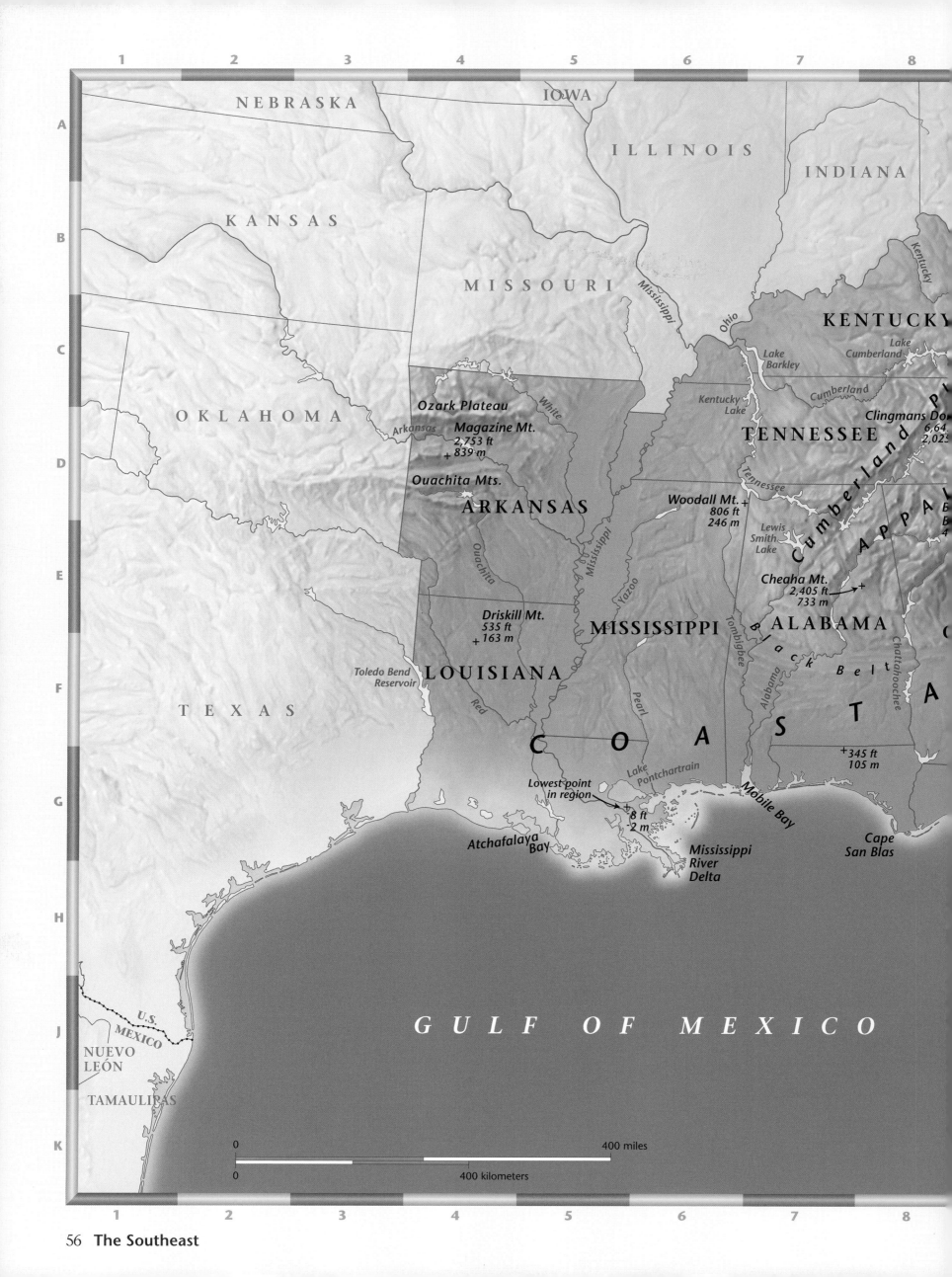

NEBRASKA

IOWA

ILLINOIS

INDIANA

KANSAS

MISSOURI

Mississippi

Ohio

KENTUCKY

Lake
Barkley

Lake
Cumberland

OKLAHOMA

Arkansas

Ozark Plateau
Magazine Mt.
2,753 ft
+ 839 m

White

Kentucky
Lake

Cumberland

TENNESSEE

Clingmans Do...
6,64...
2,025...

Ouachita Mts.

ARKANSAS

Ouachita

Mississippi

Woodall Mt. +
806 ft
246 m

Tennessee

Cumberland Pl...

APPAL...

B...
4...

Driskill Mt.
535 ft
+ 163 m

Yazoo

MISSISSIPPI

Lewis
Smith
Lake

Cheaha Mt.
2,405 ft
733 m

ALABAMA

Black

Belt

+

Toledo Bend
Reservoir

LOUISIANA

Tombigbee

Alabama

Chattahoochee

TEXAS

Red

Pearl

C   O   A   S   T

A

+ 345 ft
105 m

Lake
Pontchartrain

Lowest point
in region

+ 8 ft
- 2 m

Mobile Bay

Cape
San Blas

Atchafalaya
Bay

Mississippi
River
Delta

U.S.
MEXICO

NUEVO
LEÓN

GULF   OF   MEXICO

TAMAULIPAS

0   400 miles

0   400 kilometers

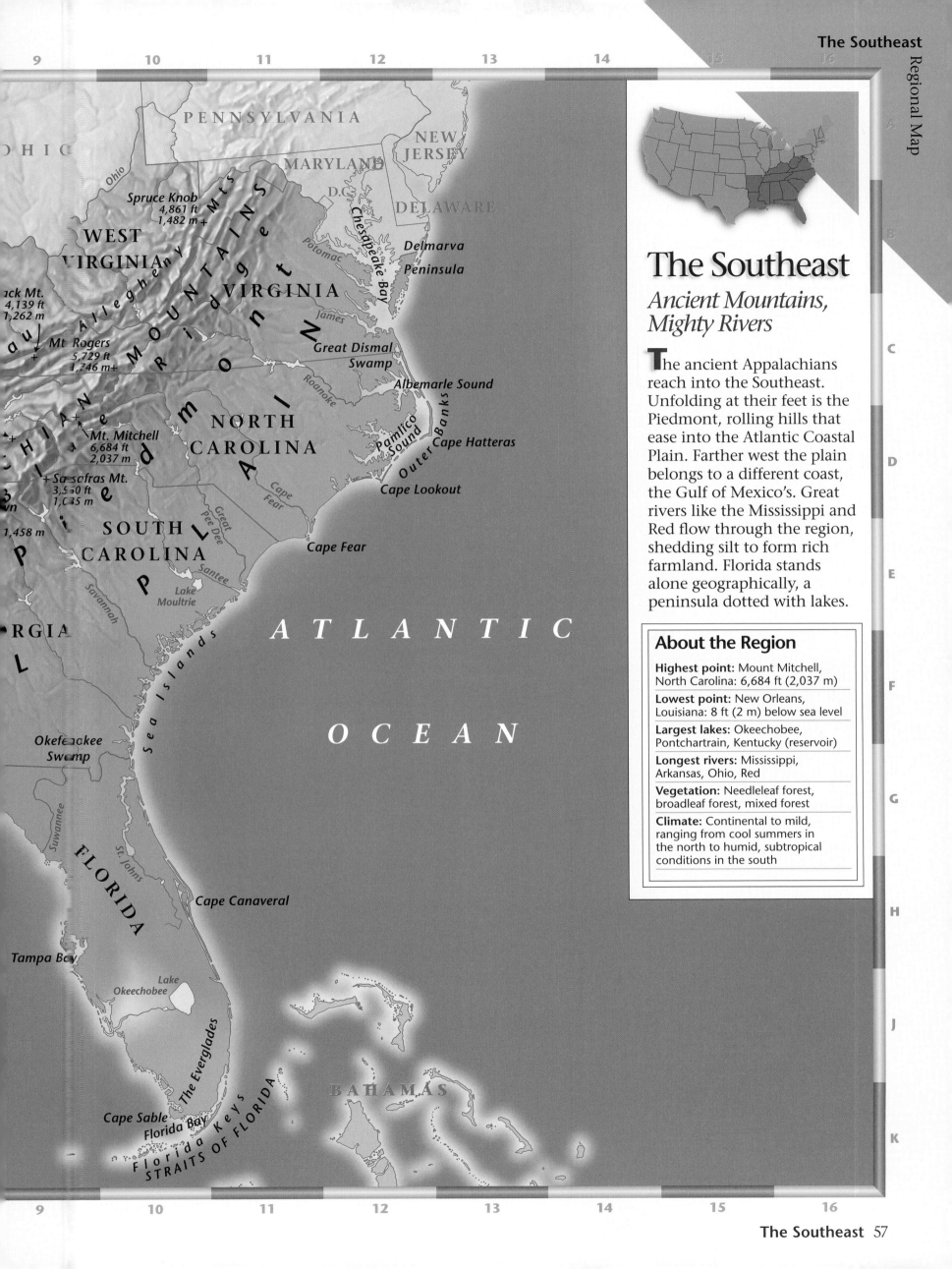

The Southeast
Ancient Mountains, Mighty Rivers

The ancient Appalachians reach into the Southeast. Unfolding at their feet is the Piedmont, rolling hills that ease into the Atlantic Coastal Plain. Farther west the plain belongs to a different coast, the Gulf of Mexico's. Great rivers like the Mississippi and Red flow through the region, shedding silt to form rich farmland. Florida stands alone geographically, a peninsula dotted with lakes.

About the Region

Highest point: Mount Mitchell, North Carolina: 6,684 ft (2,037 m)

Lowest point: New Orleans, Louisiana: 8 ft (2 m) below sea level

Largest lakes: Okeechobee, Pontchartrain, Kentucky (reservoir)

Longest rivers: Mississippi, Arkansas, Ohio, Red

Vegetation: Needleleaf forest, broadleaf forest, mixed forest

Climate: Continental to mild, ranging from cool summers in the north to humid, subtropical conditions in the south

The Southeast
Tradition Meets Technology

The Southeast is a blend of old and new: old mountains and artificial lakes, single-crop farming and multi-crop fields, time-honored crafts and high-tech industry. In the eastern part of the region, early settlers moved into Appalachian valleys, building independent communities. Their descendants preserve this mountain heritage in music and art. Cities grew up on the coast and along the fall line. Here, rivers drop from the highlands to the flat Atlantic Coastal Plain. Energy produced from the falling water powered early factories.

Cotton once ruled the fertile lands of the Deep South. In the early 1900s, after the destructive boll weevil ruined this crop, farmers began to plant a wider variety of plants and started fish farms on flooded fields. Rich with shellfish and petroleum, the Gulf of Mexico in the far south provides a living for many. In Florida, land once covered by water is now covered with orchards that are the source of the state's famous orange juice.

▲ **TRADITIONAL MUSIC-MAKING** *fills leisure hours in communities of the Appalachian Mountains. Tunes played there often reflect the settlers' Scottish and Irish roots.*

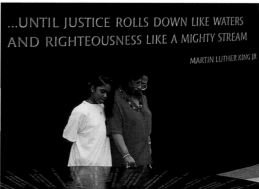

...UNTIL JUSTICE ROLLS DOWN LIKE WATERS AND RIGHTEOUSNESS LIKE A MIGHTY STREAM

MARTIN LUTHER KING JR

◀ **POWERFUL WORDS** *on the Civil Rights Memorial in Montgomery, Alabama, echo a speech by Dr. Martin Luther King, Jr., civil rights crusader.*

▼ **FUN IN THE SUN** *takes many forms on Florida's Marco Island and in other resorts that line the Gulf of Mexico.*

▶ **RED AND READY,** *steamed crawfish form the basis of many Cajun dishes. Louisiana's diverse culture is reflected in its colorful, spicy cooking.*

◀ **THOROUGHBRED HORSES** *thunder from the starting gate at Churchill Downs, home of the famous Kentucky Derby, in Louisville. Horse breeding and racing is a valuable industry in many southeastern states.*

▲ **PURPLE HAZE** *covers the slopes of the Great Smoky Mountains, which straddle the border between North Carolina and Tennessee.*

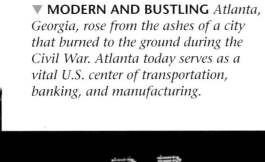

◀ **SHOULDER-HIGH** *in white fluff, Alabama farmers inspect a field of cotton, still an important crop in the Southeast.*

▼ **MODERN AND BUSTLING** *Atlanta, Georgia, rose from the ashes of a city that burned to the ground during the Civil War. Atlanta today serves as a vital U.S. center of transportation, banking, and manufacturing.*

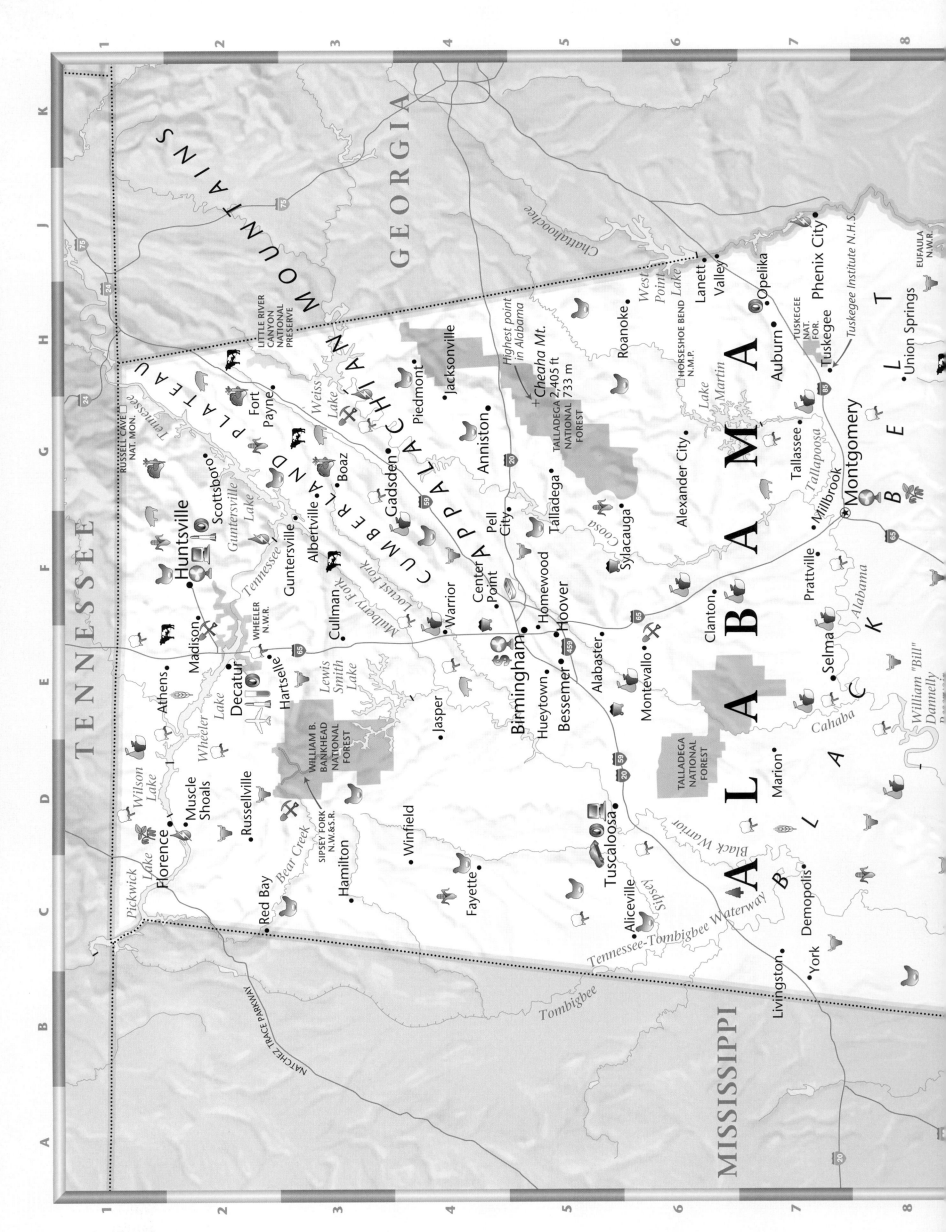

Heart of Dixie

Alabama

Just like a karate expert, the state of Alabama has a black belt. Alabama's belt is a broad strip of dark, fertile soil in the state's center where farmers grow cotton, peanuts, soybeans, and corn. Two-thirds of the state is forested, providing wood for paper and other wood products that form one of the state's most profitable industries.

Alabama was one of the first southern states to industrialize. Iron ore, coal, and limestone mined from the ridges of the Appalachian Mountains made Birmingham a steelmaking center. High-tech business has a home in Huntsville, the headquarters of the state's space industry. Here, Saturn rockets and many other advances in spaceflight were developed.

Alabama products travel through the state on its many navigable rivers. The Tennessee-Tombigbee Waterway, which connects the Tennessee and Tombigbee river systems, has increased the importance of Mobile. Goods from all over the East can reach this port city. Deep shipping lanes allow oceangoing ships to dock in Mobile's waters, giving the city international connections.

Area: 52,237 sq mi (135,293 sq km)

Population: 4,352,000

Capital: Montgomery, pop. 196,400

Largest city: Birmingham, pop. 258,500

Industry: retail and wholesale trade, services, government, finance, insurance, real estate, transportation, construction, electrical equipment

Agriculture: poultry, forest products, cattle, nursery stock, cotton, eggs, peanuts, soybeans

Statehood: December 14, 1819; 22nd state

Nickname: Heart of Dixie

More about Alabama

■ The town of Enterprise erected a monument to the boll weevil, a cotton-destroying insect, because the weevil's attack on cotton early in the 20th century forced farmers to grow new kinds of crops.

■ George Washington Carver, an agricultural scientist, discovered 300 uses for the peanut and 100 uses for the sweet potato while working at the Tuskegee Institute.

■ The building of the Tenn-Tom waterway moved more earth than the excavation of the Panama Canal.

■ Montgomery resident Rosa Parks sparked a boycott of the bus system when she was ejected from a bus after refusing to give her seat to a white person. The boycott became a major event in the civil rights movement.

■ Mobile shares the tradition of Mardi Gras, a pre-Lenten festival, with New Orleans.

Northern Flicker

Camellia

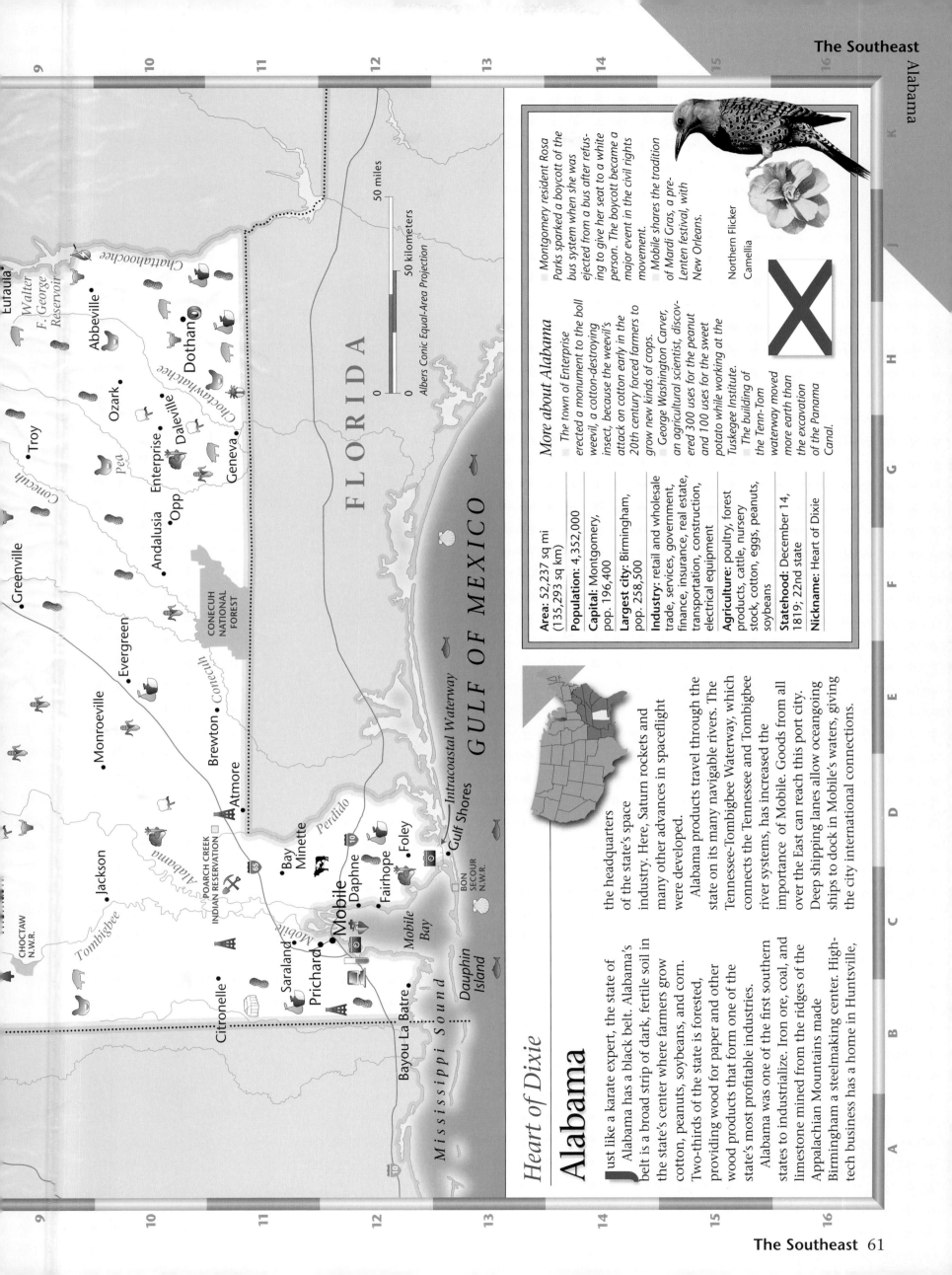

MISSISSIPPI ... *MISSOURI*

| | 1 | 2 | 3 | 4 | 5 | 6 | 7 | 8 |

A

Bella Vista
PEA RIDGE N.M.P.
Eureka Springs
White
Bull Shoals Lake
Norfork Lake
MAMMOTH SPRING S.P.
Cherokee Village
Bentonville
Berryville
Mountain Home
Horseshoe Bend

B

Rogers
Siloam Springs
Beaver Lake
Harrison
Springdale
Fayetteville
OZARK N.F.
BUFFALO N.W.&S.R.
OZARK N.F.
BUFFALO NATIONAL RIVER
OZARK NATIONAL FOREST
White
NORTH SYLAMORE CREEK NATIONAL WILD & SCENIC RIVER

C

OZARK PLATEAU
540
OZARK N.F.
Boston Mountains
HURRICANE CR. N.W.&S.R.
RICHLAND CREEK NATIONAL WILD & SCENIC RIVER
Mountain View
Batesville
OZARK NATIONAL FOREST
Mulberry
MULBERRY NATIONAL WILD & SCENIC RIVER
BIG PINEY CREEK NATIONAL WILD & SCENIC RIVER
Fairfield Bay
Clinton
Greers Ferry Lake

D

Fort Smith N.H.S.
40
Van Buren
Ozark
Clarksville
Big Piney Cr.
Heber Springs
Bald Knob
Little Red
Fort Smith
Arkansas
Lake Dardanelle
Paris
Highest point in Arkansas
OZARK N.F.
Dardanelle
Russellville
Greenbrier
Searcy
Greenwood
Magazine Mt. 2,753 ft 839 m
40
Morrilton
Conway
Beebe

E

Booneville
HOLLA BEND N.W.R.
Cabot
CACHE RIVER N.W.R.
Waldron
Little Rock Central High School N.H.S.
Maumelle
Jacksonville

F

OKLAHOMA
Ouachita Mountains
OUACHITA NATIONAL FOREST
ARKANSAS
Little Rock
North Little Rock
Mena
Lake Ouachita
HOT SPRINGS N.P.
Hot Springs
Bryant
Benton
England
Stuttgart

G

LITTLE MISSOURI N.W.&S.R.
De Gray Lake
Malvern
Sheridan
COSSATOT NATIONAL WILD & SCENIC RIVER
Lake Greeson
Pine Bluff
De Queen
Cossatot
Murfreesboro
Arkadelphia
Saline
Arkansas
Bayou Bartholomew

H

Nashville
CRATER OF DIAMONDS S.P.
30
Gurdon
Fordyce
Dumas
COSSATOT N.W.R.
Little Missouri
Prescott
Ashdown
Millwood Lake
Little
White Oak Lake
Warren
Monticello
McGehe

J

Red
Hope
Camden
Ouachita
Dermott
Texarkana
Stamps
Birthplace of President Clinton
Smackover

K

TEXAS
Magnolia
El Dorado
FELSENTHAL N.W.R.
Hamburg
Lake Erling
Red
Lake Jack Lee
OVERFLOW N.W.R.
Crossett

| | 1 | 2 | 3 | 4 | 5 | 6 | 7 | 8 |

LOUISIANA

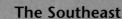

Natural State

Arkansas

Although it is the smallest mainland state west of the Mississippi, Arkansas, called the Natural State, enjoys stunning scenery. Rugged highlands of the Ozark Plateau in the north contain lush forests, gentle valleys, and rivers both wild and tame. Natural hot springs in the Ouachita Mountains attract more than a million visitors seeking either cures for their ailments or just plain relaxation. Hot Springs National Park, in the city of Hot Springs, is the most famous collection of these popular springs as well as the only national park in a city.

Chickens rule the roost in the economy of Arkansas. No other state produces more broilers, fryers, chicken parts, and processed chicken products. One job in every 12 in Arkansas is in the chicken business. Farmers in the fertile eastern Mississippi plain raise rice, making Arkansas the nation's leading rice producer. Cotton, soybeans, and cattle are other important farm products. Arkansas also boasts mineral wealth ranging from coal and oil to diamonds.

Area: 53,182 sq mi (137,742 sq km)

Population: 2,538,000

Capital: Little Rock, pop. 175,800

Largest city: Little Rock, pop. 175,800

Industry: services, food processing, paper products, transportation, metal products, machinery, electronics

Agriculture: poultry and eggs, rice, soybeans, cotton, wheat

Statehood: June 15, 1836; 25th state

Nickname: Natural State

More about Arkansas

■ The city of Texarkana is divided by the Texas-Arkansas border. It has two governments, one for each state.

■ A total of one million gallons a day pour out of the 47 springs in Hot Springs National Park.

■ Crater of Diamonds State Park, near Murfreesboro, is the only working diamond mine in the United States.

■ A system of locks and dams makes it possible for the Arkansas River to carry barges all the way from the Mississippi River to Tulsa, Oklahoma.

Mockingbird
Apple Blossom

Map labels

KY.

Corning

Pocahontas

Paragould

Walnut Ridge

Black

Jonesboro

Tuckerman

Newport

CACHE RIVER N.W.R.

St. Francis

BIG LAKE N.W.R.

Blytheville

Manila

Trumann

Osceola

TENNESSEE

Marked Tree

55

WAPANOCCA N.W.R.

Earle

L'Anguille

Crowleys Ridge

Wynne

West Memphis

CACHE RIVER W.R.

Forrest City

40

Brinkley

St. Francis

Marianna

CACHE RIVER N.W.R.

ST. FRANCIS NATIONAL FOREST

S

West Helena

Helena

White

De Witt

WHITE RIVER N.W.R.

55

ARKANSAS POST NAT. MEM.

Mississippi

MISSISSIPPI

Lake Village

Eudora

0   50 miles

0   50 kilometers

Albers Conic Equal-Area Projection

MISSISSIPPI

ALABAMA

GEOR

LOUISIANA

Perdido

Highest point in Florida +345 ft 105 m

Crestview •

Marianna •

Lake Seminole

Niceville •

Pensacola •

Fort Walton Beach •

Choctawhatchee

Tallahassee

Fort Pickens

GULF ISLANDS NATIONAL SEASHORE

Panama City •

Intracoastal Waterway

Apalachicola

Ochlockonee

APALACHICOLA NATIONAL FOREST

ST. MARKS N.W.R.

Perry •

F L O R

ST. VINCENT N.W.R.

G U L F

O F

M E X I C O

0   100 miles

0   100 kilometers

Albers Conic Equal-Area Projection

ATLANTIC OCEAN

GEORGIA

OKEFENOKEE N.W.R.

OSCEOLA NATIONAL FOREST

Live Oak

Lake City

Jacksonville

FLORIDA

St. Marys

Fernandina Beach

TIMUCUAN ECOLOGICAL AND HISTORIC PRESERVE

FORT CAROLINE NAT. MEM.

Jacksonville Beach

CASTILLO DE SAN MARCOS NAT. MON.

St. Augustine ← Oldest permanent European settlement on the continent, est. 1565

FORT MATANZAS NAT. MON.

Palatka

Gainesville

Palm Coast

Suwannee

LOWER SUWANNEE N.W.R.

Ocala

Lake George

OCALA NATIONAL FOREST

LAKE WOODRUFF N.W.R.

Daytona Beach

New Smyrna Beach

CEDAR KEYS N.W.R.

CRYSTAL RIVER N.W.R.

De Land

Deltona

HOMOSASSA SPRS.

WACCASASSA N.W.R.

Leesburg

Sanford

St. Johns

CANAVERAL NATIONAL SEASHORE

Titusville

MERRITT ISLAND N.W.R.

John F. Kennedy Space Center

Spring Hill

Walt Disney World & EPCOT Center

Orlando

Cape Canaveral

Bayonet Point

Kissimmee

Merritt Island

Tarpon Springs

Haines City

Melbourne

Lakeland

Winter Haven

FLORIDA'S TURNPIKE

Palm Bay

Clearwater

St. Petersburg

Tampa

Tampa Bay

Kissimmee

PELICAN ISLAND N.W.R.

Vero Beach

Sebring

PINELLAS N.W.R.

EGMONT KEY N.W.R.

DE SOTO NAT. MEM.

Bradenton

Fort Pierce

Port St. Lucie

LOXAHATCHEE NAT. WILD & SCENIC RIVER

Sarasota

Arcadia

Peace

St. Lucie Canal

HOBE SOUND N.W.R.

Venice

BRIGHTON SEMINOLE I.R.

Jupiter

Port Charlotte

Punta Gorda

Lake Okeechobee

West Palm Beach

Charlotte Harbor

Caloosahatchee

Belle Glade

Fort Myers

Miami Canal

ARTHUR R. MARSHALL LOXAHATCHEE N.W.R.

Delray Beach

Cape Coral

Boca Raton

J. N. "DING" DARLING N.W.R.

Immokalee

BIG CYPRESS SEMINOLE I.R.

Coral Springs

Fort Lauderdale

Sanibel Island

Big Cypress Swamp

MICCOSUKEE STATE I.R.

Hollywood

Naples

BIG CYPRESS NATIONAL PRESERVE

HOLLYWOOD I.R.

Hollywood

Miami

Ten Thousand Islands

The Everglades

Hialeah

Kendall

Miami Beach

Biscayne Bay

Homestead

BISCAYNE N.P.

EVERGLADES NATIONAL PARK

← Largest subtropical wilderness in the 48 contiguous states

Cape Sable

Florida Bay

Key Largo

Southernmost point in the 48 contiguous states

NAT. KEY DEER REFUGE

FLORIDA KEYS

DRY TORTUGAS NATIONAL PARK

GREAT WHITE HERON N.W.R.

KEY WEST N.W.R.

Marathon

Key West

FLORIDA KEYS NATIONAL MARINE SANCTUARY

STRAITS OF FLORIDA

Sunshine State

Florida

Water is everywhere in Florida, the country's southernmost mainland state. The peninsula was once a seabed. As ocean levels dropped, it became exposed, creating some 8,500 miles (13,679 km) of shoreline as well as springs, lakes, rivers, marshes, creeks, and ponds. Drained wetlands are now farms that produce most of the country's oranges as well as other fruits and vegetables. In recent years electronics has joined agriculture as a major Florida industry.

Each year Florida receives about 40 million visitors drawn by warm temperatures, sunny skies, sandy beaches, and the state's many popular attractions. The Orlando area alone lures millions, mostly to Disney-sponsored sites. Tourists like to explore the unusual ecosystem of the Everglades, a freshwater wetland that spills southward from Lake Okeechobee for some 100 miles (160 km).

Some visitors never leave. Florida's fast-growing population includes many retirees from the north as well as refugees from Cuba, Haiti, and Central American countries.

Area: 59,928 sq mi (155,214 sq km)

Population: 14,916,000

Capital: Tallahassee, pop. 136,800

Largest city: Jacksonville, pop. 679,800

Industry: health services, business services, communications, banking, electronic equipment, insurance, tourism

Agriculture: citrus, vegetables, field crops, nursery stock, cattle, dairy products

Statehood: March 3, 1845; 27th state

Nickname: Sunshine State

More about Florida

■ *Florida has the oldest population in the U.S. One in 5 residents is over 65.*

■ *Ninety percent of the orange juice consumed in the U.S. is made from Florida oranges.*

■ *Spanish explorer Ponce de Leon was one of Florida's earliest European visitors. He came to the area in the 1600s in search of a legendary Fountain of Youth.*

■ *Each American journey into space begins at the Kennedy Space Center at Cape Canaveral.*

■ *The Florida Keys are a 150-mile (241-km) chain of islands off the state's southern tip.*

Mockingbird
Orange Blossom

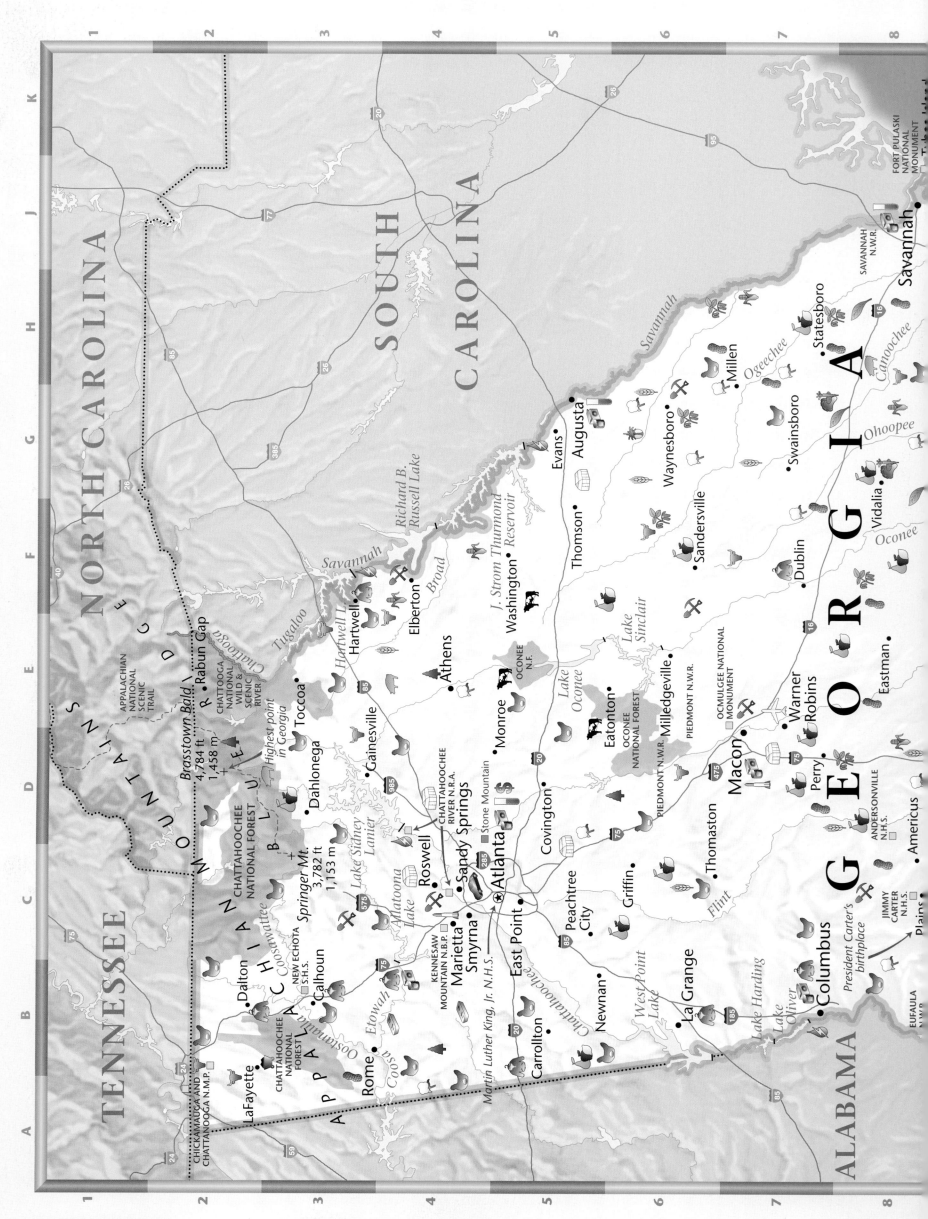

NORTH CAROLINA

TENNESSEE

SOUTH CAROLINA

GEORGIA

ALABAMA

APPALACHIAN MOUNTAINS

BLUE RIDGE

CHATTAHOOCHEE NATIONAL FOREST

APPALACHIAN NATIONAL SCENIC TRAIL

CHATTOOGA NATIONAL WILD & SCENIC RIVER

Rabun Gap

Brasstown Bald
4,784 ft
1,458 m
Highest point
in Georgia

CHATTAHOOCHEE NATIONAL FOREST

Springer Mt.
3,782 ft
1,153 m

CHICKAMAUGA AND
CHATTANOOGA N.M.P.

LaFayette

Dalton

Rome

Calhoun

NEW ECHOTA
S.H.S.

Toccoa

Dahlonega

Gainesville

Lake Sidney
Lanier

Allatoona
Lake

Roswell

Sandy Springs

Marietta

Smyrna

East Point

KENNESAW
MOUNTAIN N.B.P.

Martin Luther King, Jr. N.H.S.

Atlanta

Stone Mountain

CHATTAHOOCHEE
RIVER N.R.A.

Monroe

Athens

Elberton

Hartwell L.

Hartwell

Richard B.
Russell Lake

J. Strom Thurmond
Reservoir

Washington

Evans

Augusta

Thomson

Waynesboro

Sandersville

Millen

Swainsboro

Statesboro

Savannah

SAVANNAH
N.W.R.

FORT PULASKI
NATIONAL
MONUMENT

OCONEE
N.F.

Lake
Oconee

Lake
Sinclair

OCONEE
NATIONAL FOREST

Eatonton

Milledgeville

PIEDMONT N.W.R.

PIEDMONT N.W.R.

OCMULGEE NATIONAL
MONUMENT

Macon

Warner
Robins

Perry

Dublin

Eastman

Vidalia

Covington

Peachtree
City

Griffin

Thomaston

Newnan

La Grange

West Point
Lake

Carrollton

Columbus

President Carter's
birthplace

JIMMY
CARTER
N.H.S.

Plains

ANDERSONVILLE
N.H.S.

Americus

Lake Harding

Lake
Oliver

EUFAULA
N.W.R.

Savannah

Broad

Tugaloo

Chattooga

Coosawattee

Coosa

Etowah

Oostanaula

Chattahoochee

West Point
Lake

Flint

Ogeechee

Canoochee

Ohoopee

Oconee

Savannah

Oconee

Tybee Island

66 The Southeast

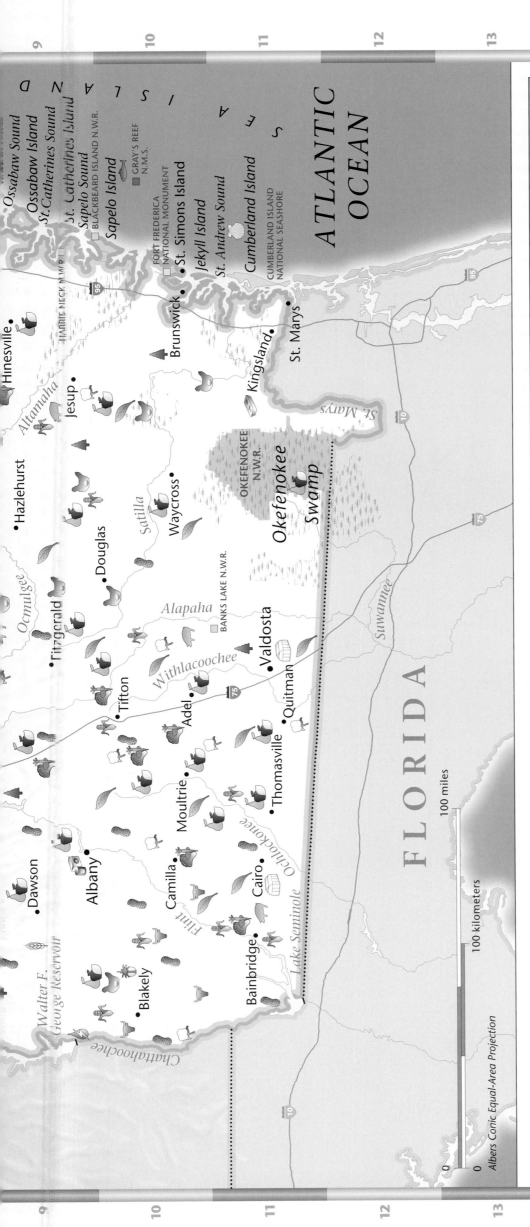

Georgia

Empire State of the South

The land slopes from northwest to southeast in Georgia, one of the largest states east of the Mississippi River. The ridges, plateaus, and foothills of the Appalachian Mountains give way to the Atlantic Coastal Plain.

Quarrying (mining for granite and marble) and lumbering supply jobs in the north. Most of the nation's carpeting is produced in mills around Dalton, as are a good portion of its cotton textiles. Agriculture takes over in the southern plains. The state is famous for its peaches, harvested by the ton in Peach County. The area around Vidalia produces Vidalia onions, sweet enough to be eaten raw. These eatables and Georgia's famous "goobers," or peanuts, are among the state's chief food crops. Tobacco grows well in the region, and Georgia ranks as a leading U.S. producer of eggs and broiler chickens.

Two out of every five Georgians live in or around Atlanta, the state's capital and one of the fastest growing metropolitan areas in the country. The bustling, modern city is one of the South's major financial and transportation centers.

Area: 58,977 sq mi (152,750 sq km)

Population: 7,642,000

Capital: Atlanta, pop. 401,900

Largest city: Atlanta, pop. 401,900

Industry: textiles and clothing, transportation equipment, food processing, paper products, chemicals, electrical equipment, tourism

Agriculture: poultry and eggs, cotton, peanuts, vegetables, sweet corn, melons, cattle

Statehood: January 2, 1788; 4th state

Nickname: Empire State of the South

More about Georgia

- Dahlonega, in northern Georgia, was the site of the first U.S. gold rush in 1828.
- President Jimmy Carter, born in Plains, Georgia, ran a successful peanut farm until he entered politics in the 1960s.
- Georgia is so well known for its flavorful peaches that one of its nicknames is Peach State.
- Stone Mountain is the site of an enormous Confederate monument. Reliefs of Jefferson Davis, Robert E. Lee, and Stonewall Jackson on horseback are carved into the mountain.
- The recipe for Coca-Cola was formulated by an Atlanta druggist more than a century ago. The company is now a multi-national corporation headquartered in Atlanta.
- Springer Mountain marks the southern end of the Appalachian National Scenic Trail.

Brown Thrasher
Cherokee Rose

ATLANTIC OCEAN

FLORIDA

Okefenokee Swamp

100 miles
100 kilometers

Albers Conic Equal-Area Projection

Bluegrass State

Kentucky

Like other professional athletes, Kentucky thoroughbred horses often bring in more than $1 million apiece. The valuable animals grow up on the rolling pastures of the Bluegrass region where underground limestone makes the grass rich in bone-strengthening lime and calcium. Each year the city of Louisville shows off the speed of these horses when it hosts the famous Kentucky Derby horse race. Kentucky's fertile soil also helps farmers raise cattle and grow light-bodied burley tobacco, corn, and soybeans.

In the east lie the Appalachian Mountains and the Cumberland Plateau, with their heavily forested ridges and peaks, fast rivers, and narrow valleys. Scotch-Irish people settled these lands, followed by southern and eastern European immigrants who mined the soft bituminous coal found in this region and the western part of the state.

Rivers lace the interior of the state, too, and one—the Ohio—forms its northern boundary. Altogether, Kentucky has more than a thousand miles of rivers.

Area: 40,411 sq mi (104,665 sq km)

Population: 3,937,000

Capital: Frankfort, pop. 26,700

Largest city: Louisville, pop. 271,000

Industry: manufacturing, services, government, finance, insurance, real estate, retail trade, transportation, wholesale trade, construction, mining

Agriculture: tobacco, horses, cattle, corn, dairy products

Statehood: June 1, 1792; 15th state

Nickname: Bluegrass State

More about Kentucky

■ Kentucky bluegrass is green not blue. It gets its name from the tiny bluish flowers that bloom briefly each May.

■ U.S. President Abraham Lincoln and Confederate President Jefferson Davis were both born in Kentucky less than 100 miles (160 km) apart.

■ Fort Knox contains more than $6 billion in gold bullion, deposited there by the U.S. government and representing nearly all the gold belonging to the country.

■ In 1775 Daniel Boone led pioneers from Tennessee into Kentucky via the Cumberland Gap. They named their town Boonesborough.

Cardinal
Goldenrod

9 10 11 12 13 14 15 16

A

OHIO

B

INDIANA

C

Newport
Covington
Florence
BIG BONE
LICK S.P.

Ohio
Licking

D

Williamstown
Maysville
Vanceburg
Flatwoods
Ashland
North Fork
Licking

WEST
VIRGINIA

E

La Grange
BLUEGRASS
Shelbyville
Frankfort
Paris
Cynthiana
Morehead
Cave Run
Lake

Kentucky
Eagle Creek
South Fork

Jeffersontown
Versailles
Georgetown
DANIEL BOONE
NATIONAL
FOREST

Little Sandy
Big Sandy

F

Salt
Lawrenceburg
Lexington
Winchester
RED NATIONAL WILD
& SCENIC RIVER
Red

Levisa Fork
Tug Fork

REGION

Bardstown
BLUE GRASS PARKWAY
FORT
BOONESBOROUGH
S.P.
COMBS MOUNTAIN PARKWAY

G

Harrodsburg
Richmond
North Fork
Prestonsburg

TUCKY

Danville
Berea
Jackson
Middle Fork
Pikeville

ABRAHAM LINCOLN
BIRTHPLACE N.H.S.
Rolling Fork

Lebanon
PLATEAU
BREAKS
INTERSTATE
PARK

H

Campbellsville
Mount Vernon
Rockcastle
S. Fk.
Hazard
Mountain
JEFFERSON
NATIONAL
FOREST

Green River
Lake
DANIEL
BOONE
NATIONAL
FOREST
DANIEL BOONE
PARKWAY

CUMBERLAND PARKWAY
London
DANIEL BOONE
NATIONAL FOREST
Cumberland
Pine
Black Mt.
4,139 ft
1,262 m

Somerset
VIRGINIA

Corbin

Cumberland
Lake
Cumberland
Cumberland Mt.
Highest point
in Kentucky

J

Williamsburg
CUMBERLAND GAP
N.H.P.
Middlesboro

Albany
Cumberland Gap

Dale Hollow
Lake
BIG SOUTH FORK
NATIONAL RIVER AND
RECREATION AREA
CUMBERLAND
APPALACHIAN MTS.

K

ESSEE

9 10 11 12 13 14 15 16

0 100 miles
0 100 kilometers
Albers Conic Equal-Area Projection

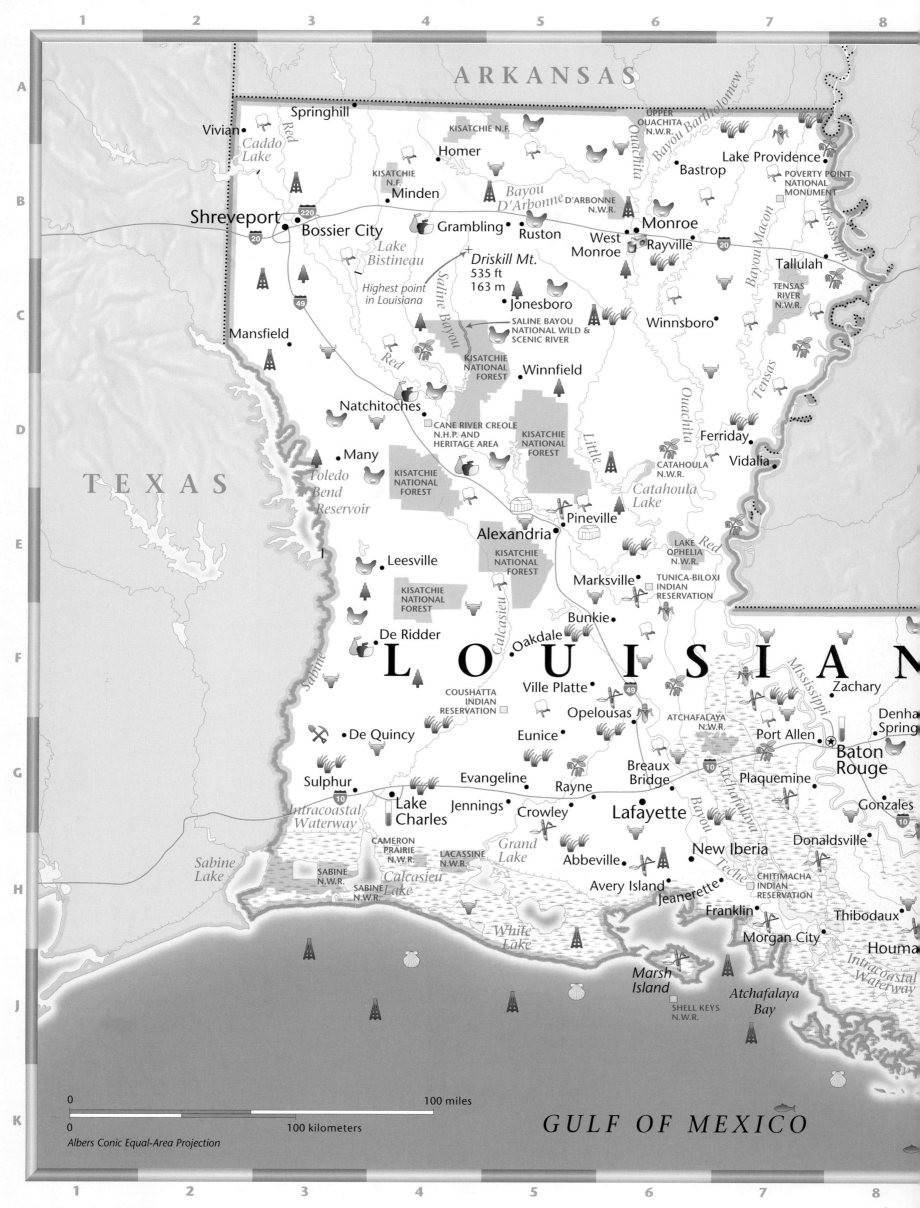

ARKANSAS

Vivian
Springhill
KISATCHIE N.F.
Homer
Caddo Lake
Red
KISATCHIE N.F.
Bayou D'Arbonne
D'ARBONNE N.W.R.
Minden
Bastrop
UPPER OUACHITA N.W.R.
Lake Providence
POVERTY POINT NATIONAL MONUMENT
Shreveport
220
Grambling
Ruston
Monroe
West Monroe
Rayville
Bossier City
Lake Bistineau
Saline Bayou
Driskill Mt.
535 ft
163 m
Highest point in Louisiana
Jonesboro
Winnsboro
Tallulah
TENSAS RIVER N.W.R.
Mississippi
Bayou Macon
Ouachita
49
Mansfield
Red
Winnfield
Tensas
Natchitoches
CANE RIVER CREOLE N.H.P. AND HERITAGE AREA
KISATCHIE NATIONAL FOREST
KISATCHIE NATIONAL FOREST
Ouachita
Ferriday
Vidalia
Many
Toledo Bend Reservoir
CATAHOULA N.W.R.
Catahoula Lake
Little
Red

TEXAS

KISATCHIE NATIONAL FOREST
Alexandria
Pineville
Lake Ophelia N.W.R.
Leesville
KISATCHIE NATIONAL FOREST
Marksville
TUNICA-BILOXI INDIAN RESERVATION
KISATCHIE NATIONAL FOREST
Bunkie
De Ridder
Calcasieu
Oakdale

L O U I S I A N

COUSHATTA INDIAN RESERVATION
Ville Platte
Opelousas
ATCHAFALAYA N.W.R.
Zachary
Denha Spring
De Quincy
Eunice
49
Port Allen
Baton Rouge
Sabine
Evangeline
Rayne
Breaux Bridge
Lafayette
Plaquemine
Gonzales
10
Sulphur
10
Lake Charles
Jennings
Crowley
Atchafalaya
Donaldsville
Intracoastal Waterway
Grand Lake
Abbeville
New Iberia
CAMERON PRAIRIE N.W.R.
LACASSINE N.W.R.
Avery Island
Bayou Teche
CHITIMACHA INDIAN RESERVATION
Sabine Lake
SABINE N.W.R.
Calcasieu Lake
Jeanerette
Franklin
Thibodaux
SABINE N.W.R.
White Lake
Morgan City
Houma
Marsh Island
Intracoastal Waterway
SHELL KEYS N.W.R.
Atchafalaya Bay

0   100 miles
0   100 kilometers
Albers Conic Equal-Area Projection

GULF OF MEXICO

Pelican State

Louisiana

Louisiana is a southeastern state with a difference. It was founded by the French, and today more than a quarter of its residents speak French as well as English. French Canadians who settled in the marshy creeks, or bayous, of southern Louisiana are known as Cajuns.

The land of Louisiana was built up by silt left by the Mississippi and other rivers when they overflowed. Large deposits of oil and natural gas occur throughout the state and in the Gulf of Mexico. Refining oil and gas is a big industry from New Orleans to Shreveport.

Louisiana farmers grow mainly cotton and soybeans in the north and rice and sugarcane in the south. Fish farmers raise catfish and crawfish, a state delicacy, in flooded fields. Gulf fishermen add to the harvest with huge catches of shrimp and oysters.

Each year near the end of winter, millions of tourists come to the port city of New Orleans to celebrate Mardi Gras. Two weeks of parades and parties highlight the city's blend of French, Spanish, and African cultures.

Area: 49,651 sq mi (128,595 sq km)

Population: 4,369,000

Capital: Baton Rouge, pop. 215,900

Largest city: New Orleans, pop. 476,600

Industry: chemicals, petroleum products, paper products, food processing, health services, tourism, oil and natural gas extraction

Agriculture: forest products, poultry, marine fisheries, sugarcane, rice, dairy products, cotton, cattle, aquaculture

Statehood: April 30, 1812; 18th state

Nickname: Pelican State

More about Louisiana

■ *Tabasco sauce originated on Avery Island, a huge salt dome that rises from a salt marsh in southern Louisiana. The fiery sauce is made from tabasco peppers whose seeds were originally brought from Mexico.*

■ *New Orleans, the lowest point in the state, is eight feet (2.4 m) below sea level. In some places it is lower than the Mississippi River, which runs past it but which is contained by levees.*

■ *New Orleans is famous for its jazz musicians. Trumpeter and jazz pioneer Louis Armstrong got his start in the city in the early years of the century.*

Brown Pelican
Magnolia

Map labels:

MISSISSIPPI

ALABAMA

Tangipahoa

Bogalusa

Bogue Chitto

BOGUE CHITTO N.W.R.

Hammond

Covington

Lake Maurepas

Mandeville

Slidell

Lake Pontchartrain

Metairie

Kenner

New Orleans

Chalmette

BAYOU SAUVAGE N.W.R.

Lake Borgne

Mississippi Sound

Chandeleur Sound

Chandeleur Islands

BRETON N.W.R.

Racelanc

L Salvador

Larose

Bayou Lafourche

Port Sulphur

Barataria Bay

Grand Isle

Timbalier Bay

Terrebonne Bay

Lowest point in Louisiana, 8 feet below sea level; Jean Lafitte N.H.P. and Preserve; New Orleans Jazz N.H.P.

Breton Sound

BRETON N.W.R.

Breton Islands

DELTA N.W.R.

Mississippi River Delta

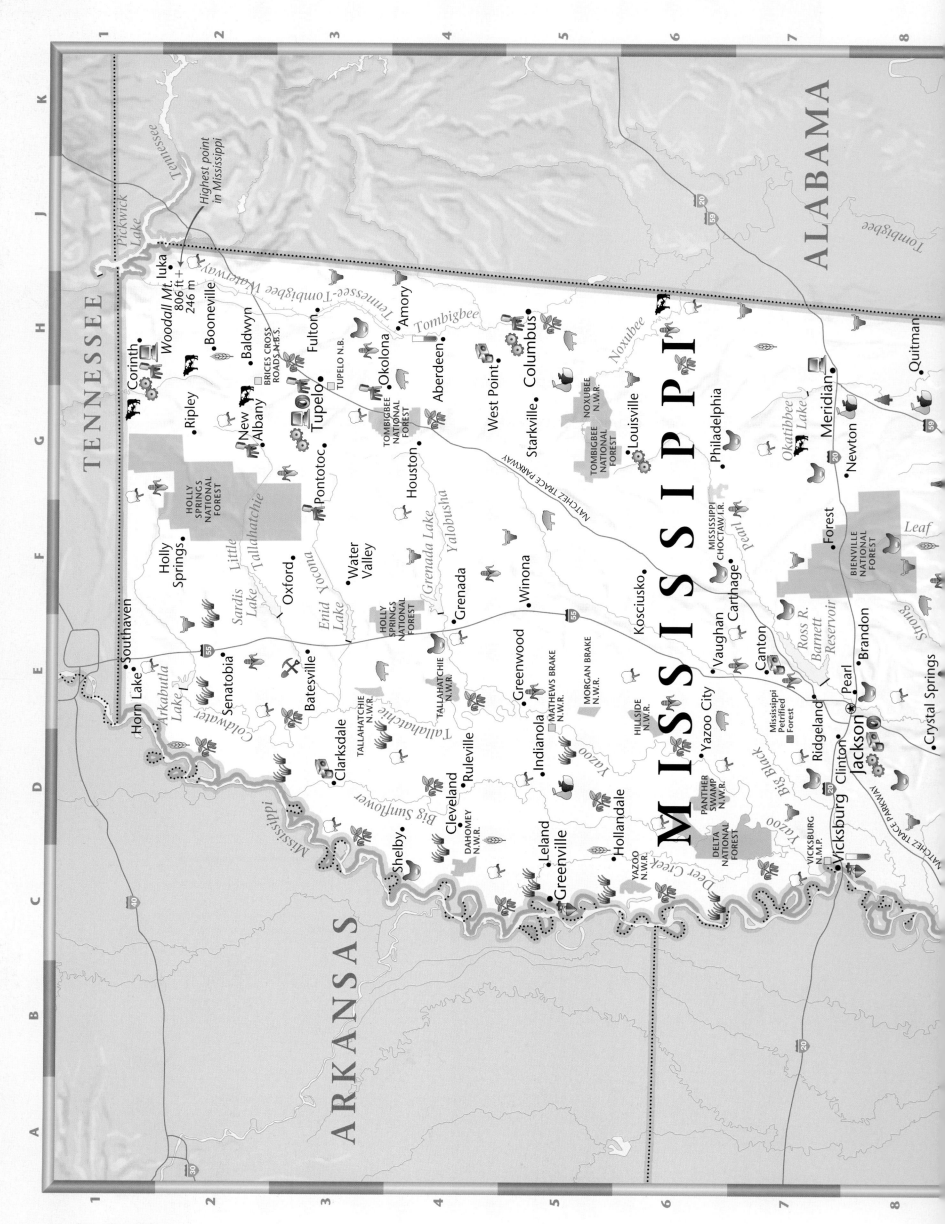

TENNESSEE

ALABAMA

ARKANSAS

MISSISSIPPI

Pickwick Lake

Tennessee

Highest point
in Mississippi

Woodall Mt.
806 ft +
246 m

Iuka

Corinth

Ripley

Booneville

Baldwyn

Tennessee-Tombigbee Waterway

BRICES CROSS
ROADS N.B.S.

New
Albany

Fulton

Tombigbee

Amory

TUPELO N.B.

Tupelo

Okolona

Aberdeen

West Point

Noxubee

Starkville

Columbus

NOXUBEE
N.W.R.

Louisville

TOMBIGBEE
NATIONAL
FOREST

Philadelphia

*Okatibbee
Lake*

Meridian

Quitman

59

20

Holly
Springs

HOLLY
SPRINGS
NATIONAL
FOREST

Pontotoc

Little Tallahatchie

TOMBIGBEE
NATIONAL
FOREST

Houston

Oxford

Water
Valley

*Enid Yocona
Lake*

Yalobusha

Grenada Lake

Grenada

Winona

NATCHEZ TRACE PARKWAY

Kosciusko

MISSISSIPPI
CHOCTAW I.R.

Carthage

Forest

BIENVILLE
NATIONAL
FOREST

Leaf

Newton

20

Sardis
Lake

Senatobia

Batesville

HOLLY
SPRINGS
NATIONAL
FOREST

Greenwood

Vaughan

Pearl

Canton

Ross R.
Barnett
Reservoir

Brandon

Strong

Horn Lake

Southaven

*Arkabutla
Lake*

Coldwater

Clarksdale

TALLAHATCHIE
N.W.R.

Tallahatchie

Ruleville

Indianola

MATHEWS BRAKE
N.W.R.

MORGAN BRAKE
N.W.R.

HILLSIDE
N.W.R.

Yazoo City

Mississippi
Petrified
Forest

Ridgeland

Clinton

Jackson

Pearl

Crystal
Springs

55

40

Mississippi

Shelby

Cleveland

DAHOMEY
N.W.R.

Big Sunflower

Leland

Greenville

Hollandale

Deer Creek

YAZOO
N.W.R.

PANTHER
SWAMP
N.W.R.

Yazoo

DELTA
NATIONAL
FOREST

Big Black

Yazoo

Vicksburg

VICKSBURG
N.M.P.

NATCHEZ TRACE PARKWAY

20

55

20

59

30

1   2   3   4   5   6   7   8

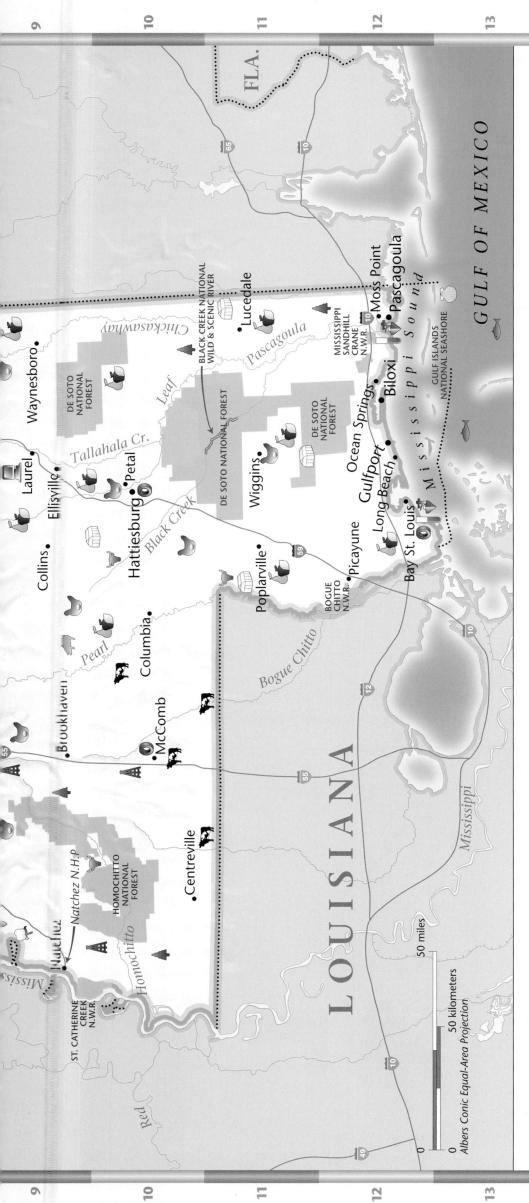

Mississippi

Magnolia State

Mississippi takes its name from the mighty river that forms its western boundary. Over thousands of years the river's flooding has laid down a thick deposit of dark soil to create a flat, fertile plain known locally as the delta. It was and still is perfect land for growing cotton, although farmers have added soybeans, rice, wheat, and other crops, including farm-raised catfish.

Farms also spread throughout other regions of Mississippi, including the Gulf Coastal Plain and the northeast. Farmers raise cattle, poultry, and hay in those areas.

The pine forests of the southeast yield lumber and other forest products. Mississippi is a rural state, with more than half the population living in the countryside or in small towns.

Though only 44 miles (71 km) long, Mississippi's Gulf Coast brings in a sizeable amount of income. Warm weather and wide beaches attract tourists. Gulf waters teem with fish and shellfish. Shipping and shipbuilding bolster the economy, as do petroleum refineries that process the state's valuable deposits of oil and natural gas.

Area: 48,286 sq mi (125,060 sq km)

Population: 2,752,000

Capital: Jackson, pop. 192,900

Largest city: Jackson, pop. 192,900

Industry: real estate, health services, electronic equipment, transportation, banking, forest products, communications

Agriculture: poultry and eggs, cotton, catfish, soybeans, cattle, rice, dairy products

Statehood: December 10, 1817; 20th state

Nickname: Magnolia State

More About Mississippi

Pioneers, soldiers, and merchants in the late 18th and early 19th centuries traveled the Natchez Trace, which connected Natchez, Mississippi, and Nashville, Tennessee.

The Petrified Forest north of Jackson contains fallen trees that are 30 million years old.

At the time of the Civil War, Vicksburg stood on a bluff overlooking the Mississippi River. But in 1876 the river changed course, leaving Vicksburg high and dry.

Mississippi's western border has many oxbow lakes that form when the Mississippi River changes its path and cuts off loops of its previous course.

The Pascagoula River is called the Singing River because it makes a singing or buzzing sound.

Mississippi has a state water mammal—the bottlenosed dolphin.

Mockingbird

Magnolia

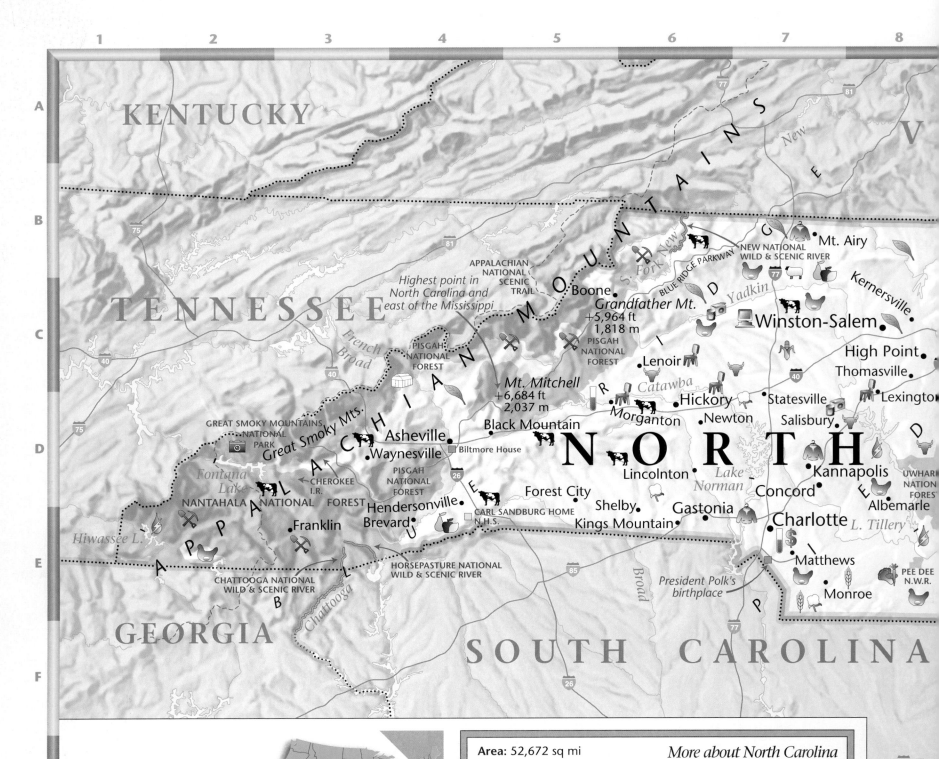

Map labels

KENTUCKY

TENNESSEE

GEORGIA

SOUTH CAROLINA

V

New

Mt. Airy

Kernersville

APPALACHIAN NATIONAL SCENIC TRAIL

S. Fork New

NEW NATIONAL WILD & SCENIC RIVER

BLUE RIDGE PARKWAY

Highest point in North Carolina and east of the Mississippi

Boone

Grandfather Mt. +5,964 ft 1,818 m

Yadkin

Winston-Salem

High Point

PISGAH NATIONAL FOREST

French Broad

PISGAH NATIONAL FOREST

Lenoir

Thomasville

Catawba

Mt. Mitchell +6,684 ft 2,037 m

Hickory

Statesville

Lexington

GREAT SMOKY MOUNTAINS NATIONAL PARK

Great Smoky Mts.

Black Mountain

Morganton

Newton

Salisbury

N O R T H

Asheville

Waynesville

Biltmore House

Lincolnton

Lake Norman

Kannapolis

UWHARRIE NATIONAL FOREST

Fontana Lake

CHEROKEE I.R.

PISGAH NATIONAL FOREST

Forest City

Concord

Albemarle

NANTAHALA NATIONAL FOREST

Hendersonville

Shelby

Gastonia

Charlotte

L. Tillery

Franklin

Brevard

CARL SANDBURG HOME N.H.S.

Kings Mountain

Hiwassee L.

Matthews

PEE DEE N.W.R.

CHATTOOGA NATIONAL WILD & SCENIC RIVER

HORSEPASTURE NATIONAL WILD & SCENIC RIVER

Chattooga

President Polk's birthplace

Broad

Monroe

APPALACHIAN MOUNTAINS

VIRGINIA

Eden
Dan
Reidsville Roxboro
GUILFORD
COURTHOUSE
N.M.P.
Burlington
Greensboro
Chapel Hill
Asheboro
B. Everett
Jordan
Lake
Cary
Haw
Deep

Oxford
Henderson
President Andrew
Johnson's birthplace
Falls L.
Durham
Raleigh
Garner
Smithfield

John H. Kerr
Reservoir
Lake
Gaston
Roanoke Rapids
Rocky Mount
Tarboro
Williamston
Wilson
Greenville
Goldsboro

Ahoskie
Roanoke
Tar
Neuse
Washington

Chowan
Great
Dismal
Swamp
GREAT
DISMAL
SWAMP
N.W.R.
Elizabeth City
Edenton
Albemarle Sound
ROANOKE
RIVER
N.W.R.
POCOSIN
LAKES
N.W.R.
MATTAMUSKEET
N.W.R.
SWANQUARTER
N.W.R.

MACKAY ISLAND N.W.R.
CURRITUCK N.W.R.
Kitty Hawk
WRIGHT BROTHERS
NAT. MEM.
FORT RALEIGH N.H.S.
Roanoke Island
PEA ISLAND
N.W.R.
Hatteras
Island
CAPE
HATTERAS
NATIONAL
SEASHORE
Cape
Hatteras

Currituck Sound
Alligator R.
ALLIGATOR
RIVER
N.W.R.
Pamlico Sound
Outer Banks

CAROLINA

Sanford
Pinehurst
Southern
Pines
Spring
Lake
Fayetteville
Hope Mills
Rockingham
LaurinEurg
Lumberton

Dunn
Clinton
Kinston
New Bern
Havelock
CROATAN
NATIONAL
FOREST
Morehead City

Pamlico R.
Neuse R.
CEDAR
ISLAND
N.W.R.
Core Sound
CAPE
LOOKOUT
NATIONAL
SEASHORE
Cape
Lookout
Ocracoke
Island
Raleigh Bay

LUMBER NATIONAL
WILD & SCENIC RIVER
Lumber
South
Cape Fear
MOORES CREEK
NATIONAL
BATTLEFIELD
Lake
Waccamaw
Whiteville
Wilmington
Green
Swamp
Wrightsville
Beach
Onslow Bay
Jacksonville

Little Pee Dee
Great Pee Dee
Waterway
Intracoastal
Long Bay
Southport
Cape Fear

ATLANTIC OCEAN

0   100 miles
0   100 kilometers
Albers Conic Equal-Area Projection

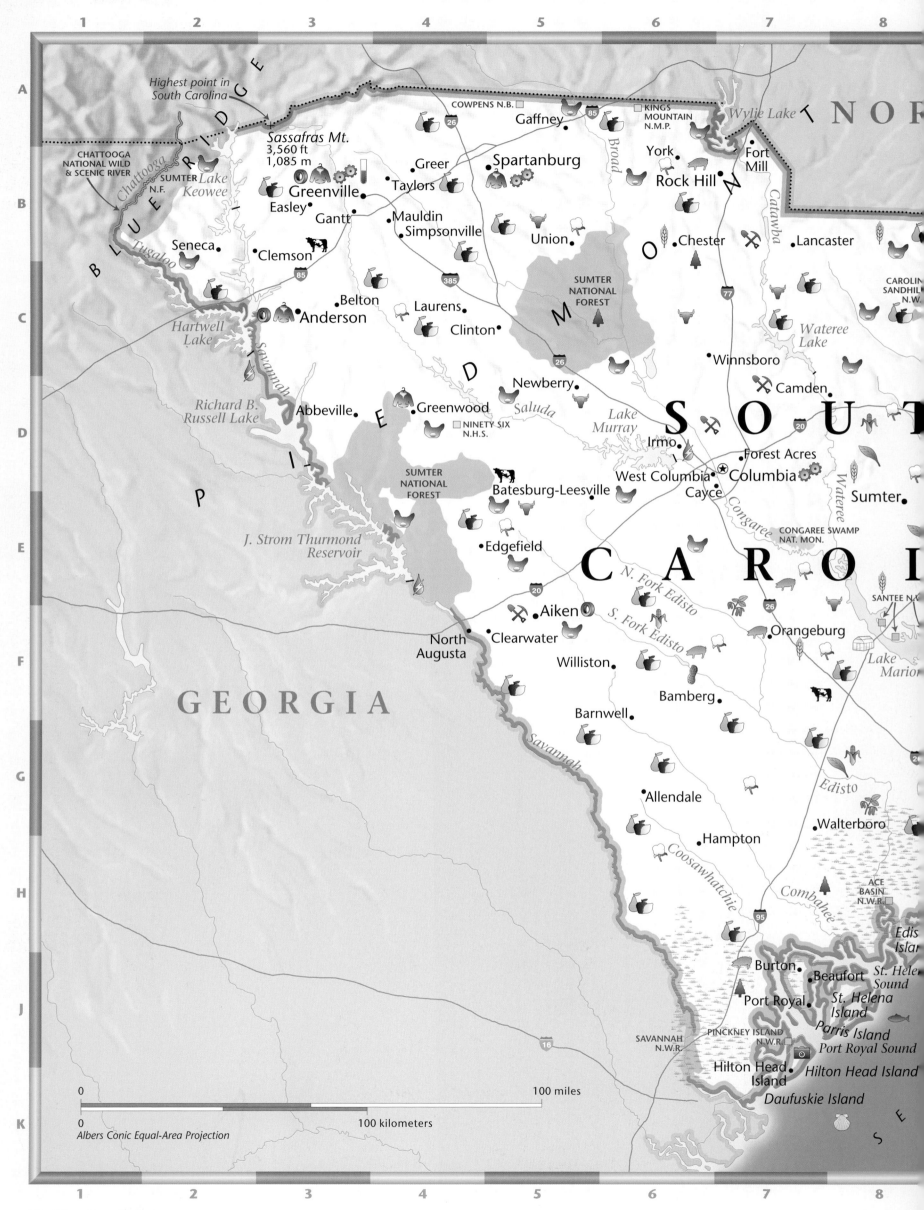

A 1 2 3 4 5 6 7 8

Highest point in South Carolina

COWPENS N.B. □ Gaffney

KINGS MOUNTAIN N.M.P. □

85

Wylie Lake

NOR

CHATTOOGA NATIONAL WILD & SCENIC RIVER

Sassafras Mt. 3,560 ft 1,085 m

26

Greer

Spartanburg

York

Fort Mill

Rock Hill

SUMTER N.F.

Lake Keowee

Greenville

Taylors

B

Easley

Gantt

Mauldin

Simpsonville

Chester

Lancaster

Broad

Catawba

N

Seneca

Clemson

85

Union

SUMTER NATIONAL FOREST

77

CAROLINA SANDHIL N.W.

Tugaloo

385

M

C

Hartwell Lake

Belton

Anderson

Laurens

Clinton

Newberry

26

Winnsboro

Wateree Lake

Camden

Richard B. Russell Lake

Abbeville

Greenwood

NINETY SIX N.H.S. □

Saluda

Lake Murray

SOUT

D

E

Irmo

20

Forest Acres

Columbia

West Columbia

Cayce

Wateree

Sumter

P

J. Strom Thurmond Reservoir

SUMTER NATIONAL FOREST

Batesburg-Leesville

CONGAREE SWAMP NAT. MON.

CARO

E

Edgefield

C

N. Fork Edisto

Congaree

SANTEE N.W

20

26

Aiken

S. Fork Edisto

Orangeburg

North Augusta

Clearwater

Lake Mario

F

Williston

Bamberg

GEORGIA

Savannah

Barnwell

Lake Marion

G

Allendale

Edisto

Walterboro

Hampton

Coosawhatchie

ACE BASIN N.W.R. □

H

Combahee

95

Edis Islan

Burton

Beaufort

St. Hele Sound

J

Port Royal

St. Helena Island

Parris Island

SAVANNAH N.W.R.

PINCKNEY ISLAND N.W.R.

Port Royal Sound

16

Hilton Head Island

Hilton Head Island

Daufuskie Island

K

0   100 miles

0   100 kilometers

Albers Conic Equal-Area Projection

H CAROLINA

South Carolina

Palmetto State

For one of the smallest states in the Southeast, South Carolina has had a big historical impact. In 1860 it was the first state to secede, or withdraw, from the Union. Charleston harbor was the site of the first shots of the Civil War when the Confederates fired on Fort Sumter in 1861.

Textiles and chemical manufacturing, including the making of dyes for cloth, are South Carolina's chief industries. The port city of Charleston, with its fine old houses and beautiful gardens, is a textile center.

The two-thirds of the state in the Atlantic Coastal Plain is called the Low Country. Farmers there grow cotton, tobacco, and soybeans. The rest of the state is known as Up Country and includes the Piedmont and the Blue Ridge Mountains. Swift Up Country rivers provide power for textile mills.

More than 200 years ago, pirates hid out in the many bays and inlets of South Carolina's winding coastline. Today, it is tourists who flock to warm, year-round seaside resorts such as Hilton Head and Myrtle Beach.

Area: 31,189 sq mi (80,779 sq km)	
Population: 3,836,000	
Capital: Columbia, pop. 112,800	

Largest city: Columbia, pop. 112,800

Industry: textiles, chemicals, paper products, machinery, tourism

Agriculture: tobacco, horses, cattle, corn, dairy products

Statehood: May 23, 1788; 8th state

Nickname: Palmetto State

More about South Carolina

■ South Carolina's many swamps gave shelter to General Francis Marion, known as Swamp Fox. The daring soldier led raids against the British during the Revolutionary War, escaping capture by disappearing into the swamps.

■ South Carolina had so much timber in its early days that settlers built their houses only from the hard "hearts of pine."

■ Some residents of the state's southeastern Sea Islands speak a language known as Gullah, a mixture of English and West African languages.

■ After South Carolina won a Revolutionary War battle from a fort made of palmetto logs (a palmetto is a kind of palm tree), the state picked up the nickname Palmetto State.

Carolina Wren
Yellow Jessamine

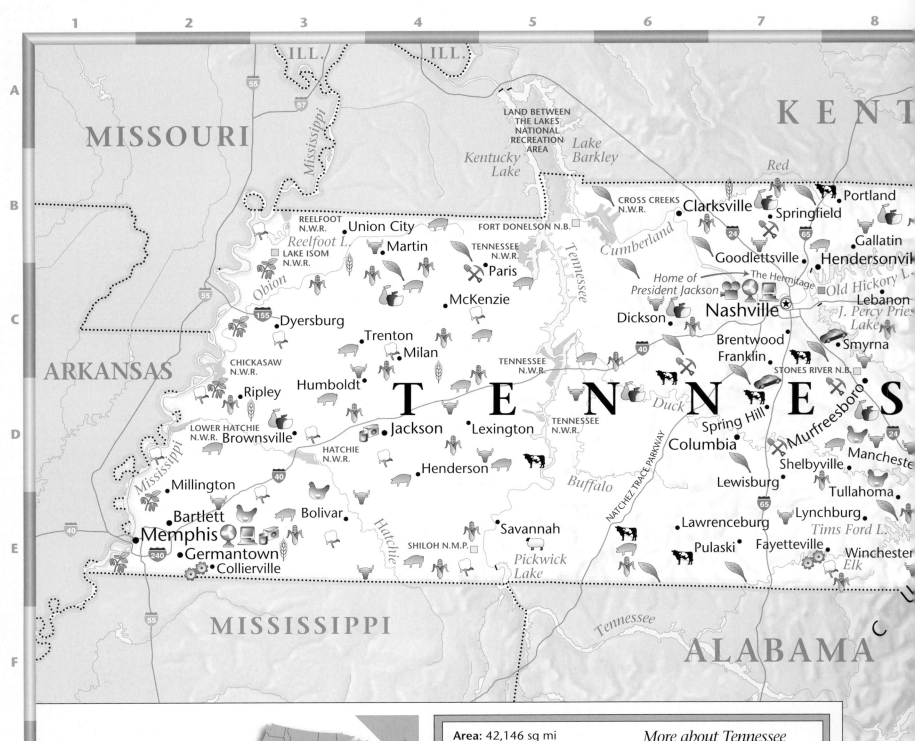

MISSOURI

ILL.

ILL.

KENT

LAND BETWEEN THE LAKES NATIONAL RECREATION AREA

Kentucky Lake

Lake Barkley

Red

REELFOOT N.W.R.

Reelfoot L.

LAKE ISOM N.W.R.

Obion

CROSS CREEKS N.W.R.

Clarksville

Portland

Springfield

Gallatin

• Union City

• Martin

FORT DONELSON N.B.

TENNESSEE N.W.R.

Cumberland

Goodlettsville

Hendersonvil

• Paris

Home of President Jackson

The Hermitage

Old Hickory L.

McKenzie

Tennessee

Dickson

Nashville

J. Percy Pries Lake

Lebanon

Dyersburg

• Trenton

• Milan

Brentwood

Franklin

Smyrna

ARKANSAS

CHICKASAW N.W.R.

Humboldt

TENNESSEE N.W.R.

STONES RIVER N.B.

Ripley

T E N N E S S

Duck

Spring Hill

Murfreesboro

LOWER HATCHIE N.W.R.

Brownsville

HATCHIE N.W.R.

Jackson

Lexington

TENNESSEE N.W.R.

Columbia

NATCHEZ TRACE PARKWAY

Shelbyville

Manchester

Henderson

Buffalo

Lewisburg

Millington

Tullahoma

Mississippi

Bartlett

Bolivar

Hatchie

Savannah

Lynchburg

Memphis

Lawrenceburg

Tims Ford L.

Germantown

SHILOH N.M.P.

Pulaski

Fayetteville

Winchester

Collierville

Pickwick Lake

Elk

MISSISSIPPI

Tennessee

ALABAMA

Volunteer State

Tennessee

Tennessee stretches from the Appalachians in the east to the Mississippi River in the west. Tennessee's Appalachians include the Blue Ridge and the Great Smoky Mountains. The Smokies get their name from the mixture of mist and evaporating plant oils that creates a bluish haze over them. Hydroelectric dams built along many of Tennessee's rivers as part of the Tennessee Valley Authority (TVA) helped industry develop here.

Middle Tennessee is a large oval basin rimmed by highlands. It has prize farmland, enriched by limestone bedrock. Farmers here raise dairy and beef cows as well as chickens and tobacco. The area also is home to big automobile factories in Spring Hill and Smyrna. Nashville is the region's main city. It is both the state capital and world capital of country music. It is a center for computers and electronics as well as the recording industry.

Small farms abound in the west. The port of Memphis is a center of biomedical research and communications.

Area: 42,146 sq mi (109,158 sq km)

Population: 5,431,000

Capital: Nashville, pop. 511,300

Largest city: Nashville, pop. 511,300

Industry: electrical machinery, transportation equipment, non-electrical machinery, chemicals, food processing

Agriculture: cattle, cotton, soybeans, dairy products, broilers, tobacco, corn, nursery stock

Statehood: June 1, 1796; 16th state

Nickname: Volunteer State

More about Tennessee

■ The Tennessee Aquarium, in Chattanooga, is the world's largest freshwater aquarium.
■ During WWII scientists developed atomic bombs in secret research laboratories in Oak Ridge.
■ In the late 18th century a section of northeastern Tennessee tried to become the separate state of Franklin, named for Benjamin Franklin.
■ Tennessee volunteer troops fought so bravely in the war of 1812 that the state earned the nickname Volunteer State.
■ Reelfoot Lake is the state's only large natural lake. It was formed when an earthquake caused the Mississippi River to fill a low area.

Mockingbird

Iris

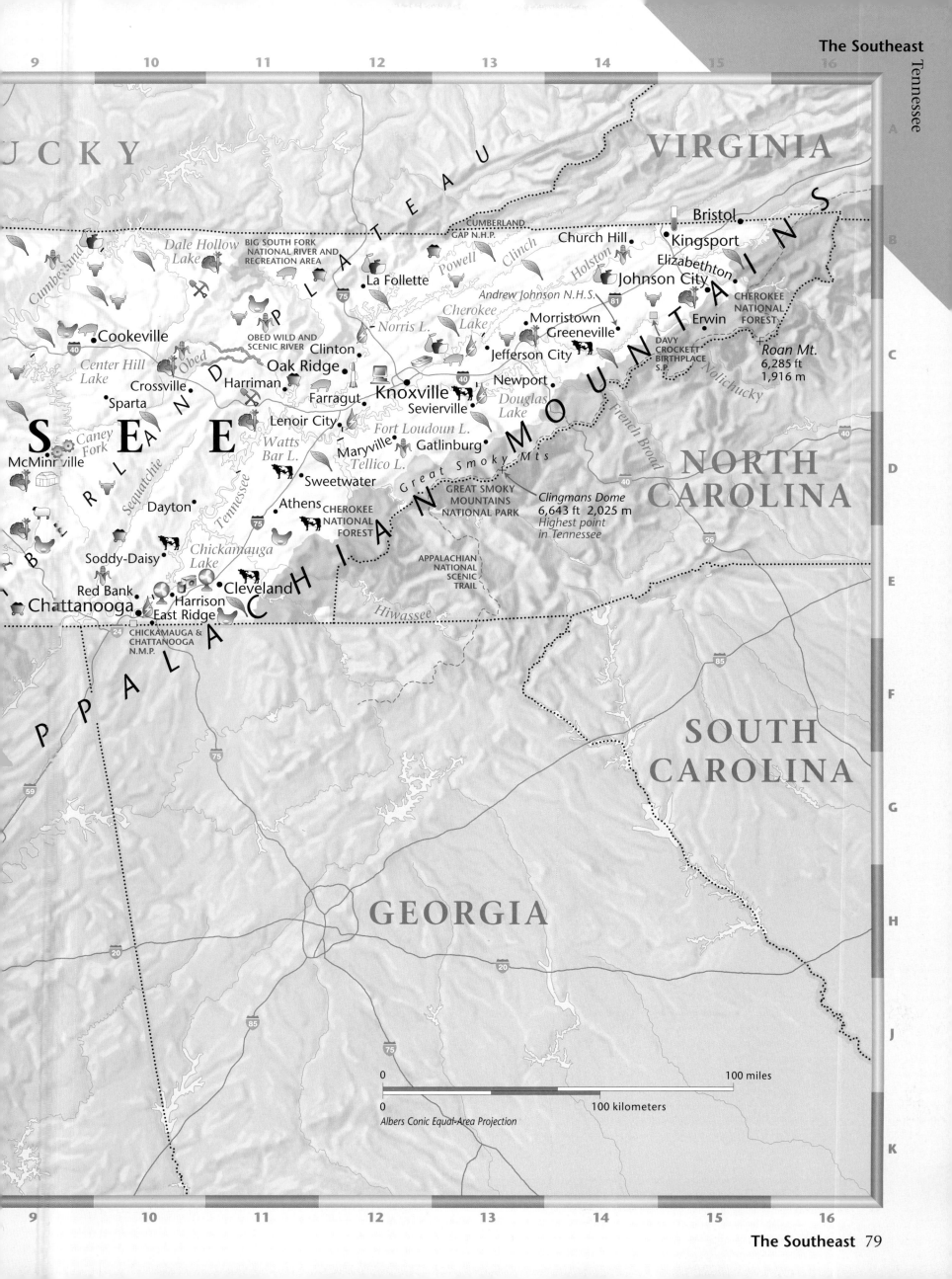

9 10 11 12 13 14 15 16

A

VIRGINIA

UCKY

B

Bristol

CUMBERLAND
GAP N.H.P.

Church Hill

Kingsport

Dale Hollow
Lake

BIG SOUTH FORK
NATIONAL RIVER AND
RECREATION AREA

Elizabethton

Powell

Clinch

Holston

Johnson City

La Follette

Cumberland

CHEROKEE
NATIONAL
FOREST

Cookeville

Andrew Johnson N.H.S.

Cherokee
Lake

Morristown

Erwin

OBED WILD AND
SCENIC RIVER

Norris L.

Greeneville

C

Center Hill
Lake

Obed

Clinton

Jefferson City

DAVY
CROCKETT
BIRTHPLACE
S.P.

Roan Mt.
6,285 ft
1,916 m

Crossville

Oak Ridge

Harriman

Nolichucky

Sparta

Knoxville

Newport

Sevierville

Douglas
Lake

French Broad

NORTH
CAROLINA

Caney
Fork

Farragut

Lenoir City

Fort Loudoun L.

D

McMinnville

Watts
Bar L.

Maryville

Gatlinburg

Sequatchie

Tellico L.

Great Smoky Mts

Dayton

Athens

Sweetwater

Great Smoky Mtns

GREAT SMOKY
MOUNTAINS
NATIONAL PARK

Clingmans Dome
6,643 ft 2,025 m
Highest point
in Tennessee

Tennessee

CHEROKEE
NATIONAL
FOREST

E

Soddy-Daisy

Chickamauga
Lake

APPALACHIAN
NATIONAL
SCENIC
TRAIL

Red Bank

Cleveland

Chattanooga

Harrison

East Ridge

Hiwassee

CHICKAMAUGA &
CHATTANOOGA
N.M.P.

SOUTH
CAROLINA

F

APPALACHIAN MOUNTAINS

PLATEAU

CUMBERLAND

G

GEORGIA

H

J

0   100 miles

0   100 kilometers

Albers Conic Equal-Area Projection

K

9 10 11 12 13 14 15 16

Old Dominion

Virginia

Virginia has witnessed many key events in the nation's history. Jamestown, for instance, was the first permanent English settlement in 1607. The American Revolution ended at Yorktown in 1781, and the Civil War came to a close at Appomattox in 1865.

Virginia's eastern third lies on the Atlantic Coastal Plain, where most of its chief rivers flow into the Chesapeake Bay. The pull of ocean tides earns the area the name Tidewater. Here most of the state's tobacco is grown. Shipbuilding is the major industry in Newport News, and Norfolk has the country's largest operating naval base.

The Piedmont fills Virginia's middle, where food processing is a major part of the economy. The fertile Shenandoah Valley, between the Alleghenies and the Blue Ridge, has most of Virginia's dairy farms and apple orchards.

Government is also big business, especially in Northern Virginia, next door to the District of Columbia. Internet and software businesses flourish in the region as well.

Area: 42,326 sq mi (109,625 sq km)

Population: 6,791,000

Capital: Richmond, pop. 198,300

Largest city: Virginia Beach, pop. 430,400

Industry: food processing, transportation equipment, printing, textiles, electrical equipment, industrial machinery

Agriculture: poultry, cattle, dairy products, tobacco, hogs, soybeans

Statehood: June 25, 1788; 10th state

Nickname: Old Dominion

More about Virginia

■ Virginia is called the Mother of Presidents because eight Presidents were born there: Washington, Jefferson, Madison, Monroe, William Henry Harrison, Tyler, Taylor, and Wilson.

■ The College of William and Mary, founded in Williamsburg in 1693, is the country's second oldest institute of higher learning.

■ The Pentagon, located in Arlington, is headquarters of the Department of Defense. It is one of the world's largest office buildings, with about 25,000 workers.

■ Virginia is one of four states called a commonwealth. The other three are Kentucky, Pennsylvania, and Massachusetts.

■ The Chesapeake Bay Bridge-Tunnel runs 17.6 miles (28.3 km) from the tip of the Delmarva Peninsula to the shore near Norfolk.

Cardinal
Flowering Dogwood

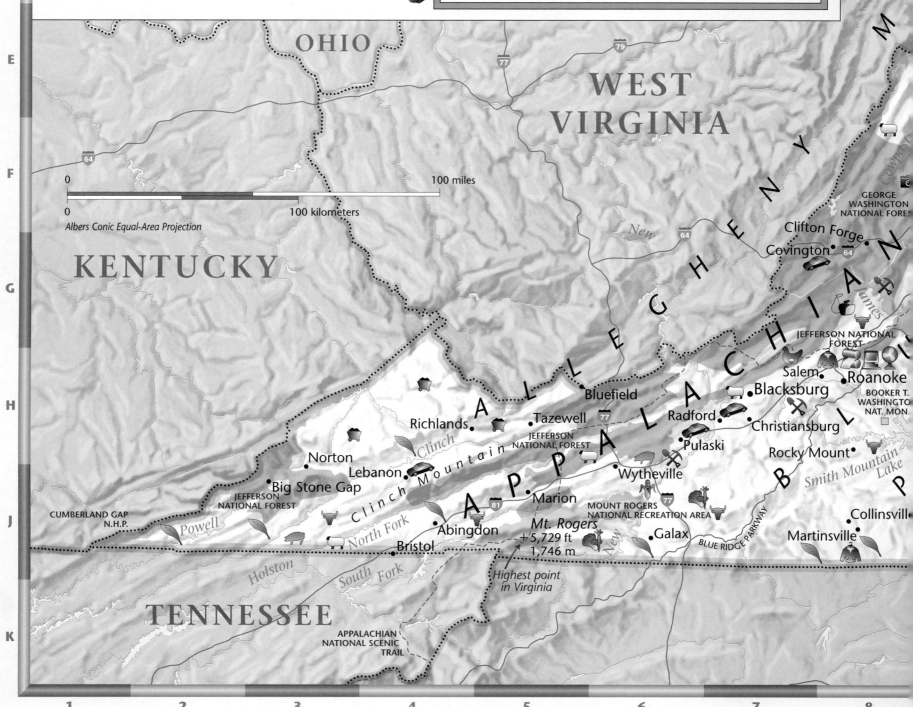

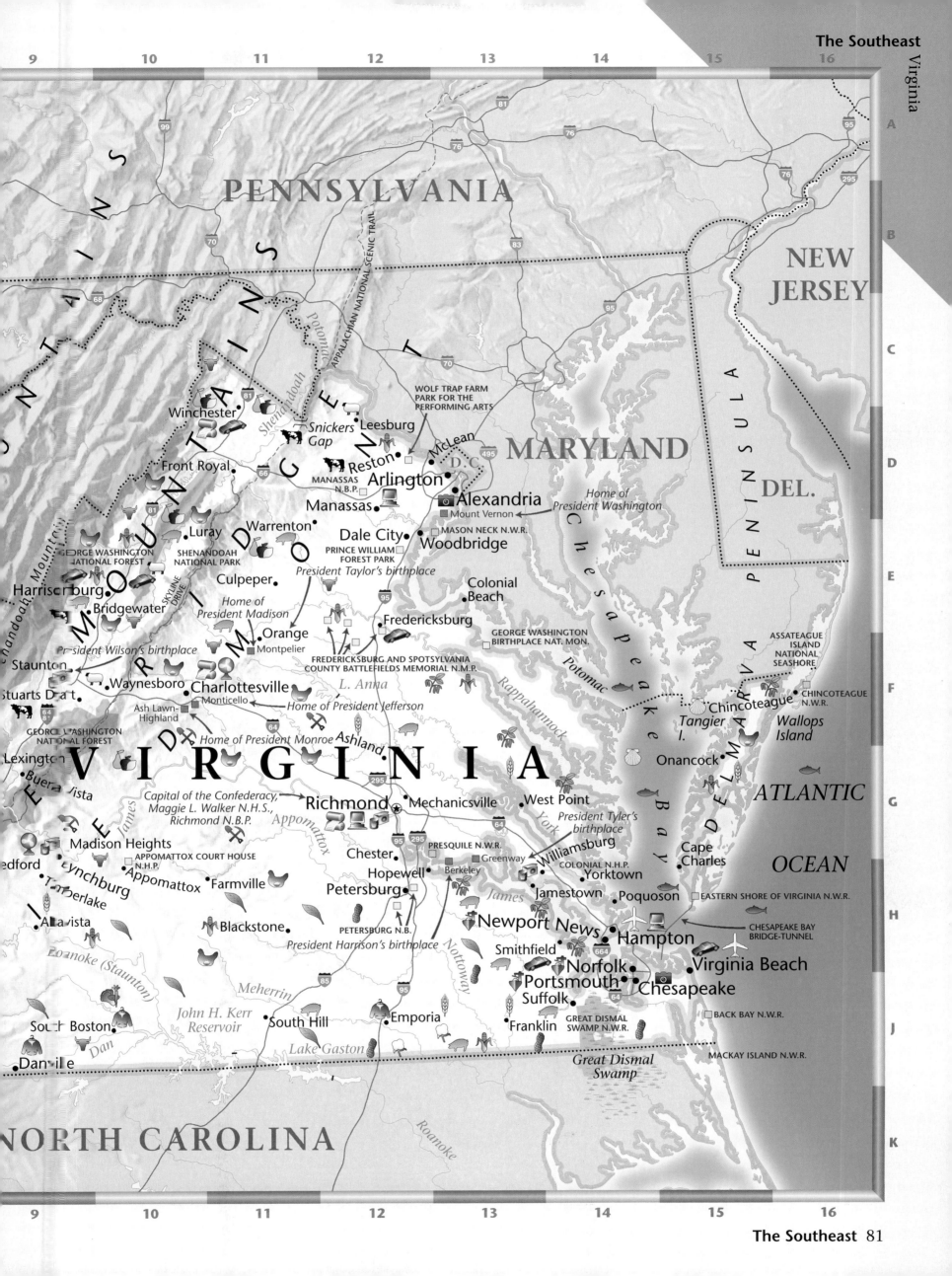

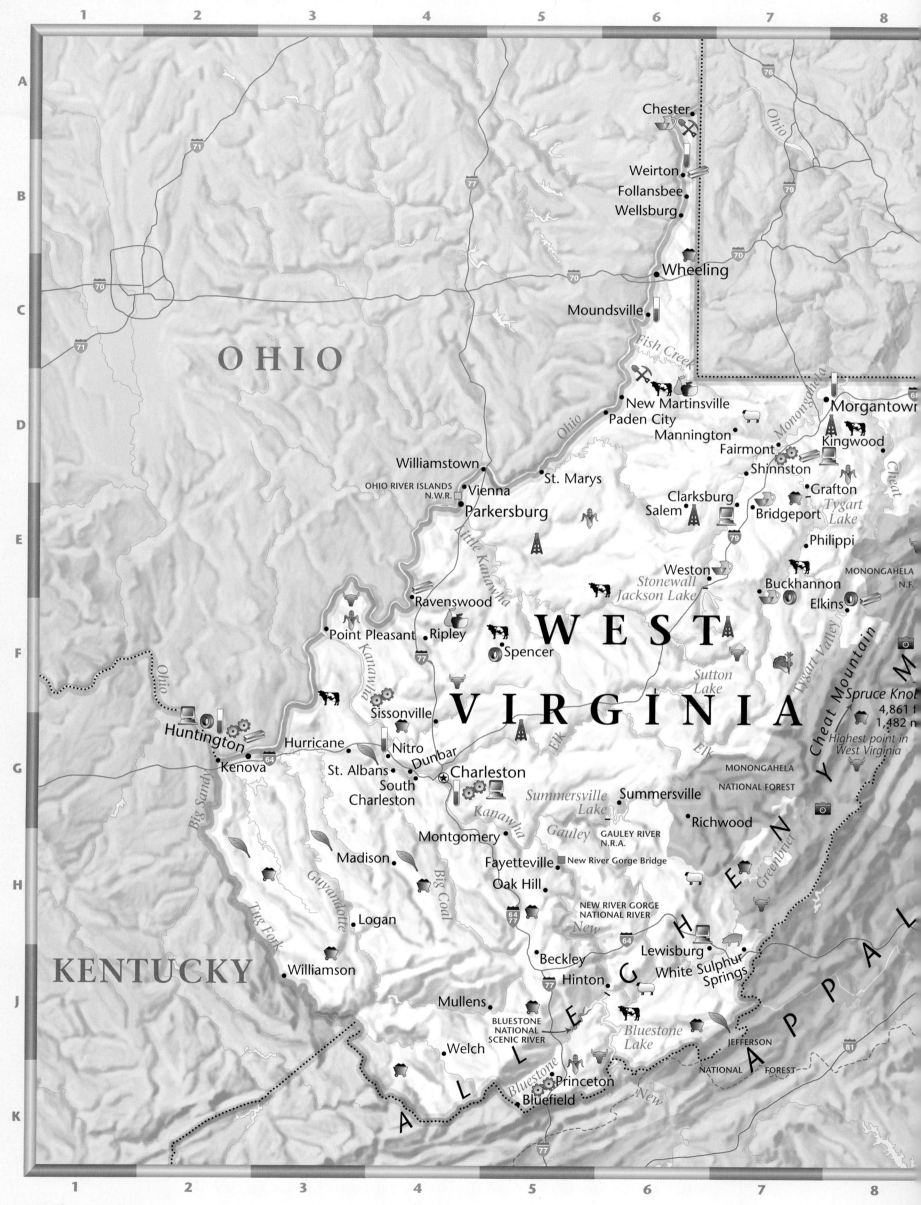

OHIO

KENTUCKY

WEST VIRGINIA

Chester

Weirton
Follansbee
Wellsburg

Wheeling

Moundsville

Fish Creek

New Martinsville
Paden City
Mannington
Morgantown

Williamstown

St. Marys
Fairmont
Kingwood

OHIO RIVER ISLANDS
N.W.R.
Vienna
Shinnston

Parkersburg
Clarksburg
Grafton
Tygart
Lake

Salem
Bridgeport

Philippi

Weston

Stonewall
Jackson Lake
Buckhannon

MONONGAHELA
N.F.

Ravenswood
Elkins

Point Pleasant
Ripley

Spencer

Sutton
Lake

Sissonville

Huntington

Hurricane
Nitro
Dunbar
Charleston
Summersville
Lake
Summersville

MONONGAHELA
NATIONAL FOREST

Kenova

St. Albans
South
Charleston
Richwood

Gauley
GAULEY RIVER
N.R.A.

Montgomery

Madison
Fayetteville
New River Gorge Bridge

Oak Hill

NEW RIVER GORGE
NATIONAL RIVER

Logan
New

Lewisburg

Williamson
Beckley
White Sulphur
Springs

Hinton

Mullens

BLUESTONE
NATIONAL
SCENIC RIVER
Bluestone
Lake

JEFFERSON

NATIONAL FOREST

Welch

Bluestone
Princeton

Bluefield
New

Spruce Knob
4,861 ft
1,482 m
Highest point in
West Virginia

Cheat Mountain

Little Kanawha

Kanawha

Kanawha

Elk

Elk

Gauley

Big Coal

Guyandotte

Tug Fork

Big Sandy

Ohio

Ohio

Ohio

Monongahela

Cheat

Tygart Valley

Greenbrier

Mountain State

West Virginia

Though it is the 41st state in size, West Virginia actually has a lot of land if all the folds and hills and ridges of the Appalachian Mountains could be stretched and flattened.

Geology influences almost everything in West Virginia. Vast amounts of minerals lie within its rocks, with deposits of soft bituminous coal under about half the state. Mining began in the mid-1800s, and production is higher than ever, although it uses fewer miners these days. West Virginia contains large deposits of silica and sand that support its glass-manufacturing industry. The state also has big salt deposits. Chemical companies use the salt in plastics and other products, and the chemical industry in Charleston is one of the largest in the U.S.

West Virginia has ties in many directions. In the west, the Ohio River links the state to the Mississippi River system. The northern panhandle draws on Pittsburgh for jobs, while the eastern panhandle is a fast-growing outer edge of the Washington, D.C., area.

Area: 24,231 sq mi (62,759 sq km)

Population: 1,811,000

Capital: Charleston, pop. 56,100

Largest city: Charleston, pop. 56,100

Industry: coal mining, chemicals, metal manufacturing, forest products, stone, clay, oil, and glass products

Agriculture: poultry and eggs, cattle, dairy products, apples

Statehood: June 20, 1863; 35th state

Nickname: Mountain State

More about West Virginia

■ West Virginia was part of Virginia until 1863. It became a separate state because most of its people supported the Union during the Civil War.

■ West Virginia took the name Kanawha for a few months when it first became a state. The name comes from an Indian word meaning "place of white stone," which may refer to the state's large salt deposits.

■ A coal mine explosion in 1968 that killed 78 people led to national mine safety laws.

■ The state is the largest producer of glass marbles in the country.

Cardinal
Rhododendron

Map labels

PENNSYLVANIA

MARYLAND

VIRGINIA

MOUNTAINS

APPALACHIAN MOUNTAINS

Keyser
Romney
Martinsburg
Charles Town
Moorefield
Petersburg

North Branch Potomac
South Branch Potomac
Potomac
Cacapon
Potomac
Shenandoah

HARPERS FERRY NATIONAL HISTORICAL PARK

APPALACHIAN NATIONAL SCENIC TRAIL

SPRUCE KNOB-SENECA ROCKS R.A.

GEORGE WASHINGTON NATIONAL FOREST

D.C.

100 miles

100 kilometers

Albers Conic Equal-Area Projection

The Midw

est

Illinois
Indiana
Iowa
Kansas
Michigan
Minnesota
Missouri
Nebraska
North Dakota
Ohio
South Dakota
Wisconsin

A combine harvests wheat in Minnesota (left). Fertile Midwest farms grow much of the nation's food. The region's cities, on the other hand, host some major industries. Above, a factory worker in Ohio checks a sampling of molten iron.

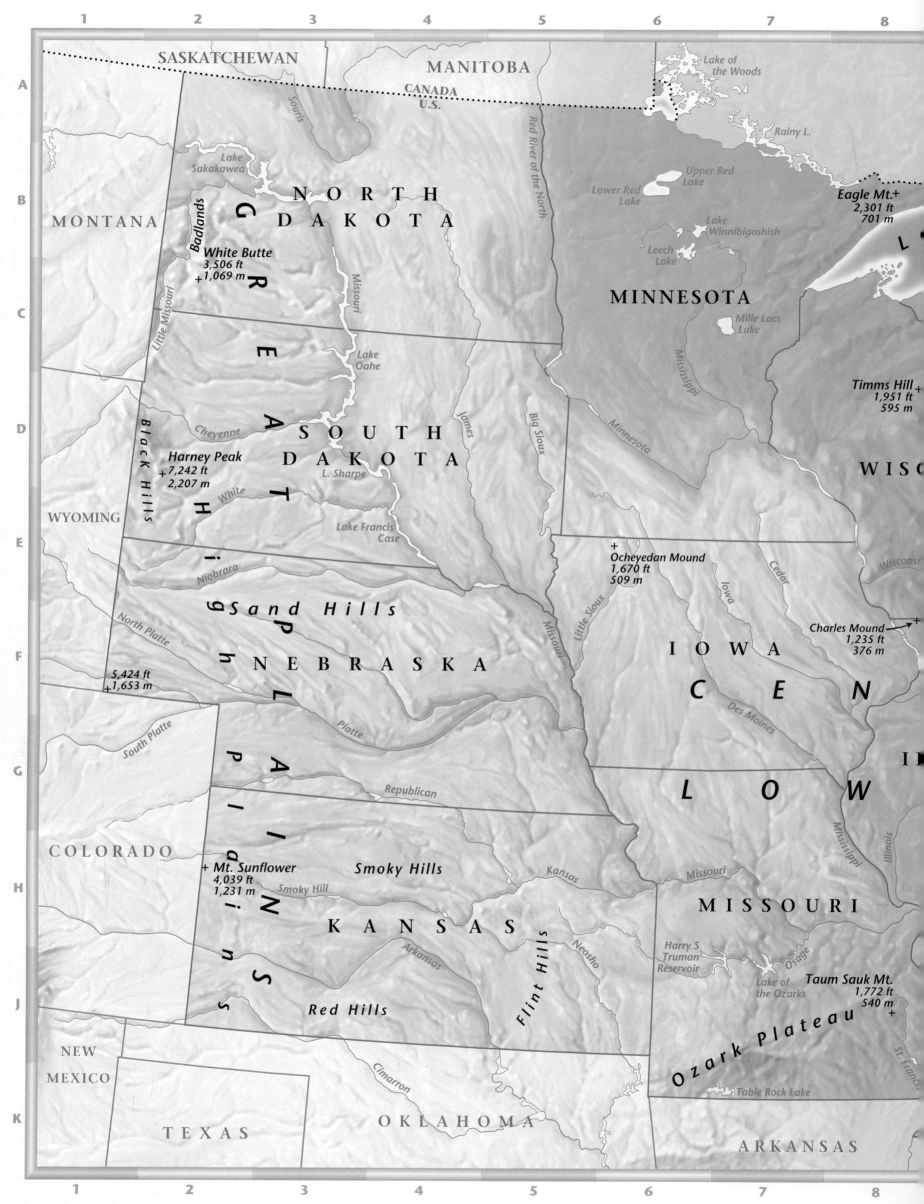

SASKATCHEWAN

MANITOBA

Lake of
the Woods

CANADA
U.S.

Rainy L.

NORTH
DAKOTA

Souris

MONTANA

Lake
Sakakawea

Badlands

White Butte
3,506 ft
+1,069 m

Upper Red
Lake

Lower Red
Lake

Lake
Winnibigoshish

Leech
Lake

Eagle Mt.+
2,301 ft
701 m

Missouri

Little Missouri

MINNESOTA

Mille Lacs
Lake

Lake
Oahe

Cheyenne

SOUTH
DAKOTA

James

Mississippi

Minnesota

Big Sioux

Timms Hill
1,951 ft
595 m

WISCO

Harney Peak
+7,242 ft
2,207 m

L. Sharpe

Black Hills

White

WYOMING

Lake Francis
Case

Niobrara

Ocheyedan Mound
1,670 ft
509 m

Cedar

Iowa

Wisconsi

Sand Hills

North Platte

G
R
E
A
T

H
i
g
h

P
L
A
I
N
S

Little Sioux

Missouri

IOWA

CEN

Charles Mound
1,235 ft
376 m

5,424 ft
+1,653 m

NEBRASKA

Des Moines

LOW

South Platte

Platte

Republican

Missouri

Illinois

Mississippi

Mt. Sunflower
4,039 ft
1,231 m

Smoky Hills

Kansas

COLORADO

Smoky Hill

MISSOURI

KANSAS

Arkansas

Neosho

Harry S
Truman
Reservoir

Osage

Taum Sauk Mt.
1,772 ft
540 m

Flint Hills

Lake of
the Ozarks

Red Hills

NEW
MEXICO

Cimarron

Ozark Plateau

St. Franci

Table Rock Lake

TEXAS

OKLAHOMA

ARKANSAS

ONTARIO

0   200 miles
0   200 kilometers
Albers Conic Equal-Area Projection

QUEBEC

Isle Royale

e **S u p e r i o r**

Keweenaw
Peninsula

Mt. Arvo
1,979
603

M Upper Peninsula

Menominee

Strs. of Mackinac

Lake Huron

Green Bay
Door Pen.

C

H

I

Lower

Saginaw Bay

ONSIN

Lake
Winnebago

L a k e   M i c h i g a n

Muskegon

G

Peninsula

A

N

Grand

Lake
St. Clair

Rock

Fox

Lake Erie

N.Y.

C

E

N

Maumee

PENN.

T

R

A

L

LINOIS

L

A

N

D

O H I O

+Campbell Hill
1,549 ft
472 m

Muskingum

Wabash

1,257 ft +
383 m

Great Miami

Scioto

Ohio

I N D I A N A

White

Ohio

WEST

VIRGINIA

Ohio

VIRGINIA

K E N T U C K Y

Ohio

T E N N E S S E E

NORTH

CAROLINA

The Midwest
Great Lakes,
Great Rivers

Reaching across the central
United States, the Midwest
is a land of rolling hills and
grassy plains. Glaciers
smoothed much of the land
long ago, leaving behind rich
soil in the eastern regions.
Glaciers also scooped out
holes that became lakes,
including the huge Great
Lakes. The region is drained
by the Mississippi and two
of its largest tributaries, the
Ohio and the Missouri.

About the Region

Highest point: Harney Peak,
South Dakota: 7,242 ft (2,207 m)

Lowest point: St. Francis River,
Missouri: 230 ft (70 m)

Largest lakes: Superior, Michigan,
Huron, Erie

Longest rivers: Mississippi, Missouri,
Arkansas, Ohio

Vegetation: Grassland, broadleaf
forest, needleleaf forest, mixed forest

Climate: Continental to mild,
ranging from cold winters and cool
summers in the north to mild winters
and humid summers in the south.

The Midwest
The Heartland

A region of wide open lands and great inland waters, the Midwest spreads from the Great Lakes to the eastern foothills of the Rocky Mountains.

To pioneers moving west, the land looked like a sea of grass. Many thought the drier western part of the region was a desert. Today, farmed fields cover the land like a quilt. Rich soil, plentiful rain in the east, and vast underground reservoirs in the west make this the nation's corn and wheat belt—its breadbasket—and a major source of milk, cheese, beef, and pork. Its people include descendants of European immigrants as well as Native Americans, Hispanics, and African-Americans.

The Great Lakes form the world's largest body of fresh water. A series of locks makes it possible for ships and barges to carry goods between the Midwest and the Atlantic Ocean via the St. Lawrence River. This transportation network, linked to railroads, led to the growth of such industrial cities as Chicago, Gary, Detroit, and Cleveland.

▲ **AN ORE FREIGHTER** *travels between Lakes Superior and Huron on the Soo Canals. Great Lakes ships carry iron ore, coal, and grain to the Atlantic Ocean.*

▶ **BUSY TRADERS** *crowd the floor of the Chicago Board of Trade, where they buy and sell contracts for grain, cattle, and other items. Chicago is the Midwest's finance capital.*

◀ **DAIRY COWS** *peer through a fence on a Wisconsin farm. The state is a leading producer of milk, butter, and cheese— a business worth millions of dollars. Livestock, including cattle and hogs, are an important part of the midwestern economy.*

◄ **GRANITE FACES** *of Presidents George Washington, Thomas Jefferson, Theodore Roosevelt, and Abraham Lincoln rise 60 feet (18 m) high on Mount Rushmore, in South Dakota.*

▲ **A MIDWESTERN GIRL** *enjoys corn on the cob. Three-fourths of U.S. corn is grown from Ohio to Nebraska.*

▲ **ROBOTS WELD** *new car frames in an auto plant in Illinois. Midwest assembly lines turn out thousands of vehicles a day for sale in the U.S. and abroad.*

▼ **A SOARING SPAN** *of steel, the Gateway Arch, in St. Louis, Missouri, rises 630 feet (192 m) along the waterfront.*

► **A PRAIRIE DOG** *pup greets its mother by nuzzling her. These burrowing animals live in large underground "towns."*

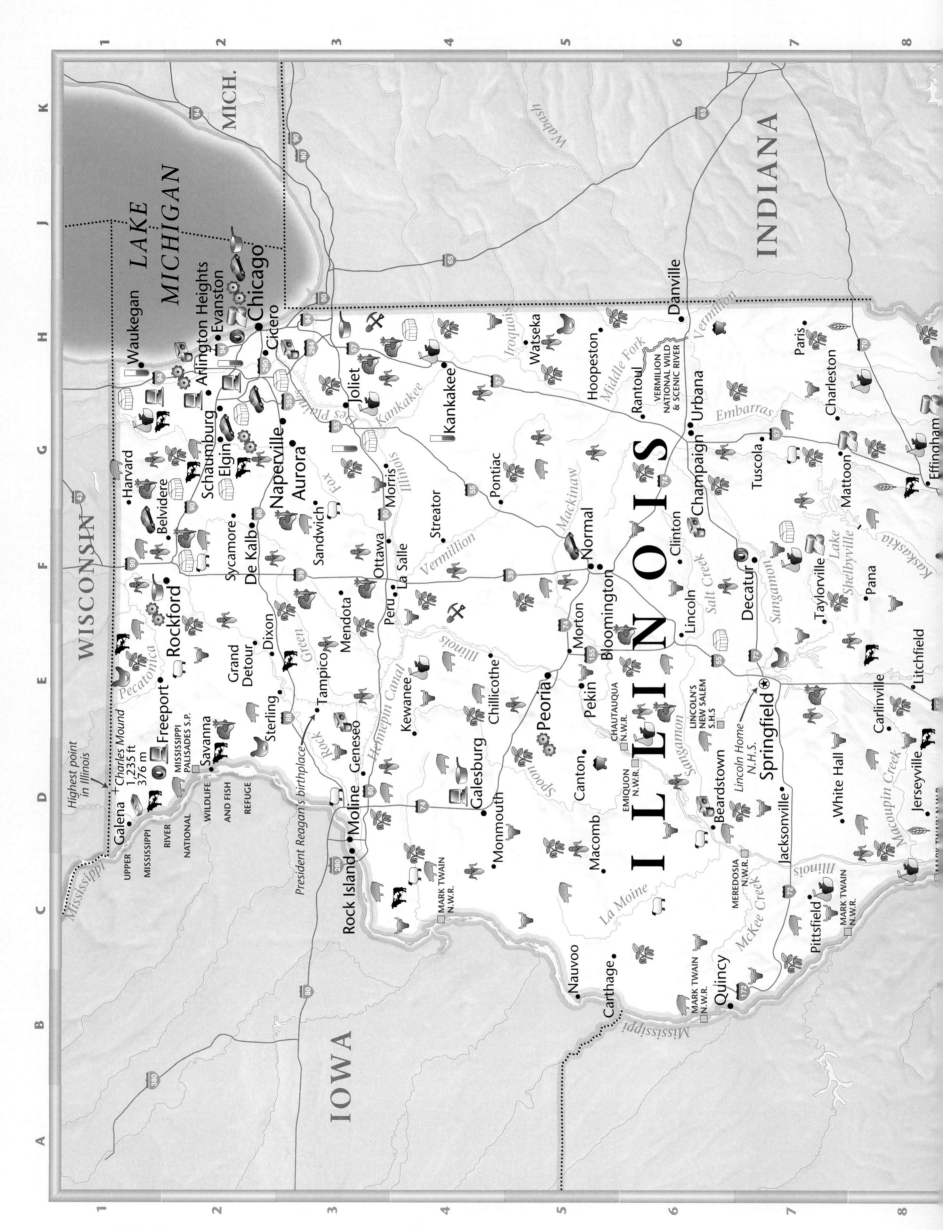

LAKE MICHIGAN

MICH.

WISCONSIN

IOWA

INDIANA

ILLINOIS

Waukegan
Arlington Heights
Evanston
Chicago
Cicero
Harvard
Belvidere
Schaumburg
Elgin
Rockford
Sycamore
Naperville
De Kalb
Aurora
Joliet
Kankakee
Sandwich
Morris
Ottawa
Streator
Pontiac
La Salle
Peru
Vermillion
Mendota
Dixon
Grand Detour
Sterling
Tampico
Geneseo
Moline
Rock Island
Monmouth
Galesburg
Kewanee
Chillicothe
Normal
Bloomington
Morton
Lincoln
Pekin
Peoria
Canton
Macomb
Beardstown
Jacksonville
Springfield
White Hall
Carlinville
Jerseyville
Pittsfield
Quincy
Carthage
Nauvoo
Freeport
Galena
Savanna
Danville
Hoopeston
Watseka
Rantoul
Urbana
Champaign
Tuscola
Clinton
Decatur
Taylorville
Pana
Litchfield
Mattoon
Charleston
Paris
Effingham

Highest point
in Illinois
Charles Mound
1,235 ft
376 m

UPPER
MISSISSIPPI
RIVER
NATIONAL
WILDLIFE
AND FISH
REFUGE

MISSISSIPPI PALISADES S.P.

President Reagan's birthplace

Hennepin Canal

LINCOLN'S NEW SALEM S.H.S

Lincoln Home N.H.S.

CHAUTAUQUA N.W.R.
EMIQUON N.W.R.
MEREDOSIA N.W.R.
MARK TWAIN N.W.R.

VERMILION NATIONAL WILD & SCENIC RIVER

Mississippi
Pecatonica
Green
Rock
Illinois
Fox
Des Plaines
Kankakee
Iroquois
Vermillion
Mackinaw
Salt Creek
Sangamon
Spoon
La Moine
McKee Creek
Macoupin Creek
Illinois
Middle Fork
Vermilion
Embarras
Kaskaskia
Lake Shelbyville
Wabash

Lake Michigan

90   The Midwest

Land of Lincoln

Illinois

Except for a few areas in the northwest and southwest, most of Illinois is flat. Once, tall prairie grass grew in the rich soil left by glaciers. Today, cornfields cover much of Illinois, making it one of the country's top corn-growing states. Northeastern Illinois is also located along the old industrial core of America, a string of cities that runs from the Northeast into the Midwest. The state's biggest city by far—and the nation's third largest metropolitan area—is Chicago, on Lake Michigan. The Chicago region is known for factories that make processed foods, steel, and machinery.

Chicago is a major transportation center. It is linked to the Mississippi River in the west by a system of waterways and to eastern ports via the Great Lakes and the St. Lawrence River. Chicago is also a hub for railroads and airlines. The city is famous for its museums, sports teams, and skyscrapers: The Sears Tower in downtown Chicago is the tallest building in the U.S.

Illinois is known as the land of Lincoln because President Abraham Lincoln lived much of his life here. He is buried in Springfield.

More about Illinois

- Illinois gets its name from Indians called the Illini, who used to live in the region.
- Disaster struck Chicago on October 8, 1871, when a fire started in Kate O'Leary's barn. The fire spread quickly, killing hundreds of people and destroying thousands of buildings in 31 hours.
- Illinois has some of the nation's biggest deposits of bituminous (soft) coal, which is burned to produce electricity.
- The world's first skyscraper, Chicago's ten-story Home Insurance Building, was finished in 1885.
- In 1837 John Deere of Grand Detour, Illinois, invented a steel plow that could cut through prairie sod better than existing plows.
- On March 18, 1925, the most deadly tornado in history roared across southern Illinois. Called the Tri-State Tornado, it killed more than 600 people in Illinois and 100 more in Missouri and Indiana.

Area: 57,918 sq mi (150,007 sq km)

Population: 12,045,000

Capital: Springfield, pop. 112,900

Largest city: Chicago, pop. 2,768,500

Industry: Industrial machinery, electronic equipment, food processing, chemicals, metals, printing and publishing, rubber and plastics, motor vehicles

Agriculture: corn, soybeans, hogs, cattle, dairy products, nursery stock

Statehood: December 3, 1818; 21st state

Nickname: Land of Lincoln

Cardinal

Violet

ILLINOIS

MISSOURI

KENTUCKY

Wabash

Embarras

Olney

Lawrenceville

Mt. Carmel

Carmi

Shawneetown

Little Wabash

Flora

Fairfield

Saline

Mt. Vernon

Salem Fork

West Frankfort

Harrisburg

Benton

Marion

Centralia

Nashville

SHAWNEE NATIONAL FOREST

CRAB ORCHARD N.W.R.

Carbondale

Murphysboro

Du Quoin

Chester

Red Bud

Anna

SHAWNEE N.F.

CYPRESS CREEK N.W.R.

Metropolis

Cairo

Ohio

Mississippi

Kaskaskia

Kaskaskia Island

Big Muddy

Rend Lake

Carlyle Lake

Skillet Fork

Belleville

Granite City

East St. Louis

Edwardsville

Alton

N.W.R.

Albers Conic Equal-Area Projection

0   100 miles

0   100 kilometers

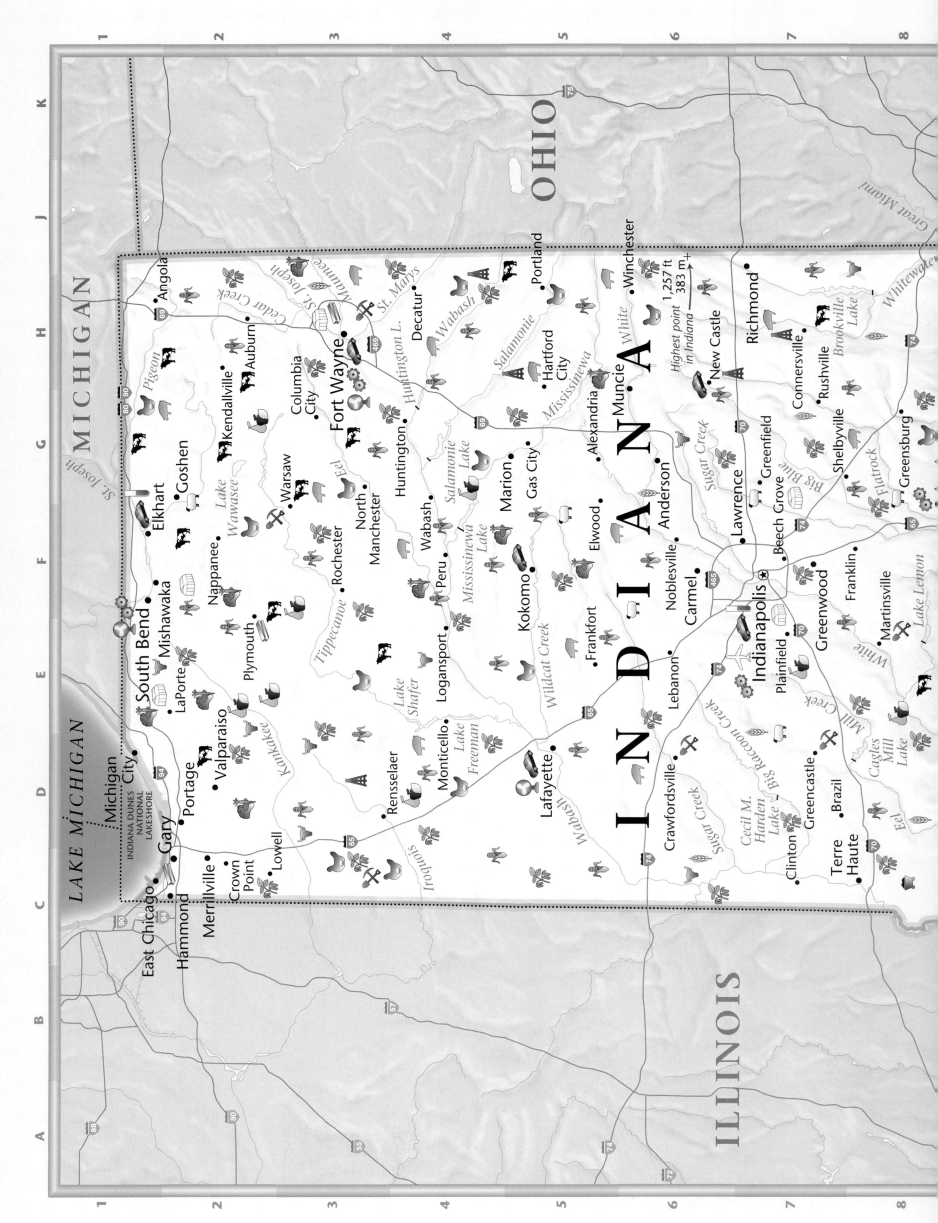

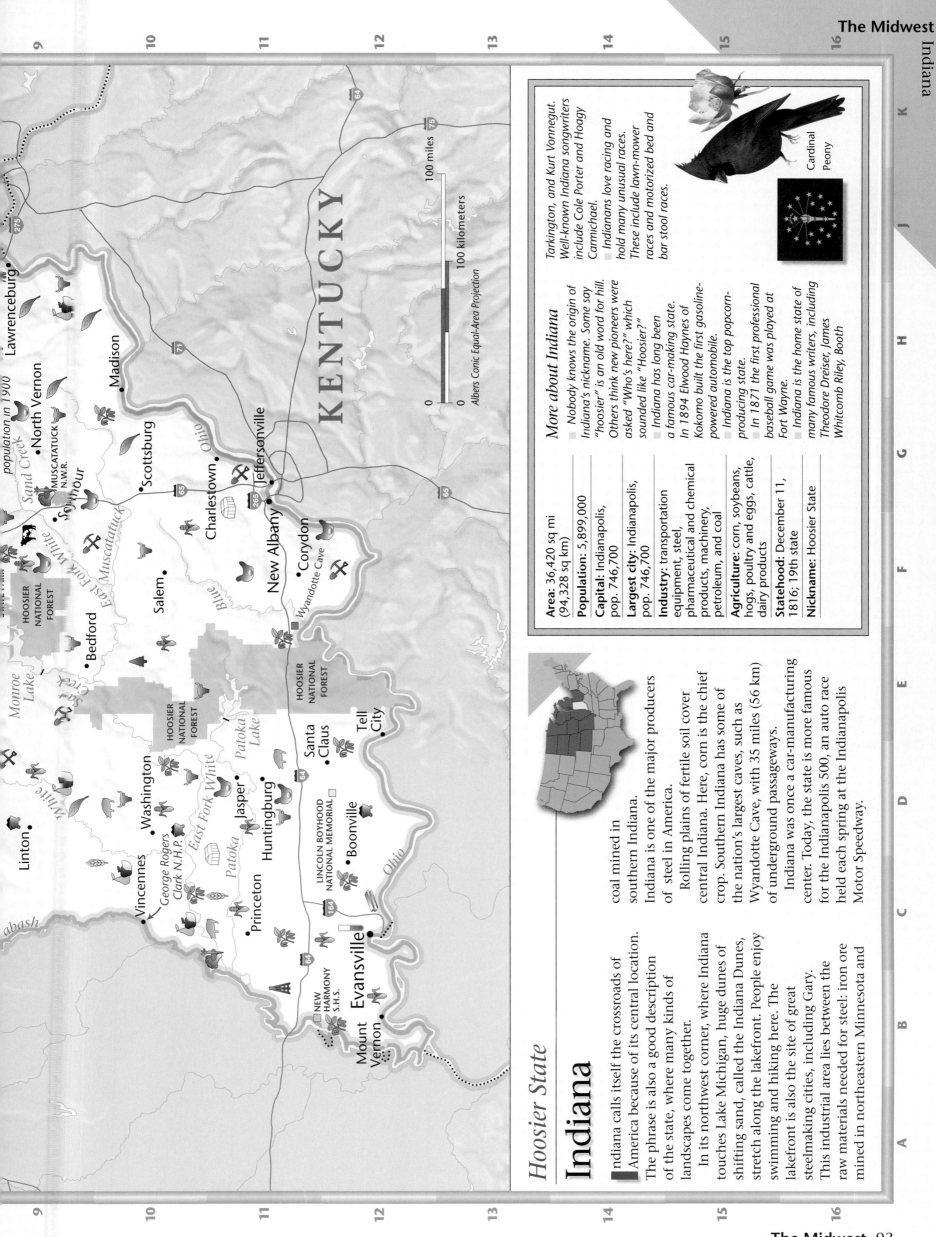

Hoosier State

Indiana

Indiana calls itself the crossroads of America because of its central location. The phrase is also a good description of the state, where many kinds of landscapes come together.

In its northwest corner, where Indiana touches Lake Michigan, huge dunes of shifting sand, called the Indiana Dunes, stretch along the lakefront. People enjoy swimming and hiking here. The lakefront is also the site of great steelmaking cities, including Gary. This industrial area lies between the raw materials needed for steel: iron ore mined in northeastern Minnesota and

coal mined in southern Indiana.

Indiana is one of the major producers of steel in America.

Rolling plains of fertile soil cover central Indiana. Here, corn is the chief crop. Southern Indiana has some of the nation's largest caves, such as Wyandotte Cave, with 35 miles (56 km) of underground passageways.

Indiana was once a car-manufacturing center. Today, the state is more famous for the Indianapolis 500, an auto race held each spring at the Indianapolis Motor Speedway.

More about Indiana

■ Nobody knows the origin of Indiana's nickname. Some say "hoosier" is an old word for hill. Others think new pioneers were asked "Who's here?" which sounded like "Hoosier?"

■ Indiana has long been a famous car-making state. In 1894 Elwood Haynes of Kokomo built the first gasoline-powered automobile.

■ Indiana is the top popcorn-producing state.

■ In 1871 the first professional baseball game was played at Fort Wayne.

■ Indiana is the home state of many famous writers, including Theodore Dreiser, James Whitcomb Riley, Booth Tarkington, and Kurt Vonnegut. Well-known Indiana songwriters include Cole Porter and Hoagy Carmichael.

■ Indianans love racing and hold many unusual races. These include lawn-mower races and motorized bed and bar stool races.

Area: 36,420 sq mi (94,328 sq km)

Population: 5,899,000

Capital: Indianapolis, pop. 746,700

Largest city: Indianapolis, pop. 746,700

Industry: transportation equipment, steel, pharmaceutical and chemical products, machinery, petroleum, and coal

Agriculture: corn, soybeans, hogs, poultry and eggs, cattle, dairy products

Statehood: December 11, 1816; 19th state

Nickname: Hoosier State

Cardinal
Peony

0   100 miles
0   100 kilometers
Albers Conic Equal-Area Projection

Map labels

KENTUCKY

Lawrenceburg
North Vernon
Madison
Sand Creek
MUSCATATUCK N.W.R.
Seymour
Scottsburg
Ohio
Jeffersonville
Charlestown
New Albany
Corydon
Wyandotte Cave
Salem
Bedford
Monroe Lake
HOOSIER NATIONAL FOREST
East Fork White
Blue
HOOSIER NATIONAL FOREST
Patoka Lake
Santa Claus
Tell City
Washington
Vincennes
George Rogers Clark N.H.P.
Jasper
Huntingburg
Princeton
Boonville
LINCOLN BOYHOOD NATIONAL MEMORIAL
Mount Vernon
Evansville
NEW HARMONY S.H.S.
Linton
White
Wabash
Ohio
East Fork White
Patoka
population in 1900

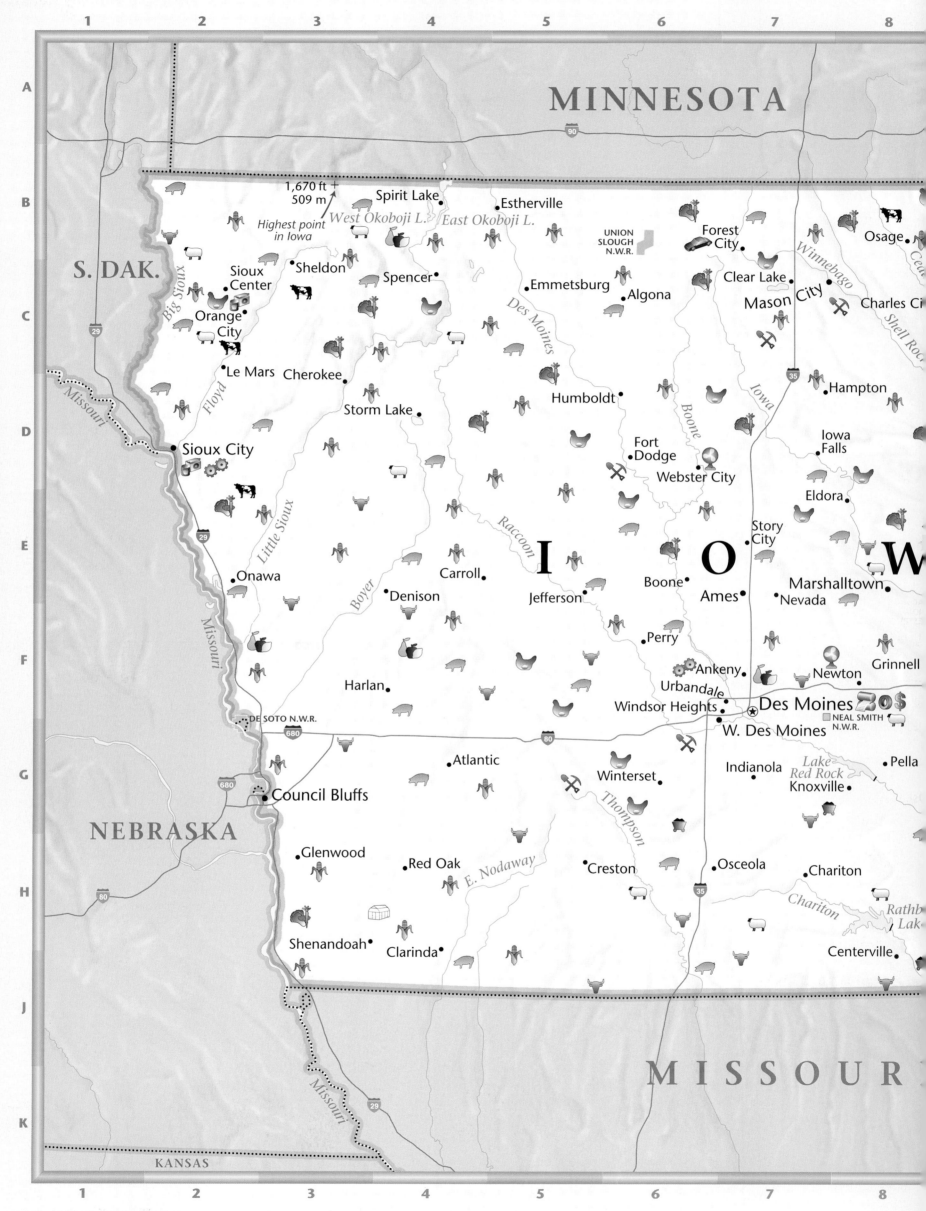

MINNESOTA

S. DAK.

1,670 ft +
509 m
Highest point in Iowa

Spirit Lake
West Okoboji L. *East Okoboji L.*
Estherville

UNION SLOUGH N.W.R.

Forest City

Osage

Sioux Center
Sheldon
Spencer
Emmetsburg
Algona

Clear Lake
Mason City

Charles Ci

Orange City

Le Mars
Cherokee

Humboldt

Hampton

Big Sioux
Floyd

Storm Lake

Fort Dodge
Webster City

Iowa Falls

Missouri

Sioux City

Eldora

Little Sioux

Boone

Story City

I O W

Onawa
Carroll

Boone
Ames

Marshalltown
Nevada

Boyer
Denison
Jefferson

Raccoon

Perry

Iowa

Grinnell

Harlan

Ankeny
Urbandale
Newton

Missouri

Windsor Heights
Des Moines
W. Des Moines

NEAL SMITH N.W.R.

DE SOTO N.W.R.

Atlantic

Winterset
Indianola

Lake Red Rock
Pella

Council Bluffs

Knoxville

NEBRASKA

Glenwood
Red Oak

E. Nodaway
Creston

Thompson

Osceola
Chariton

Shenandoah
Clarinda

Chariton

Rathb Lak

Centerville

M I S S O U R I

Missouri

KANSAS

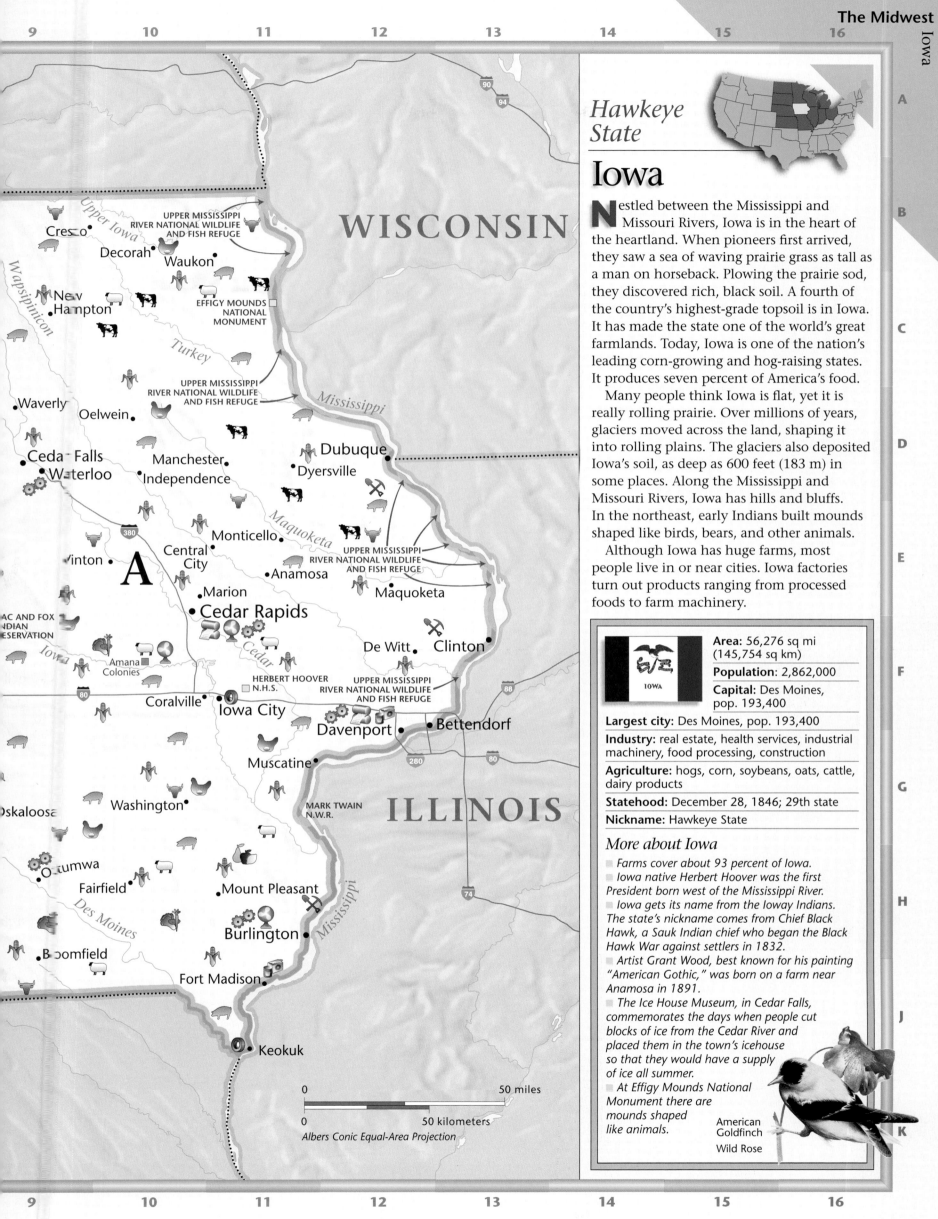

WISCONSIN

ILLINOIS

Hawkeye State

Iowa

Nestled between the Mississippi and Missouri Rivers, Iowa is in the heart of the heartland. When pioneers first arrived, they saw a sea of waving prairie grass as tall as a man on horseback. Plowing the prairie sod, they discovered rich, black soil. A fourth of the country's highest-grade topsoil is in Iowa. It has made the state one of the world's great farmlands. Today, Iowa is one of the nation's leading corn-growing and hog-raising states. It produces seven percent of America's food.

Many people think Iowa is flat, yet it is really rolling prairie. Over millions of years, glaciers moved across the land, shaping it into rolling plains. The glaciers also deposited Iowa's soil, as deep as 600 feet (183 m) in some places. Along the Mississippi and Missouri Rivers, Iowa has hills and bluffs. In the northeast, early Indians built mounds shaped like birds, bears, and other animals.

Although Iowa has huge farms, most people live in or near cities. Iowa factories turn out products ranging from processed foods to farm machinery.

Area: 56,276 sq mi (145,754 sq km)

Population: 2,862,000

Capital: Des Moines, pop. 193,400

Largest city: Des Moines, pop. 193,400

Industry: real estate, health services, industrial machinery, food processing, construction

Agriculture: hogs, corn, soybeans, oats, cattle, dairy products

Statehood: December 28, 1846; 29th state

Nickname: Hawkeye State

More about Iowa

■ Farms cover about 93 percent of Iowa.
■ Iowa native Herbert Hoover was the first President born west of the Mississippi River.
■ Iowa gets its name from the Ioway Indians. The state's nickname comes from Chief Black Hawk, a Sauk Indian chief who began the Black Hawk War against settlers in 1832.
■ Artist Grant Wood, best known for his painting "American Gothic," was born on a farm near Anamosa in 1891.
■ The Ice House Museum, in Cedar Falls, commemorates the days when people cut blocks of ice from the Cedar River and placed them in the town's icehouse so that they would have a supply of ice all summer.
■ At Effigy Mounds National Monument there are mounds shaped like animals.

American Goldfinch

Wild Rose

MARK TWAIN N.W.R.

Albers Conic Equal-Area Projection

NEBRASKA

Little Blue

COLORADO

South Fork Republican

P L A I N S

Sappa Creek

Oberlin · Prairie Dog Creek · Norton

Beaver Creek

Geographic center of the 48 contiguous states → ■ ·Lebanon

Belleville

·Phillipsburg

KIRWIN N.W.R. *Kirwin Reservoir*

Waconda Lake Concordia

·Beloit

Goodland · Colby

NICODEMUS N.H.S.

North Fork Solomon

South Fork Solomon

Solomon

Highest point in Kansas

·Plainville

S m o k y   H i l l s

Oakley ·

I-70

·WaKeeney

Wilson Lake Minneapolis

+ Mt. Sunflower 4,039 ft 1,231 m

Smoky Hill

Cedar Bluff Reservoir

·Hays · Russell

Saline

I-70

· Salina

Smoky Hill

White Woman Creek

Ladder Creek

K   A   N

Ellsworth ·

Kanopolis Lake Lindsb

·Scott City

Ness City

Walnut Creek

Hoisington ·

· Great Bend

Cheyenne Bottoms

McPherson ·

·Lyons

·Hessto

Arkansas

Pawnee

Larned ·

■ FORT LARNED N.H.S.

QUIVIRA N.W.R.

·Lakin

·Garden City

Buckner Creek

·Hutchinson

Arkansas

·Kinsley

·Dodge City

·Pratt

Cheney Reservoir

·Ulysses

·Kingman

North Fork

H   I   G   H

Cimarron

·Greensburg

·Medicine Lodge

Bear Creek

·Meade

Crooked Creek

R e d   H i l l s

Medicine Lodge

·Wellingt

CIMARRON NATIONAL GRASSLAND

·Hugoton

·Anthony

·Elkhart ·Liberal

H

Cimarron

OKLAH

TEXAS

| 0 | | 100 miles |
| 0 | | 100 kilometers |

Albers Conic Equal-Area Projection

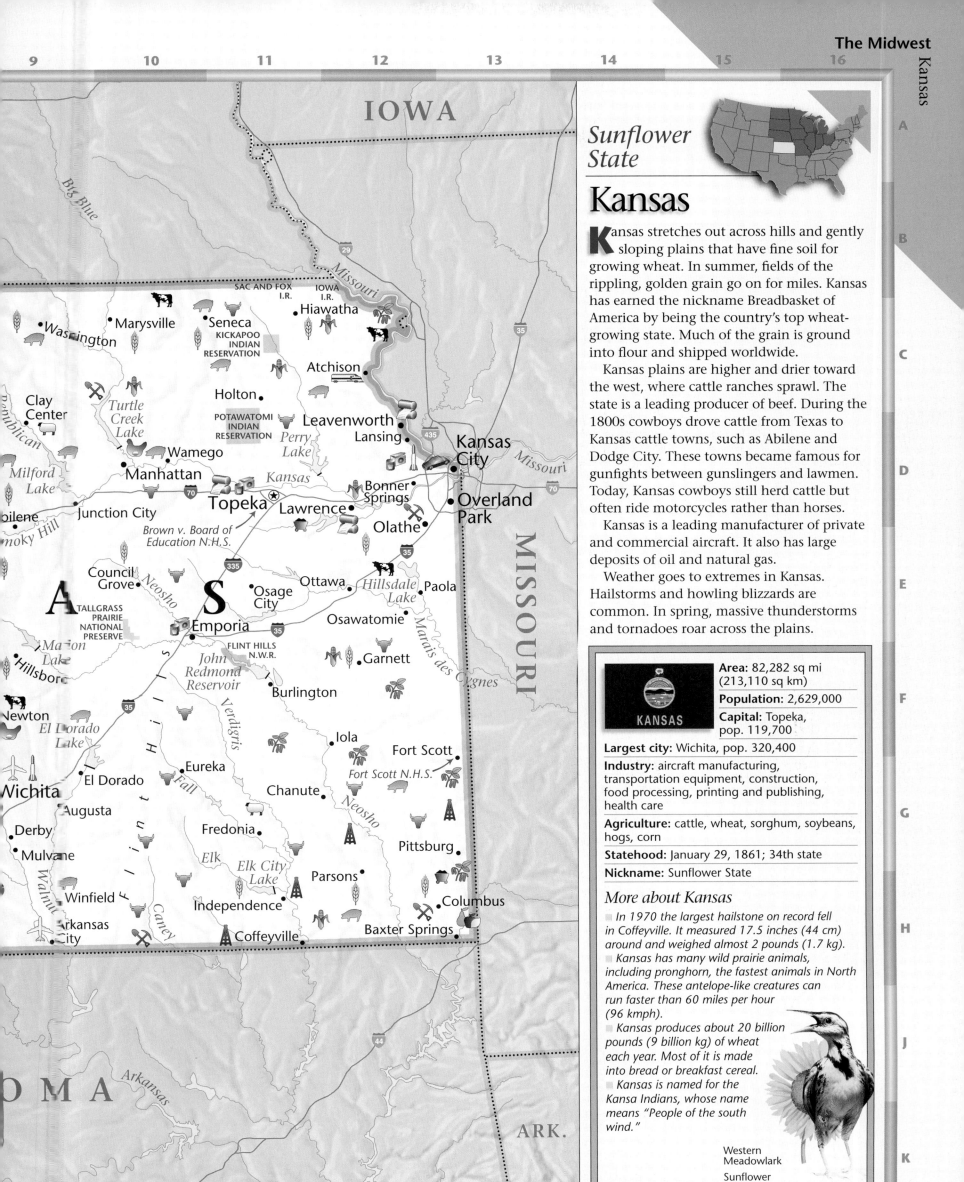

Kansas

Sunflower State

Kansas stretches out across hills and gently sloping plains that have fine soil for growing wheat. In summer, fields of the rippling, golden grain go on for miles. Kansas has earned the nickname Breadbasket of America by being the country's top wheat-growing state. Much of the grain is ground into flour and shipped worldwide.

Kansas plains are higher and drier toward the west, where cattle ranches sprawl. The state is a leading producer of beef. During the 1800s cowboys drove cattle from Texas to Kansas cattle towns, such as Abilene and Dodge City. These towns became famous for gunfights between gunslingers and lawmen. Today, Kansas cowboys still herd cattle but often ride motorcycles rather than horses.

Kansas is a leading manufacturer of private and commercial aircraft. It also has large deposits of oil and natural gas.

Weather goes to extremes in Kansas. Hailstorms and howling blizzards are common. In spring, massive thunderstorms and tornadoes roar across the plains.

Area: 82,282 sq mi (213,110 sq km)

Population: 2,629,000

Capital: Topeka, pop. 119,700

Largest city: Wichita, pop. 320,400

Industry: aircraft manufacturing, transportation equipment, construction, food processing, printing and publishing, health care

Agriculture: cattle, wheat, sorghum, soybeans, hogs, corn

Statehood: January 29, 1861; 34th state

Nickname: Sunflower State

More about Kansas

■ In 1970 the largest hailstone on record fell in Coffeyville. It measured 17.5 inches (44 cm) around and weighed almost 2 pounds (1.7 kg).
■ Kansas has many wild prairie animals, including pronghorn, the fastest animals in North America. These antelope-like creatures can run faster than 60 miles per hour (96 kmph).
■ Kansas produces about 20 billion pounds (9 billion kg) of wheat each year. Most of it is made into bread or breakfast cereal.
■ Kansas is named for the Kansa Indians, whose name means "People of the south wind."

Western Meadowlark

Sunflower

LAKE SUPERIOR

LAKE HURON

ONTARIO

CANADA
U.S.

MINN.

WISCONSIN

MICHIGAN

UPPER PENINSULA

Isle Royale

ISLE ROYALE
NATIONAL PARK

Isle Royale

KEWEENAW
N.H.P.

Keweenaw
Peninsula

Laurium

Houghton

ONTONAGON
INDIAN
RESERVATION

STURGEON
NATIONAL WILD &
SCENIC RIVER

HURON
N.W.R.

Mt. Arvon
1,979 ft
+603 m
Highest point
in Michigan

L'Anse
L'ANSE
I.R.

YELLOW DOG
N.W.&S.R.

OTTAWA
N.F.

PORCUPINE
MOUNTAINS
STATE PARK

BLACK
N.W.&S.R.

Ironwood

OTTAWA NATIONAL FOREST

ONTONAGON
N.W.&S.R.

PAINT
N.W.&S.R.

LAC VIEUX DESERT I.R.

PRESQUE ISLE
N.W.&S.R.

Marquette

GRAND
ISLAND
N.R.A.

PICTURED
ROCKS
NATIONAL
LAKESHORE

Munising

Ishpeming

INDIAN
N.W.&S.R.

WHITEFISH
N.W.&S.R.

HIAWATHA
NATIONAL
FOREST

SENEY
N.W.R.

STURGEON
NATIONAL WILD &
SCENIC RIVER

Manistique

Gladstone

Escanaba

Garden
Peninsula

Cedar

HANNAHVILLE
I.R.

Menominee

Iron
Mountain

Brule

Ford

Menominee

TAHQUAMENON
FALLS S.P.

TAHQUAMENON
(EAST BRANCH)
N.W.&S.R.

Whitefish
Bay

HIAWATHA
NATIONAL
FOREST

CARP
N.W.&S.R.

Sault Sainte Marie

St. Marys

BAY MILLS
I.R.

HARBOR ISLAND N.W.R.

Drummond
Island

Soo Canals: among the busiest ship
canals in the Western Hemisphere

75

Mackinac I.

Bois Blanc I.

Cheboygan

St. Ignace

Straits of Mackinac

Mullett
L.

Burt
Lake

Beaver I.

Grand
Traverse
Bay

Grand
Traverse I.R.

Manitou
Islands

Manitou Passage

SLEEPING
BEAR DUNES
NAT. LAKESHORE

Site of at least
50 shipwrecks

Green Bay

Boyne City

Petoskey

Rogers City

Alpena

Thunder Bay

Hubbard L.

Mio

AU SABLE NATIONAL
WILD & SCENIC RIVER

HURON NATIONAL FOREST

Gaylord

Au Sable

Pigeon

Thunder
Bay

Tawas
City

Rifle

Houghton Lake

Houghton
Lake

Kalkaska

Cadillac

PINE
N.W.&S.R.

MANISTEE NATIONAL

Manistee

Traverse City

Manistee

BEAR CREEK
N.W.&S.R.

75

75

43

35

Albers Conic Equal-Area Projection

100 miles

100 kilometers

0

0

98 The Midwest

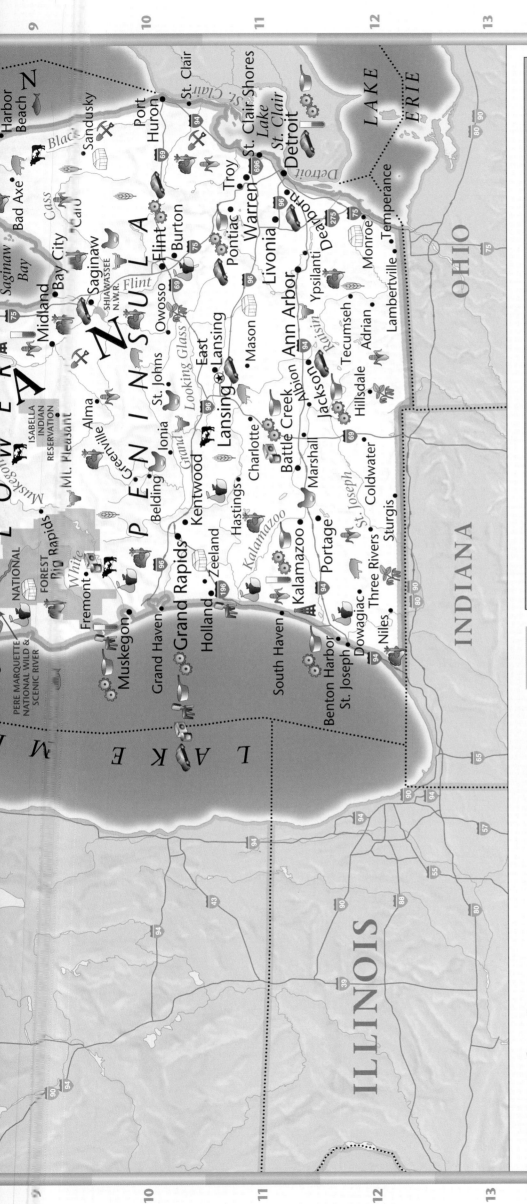

The Midwest

Michigan

N

LAKE SUPERIOR M

U P P E R   P E N I N S U L A

PERE MARQUETTE NATIONAL WILD & SCENIC RIVER

NATIONAL FOREST

L O W E R   P E N I N S U L A

Harbor Beach

Sandusky

Bad Axe

Saginaw Bay

Cass

Black

Cass

Cass

St. Clair

Port Huron

St. Clair Shores

Lake St. Clair

Detroit

Dearborn

LAKE ERIE

OHIO

Troy
Warren
Pontiac
Livonia
Ypsilanti
Ann Arbor
Temperance
Lambertville
Monroe

Burton
Flint
SHIAWASSEE N.W.R.
Flint
Owosso
Saginaw
Bay City
Midland
Alma
Mt. Pleasant
ISABELLA INDIAN RESERVATION
Muskegon
Greenville
Belding
Ionia
St. Johns
East Lansing
Lansing
Mason
Charlotte
Battle Creek
Marshall
Albion
Jackson
Hillsdale
Adrian
Tecumseh
Coldwater
Sturgis
Three Rivers
Kalamazoo
Portage
Dowagiac
Niles
Benton Harbor
St. Joseph
South Haven
Holland
Zeeland
Grand Rapids
Kentwood
Hastings
Grand Haven
Muskegon
Fremont
White
Big Rapids
White

Looking Glass
Grand
St. Joseph
Kalamazoo
Raisin
Saginaw
Flint

INDIANA

ILLINOIS

LAKE MICHIGAN

Great Lakes State

Michigan

Michigan is made up of two parts: the populous Lower Peninsula and the sparsely populated Upper Peninsula. Water surrounds most of the state, which borders four of the five Great Lakes—Michigan, Huron, Superior, and Erie. The lakes not only define the state's shape, but also help economically by providing a route for raw materials and goods to move in and out of the state.

Detroit, the largest city, was founded by a Frenchman named Cadillac. Steel production in the area attracted job-seeking immigrants from Germany, Poland, Hungary, and other European countries in the 19th century. By 1896 Henry Ford began making cars in Detroit, followed by Ransom Olds, David Buick, and the Dodge brothers. Despite tough times caused by foreign competition, Michigan still leads the nation in producing cars and trucks. Southern Michigan is also a top producer of cherries and other fruits grown along Lake Michigan's shores.

The Upper Peninsula is famous as a vacation land. Its attractions include forests, streams, and nearby islands such as Isle Royale in Lake Superior.

More about Michigan

Area: 96,705 sq mi (250,465 sq km)

Population: 9,817,000

Capital: Lansing, pop. 125,700

Largest city: Detroit, pop. 1,012,100

Industry: motor vehicles and parts, machinery, metal products, office furniture, tourism, chemicals

Agriculture: dairy products, cattle, vegetables, hogs, corn, nursery stock, soybeans

Statehood: January 26, 1837; 26th state

Nickname: Great Lakes State

■ Michigan's shoreline measures 3,288 miles (5,291 km), longer than any other inland state's.

■ No place in Michigan is more than a few minutes from a lake.

■ Another nickname for Michigan is Wolverine State. Early trappers traded many valuable wolverine pelts.

■ Because Lake Superior is 20 feet (6 m) higher than Lake Huron, engineers built canals and locks at Sault Sainte Marie in 1855 to allow ships to pass between the two lakes.

■ The five-mile (8-km)-long Mackinac Bridge, built across the Straits of Mackinac in 1957, links the Lower and Upper Peninsulas.

■ The Upper Peninsula of Michigan is sometimes called the "land of Hiawatha," because poet Henry Wadsworth Longfellow described it in his poem The Song of Hiawatha.

Robin
Apple Blossom

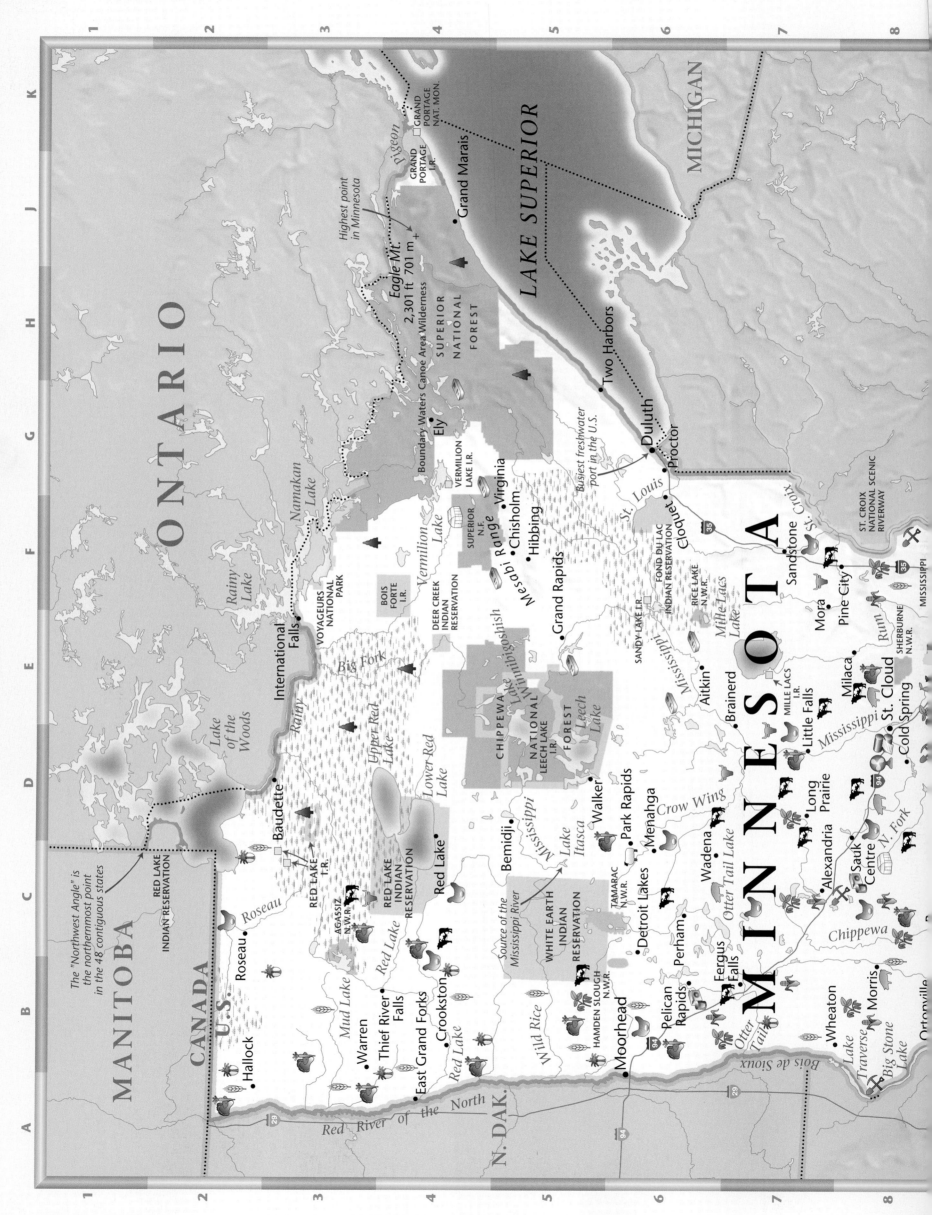

MANITOBA

CANADA
U.S.

ONTARIO

LAKE SUPERIOR

MICHIGAN

MINNESOTA

N. DAK.

The "Northwest Angle" is
the northernmost point
in the 48 contiguous states

RED LAKE
INDIAN RESERVATION

Lake of
the Woods

Roseau

Hallock

Warren

Thief River
Falls

Baudette

Mud Lake

AGASSIZ
N.W.R.

RED LAKE
I.R.

RED LAKE
INDIAN
RESERVATION

Red Lake

Upper Red
Lake

Lower Red
Lake

Roseau

Red Lake

Rainy

International
Falls

Big Fork

VOYAGEURS
NATIONAL
PARK

Namakan
Lake

Rainy
Lake

Vermilion
Lake

BOIS
FORTE
I.R.

DEER CREEK
INDIAN
RESERVATION

Ely

VERMILION
LAKE I.R.

SUPERIOR
N.F.

Virginia
Chisholm
Hibbing

Mesabi Range

Grand Rapids

Lake
Winnibigoshish

CHIPPEWA

NATIONAL

LEECH LAKE
FOREST
I.R.

Leech
Lake

Boundary Waters Canoe Area Wilderness

SUPERIOR
NATIONAL
FOREST

Eagle Mt.
2,301 ft 701 m +

Highest point
in Minnesota

GRAND
PORTAGE
I.R.

GRAND
PORTAGE
NAT. MON.

Grand Marais

Pigeon

Two Harbors

Duluth

Proctor

St. Louis

Busiest freshwater
port in the U.S.

Cloquet

FOND DU LAC
INDIAN RESERVATION

SANDY LAKE I.R.

RICE LAKE
N.W.R.

Mille Lacs
Lake

MILLE
LACS
I.R.

Sandstone

St. Croix

St. Croix

ST. CROIX
NATIONAL SCENIC
RIVERWAY

MISSISSIPPI

Mora

Pine City

Milaca

Cold Spring

St. Cloud

SHERBURNE
N.W.R.

Rum

N. Fork

Mississippi

Little Falls

Aitkin

Brainerd

Crow Wing

Mississippi

Source of the
Mississippi River

Lake
Itasca

Bemidji

WHITE EARTH
INDIAN
RESERVATION

TAMARAC
N.W.R.

HAMDEN SLOUGH
N.W.R.

Wild Rice

Walker

Park Rapids

Menahga

Detroit Lakes

Perham

Wadena

Long
Prairie

Sauk
Centre

Alexandria

Otter Tail Lake

Otter
Tail

Chippewa

Pelican
Rapids

Fergus
Falls

Moorhead

East Grand Forks

Crookston

Red Lake

Red River of the North

Bois de Sioux

Wheaton

Morris

Ortonville

Big Stone
Lake

Traverse
Lake

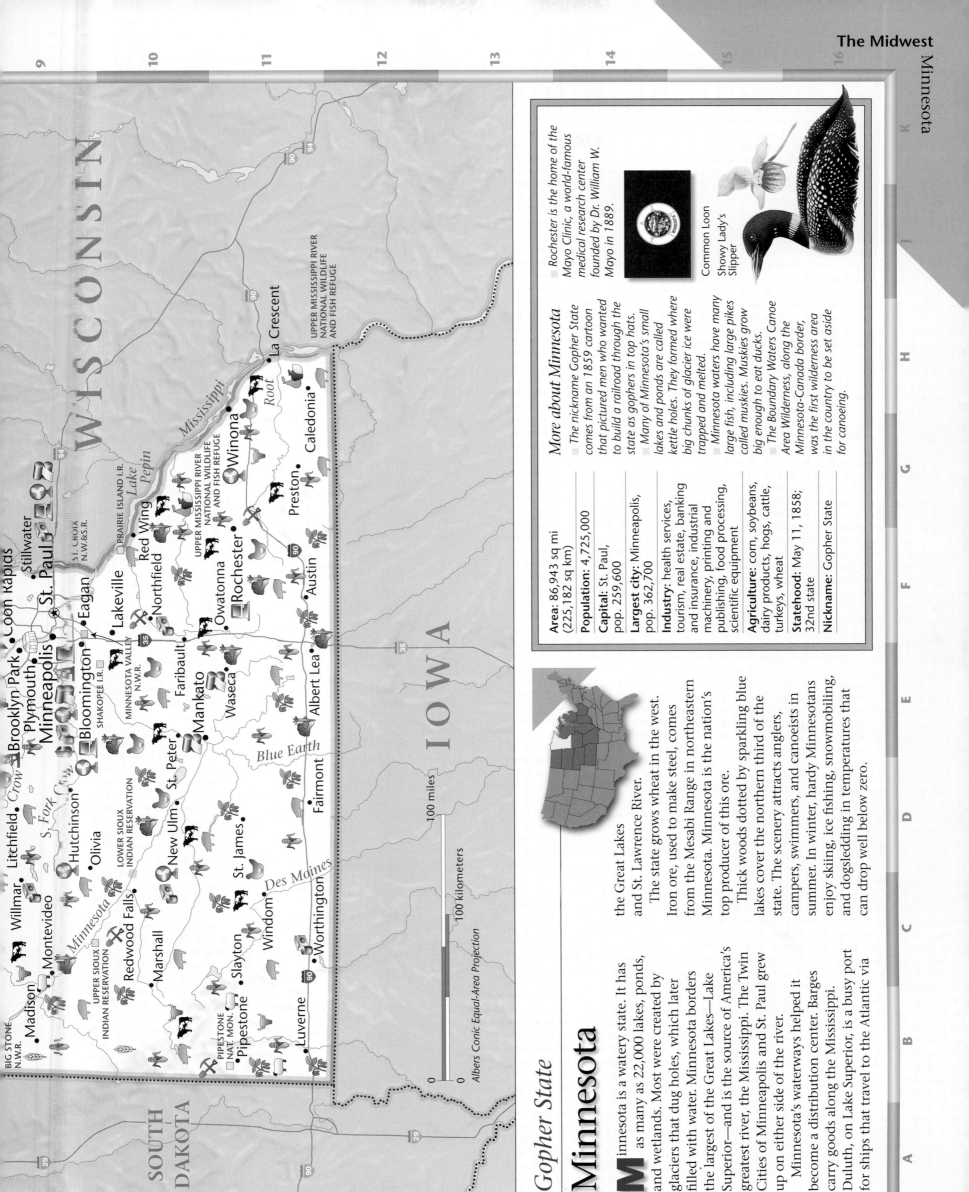

Gopher State

Minnesota

Minnesota is a watery state. It has as many as 22,000 lakes, ponds, and wetlands. Most were created by glaciers that dug holes, which later filled with water. Minnesota borders the largest of the Great Lakes—Lake Superior—and is the source of America's greatest river, the Mississippi. The Twin Cities of Minneapolis and St. Paul grew up on either side of the river.

Minnesota's waterways helped it become a distribution center. Barges carry goods along the Mississippi. Duluth, on Lake Superior, is a busy port for ships that travel to the Atlantic via the Great Lakes and St. Lawrence River.

The state grows wheat in the west. Iron ore, used to make steel, comes from the Mesabi Range in northeastern Minnesota. Minnesota is the nation's top producer of this ore.

Thick woods dotted by sparkling blue lakes cover the northern third of the state. The scenery attracts anglers, campers, swimmers, and canoeists in summer. In winter, hardy Minnesotans enjoy skiing, ice fishing, snowmobiling, and dogsledding in temperatures that can drop well below zero.

Area: 86,943 sq mi (225,182 sq km)

Population: 4,725,000

Capital: St. Paul, pop. 259,600

Largest city: Minneapolis, pop. 362,700

Industry: health services, tourism, real estate, banking and insurance, industrial machinery, printing and publishing, food processing, scientific equipment

Agriculture: corn, soybeans, dairy products, hogs, cattle, turkeys, wheat

Statehood: May 11, 1858; 32nd state

Nickname: Gopher State

More about Minnesota

■ The nickname Gopher State comes from an 1859 cartoon that pictured men who wanted to build a railroad through the state as gophers in top hats.

■ Many of Minnesota's small lakes and ponds are called kettle holes. They formed where big chunks of glacier ice were trapped and melted.

■ Minnesota waters have many large fish, including large pikes called muskies. Muskies grow big enough to eat ducks.

■ The Boundary Waters Canoe Area Wilderness, along the Minnesota-Canada border, was the first wilderness area in the country to be set aside for canoeing.

■ Rochester is the home of the Mayo Clinic, a world-famous medical research center founded by Dr. William W. Mayo in 1889.

Common Loon

Showy Lady's Slipper

100 miles

100 kilometers

Albers Conic Equal-Area Projection

NEBRASKA

IOWA

1 2 3 4 5 6 7 8

A

Maryville

Bethany

Thompson

Weldon

Kirksville

Locust Creek

Middle Fabius

Wyaconda

Canton

B

One Hundred and Two

Platte

Grand

Trenton

South Fabius

Salt

SQUAW CREEK N.W.R.

Savannah

Missouri

St. Joseph

Gallatin

Cameron

Chillicothe

Brookfield

SWAN LAKE N.W.R.

Macon

Boyhood home of Mark Twain

Hannibal

C

Jesse James Farm and Museum

Chariton

Moberly

Mark Twain Lake

Liberty

Richmond

Harry S Truman N.H.S.

Missouri

Centralia

Mexico

Kansas City

Independence

Marshall

Boonville

Columbia

Salt

D

KANSAS

Blue Springs

Lees Summit

Blackwater

BIG MUDDY N.W.R.

MARK TWAIN NATIONAL FOREST

Fulton

Belton

Warrensburg

Sedalia

California

Hermann

Harrisonville

Jefferson City

E

South Grand

MISSOURI

Clinton

Eldon

Butler

Harry S Truman Reservoir

Osage

Marais des Cygnes

Osage

Lake of the Ozarks

Gasconade

Rolla

St. Jam

F

Nevada

Osage

Sac

Niangua

Waynesville

Salem

Stockton Lake

Bolivar

Lebanon

Osage Fork

MARK TWAIN NATIONAL FOREST

Current

G

Little Sac

Gasconade

Big Piney

OZARK NATIONAL SCENIC RIVERWAYS

Webb City

Carthage

Springfield

Seymour

Mountain Grove

Jacks Fo

H

Joplin

Republic

WILSON'S CREEK N.B.

Ava

MARK TWAIN NATIONAL FOREST

Eleven Point

West Plains

GEORGE WASHINGTON CARVER NATIONAL MONUMENT

Aurora

Monett

Bryant Creek

Neosho

Table Rock Lake

Branson

MARK TWAIN NATIONAL FOREST

ELEVEN POINT NATIONAL WILD & SCENIC RIVER

J

OKLAHOMA

O

Only extensive highlands in the central U.S.

White

Bull Shoals Lake

ARKANSAS

K

0   100 miles

0   100 kilometers

Albers Conic Equal-Area Projection

Map labels

9 10 11 12 13 14 15 16

A
B
C
D
E
F
G
H
J
K

Louisiana

CLARENCE CANNON N.W.R.

Cuivre

ILLINOIS

St. Charles
St. Peters
Florissant
Ferguson
University City
Kirkwood
St. Louis ←
Washington
Union
ULYSSES S. GRANT N.H.S.

Jefferson National Expansion Memorial includes Gateway Arch

Sullivan
Festus
De Soto

U.S. center of population, 1990

Park Hills
Farmington
Perryville
Taum Sauk Mt. 1,772 ft +540 m
Fredericktown
Jackson
Cape Girardeau

MARK TWAIN NATIONAL FOREST

Highest point in Missouri

OZARK NATIONAL SCENIC RIVERWAYS

MINGO N.W.R.

MARK TWAIN NATIONAL FOREST

MARK TWAIN NATIONAL FOREST

Poplar Bluff
Sikeston
Dexter

St. Francis

Charleston

KENTUCKY

Severe earthquakes in 1811–12 changed the course of the Mississippi River

New Madrid
Malden

Current

Black

Kennett
Caruthersville

TENNESSEE

Mississippi

IND.

Show Me State

Missouri

Two great rivers frame Missouri. The Mississippi River forms the state's eastern border; the Missouri River, known as Big Muddy, forms part of the western border. The fact that these two major rivers meet near St. Louis, in eastern Missouri, has made the state a transportation hub since pioneer days. Both St. Louis and Kansas City, which grew up across the state on the Missouri River, are now manufacturing centers, making products ranging from jet aircraft to processed foods.

Several historic trails West began in Missouri. Both the Oregon and the Santa Fe Trails began in Independence. In the 1800s many pioneers also stopped in St. Louis to get supplies for the long trek westward. Today, the Gateway Arch towers over the city, a symbol of the city's role as a gate to the West.

Missouri has many different landscapes. The north has fertile cornfields, and the southeast grows cotton and rice on low plains. The Ozark Plateau covers much of the south. Caves, springs, lakes, and swift streams make the area a favorite vacation spot.

Area: 69,709 sq mi (180,546 sq km)

Population: 5,439,000

Capital: Jefferson City, pop. 36,100

Largest city: Kansas City, pop. 431,600

Industry: transportation equipment, food processing, chemicals, electrical equipment, metal products

Agriculture: cattle, soybeans, hogs, corn, poultry and eggs, dairy products

Statehood: August 10, 1821; 24th state

Nickname: Show Me State

More about Missouri

■ The state's nickname, Show Me State, comes from a speech by Missouri Congressman Willard Duncan Vandiver in 1899. He said "I am from Missouri. You have got to show me."

■ The first ice-cream cones were served in 1904 at the Louisiana Purchase Exposition world's fair in St. Louis.

■ In late 1811 and early 1812, three of the strongest earthquakes in U.S. history rocked Missouri near New Madrid. The quakes, which scientists believe measured 8 on the Richter scale, caused the Mississippi River to flow backward temporarily.

■ Because it was a jumping-off point for so many pioneers, Missouri is sometimes called "The Mother of the West."

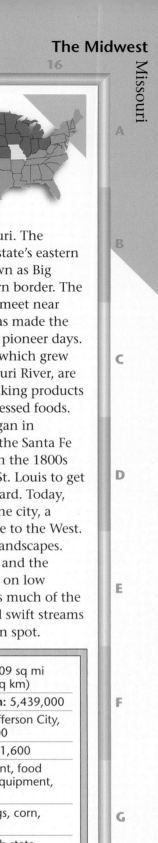

Eastern Bluebird
Hawthorn

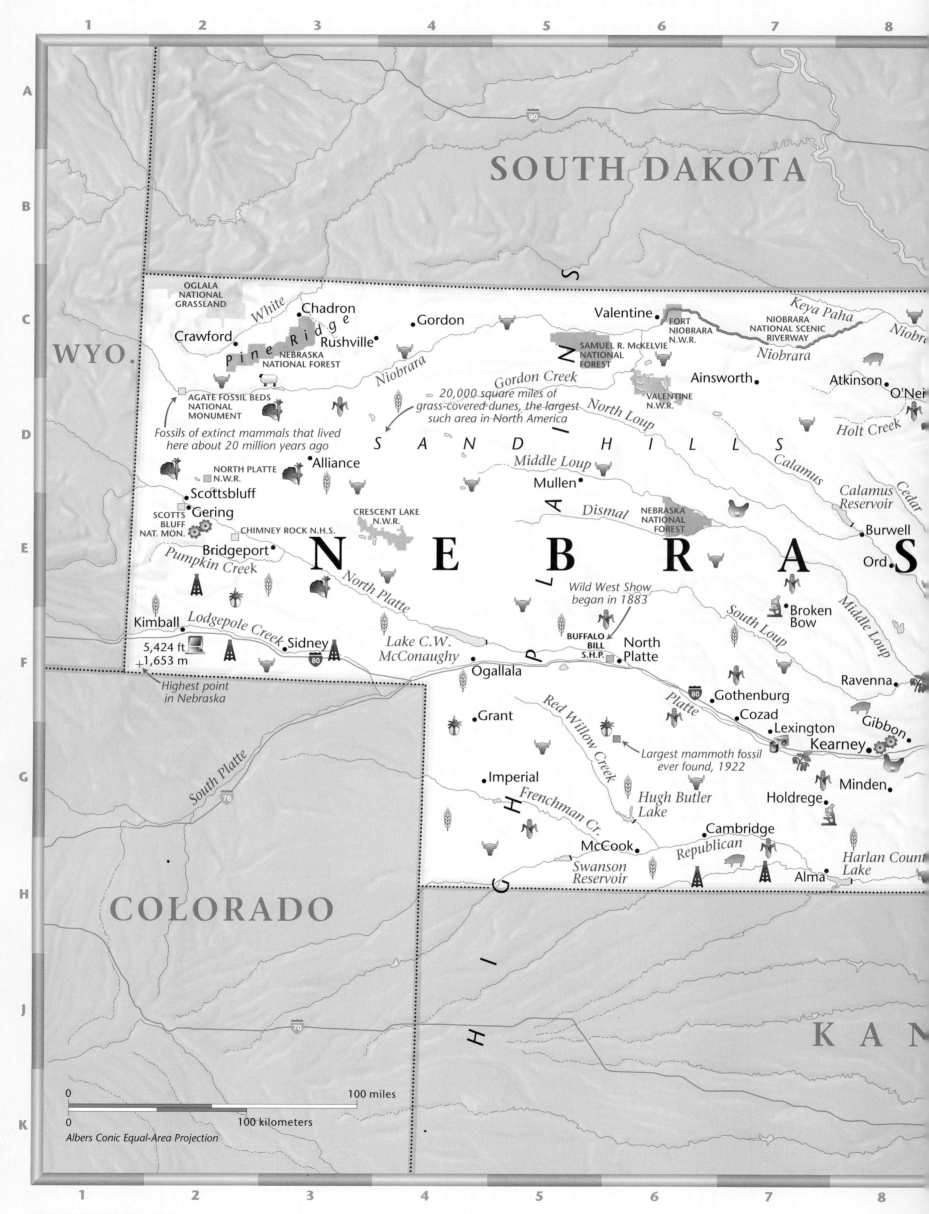

SOUTH DAKOTA

WYO.

OGLALA NATIONAL GRASSLAND

Crawford
Chadron
Gordon
Valentine
FORT NIOBRARA N.W.R.
NIOBRARA NATIONAL SCENIC RIVERWAY

White
Pine Ridge
Rushville
NEBRASKA NATIONAL FOREST

SAMUEL R. McKELVIE NATIONAL FOREST

Ainsworth
Atkinson
O'Nei

Keya Paha

Niobra

Niobrara

AGATE FOSSIL BEDS NATIONAL MONUMENT

Gordon Creek

20,000 square miles of grass-covered dunes, the largest such area in North America

VALENTINE N.W.R.

Holt Creek

Fossils of extinct mammals that lived here about 20 million years ago

North Loup

Calamus

S A N D   H I L L S

Alliance
NORTH PLATTE N.W.R.

Middle Loup
Mullen

Calamus Reservoir

Scottsbluff
Gering
SCOTTS BLUFF NAT. MON.
CHIMNEY ROCK N.H.S.

CRESCENT LAKE N.W.R.

Dismal
NEBRASKA NATIONAL FOREST

Burwell

Bridgeport

N   E   B   R   A   S

Ord

Pumpkin Creek

North Platte

Wild West Show began in 1883

Broken Bow

South Loup

Middle Loup

Kimball

Lodgepole Creek
Sidney

Lake C.W. McConaughy

BUFFALO BILL S.H.P.
North Platte

Ravenna

5,424 ft +1,653 m

80

Ogallala
Gothenburg
Cozad
Lexington
Gibbon

Highest point in Nebraska

Grant

Red Willow Creek

Platte

Kearney

Largest mammoth fossil ever found, 1922

Minden

South Platte

76

Imperial

Frenchman Cr.

Hugh Butler Lake

Holdrege

70

Cambridge

McCook
Republican

Swanson Reservoir

Alma

Harlan Count Lake

COLORADO

H   I   G   H

K A N

0   100 miles

0   100 kilometers

Albers Conic Equal-Area Projection

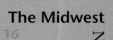

MINNESOTA

IOWA

MISSOURI

Lewis and Clark Lake

MISSOURI NATIONAL RECREATION RIVER

MISSOURI NATIONAL RECREATION RIVER

SANTEE INDIAN RESERVATION

Verdigre Cr.

Hartington

Logan Creek

Missouri

Elkhorn

Wayne

WINNEBAGO I.R.

South Sioux City

Neligh

Norfolk

Pender

OMAHA I.R.

Madison

West Point

Tekamah

K

Albion

Shell Cr.

A

Blair

DE SOTO N.W.R.

Schuyler

Fremont

BOYER CHUTE N.W.R.

Columbus

Fullerton

Loup

David City

Wahoo

Omaha

St. Paul

Central City

Big Blue

Papillion

Bellevue

President Ford's birthplace

Grand Island

Seward

Ashland

Waverly

Platte

Plattsmouth

York

Nine-Mile Prairie

Lincoln

Aurora

Milford

Nebraska City

Crete

Hastings

Geneva

Wilber

Auburn

Missouri

Little Blue

HOMESTEAD NAT. MON. OF AMERICA

Beatrice

Hebron

ed Cloud

Fairbury

Big Nemaha

Falls City

Superior

SAC AND FOX I.R.

IOWA I.R.

SAS

Cornhusker State

Nebraska

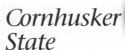

Before settlers came to Nebraska in the 19th century, this land was a nearly treeless grassland. In 1820 U.S. Army Major Stephen H. Long led an expedition along the Platte River during a severe drought. He called the land a "Great American Desert" and "almost wholly unfit for farming."

Today, farms and ranches cover about 95 percent of Nebraska's open, rolling land, a greater share than in any other state. Corn grows in the fertile soil of the east, which is bordered by the Missouri River. On the drier western plains, wheat thrives with irrigation. And on low, grass-covered sand dunes called the Sand Hills, herds of cattle graze. Nebraska is a top beef-producing state.

In the mid-1800s thousands of pioneers followed Nebraska's Platte River west along the Mormon and Oregon Trails. Their wagon wheels wore deep ruts that can be seen today.

Omaha is Nebraska's biggest city. It is among the Midwest's leading finance and insurance centers as well as a major meatpacking and food-processing center.

Area: 77,358 sq mi (200,358 sq km)

Population: 1,663,000

Capital: Lincoln, pop. 209,200

Largest city: Omaha, pop. 339,700

Industry: food processing, machinery, electrical equipment, printing and publishing

Agriculture: cattle, corn, hogs, soybeans, wheat, sorghum

Statehood: March 1, 1867; 37th state

Nickname: Cornhusker State

More about Nebraska

■ *Many of Nebraska's early settlers were called sodbusters because they cut sod—chunks of the grassy prairie surface—to build houses. The sod became known as "Nebraska marble."*

■ *Cattle outnumber people in Nebraska by more than four to one.*

■ *The state's nickname, Cornhusker State, refers to its chief crop and to early cornhusking contests held in many areas.*

■ *At Nine-Mile Prairie, near Lincoln, visitors can see 230 acres (93 ha) of unspoiled prairie, along with more than 300 species of native prairie grasses and wildflowers.*

■ *Nebraska is the only state with a one-house legislature. All 49 members are called senators.*

Western Meadowlark
Goldenrod

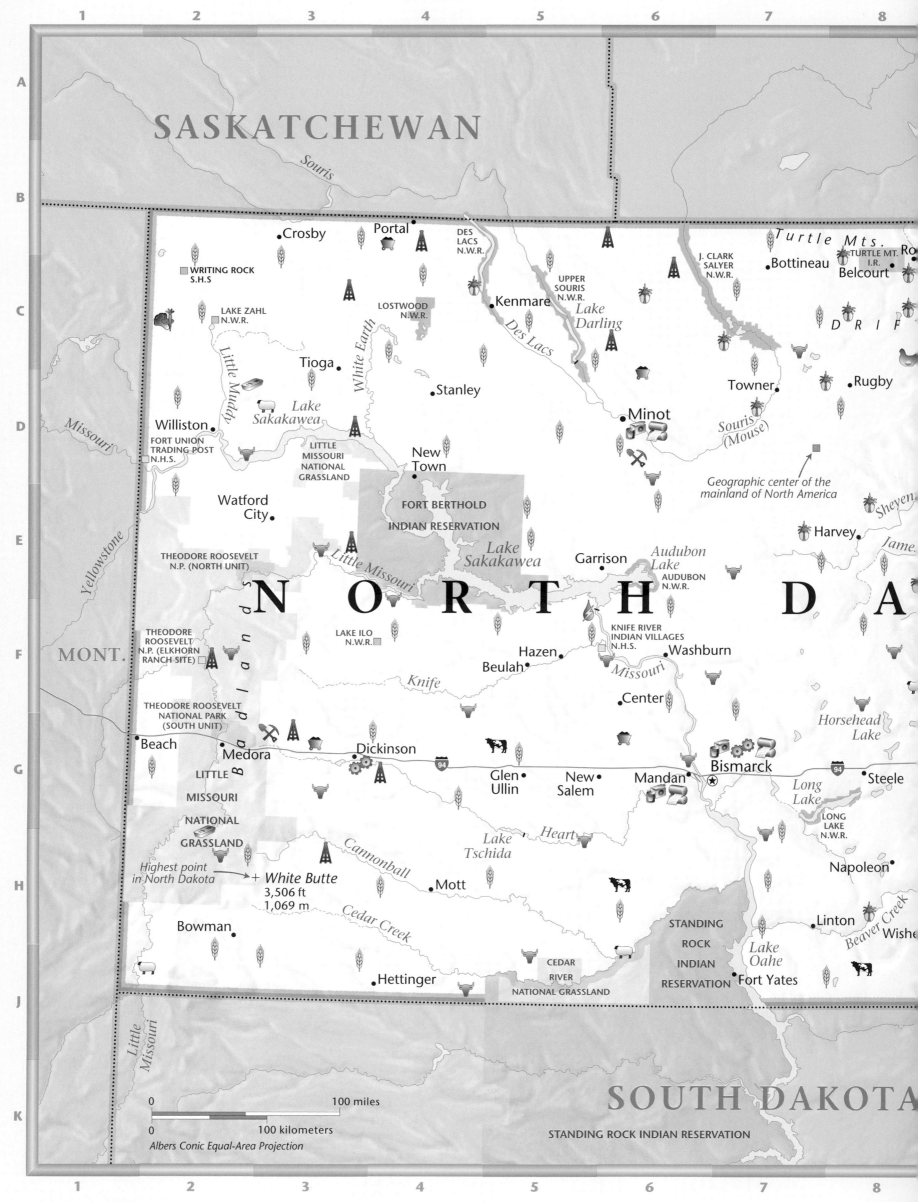

SASKATCHEWAN

Souris

Crosby
Portal
DES LACS N.W.R.

WRITING ROCK S.H.S
LAKE ZAHL N.W.R.
LOSTWOOD N.W.R.
Kenmare
UPPER SOURIS N.W.R.
Lake Darling
J. CLARK SALYER N.W.R.
Turtle Mts.
TURTLE MT. I.R.
Bottineau
Belcourt
Ro

Little Muddy
Tioga
White Earth
Stanley
Minot
Souris (Mouse)
Towner
D R I F
Rugby

Williston
Lake Sakakawea
FORT UNION TRADING POST N.H.S.
LITTLE MISSOURI NATIONAL GRASSLAND
New Town
Geographic center of the mainland of North America

Missouri

Watford City
FORT BERTHOLD INDIAN RESERVATION
Lake Sakakawea
Garrison
Audubon Lake
AUDUBON N.W.R.
Harvey
Sheyen
James.

THEODORE ROOSEVELT N.P. (NORTH UNIT)
Little Missouri

N O R T H   D A

Yellowstone

MONT.
THEODORE ROOSEVELT N.P. (ELKHORN RANCH SITE)
LAKE ILO N.W.R.
KNIFE RIVER INDIAN VILLAGES N.H.S.
Hazen
Beulah
Washburn
Missouri

THEODORE ROOSEVELT NATIONAL PARK (SOUTH UNIT)
Knife
Center
Horsehead Lake

Beach
Medora
Badlands
Dickinson
94
Glen Ullin
New Salem
Mandan
Bismarck
94
Steele
Long Lake
LONG LAKE N.W.R.

LITTLE MISSOURI NATIONAL GRASSLAND
Cannonball
Lake Tschida
Heart
Napoleon

Highest point in North Dakota
+ White Butte
3,506 ft
1,069 m
Mott
Linton
Beaver Creek
Wishe

Bowman
Cedar Creek
STANDING ROCK INDIAN RESERVATION
Lake Oahe
Fort Yates

Hettinger
CEDAR RIVER NATIONAL GRASSLAND

0   100 miles
0   100 kilometers
Albers Conic Equal-Area Projection

SOUTH DAKOTA

STANDING ROCK INDIAN RESERVATION

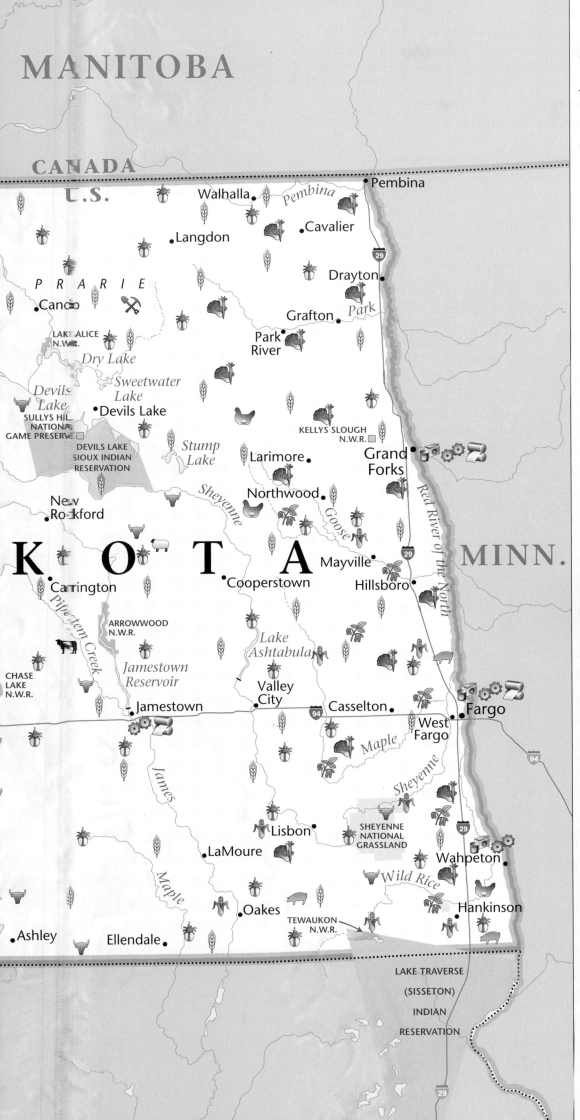

MANITOBA

CANADA
U.S.

PRARIE
DAKOTA

Cando
LAKE ALICE N.W.R.
Dry Lake
Devils Lake
Sweetwater Lake
SULLYS HILL NATIONAL GAME PRESERVE
DEVILS LAKE SIOUX INDIAN RESERVATION
New Rockford
Carrington
Pipestem Creek
ARROWWOOD N.W.R.
CHASE LAKE N.W.R.
Jamestown Reservoir
Jamestown
James
Stump Lake
Sheyenne
Larimore
Northwood
Goose
Cooperstown
Mayville
Lake Ashtabula
Valley City
Casselton
Maple
Lisbon
LaMoure
Maple
Oakes
Ashley
Ellendale
TEWAUKON N.W.R.

Walhalla
Langdon
Cavalier
Pembina
Drayton
Park
Grafton
Park River
KELLYS SLOUGH N.W.R.
Grand Forks
Hillsboro
Red River of the North
MINN.
94
West Fargo
Fargo
Sheyenne
SHEYENNE NATIONAL GRASSLAND
Wahpeton
Wild Rice
Hankinson
94
29

LAKE TRAVERSE (SISSETON) INDIAN RESERVATION

Flickertail State

North Dakota

You can find the geographic center of the North American continent in North Dakota south of Rugby, a small town on the windswept plains. Rugby is about 1,500 miles (2,400 km) from the Atlantic, Pacific, and Arctic Oceans and the Gulf of Mexico.

Flat or rolling plains stretch across much of North Dakota. Most North Dakotans live along the eastern border in the valley of the Red River of the North. Glaciers left rich soil east of the Missouri River. Here farmers grow huge crops of spring wheat. North Dakota leads the nation in barley, sunflower seeds, and seed flax. The Great Plains, rich in coal and oil, lie west of the Missouri River. The state capital, Bismarck, stands on the Missouri between these two regions and is the center for industries that cater to them both.

North Dakota is known for its frigid, windy winters, when temperatures may plummet as low as -60° Fahrenheit (-51°C). Without an ocean or any large lakes to moderate the climate, summer temperatures can be just as extreme, soaring to 121° Fahrenheit (49°C).

Area: 70,704 sq mi (183,123 sq km)

Population: 638,000

Capital: Bismarck, pop. 53,500

Largest city: Fargo, pop. 77,100

Industry: services, government, finance, insurance, real estate, transportation

Agriculture: wheat, cattle, sunflowers, barley, soybeans

Statehood: November 2, 1889; 39th state

Nickname: Flickertail State

More about North Dakota

■ The state's nickname, Flickertail State, comes from the many flickertail ground squirrels that live there.

■ North Dakota's capitol building, in Bismarck, is 19 stories high. It is known as the Skyscraper of the Prairies.

■ West of the Red River Valley is the Drift Prairie, pockmarked by thousand of glacially created kettle hole lakes and ponds. These regions are prime habitat for migrating ducks and geese.

■ North Dakota is the only state that shares a golf course with another country. Part of the course is in Portal, North Dakota, and the other part is in Saskatchewan, a Canadian province.

■ The Red River of the North is one of the few large north-flowing rivers in the U.S.

Western Meadowlark

Wild Prairie Rose

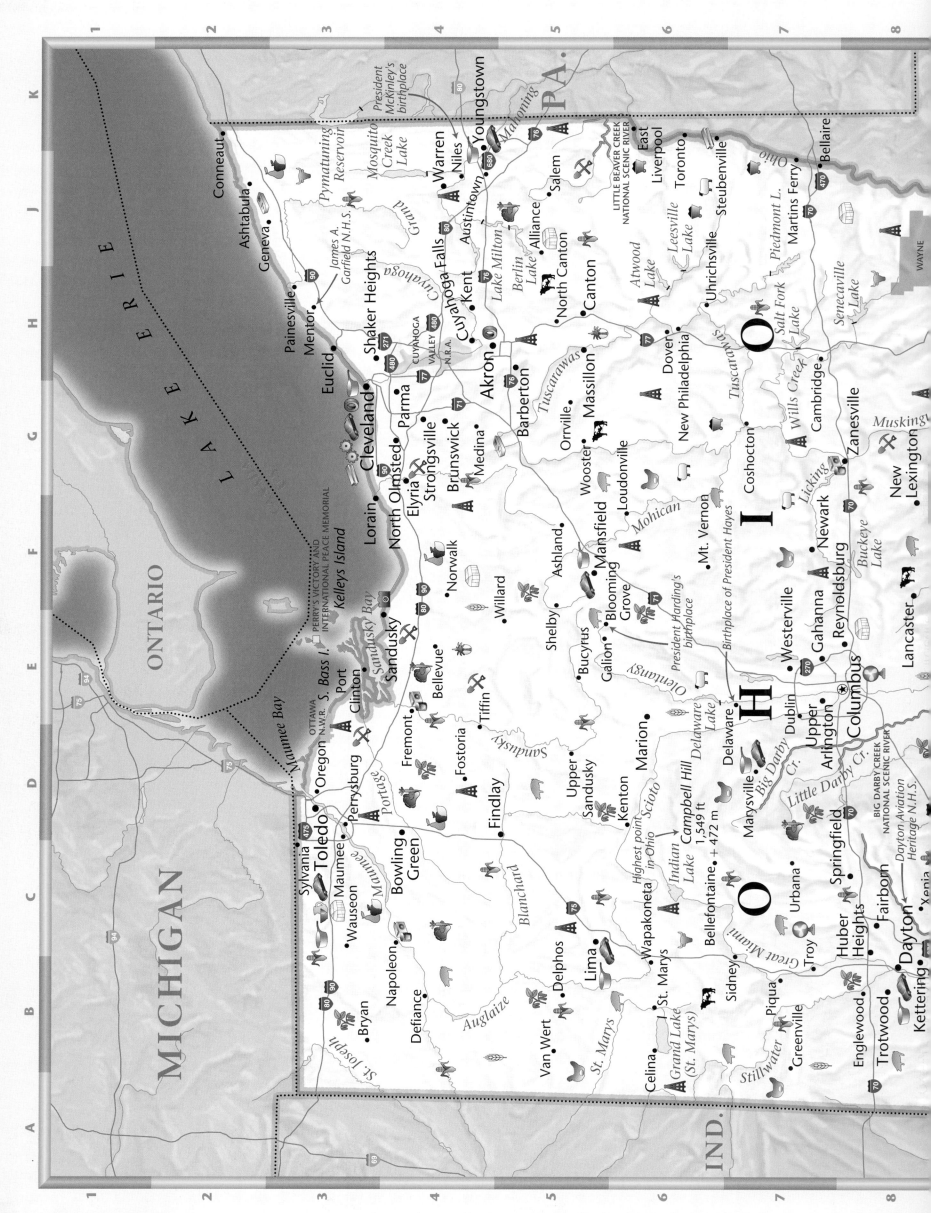

MICHIGAN

ONTARIO

L A K E   E R I E

Conneaut
Ashtabula
Geneva
Painesville
Mentor
Euclid
Shaker Heights
Cleveland
Parma
North Olmsted
Strongsville
Brunswick
Medina
Lorain
Elyria
Norwalk
Willard
Bellevue
Sandusky
Port Clinton
Oregon N.W.R.
Perrysburg
Portage
Maumee
Sylvania
Toledo
Wauseon
Napoleon
Bryan
Defiance
Bowling Green
Fostoria
Findlay
Tiffin
Fremont
Shelby
Bucyrus
Galion
Blooming Grove
Mansfield
Ashland
Wooster
Orrville
Loudonville
Mt. Vernon
Coshocton
Zanesville
New Lexington
Newark
Licking
Buckeye Lake
Gahanna
Reynoldsburg
Westerville
Dublin
Upper Arlington
Columbus
Delaware
Delaware Lake
Marysville
Marion
Kenton
Upper Sandusky
Van Wert
Delphos
Lima
St. Marys
Wapakoneta
Bellefontaine
Indian Lake
Sidney
Piqua
Troy
Urbana
Springfield
Fairborn
Huber Heights
Dayton
Kettering
Trotwood
Englewood
Greenville
Celina
Grand Lake (St. Marys)
Xenia

Pymatuning Reservoir
Mosquito Creek Lake
President McKinley's birthplace
Warren
Niles
Youngstown
Austintown
Mahoning
Lake Milton
Berlin Lake
Alliance
Salem
East Liverpool
Toronto
Steubenville
Martins Ferry
Bellaire
Kent
Cuyahoga Falls
North Canton
Canton
Massillon
Barberton
Akron
Tuscarawas
Dover
New Philadelphia
Atwood Lake
Leesville Lake
Uhrichsville
Piedmont L.
Salt Fork Lake
Wills Creek Lake
Cambridge
Senecaville Lake
Muskingum
Ohio
Little Beaver Creek National Scenic River
WAYNE

James A. Garfield N.H.S.
Grand
Cuyahoga
Cuyahoga Valley N.R.A.

Campbell Hill
Highest point in Ohio
1,549 ft
+ 472 m
President Harding's birthplace
Birthplace of President Hayes
Birthplace of President Hayes

Perry's Victory and International Peace Memorial
S. Bass I.
Kelleys Island
Sandusky Bay
Maumee Bay
Ottawa N.W.R.

Scioto
Olentangy
Big Darby
Little Darby Cr.
Big Darby Creek National Scenic River
Dayton Aviation Heritage N.H.S.

Great Miami
Stillwater
Auglaize
St. Marys
Blanchard
Sandusky
Mohican

St. Joseph
Maumee

O H I O

PA.

IND.

Ohio

Buckeye State

Ohio lies between two great bodies of water: Lake Erie on the north and the Ohio River on the south. These water highways and the canals, roads, and railways that crisscrossed the state made Ohio a major link to the West for the settlers who traveled them.

The waterways and rich natural resources also helped Ohio become a great manufacturing state. Boats carried coal, oil, and iron ore from the Appalachians in the southeast to the state's factories and carried finished products to markets.

Busy industrial cities grew up along the waterways and became famous for different products. Cincinnati, on the Ohio River, has long made soap. Cleveland, on Lake Erie at the mouth of the Cuyahoga River, smelts steel. Toledo is famous for glass; Akron for tires. Today, Ohio's leading manufactured products are cars, trucks, and machine tools.

More than half of Ohio is farmland. Much of the land is fertile rolling hills and valleys or plains. Soybeans and corn are Ohio's two biggest crops.

Area: 44,828 sq mi (116,103 sq km)

Population: 11,209,000

Capital: Columbus, pop. 657,100

Largest city: Columbus, pop. 657,100

Industry: transportation equipment, metal products, machinery, food processing, electrical equipment

Agriculture: soybeans, dairy products, corn, hogs, cattle, poultry and eggs

Statehood: March 1, 1803; 17th state

Nickname: Buckeye State

Cardinal
Scarlet Carnation

More about Ohio

- Ohio is called the Buckeye State because dense forests of buckeye (horse chestnut) trees once grew on the state's hills and plains.
- The country's first public weather forecasting service was started in Cincinnati in 1869 at the Cincinnati Observatory. The forecasts were called "probabilities."
- Early Indians built more than 10,000 mounds in Ohio, including the Serpent Mound, a quarter-mile-long structure near Hillsboro.
- Ohio is the nation's top maker of appliances, such as stoves, refrigerators, and washing machines.
- The Rock and Roll Hall of Fame and Museum is in Cleveland.

100 miles

100 kilometers

Albers Conic Equal-Area Projection

NORTH DAK

MONTANA

Little Missouri

CUSTER
NATIONAL
FOREST

•Lemmon •McIntosh

S. Fork Grand

GRAND RIVER
NATIONAL
GRASSLAND

Grand

POCASSE
N.W.R.

Buffalo•

CUSTER
NATIONAL
FOREST

CUSTER
NATIONAL
FOREST

Bison•

GRAND
RIVER N.G.

Thunder Butte Creek

STANDING ROCK
INDIAN RESERVATION

Eureka•

Mobridge•
Selby•

Timber Lake•

Moreau

Lake
Oahe

Geographic center
of the 50 states

Moreau

Sulphur Creek

Dupree•

CHEYENNE RIVER
INDIAN RESERVATION

Gettysburg•

Cherry Creek

Okobojo Creek

Belle Fourche•

Cheyenne

Onida•

•Spearfish

Belle Fourche

S O U T H   D A

Highmore•

Deadwood•
•Lead

•Sturgis

Highest mountains
east of the Rockies

Fort Pierre •Pierre

Lake
Sharpe

BLACK
HILLS

Black Hawk•

BLACK HILLS
NATIONAL
FOREST

Rapid City•

Highest point
in South Dakota

Wall•

Bad

Philip•

FORT PIERRE
NATIONAL
GRASSLAND

Fort Thompson

WYOMING

MOUNT RUSHMORE
NAT. MEM.

Crazy Horse Memorial ■

Custer•

Harney Peak
7,242 ft 2,207 m

CUSTER
S.P.

BUFFALO GAP
NATIONAL
GRASSLAND

Kadoka•

Murdo•

LOWER BRULE
INDIAN RESERVATION

Kennebec•

JEWEL CAVE
NAT. MON.

BADLANDS
NATIONAL
PARK

White

White

WIND CAVE
NATIONAL
PARK

Cheyenne

Huge rock barrier sculptured into
pinnacles and gullies by running water

White River•

Hot Springs•

Edgemont•

PINE RIDGE INDIAN RESERVATION

Little White

Winner•

BUFFALO GAP

Wounded Knee
Massacre Site ■

Rosebud•

NATIONAL

Martin•

ROSEBUD
INDIAN
RESERVATION

Gregory•

GRASSLAND

Pine Ridge•

LACREEK
N.W.R.

Keya Paha

Last major conflict of the
Indian Wars, December 1890

White

N E B R A S

0   100 miles

0   100 kilometers

Albers Conic Equal-Area Projection

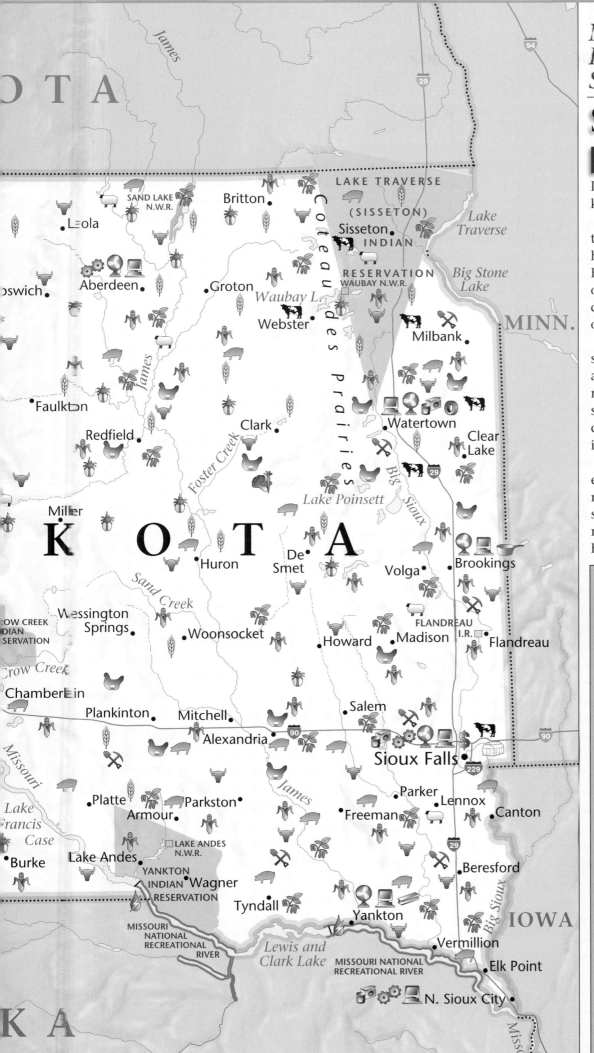

Mount Rushmore State

South Dakota

Named for the Dakota, or Sioux, Indians, South Dakota is sometimes called the Land of Infinite Variety, because of its many kinds of landscapes.

The Missouri River divides the state into two parts. East of the river is a land of rolling hills with fertile soil left by retreating glaciers. Here, farmers grow corn and soybeans. West of the river are the Great Plains. The land is drier here. Ranchers graze sheep and cattle on short grasses.

Close by is a barren rocky land with strangely shaped spires and canyons known as the Badlands. The Black Hills, beautiful mountains named for their dark pine and spruce trees, rise beyond them. Gold was discovered here in 1874, and South Dakota is still a leading gold-producing state.

Millions of visitors come to the Black Hills each year to visit Mount Rushmore and the nearby Crazy Horse Memorial, which is still under construction. Visitors to the memorial can also see one of the largest herds of bison in the United States.

Area: 77,121 sq mi (199,744 sq km)

Population: 738,000

Capital: Pierre, pop. 13,400

Largest city: Sioux Falls, pop. 105,600

Industry: finance, services, manufacturing, government, retail trade, transportation and utilities, wholesale trade, construction, mining

Agriculture: cattle, corn, soybeans, wheat, hogs, hay, dairy products

Statehood: November 2, 1889; 40th state

Nickname: Mount Rushmore State

More about South Dakota

■ Sculptors used dynamite to remove about a billion pounds of rock to make Mount Rushmore.
■ In 1876 the famous bank robber Jesse James escaped from a posse by jumping his horse across Devils Gulch, a canyon 20 feet (6 m) wide and 50 feet (15 m) deep, near Sioux Falls.
■ South Dakota has about 8,000 bison in different areas, more than any other state.
■ The domed Corn Palace, in Mitchell, is decorated with murals made of different colors of corn and other grains.
■ South Dakota's state fossil is the Triceratops.
■ Each eye in Mount Rushmore measures 11 feet (3.3 m) across.

Ring-necked Pheasant

Pasqueflower

LAKE SUPERIOR

MINNESOTA

MICHIGAN

W I S C O N S I N

Lake Superior

Apostle Islands
APOSTLE ISLANDS NATIONAL LAKESHORE
RED CLIFF INDIAN RESERVATION
Madeline Island
BAD RIVER INDIAN RESERVATION

Washburn
Ashland
Hurley

Superior

Bois Brule
St. Croix
Namekagon
ST. CROIX NATIONAL SCENIC RIVERWAY

CHEQUAMEGON NATIONAL FOREST
Turtle-Flambeau Flowage
Lake Chippewa
Park Falls
Hayward

LAC COURTE OREILLES INDIAN RESERVATION

Spooner
Rice Lake

St. Croix Falls
ST. CROIX NATIONAL SCENIC RIVERWAY

New Richmond
Hudson
River Falls
ST. CROIX N.W.&S.R.

Menomonie
Chippewa Falls
Eau Claire
Altoona
Red Cedar
Chippewa

Pepin
Lake Pepin
Mississippi
UPPER MISSISSIPPI WILDLIFE AND

Black River Falls
Black

Marshfield
Medford
Highest point in Wisconsin
+ Timms Hill 1,951ft 595 m
Tomahawk

Ladysmith
Flambeau
Jump
Yellow
Lake Wissota

Rhinelander

LAC DU FLAMBEAU INDIAN RESERVATION
CHEQUAMEGON NATIONAL FOREST

Eagle River
Land O'Lakes

Brule
Pine
Poppie
Menominee
Niagara
Peshtigo
NICOLET NATIONAL FOREST

POTAWATOMI INDIAN RESERVATION

SOKAOGON CHIPPEWA INDIAN RESERVATION
Wolf

MENOMINEE INDIAN RESERVATION
NICOLET NATIONAL FOREST
WOLF NATIONAL WILD & SCENIC RIVER

Antigo
Wolf
Shawano
STOCKBRIDGE INDIAN RESERVATION

Merrill
Wausau
Lake Du Bay

Big Eau Pleine Res.
Wisconsin
39

Stevens Point
Plover
Wisconsin Rapids
WISCONSIN WINNEBAGO INDIAN RESERVATION
NECEDAH NATIONAL WILDLIFE

New London
Waupaca
Lake
Petenwell

Washington Island
DOOR PENINSULA
Green Bay
Sturgeon Bay
Oconto
Marinette
Niagara

Algoma
Two Rivers
Green Bay
De Pere
Ashwaubenon
ONEIDA INDIAN RESERVATION
Kaukauna
Menasha
Appleton
Neenah
Fox

94
35
97

112 The Midwest

Wisconsin

Badger State

Wisconsin is sometimes called the Land of Lakes. It's easy to see why. Two great lakes—Lake Superior on the north and Lake Michigan on the east—border this midwestern state. There are also about 14,000 lakes inside the state that were formed by melting glaciers. Wisconsin's lakes and its thick northern forests, called the North Woods, make it a prime vacation spot. In summer, visitors fish, swim, and sail. In winter, they ski or go ice-fishing.

In the 1800s Wisconsin farmers began raising dairy cows. Settlers from Switzerland brought traditional cheese-making skills.

Today, Wisconsin is one of the nation's top producers of milk, cheese, and butter. It is known as America's dairyland.

Wisconsin has more people of German ancestry than any other state. Many live in Milwaukee, the state's largest city. Wisconsin's cities also make machinery and processed foods.

Forests cover half of Wisconsin. A century ago, lumberjacks there told tall tales about a giant logger named Paul Bunyan. Today, Wisconsin's huge forests make it a leading paper producer.

More about Wisconsin

- Wisconsin is nicknamed the Badger State because in the 1820s lead miners in the state lived like badgers in caves they had dug.
- Near Baraboo are the Wisconsin Dells, where the Wisconsin River has carved out gorges and unusual rock formations, including some called Witches Gulch and Devil's Elbow.
- Every February the American Birkebeiner, the largest cross-country ski race in the U.S., is held in Wisconsin.
- Nearly three-fourths of all the milk produced in the state goes into making cheese.
- Among the famous writers born in Wisconsin are novelist and playwright Thornton Wilder and Laura Ingalls Wilder, author of Little House on the Prairie. (The two writers are not related.)

Area: 65,499 sq mi (169,643 sq km)

Population: 5,224,000

Capital: Madison, pop. 197,600

Largest city: Milwaukee, pop. 617,000

Industry: industrial machinery, paper products, food processing, metal products, electronic equipment, transportation

Agriculture: dairy products, cattle, corn, poultry and eggs, soybeans

Statehood: May 29, 1848; 30th state

Nickname: Badger State

WISCONSIN 1848

Robin

Wood Violet

Map labels

LAKE

MICHIGAN

IOWA

ILLINOIS

Sheboygan
Fond du Lac
Port Washington
Mequon
Milwaukee
Wauwatosa
West Allis
S. Milwaukee
Racine
Kenosha
Burlington
Pleasant Prairie
Menomonee Falls
Brookfield
Waukesha
Fort Atkinson
Whitewater
Lake Geneva
West Bend
HORICON NATIONAL WILDLIFE REFUGE
Oshkosh
Ripon
Waupun
Beaver Dam
Sun Prairie
Watertown
Janesville
Beloit
Stoughton
Monona
Madison
Middleton
Lake Mendota
Lake Wisconsin
Baraboo
Wisconsin Dells
Reedsburg
Richland Center
Dodgeville
Lancaster
Platteville
Prairie du Chien
Taliesin
Castle Rock Lake
Tomah
Sparta
Onalaska
La Crosse
Viroqua
Monroe
Portage

Lake Winnebago
Fox
Rock
Fox
Wisconsin
Kickapoo
Pecatonica
Sugar
Rock
Mississippi

UPPER MISSISSIPPI RIVER NATIONAL WILDLIFE AND FISH REFUGE

N.W.R.

0   100 miles
0   100 kilometers

Albers Conic Equal-Area Projection

The South

west

Arizona
New Mexico
Oklahoma
Texas

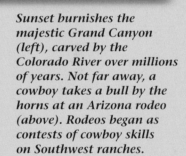

Sunset burnishes the majestic Grand Canyon (left), carved by the Colorado River over millions of years. Not far away, a cowboy takes a bull by the horns at an Arizona rodeo (above). Rodeos began as contests of cowboy skills on Southwest ranches.

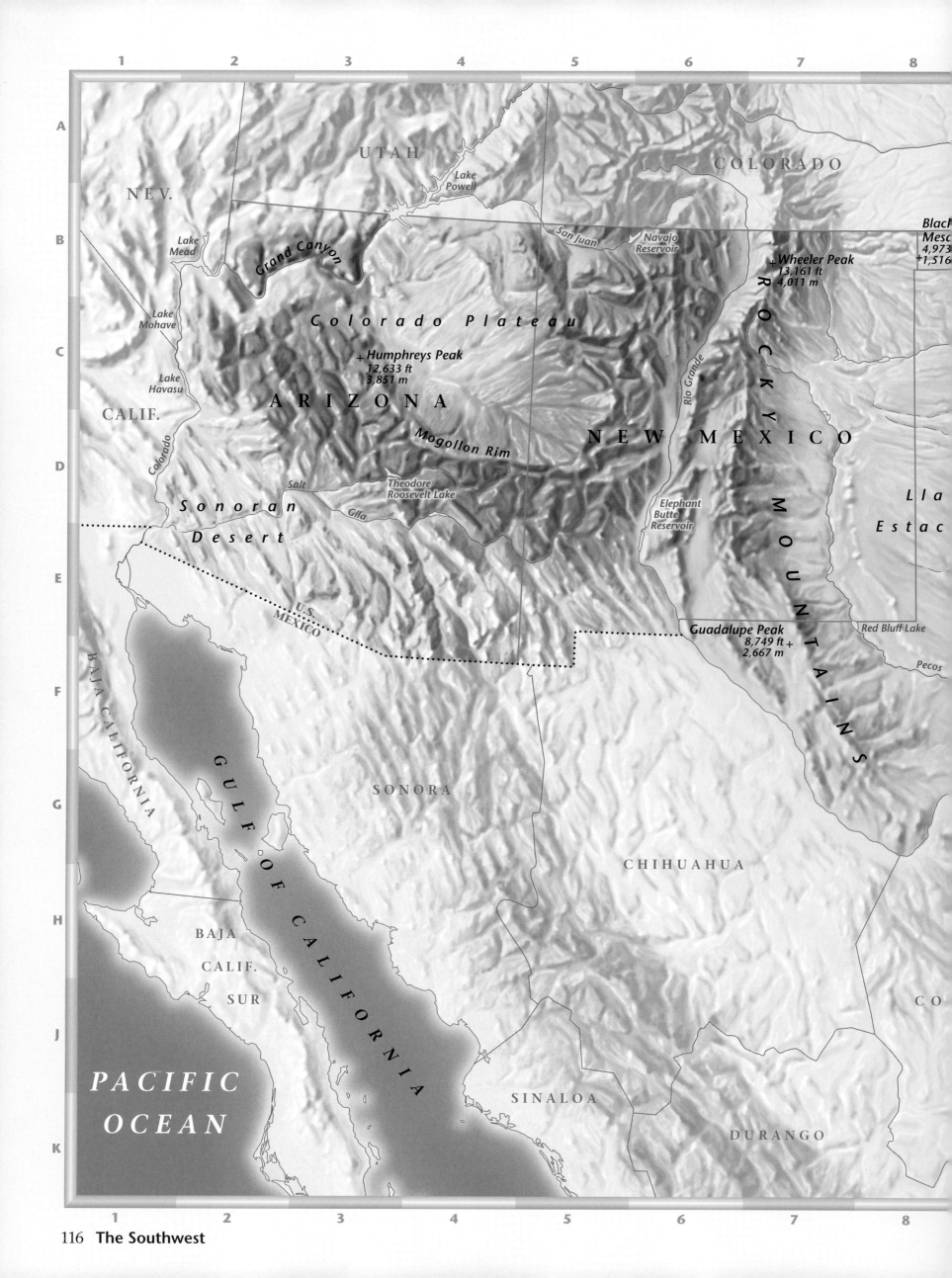

NEV.

UTAH

COLORADO

Lake
Powell

Lake
Mead

San Juan

Navajo
Reservoir

Blac
Mesc
4,973
+1,516

Grand Canyon

+ Wheeler Peak
13,161 ft
4,011 m

C o l o r a d o   P l a t e a u

Lake
Mohave

+ Humphreys Peak
12,633 ft
3,851 m

CALIF.

Lake
Havasu

A R I Z O N A

N E W   M E X I C O

Colorado

Mogollon Rim

Rio Grande

R O C K Y

Lla
Estac

Salt

Sonoran

Gila

Theodore
Roosevelt Lake

Elephant
Butte
Reservoir

M

Desert

O

U.S.
MEXICO

Guadalupe Peak
8,749 ft +
2,667 m

Red Bluff Lake

U

BAJA CALIFORNIA

N

Pecos

T

G U L F   O F   C A L I F O R N I A

S O N O R A

A

I

N

C H I H U A H U A

S

BAJA

CALIF.

SUR

C

PACIFIC
OCEAN

S I N A L O A

DURANGO

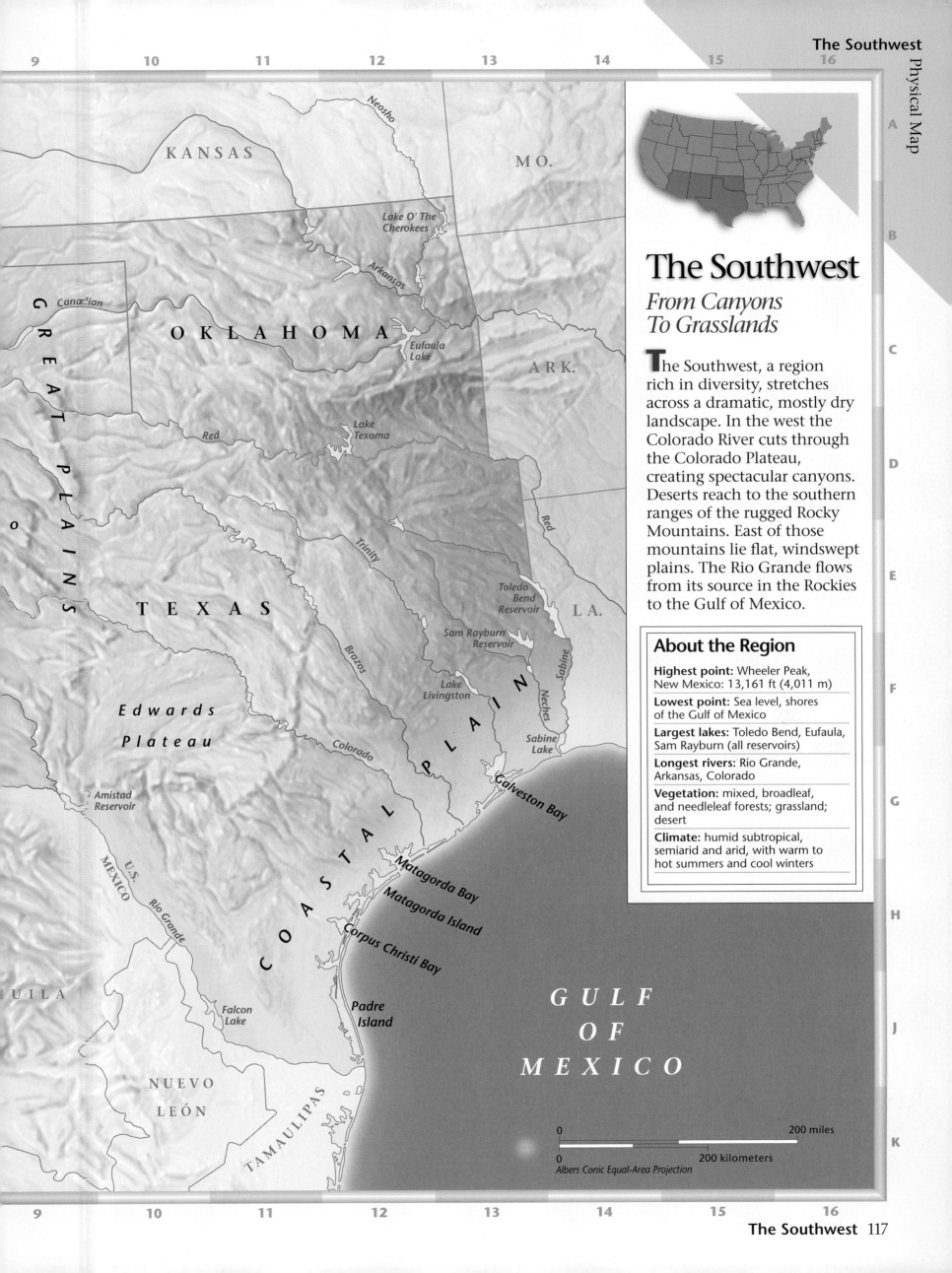

The Southwest
From Canyons To Grasslands

The Southwest, a region rich in diversity, stretches across a dramatic, mostly dry landscape. In the west the Colorado River cuts through the Colorado Plateau, creating spectacular canyons. Deserts reach to the southern ranges of the rugged Rocky Mountains. East of those mountains lie flat, windswept plains. The Rio Grande flows from its source in the Rockies to the Gulf of Mexico.

About the Region

Highest point: Wheeler Peak, New Mexico: 13,161 ft (4,011 m)

Lowest point: Sea level, shores of the Gulf of Mexico

Largest lakes: Toledo Bend, Eufaula, Sam Rayburn (all reservoirs)

Longest rivers: Rio Grande, Arkansas, Colorado

Vegetation: mixed, broadleaf, and needleleaf forests; grassland; desert

Climate: humid subtropical, semiarid and arid, with warm to hot summers and cool winters

KANSAS

MO.

OKLAHOMA

ARK.

LA.

TEXAS

GREAT PLAINS

Edwards Plateau

COASTAL PLAIN

U.S.
MEXICO

NUEVO LEÓN

TAMAULIPAS

COAHUILA

Neosho

Lake O' The Cherokees

Arkansas

Eufaula Lake

Canadian

Red

Lake Texoma

Trinity

Red

Toledo Bend Reservoir

Sam Rayburn Reservoir

Sabine

Brazos

Lake Livingston

Neches

Colorado

Sabine Lake

Galveston Bay

Amistad Reservoir

Rio Grande

Matagorda Bay

Matagorda Island

Corpus Christi Bay

Padre Island

Falcon Lake

GULF OF MEXICO

0   200 miles

0   200 kilometers
Albers Conic Equal-Area Projection

The Southwest
Land of Natural Wonders

Vast and varied, the Southwest is a land of colorful contrasts. On the wide open plains of Texas, huge wheatfields and ranches with grazing cattle sprawl for miles. Farther west, snow-capped mountains rise above busy cities. Some, such as Phoenix, are among the fastest-growing cities in the country.

The region abounds with natural wonders: the matchless spectacle of the Grand Canyon, the strange beauty of reddish sandstone spires and sentinels in Monument Valley, and the sight of deserts blooming with cactus flowers. A history of early Indian cultures, Mexican colonization, and Wild West days gives the region a rich ethnic heritage. Today, southwestern states celebrate Mexican fiestas, Indian tribal powwows, and Frontier Days. Visitors to the area can explore ghost towns near old mining sites or boomtowns where oil first gushed. In the shadow of ancient Indian cliff-dwellings, present-day Indians make fine pottery, baskets, and silver and turquoise jewelry.

▶ **GLEN CANYON** *dam, located on the Colorado River in Arizona and Utah, created Lake Powell to supply water and electricity to much of this arid region.*

◀ **GIANT SAGUARO** *cactuses tower as high as 60 feet (18 m) in Arizona's Sonoran Desert. They survive long dry spells by storing water in their trunks and branches.*

▶ **NAVAJO GIRLS** *play on their large reservation in Monument Valley. More than a hundred different tribes of Native Americans live in the Southwest.*

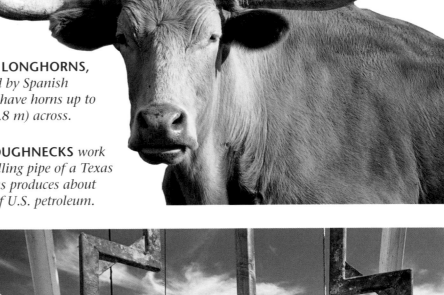

▶ **TEXAS LONGHORNS,** *introduced by Spanish explorers, have horns up to six feet (1.8 m) across.*

▼ **OIL ROUGHNECKS** *work on the drilling pipe of a Texas well. Texas produces about a fourth of U.S. petroleum.*

▲ **SAN XAVIER** *del Bac, a Spanish mission, was built about 1700 near Tucson, Arizona, by Spanish priests. It sheltered Indians learning about Christianity.*

◀ **HOT PIÑON** *chili peppers dry after harvest in New Mexico. Sold ground or whole, chili peppers add flavor to a variety of foods.*

▲ **LUSH CIRCLES OF GREEN** *are the trademark of a kind of irrigation called center pivot. Each circular field is watered by a rotating sprinkler system that draws water from a well. The system helps farmers grow crops in the dry Southwest.*

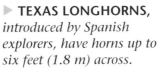

COLO.

Four Corners

Only spot in the U.S. where the borders of four states come together

NAVAJO INDIAN RESERVATION

NEW MEXICO

San Francisco

UTAH

NEVADA

CALIFORNIA

ARIZONA

Lake Powell

Page

Glen Canyon Dam

GLEN CANYON NATIONAL RECREATION AREA

Colorado

Paria

Marble Canyon

NAVAJO INDIAN RESERVATION
Monument Valley

Kayenta

NAVAJO NAT. MON.
(KEET SEEL RUIN)

NAVAJO NAT. MON.
(BETATAKIN RUIN)

Black Mesa

NAVAJO NAT. MON.
(INSCRIPTION HOUSE RUIN)

CANYON DE CHELLY NAT. MON.

Chinle Wash

Chinle

NAVAJO
INDIAN
RESERVATION

Fort Defiance

Window Rock

HUBBELL TRADING POST N.H.S.

Zuni

Little Colorado

Puerco

St. Johns

APACHE-SITGREAVES NATIONAL FOREST

Eagar

Pinetop-Lakeside

Whiteriver

White

Black

APACHE-SITGREAVES NATIONAL FOREST

Show Low

Snowflake

FORT APACHE INDIAN RESERVATION

SAN CARLOS

Salt

Hopi pueblo, oldest continuously inhabited town in U.S., dating from prehistoric times

Old Oraibi

Polacca

HOPI INDIAN RESERVATION

Earth's largest known meteor crater, one mile wide

Winslow

Holbrook

PETRIFIED FOREST N.P.

Meteor Crater

Clear Creek

Chevelon Cr.

Mogollon Rim

TONTO NAT. MON.

Theodore Roosevelt Lake

TONTO NATIONAL FOREST

Globe

Tuba City

Painted

Little Colorado

Desert

WUPATKI NAT. MON.

SUNSET CRATER VOLCANO NAT. MON.

WALNUT CANYON NAT. MON.

COCONINO NATIONAL FOREST

Payson

Verde

Kaibab Plateau

KAIBAB NATIONAL FOREST

GRAND CANYON NATIONAL PARK

Grand Canyon

Coconino Plateau

Humphreys Peak
12,633 ft
3,851 m

Highest point in Arizona

Flagstaff

N.F.

KAIBAB

Sedona

TUZIGOOT NAT. MON.

Cottonwood

Camp Verde

CAMP VERDE I.R.

MONTEZUMA CASTLE NAT. MON.

VERDE N.W. &S.R.

Campe Verde

Verde

FT. McDOWELL I.R.

SALT RIVER I.R.

Scottsdale

Mesa

PIPE SPRING NAT. MON.

KAIBAB NATIONAL FOREST

Grand Canyon

COLORADO

Kanab Cr.

KAIBAB I.R.

HAVASUPAI I.R.

P L A T E A U

Williams

Seligman

Prescott Valley

Chino Valley

PRESCOTT NATIONAL FOREST

YAVAPAI I.R.

Prescott

PRESCOTT NATIONAL FOREST

Verde

Agua Fria

Sun City

Glendale

Phoenix

Tempe

Colorado City

Aubrey

Cliffs

Grand Wash Cliffs

LAKE MEAD N.R.A.

GRAND CANYON NATIONAL PARK

HUALAPAI INDIAN RESERVATION

Big Sandy

Kingman

Wickenburg

KOFA NATIONAL WILDLIFE

Virgin

Red Lake

Dolan Springs

Black Mountains

Bill Williams City

BILL WILLIAMS RIVER N.W.R.

Bill Williams

Lake Havasu City

HAVASU N.W.R.

Parker

COLORADO RIVER INDIAN RESERVATION

Quartzsite

CIBOLA

Lake Mead

Hoover Dam

LAKE MEAD NATIONAL RECREATION AREA

Lake Mohave

Bullhead City

FT. MOJAVE I.R.

Lake Havasu

Colorado

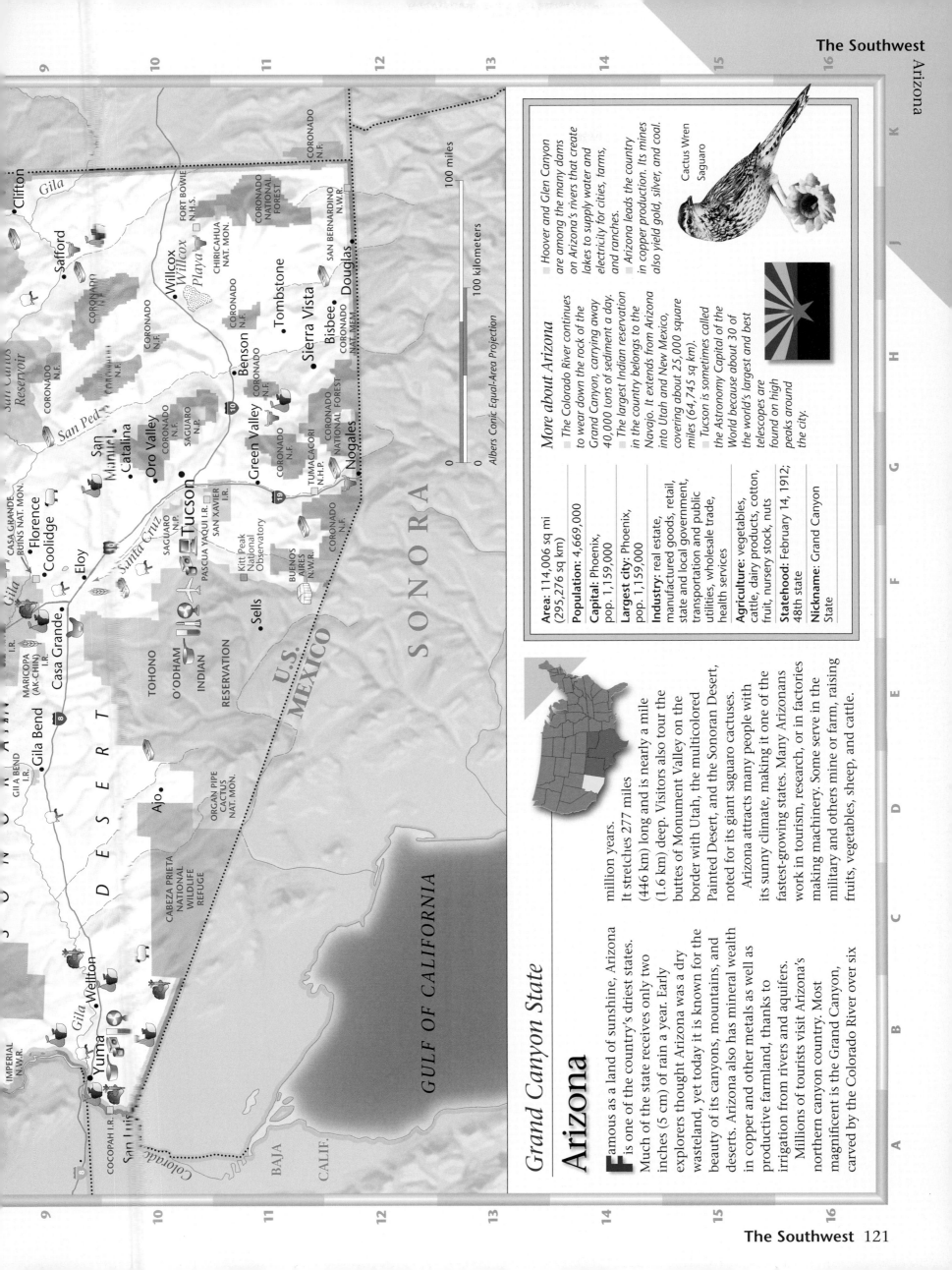

Grand Canyon State

Arizona

Famous as a land of sunshine, Arizona is one of the country's driest states. Much of the state receives only two inches (5 cm) of rain a year. Early explorers thought Arizona was a dry wasteland, yet today it is known for the beauty of its canyons, mountains, and deserts. Arizona also has mineral wealth in copper and other metals as well as productive farmland, thanks to irrigation from rivers and aquifers. Millions of tourists visit Arizona's northern canyon country. Most magnificent is the Grand Canyon, carved by the Colorado River over six million years.

It stretches 277 miles (446 km) long and is nearly a mile (1.6 km) deep. Visitors also tour the buttes of Monument Valley on the border with Utah, the multicolored Painted Desert, and the Sonoran Desert, noted for its giant saguaro cactuses. Arizona attracts many people with its sunny climate, making it one of the fastest-growing states. Many Arizonans work in tourism, research, or in factories making machinery. Some serve in the military and others mine or farm, raising fruits, vegetables, sheep, and cattle.

More about Arizona

■ The Colorado River continues to wear down the rock of the Grand Canyon, carrying away 40,000 tons of sediment a day.

■ The largest Indian reservation in the country belongs to the Navajo. It extends from Arizona into Utah and New Mexico, covering about 25,000 square miles (64,745 sq km).

■ Tucson is sometimes called the Astronomy Capital of the World because about 30 of the world's largest and best telescopes are found on high peaks around the city.

■ Hoover and Glen Canyon are among the many dams on Arizona's rivers that create lakes to supply water and electricity for cities, farms, and ranches.

■ Arizona leads the country in copper production. Its mines also yield gold, silver, and coal.

Area: 114,006 sq mi (295,276 sq km)

Population: 4,669,000

Capital: Phoenix, pop. 1,159,000

Largest city: Phoenix, pop. 1,159,000

Industry: real estate, manufactured goods, retail, state and local government, transportation and public utilities, wholesale trade, health services

Agriculture: vegetables, cattle, dairy products, cotton, fruit, nursery stock, nuts

Statehood: February 14, 1912; 48th state

Nickname: Grand Canyon State

Cactus Wren
Saguaro

Albers Conic Equal-Area Projection

100 miles

100 kilometers

UTAH

COLORADO

OKLA.

Only spot in the U.S. where the borders of four states come together

Four Corners

UTE MOUNTAIN I. R.

Ship Rock + 7,178 ft 2,188 m

Shiprock

San Juan

Farmington

Bloomfield

Aztec

AZTEC RUINS NAT. MON.

Pueblo Bonito

CHACO CULTURE N.H.P.

Cañon Largo

Continental Divide

Dulce

Chama

JICARILLA APACHE INDIAN RESERVATION

Navajo Reservoir

CARSON NATIONAL FOREST

NAVAJO INDIAN RESERVATION

Navajo

Gallup

NAVAJO I.R.

ZUNI INDIAN RESERVATION

Zuni

ZUNI I.R.

RAMAH NAVAJO INDIAN RESERVATION

Crownpoint

CIBOLA NATIONAL FOREST

Milan

Grants

EL MORRO NAT. MON.

EL MALPAIS NAT. MON.

Rio San José

ACOMA I.R.

LAGUNA I.R.

LAGUNA I.R.

CIBOLA NATIONAL FOREST

ALAMO NAVAJO I.R.

CIBOLA NATIONAL FOREST

Rio Puerco

RIO GRANDE N.W.&S.R.

Questa

Taos

TAOS I.R.

TAOS

CARSON N.F.

Wheeler Peak + 13,161 ft 4,011 m *Highest point in New Mexico*

Springer

Raton

CAPULIN VOLCANO NAT. MON.

MAXWELL N.W.R.

Dry Cimarron

Corrumpa Creek

Carrizo Creek

Ute Creek

Canadian

KIOWA NATIONAL GRASSLANDS

Clayton

KIOWA NATIONAL GRASSLANDS

PICURIS I.R.

SAN JUAN I.R.

Española

SANTA CLARA I.R.

RIO CHAMA N.W.&S.R.

Chimayo

POJOAQUE I.R.

NAMBE I.R.

TESUQUE I.R.

SANTE FE NATIONAL FOREST

JEMEZ, E. FORK N.W.&S.R.

JEMEZ I.R.

Los Alamos

BANDELIER NAT. MON.

SAN ILDEFONSO I.R.

COCHITI I.R.

SANTO DOMINGO I.R.

SANTA ANA I.R.

ZIA I.R.

SAN FELIPE I.R.

PECOS N.W.&S.R.

PECOS N.H.P.

Oldest capital city in the U.S.

Las Vegas

Santa Fe

SANTE FE N.F.

SANTA FE NATIONAL FOREST

FORT UNION NAT. MON.

Mora

Canadian

KIOWA NATIONAL GRASSLANDS

Conchas Lake

Conchas Lake

Santa Rosa Lake

Santa Rosa

Tucumcari

Pecos

Gallinas

LAS VEGAS N.W.R.

Santa Rosa Lake

Summer Lake

Fort Sumner

Summer Lake

Clovis

Portales

GRULLA N.W.R.

LLANO ESTACADO

ROCKY MOUNTAINS

Sangre de Cristo Mountains

Bernalillo

Rio Rancho

Albuquerque

SANDIA I.R.

PETROGLYPH NAT. MON.

ISLETA I.R.

Moriarty

Mountainair

Estancia

SALINAS PUEBLO MISSIONS NAT. MON.

CIBOLA NATIONAL FOREST

Los Lunas

Valencia

Belen

SALINAS PUEBLO MISSIONS NAT. MON.

Socorro

Site of first atomic bomb test, July 16, 1945

BOSQUE DEL APACHE N.W.R.

Trinity Site

Rio Grande

Gallo Arroyo

Arroyo del Macho

Roswell

Rio Hondo

SALINAS PUEBLO MISSIONS NAT. MON.

Carrizozo

LINCOLN NATIONAL FOREST

Ruidoso

Sacra

Reserve

GILA NATIONAL FOREST

GILA CLIFF DWELLINGS

San Francisco

Range

APACHE-SITGREAVES NATIONAL FOREST

ARIZ.

NEW MEXICO

MOUNTAINS

Rio Grande

Elephant Butte

CIBOLA NATIONAL FOREST

BITTER LAKE N.W.R.

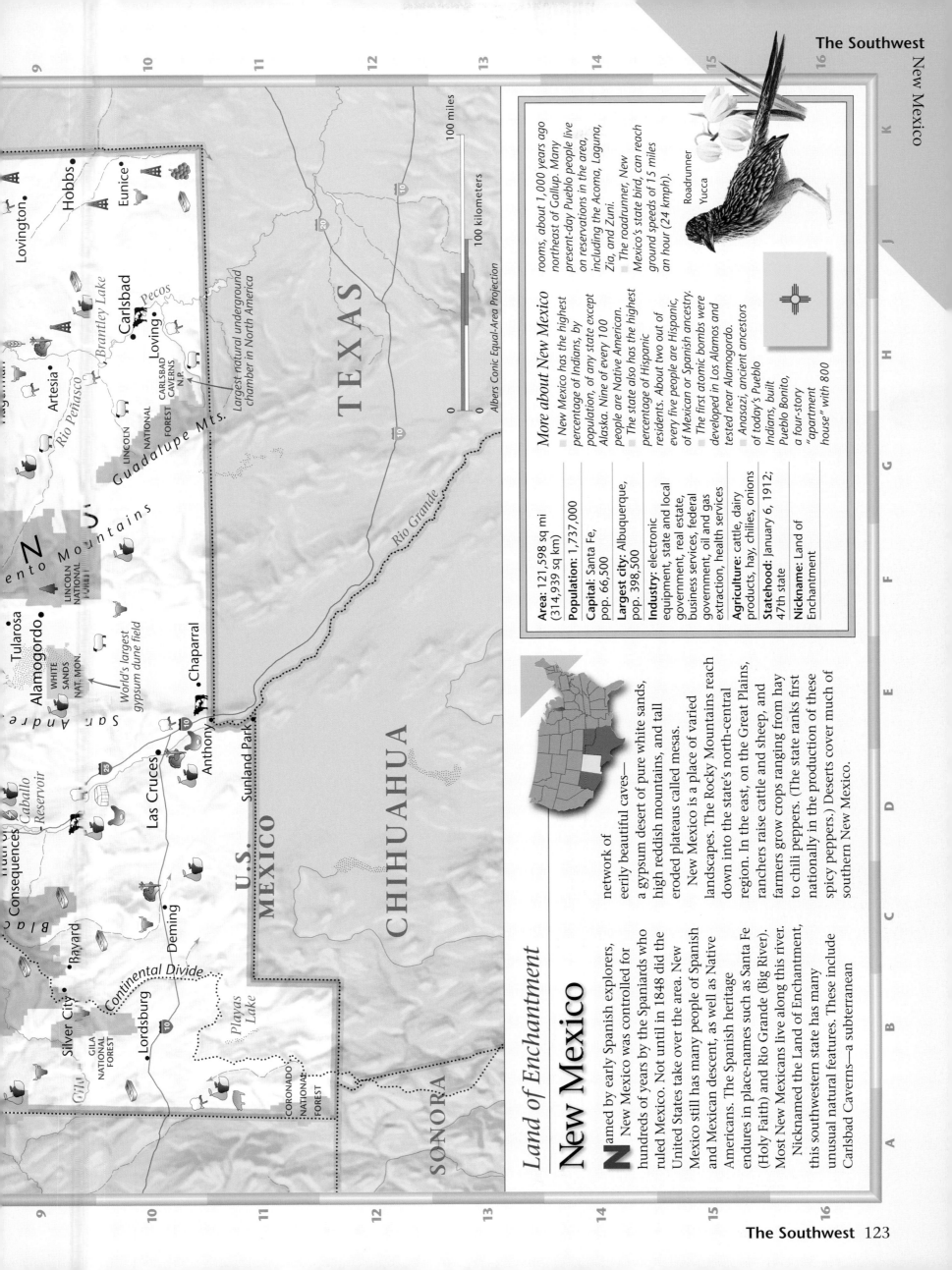

Land of Enchantment

New Mexico

Named by early Spanish explorers, New Mexico was controlled for hundreds of years by the Spaniards who ruled Mexico. Not until in 1848 did the United States take over the area. New Mexico still has many people of Spanish and Mexican descent, as well as Native Americans. The Spanish heritage endures in place-names such as Santa Fe (Holy Faith) and Rio Grande (Big River). Most New Mexicans live along this river.

Nicknamed the Land of Enchantment, this southwestern state has many unusual natural features. These include Carlsbad Caverns—a subterranean network of eerily beautiful caves—a gypsum desert of pure white sands, high reddish mountains, and tall eroded plateaus called mesas.

New Mexico is a place of varied landscapes. The Rocky Mountains reach down into the state's north-central region. In the east, on the Great Plains, ranchers raise cattle and sheep, and farmers grow crops ranging from hay to chili peppers. (The state ranks first nationally in the production of these spicy peppers.) Deserts cover much of southern New Mexico.

Area: 121,598 sq mi (314,939 sq km)

Population: 1,737,000

Capital: Santa Fe, pop. 66,500

Largest city: Albuquerque, pop. 398,500

Industry: electronic equipment, state and local government, real estate, business services, federal government, oil and gas extraction, health services

Agriculture: cattle, dairy products, hay, chilies, onions

Statehood: January 6, 1912; 47th state

Nickname: Land of Enchantment

More about New Mexico

New Mexico has the highest percentage of Indians, by population, of any state except Alaska. Nine of every 100 people are Native American.

The state also has the highest percentage of Hispanic residents. About two out of every five people are Hispanic, of Mexican or Spanish ancestry.

The first atomic bombs were developed in Los Alamos and tested near Alamogordo.

Anasazi, ancient ancestors of today's Pueblo Indians, built Pueblo Bonito, a four-story "apartment house" with 800 rooms, about 1,000 years ago northeast of Gallup. Many present-day Pueblo people live on reservations in the area, including the Acoma, Laguna, Zia, and Zuni.

The roadrunner, New Mexico's state bird, can reach ground speeds of 15 miles an hour (24 kmph).

Roadrunner
Yucca

100 miles
100 kilometers
Albers Conic Equal-Area Projection

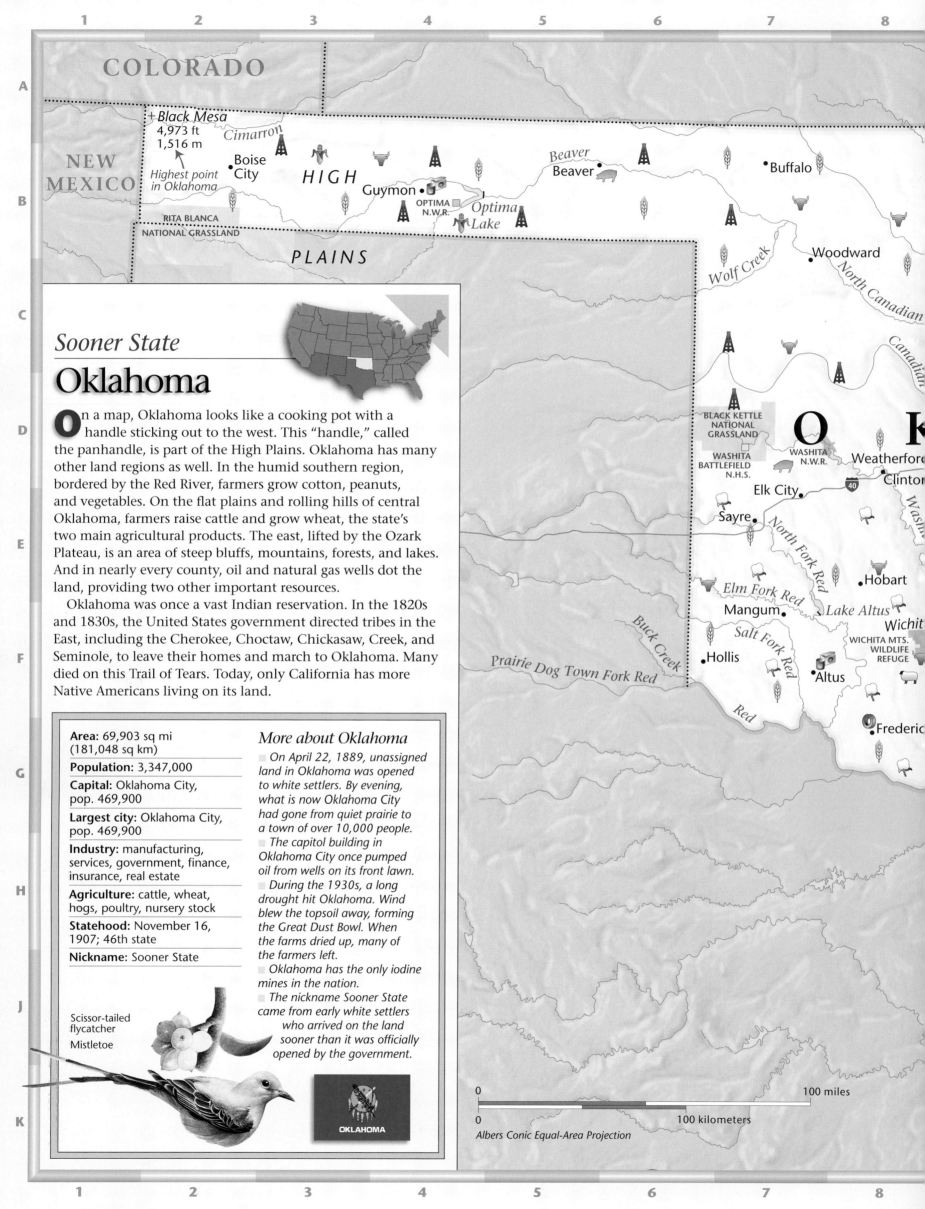

Sooner State

Oklahoma

On a map, Oklahoma looks like a cooking pot with a handle sticking out to the west. This "handle," called the panhandle, is part of the High Plains. Oklahoma has many other land regions as well. In the humid southern region, bordered by the Red River, farmers grow cotton, peanuts, and vegetables. On the flat plains and rolling hills of central Oklahoma, farmers raise cattle and grow wheat, the state's two main agricultural products. The east, lifted by the Ozark Plateau, is an area of steep bluffs, mountains, forests, and lakes. And in nearly every county, oil and natural gas wells dot the land, providing two other important resources.

Oklahoma was once a vast Indian reservation. In the 1820s and 1830s, the United States government directed tribes in the East, including the Cherokee, Choctaw, Chickasaw, Creek, and Seminole, to leave their homes and march to Oklahoma. Many died on this Trail of Tears. Today, only California has more Native Americans living on its land.

Area: 69,903 sq mi (181,048 sq km)

Population: 3,347,000

Capital: Oklahoma City, pop. 469,900

Largest city: Oklahoma City, pop. 469,900

Industry: manufacturing, services, government, finance, insurance, real estate

Agriculture: cattle, wheat, hogs, poultry, nursery stock

Statehood: November 16, 1907; 46th state

Nickname: Sooner State

Scissor-tailed flycatcher
Mistletoe

More about Oklahoma

■ On April 22, 1889, unassigned land in Oklahoma was opened to white settlers. By evening, what is now Oklahoma City had gone from quiet prairie to a town of over 10,000 people.

■ The capitol building in Oklahoma City once pumped oil from wells on its front lawn.

■ During the 1930s, a long drought hit Oklahoma. Wind blew the topsoil away, forming the Great Dust Bowl. When the farms dried up, many of the farmers left.

■ Oklahoma has the only iodine mines in the nation.

■ The nickname Sooner State came from early white settlers who arrived on the land sooner than it was officially opened by the government.

OKLAHOMA

0   100 miles
0   100 kilometers
Albers Conic Equal-Area Projection

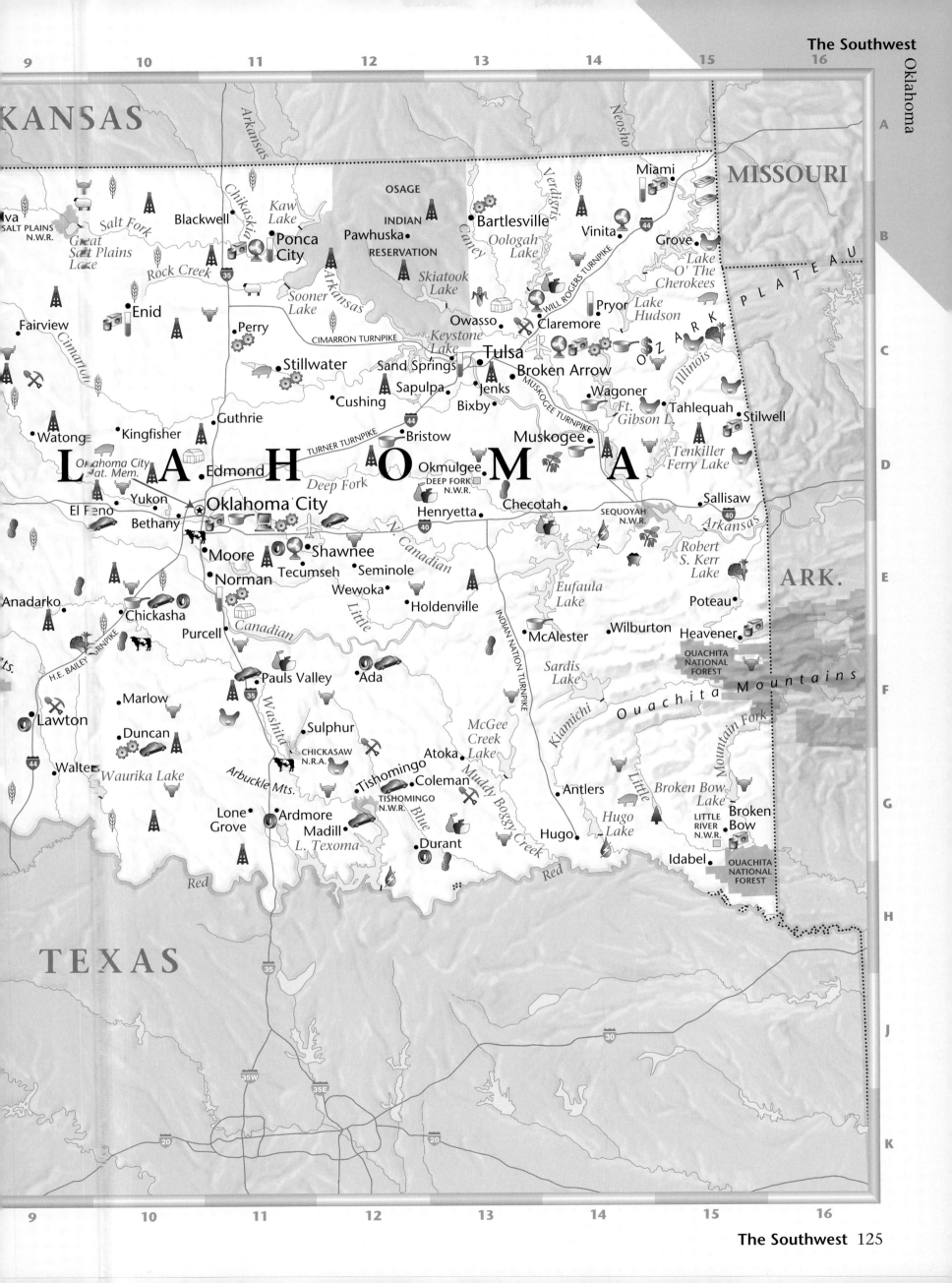

KANSAS

MISSOURI

ARK.

TEXAS

A

B

C

D

E

F

G

H

J

K

9   10   11   12   13   14   15   16

L A H O M A

Salt Fork

SALT PLAINS N.W.R.

Great Salt Plains Lake

Rock Creek

Chikaskia

Kaw Lake

Arkansas

OSAGE INDIAN RESERVATION

Pawhuska

Skiatook Lake

Oologah Lake

Caney

Verdigris

Neosho

Miami

Bartlesville

Vinita

Grove

Lake O' The Cherokees

PLATEAU

Blackwell

Ponca City

Will Rogers Turnpike

Pryor

Lake Hudson

Enid

Fairview

Cimarron

Perry

Sooner Lake

CIMARRON TURNPIKE

Owasso

Claremore

Keystone Lake

Tulsa

OZARK

Illinois

Stillwater

Sand Springs

Broken Arrow

Watonga

Kingfisher

Guthrie

Sapulpa

Jenks

Wagoner

Ft. Gibson L.

Tahlequah

Stilwell

Cushing

Bixby

Oklahoma City Nat. Mem.

Edmond

Bristow

TURNER TURNPIKE

Muskogee

Tenkiller Ferry Lake

Deep Fork

Okmulgee

DEEP FORK N.W.R.

MUSKOGEE TURNPIKE

Yukon

El Reno

Bethany

Oklahoma City

Henryetta

Checotah

SEQUOYAH N.W.R.

Sallisaw

Arkansas

Moore

Shawnee

N. Canadian

Robert S. Kerr Lake

Norman

Tecumseh

Seminole

Anadarko

Wewoka

Holdenville

Eufaula Lake

Poteau

Chickasha

Little

Canadian

McAlester

Wilburton

Heavener

Purcell

H.E. BAILEY TURNPIKE

Sardis Lake

OUACHITA NATIONAL FOREST

Pauls Valley

Ada

INDIAN NATION TURNPIKE

Mountains

Marlow

Washita

Kiamichi

Ouachita

Mountain Fork

Lawton

Duncan

Sulphur

CHICKASAW N.R.A.

McGee Creek Lake

Atoka

Walter

Waurika Lake

Arbuckle Mts.

Tishomingo

Coleman

Muddy Boggy Creek

Antlers

Broken Bow Lake

Lone Grove

Ardmore

TISHOMINGO N.W.R.

Blue

Hugo Lake

LITTLE RIVER N.W.R.

Broken Bow

Madill

L. Texoma

Durant

Hugo

Idabel

OUACHITA NATIONAL FOREST

Red

Red

Little

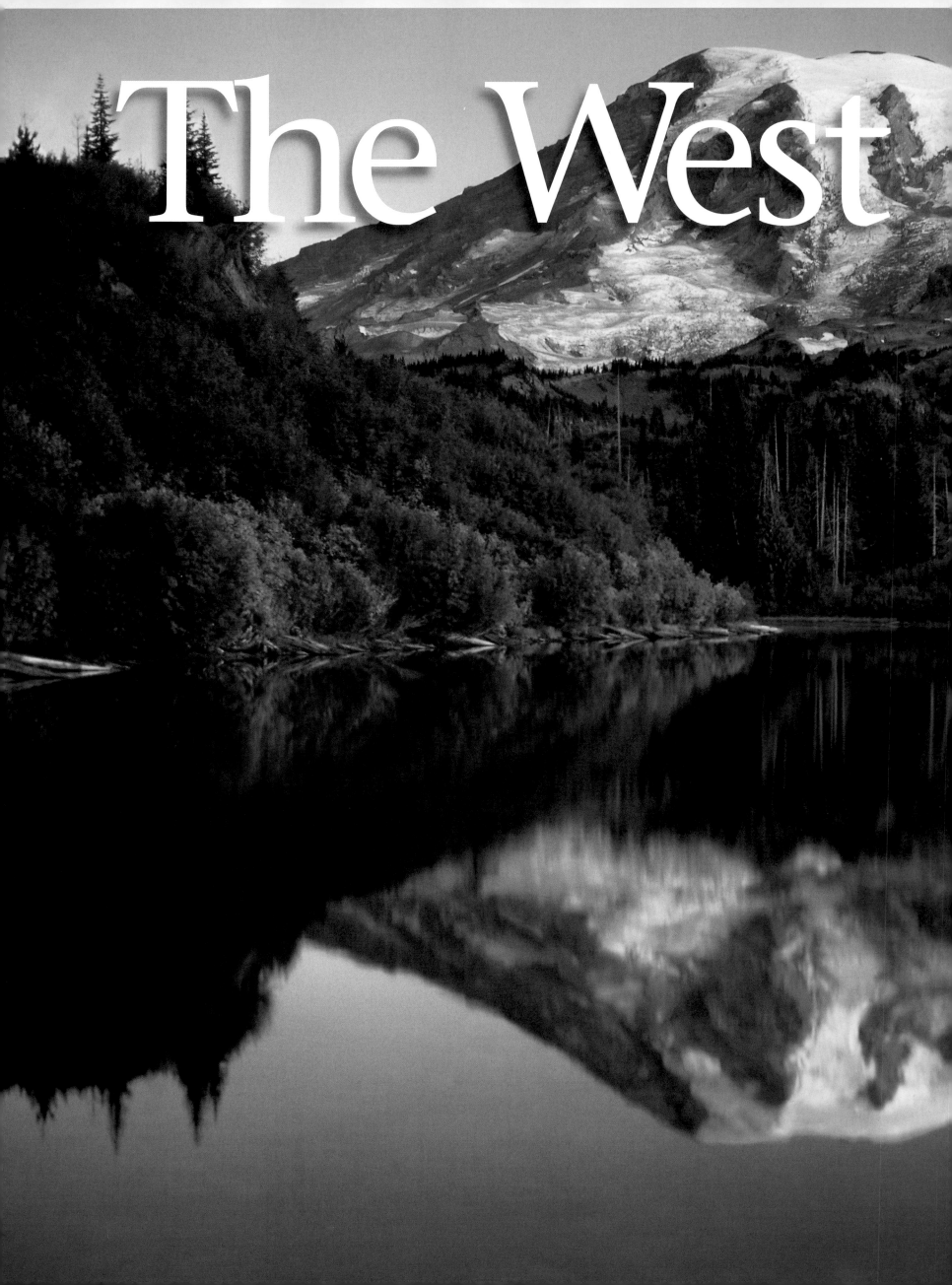

The West

The West

Alaska
California
Colorado
Hawaii
Idaho
Montana
Nevada
Oregon
Utah
Washington
Wyoming

*The peace and grandeur
of the West find expression
in Mount Rainier, here
reflected in Bench Lake near
Seattle, Washington (left).
In some areas, however,
congestion is taking its toll.
This mazelike interchange
on the Los Angeles Freeway,
in California (above),
is just one example.*

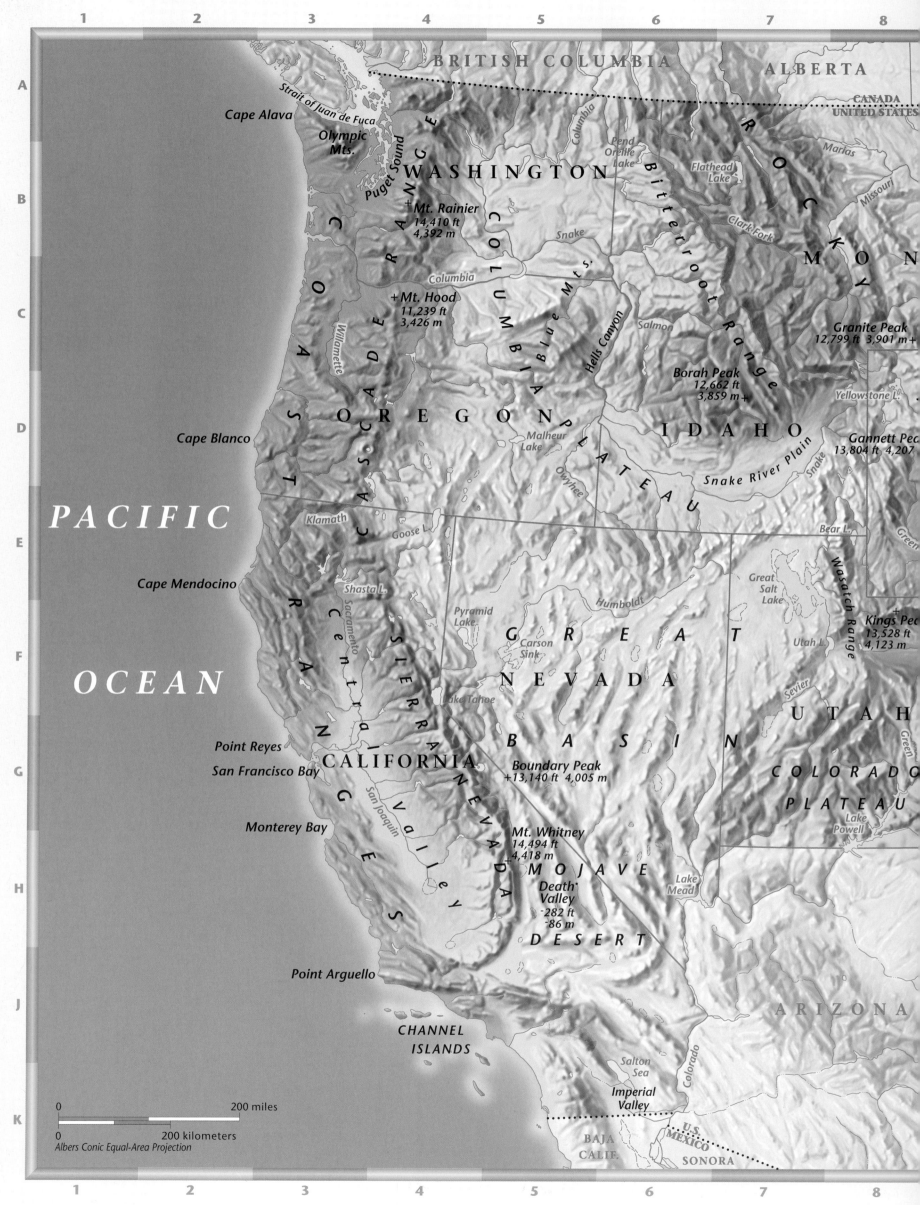

BRITISH COLUMBIA ALBERTA

CANADA
UNITED STATES

Strait of Juan de Fuca

Cape Alava

Olympic Mts.

Puget Sound

WASHINGTON

+Mt. Rainier
14,410 ft
4,392 m

Columbia

Columbia

+Mt. Hood
11,239 ft
3,426 m

Snake

Blue Mts.

Pend Orelle Lake

Flathead Lake

Marias

Missouri

Clark Fork

Bitterroot Range

ROCKY

MON

Granite Peak
12,799 ft 3,901 m +

Hells Canyon

Salmon

Borah Peak
12,662 ft
3,859 m +

IDAHO

Yellowstone L.

Willamette

CASCADE

RANGE

OREGON

PLATEAU

COLUMBIA

Malheur Lake

Owyhee

Snake River Plain

Snake

Gannett Pea
13,804 ft 4,207

Cape Blanco

Klamath

Goose L.

Bear L.

PACIFIC

Shasta L.

Cape Mendocino

Pyramid Lake

Humboldt

Great Salt Lake

Wasatch Range

Kings Pea
13,528 ft
4,123 m

OCEAN

Sacramento

COAST

SIERRA

Carson Sink

GREAT

NEVADA

BASIN

Utah L.

UTAH

Point Reyes

San Francisco Bay

CALIFORNIA

Lake Tahoe

Central Valley

Boundary Peak
+13,140 ft 4,005 m

Sevier

COLORADO

PLATEAU

Monterey Bay

San Joaquin

NEVADA

RANGES

Mt. Whitney
14,494 ft
4,418 m +

MOJAVE

Lake Powell

Death Valley
-282 ft
-86 m

DESERT

Lake Mead

Point Arguello

J

ARIZONA

CHANNEL ISLANDS

Salton Sea

Colorado

Imperial Valley

U.S.
MEXICO

BAJA CALIF.

SONORA

0   200 miles
0   200 kilometers
Albers Conic Equal-Area Projection

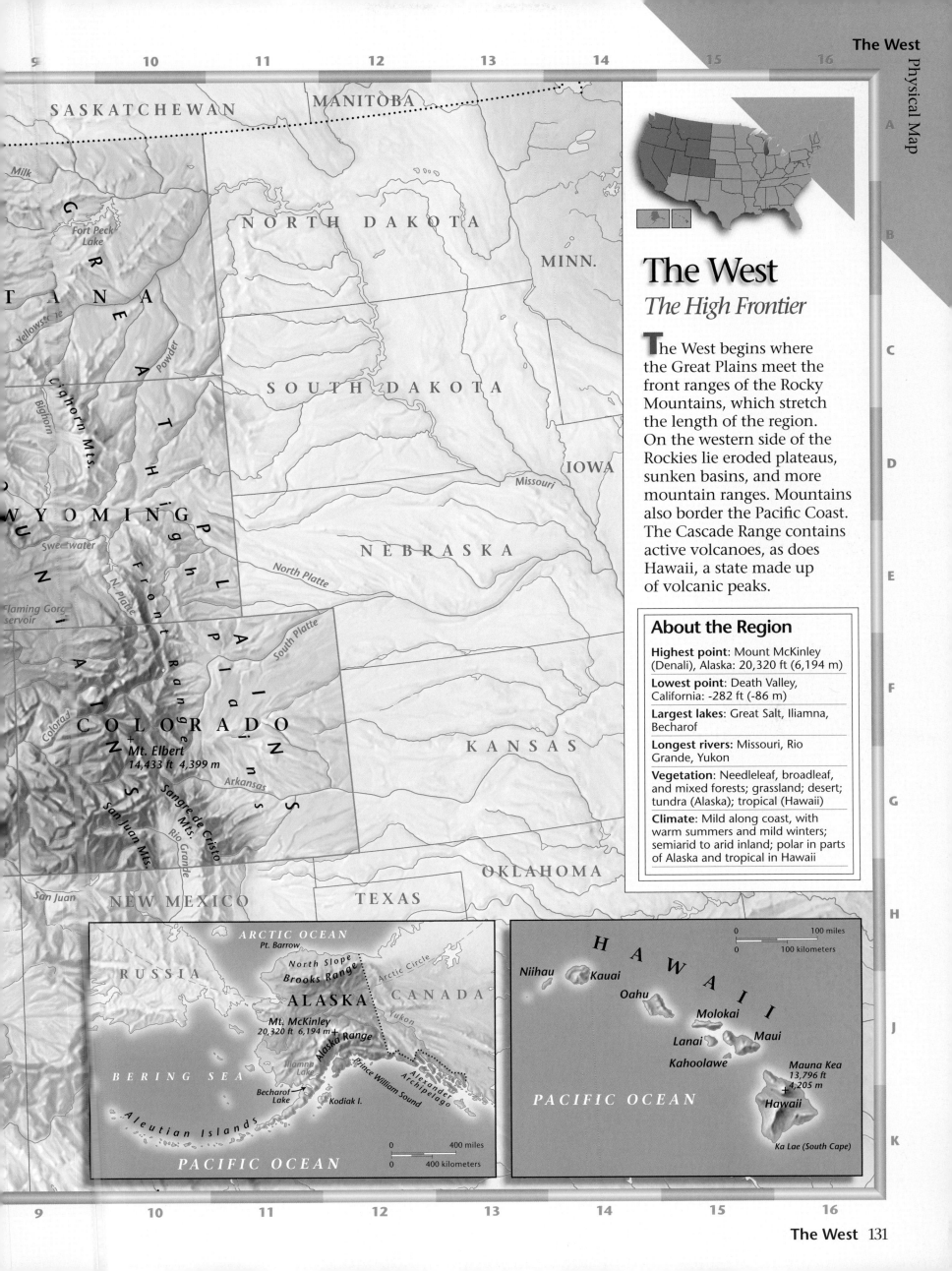

SASKATCHEWAN

MANITOBA

Milk

MONTANA

Fort Peck Lake

Yellowstone

GREAT

NORTH DAKOTA

MINN.

Bighorn Mts.

Powder

SOUTH DAKOTA

Bighorn

IOWA

WYOMING

High Plains

Missouri

Sweetwater

Front Range

N. Platte

Flaming Gorge Reservoir

NEBRASKA

North Platte

Colorado

South Platte

COLORADO

*Mt. Elbert
14,433 ft 4,399 m*

Great Plains

KANSAS

Arkansas

Sangre de Cristo Mts.

San Juan Mts.

Rio Grande

OKLAHOMA

San Juan

NEW MEXICO

TEXAS

The West
The High Frontier

The West begins where the Great Plains meet the front ranges of the Rocky Mountains, which stretch the length of the region. On the western side of the Rockies lie eroded plateaus, sunken basins, and more mountain ranges. Mountains also border the Pacific Coast. The Cascade Range contains active volcanoes, as does Hawaii, a state made up of volcanic peaks.

About the Region

Highest point: Mount McKinley (Denali), Alaska: 20,320 ft (6,194 m)

Lowest point: Death Valley, California: -282 ft (-86 m)

Largest lakes: Great Salt, Iliamna, Becharof

Longest rivers: Missouri, Rio Grande, Yukon

Vegetation: Needleleaf, broadleaf, and mixed forests; grassland; desert; tundra (Alaska); tropical (Hawaii)

Climate: Mild along coast, with warm summers and mild winters; semiarid to arid inland; polar in parts of Alaska and tropical in Hawaii

ARCTIC OCEAN
Pt. Barrow
North Slope
Brooks Range
Arctic Circle

RUSSIA

CANADA

ALASKA

*Mt. McKinley
20,320 ft 6,194 m*

Alaska Range

Yukon

Iliamna Lake

Prince William Sound

BERING SEA

Becharof Lake

Alexander Archipelago

Kodiak I.

Aleutian Islands

0   400 miles
0   400 kilometers

PACIFIC OCEAN

HAWAII

Niihau   *Kauai*

Oahu

Molokai

Lanai   *Maui*

Kahoolawe

*Mauna Kea
13,796 ft
4,205 m*

PACIFIC OCEAN

Hawaii

Ka Lae (South Cape)

0   100 miles
0   100 kilometers

The West
Land of Opportunity

Blessed with rich natural resources, the West has attracted settlers from all over the United States and the world. At different times, gold, silver—and more recently, oil—brought Easterners streaming to states such as Alaska, California, Colorado, and Nevada. Vast forests, fertile valleys, and a mild climate also lured people to California as well as to Washington and Oregon. People from Latin America and Asia came to the West Coast to find work on farms and in thriving businesses. Native Americans, the original residents, live in these states as well. In Alaska, some still hunt and fish as their ancestors did.

Except for California, most western states have few residents for their size: Giant Alaska has fewer people than tiny Rhode Island. In Wyoming and some other states, cattle nearly outnumber people. Many Westerners make their living farming, ranching, logging, and mining. But manufacturing, high-tech industries, and tourism also attract people to the West.

▲ **ARMED ONLY WITH MUSCLES AND A SPEAR,** *a Yakima Indian from Washington flings a king salmon into his boat. Using both traditional and modern methods, Western fishermen haul in catches worth millions each year.*

◀ **THE MIGHTY** *microchip has transformed the economy in much of the West, where computer hardware and software are big business.*

▲ **READY TO ROLL,** *freshly cut logs are loaded onto a waiting train. Generous rainfall nourishes forests in the Pacific Northwest, which supplies timber throughout the U.S. and to markets in Japan, China, and South Korea as well.*

 ◀ **THRILL-SEEKERS** *ski off an Alaska glacier. The West boasts the country's highest mountains, offering wild—and tame—recreation.*

▶ **THE GOLDEN GATE** *Bridge frames the skyline of San Francisco, California. This former gold rush town remains a banking center.*

◀ **THEME HOTELS,** *such as the Luxor, attract tourists to Las Vegas, a city in the Nevada desert devoted to entertainment.*

▶ **PACIFIC WAVES** *lure surfers to many Pacific beaches. In some locations, such as Hawaii's Waimea Bay, on the island of Oahu, waves can tower up to 25 feet (8 m) high.*

▼ **HMONG FARMERS** *display dikon radishes in California's San Joaquin Valley. Southeast Asians, many of whom work in high-tech businesses, form a large part of the area's immigrant population.*

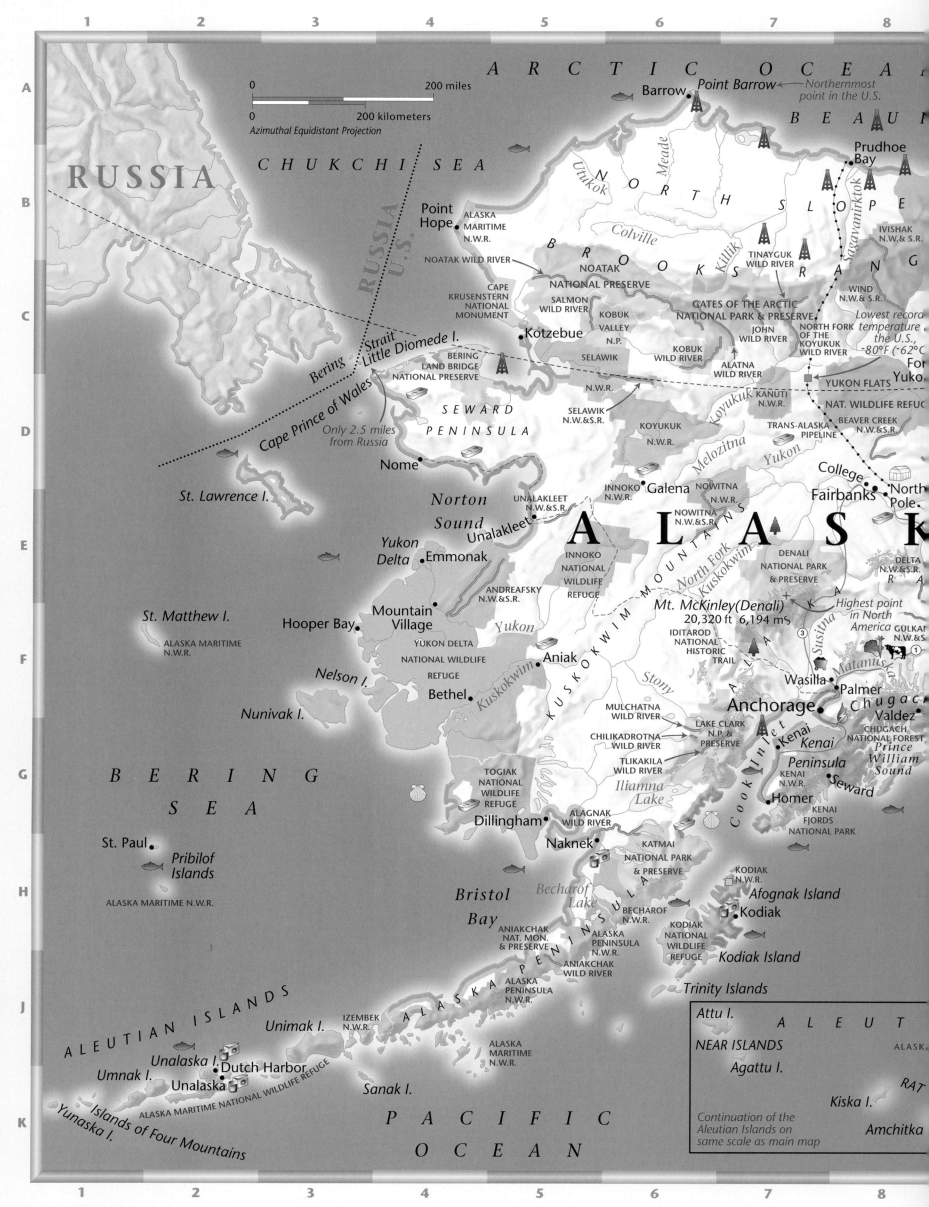

ARCTIC OCEAN

RUSSIA

CHUKCHI SEA

Barrow • Point Barrow ← Northernmost point in the U.S.

BEAU...

Prudhoe Bay

N O R T H   S L O P E

Utukok
Meade
Colville
Sagavanirktok
IVISHAK N.W. & S.R.

Point Hope •
ALASKA MARITIME N.W.R.

B R O O K S   R A N G E

Killik

NOATAK WILD RIVER
NOATAK NATIONAL PRESERVE
TINAYGUK WILD RIVER

CAPE KRUSENSTERN NATIONAL MONUMENT

SALMON WILD RIVER
NOATAK
KOBUK VALLEY N.P.
GATES OF THE ARCTIC NATIONAL PARK & PRESERVE
JOHN WILD RIVER
NORTH FORK OF THE KOYUKUK WILD RIVER
WIND N.W. & S.R.
Lowest record temperature the U.S., –80°F (–62°C)

RUSSIA
U.S.

• Kotzebue

KOBUK WILD RIVER
SELAWIK N.P.
ALATNA WILD RIVER

For Yuko...

Bering Strait
Little Diomede I.

BERING LAND BRIDGE NATIONAL PRESERVE

SELAWIK N.W.&S.R.
N.W.R.

KOYUKUK N.W.R.
KANUTI N.W.R.
YUKON FLATS
NAT. WILDLIFE REFUG...
BEAVER CREEK N.W.&S.R.

Cape Prince of Wales

SEWARD PENINSULA

Koyukuk
Melozitna
Yukon

TRANS-ALASKA PIPELINE

Only 2.5 miles from Russia

Nome •

INNOKO N.W.R.
Galena •
NOWITNA N.W.R.
NOWITNA N.W.&S.R.

College •
Fairbanks •
North...
North Pole

St. Lawrence I.

Norton Sound

UNALAKLEET N.W.&S.R.

A L A S K...

Yukon Delta
Emmonak •
Unalakleet

INNOKO NATIONAL WILDLIFE REFUGE

North Fork Kuskokwim
DENALI NATIONAL PARK & PRESERVE
DELTA N.W.&S.R.

St. Matthew I.

Hooper Bay •
Mountain Village •

ANDREAFSKY N.W.&S.R.

K U S K O K W I M   M O U N T A I N S

Mt. McKinley (Denali) 20,320 ft 6,194 m S + Highest point in North America
GULKANA N.W.&S...

ALASKA MARITIME N.W.R.

Nelson I.

YUKON DELTA NATIONAL WILDLIFE REFUGE

Yukon
• Aniak

Stony
North Fork Kuskokwim
Susitna

IDITAROD NATIONAL HISTORIC TRAIL
Wasilla •
Matanus...
Palmer •
Chugac...

Nunivak I.

Bethel •
Kuskokwim

MULCHATNA WILD RIVER
CHILIKADROTNA WILD RIVER
TLIKAKILA WILD RIVER
LAKE CLARK N.P. & PRESERVE

Anchorage
Cook Inlet
Kenai •
Kenai
Valdez •
CHUGACH NATIONAL FOREST
Prince William Sound

B E R I N G   S E A

TOGIAK NATIONAL WILDLIFE REFUGE

Iliamna Lake
Kenai Peninsula
KENAI N.W.R.
• Homer
Seward •

St. Paul •
Pribilof Islands

Dillingham •
ALAGNAK WILD RIVER
Naknek •

KENAI FJORDS NATIONAL PARK

ALASKA MARITIME N.W.R.

Bristol Bay

Becharof Lake

KATMAI NATIONAL PARK & PRESERVE

KODIAK N.W.R.

Afognak Island

BECHAROF N.W.R.
• Kodiak

ANIAKCHAK NAT. MON. & PRESERVE
ALASKA PENINSULA N.W.R.
KODIAK NATIONAL WILDLIFE REFUGE

A L A S K A   P E N I N S U L A

ANIAKCHAK WILD RIVER
ALASKA PENINSULA N.W.R.

Kodiak Island

Trinity Islands

A L E U T I A N   I S L A N D S

IZEMBEK N.W.R.
Unimak I.

ALASKA MARITIME N.W.R.

PACIFIC OCEAN

Umnak I.
Unalaska I. • Dutch Harbor
Unalaska •

Sanak I.

Islands of Four Mountains
Yunaska I.

ALASKA MARITIME NATIONAL WILDLIFE REFUGE

Attu I.
NEAR ISLANDS
Agattu I.

A L E U T...
ALASK...

RAT...
Kiska I.
Amchitka

Continuation of the Aleutian Islands on same scale as main map

0   200 miles
0   200 kilometers
Azimuthal Equidistant Projection

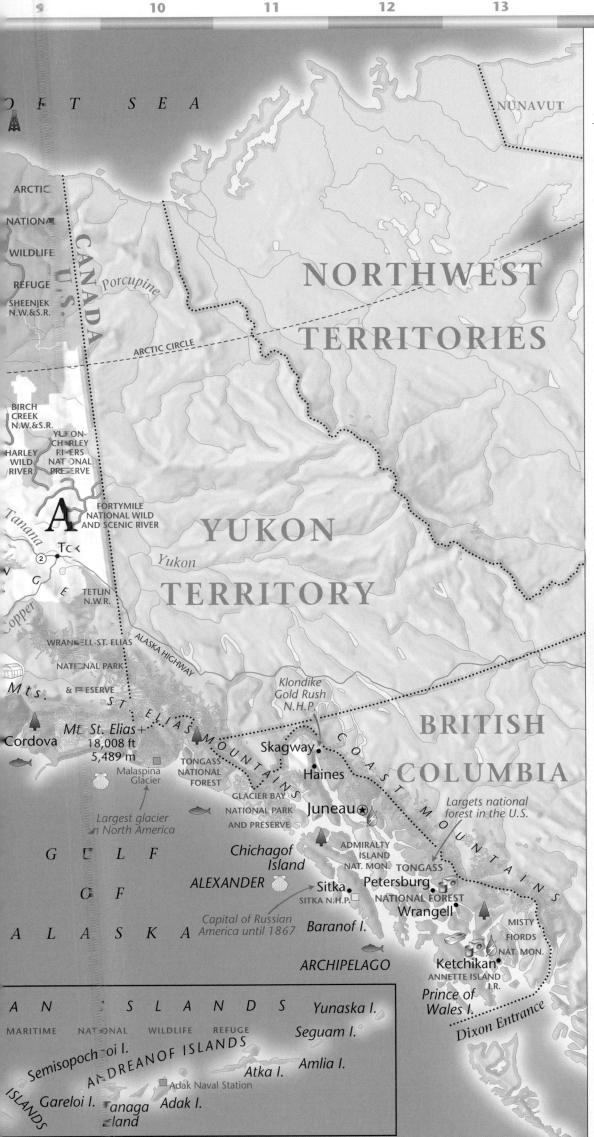

Map labels

OFT SEA

NUNAVUT

ARCTIC
NATIONAL
WILDLIFE
REFUGE
SHEENJEK
N.W.&S.R.

CANADA
U.S.

Porcupine

ARCTIC CIRCLE

NORTHWEST
TERRITORIES

BIRCH
CREEK
N.W.&S.R.

YUKON-
CHARLEY
RIVERS
NATIONAL
PRESERVE

HARLEY
WILD
RIVER

FORTYMILE
NATIONAL WILD
AND SCENIC RIVER

YUKON
TERRITORY

Tanana

TOK
2

Yukon

TETLIN
N.W.R.

Copper

WRANGELL-ST. ELIAS

NATIONAL PARK

ALASKA HIGHWAY

& RESERVE

ST. ELIAS MOUNTAINS

Klondike
Gold Rush
N.H.P.

BRITISH
COLUMBIA

COAST MOUNTAINS

Mt. St. Elias +
18,008 ft
5,489 m

Cordova

Malaspina
Glacier

Largest glacier
in North America

TONGASS
NATIONAL
FOREST

GLACIER BAY
NATIONAL PARK
AND PRESERVE

Skagway

Haines

Juneau ★

Largest national
forest in the U.S.

GULF
OF
ALASKA

Chichagof
Island

ADMIRALTY
ISLAND
NAT. MON.

ALEXANDER

Sitka
SITKA N.H.P.

Capital of Russian
America until 1867

Baranof I.

TONGASS

Petersburg

NATIONAL FOREST

Wrangell

MISTY
FIORDS
NAT. MON.

ARCHIPELAGO

Ketchikan
ANNETTE ISLAND
I.R.

Prince of
Wales I.

Dixon Entrance

AN ISLANDS

Yunaska I.

MARITIME   NATIONAL   WILDLIFE   REFUGE

Seguam I.

Semisopochnoi I.

ANDREANOF ISLANDS

Atka I.

Amlia I.

ISLANDS

Garelol I.

Adak Naval Station

Tanaga
Island

Adak I.

Great Land

Alaska

Almost everything about Alaska is big. The state is the largest in the country—more than twice the size of Texas, the second-largest state. Only the population is small, about half a million people.

Alaska is an immense peninsula with a coastline that stretches some 6,000 miles (9,700 km). In the south mountain ranges rim the Pacific Ocean. Forested islands edge the southeastern panhandle where people, many of them Native Americans, work mainly in the fishing and lumbering industries. Nineteen hours of summer daylight extend the growing time for crops in the Matanuska River Valley north of Anchorage. Volcanic eruptions, earthquakes, and storms wrack the 1,700-mile (2,736-km) Aleutian Island arc.

The Yukon River runs east to west across Alaska. South of it is North America's highest peak—Mount McKinley, or Denali. To the north spreads tundra. Oil and natural gas were discovered on the North Slope in 1968, providing most of Alaska's current wealth.

	**Area:** 615,230 sq mi (1,593,444 sq km)
	Population: 614,000
	Capital: Juneau, pop. 29,800

Largest city: Anchorage, pop. 250,500

Industry: petroleum products, state and local government, services, trade, federal government

Agriculture: shellfish, seafood, nursery stock, vegetables, dairy products, feed crops

Statehood: January 3, 1959; 49th state

Nickname: Great Land

More about Alaska

■ At their closest points, the mainlands of Alaska and Russia are only 51 miles (82 km) apart.

■ The trans-Alaska oil pipeline carries more than a million barrels of oil a day 800 miles (1,287 km) across the state from Prudhoe Bay to the ice-free port of Valdez.

■ The midsummer sun never sets on Barrow, Alaska's northernmost town.

■ A 13-year-old boy designed Alaska's flag.

■ The Aleutian islands of Attu and Kiska were the only places on the North American continent occupied by the Japanese during World War II.

■ If Alaska were placed on top of the contiguous 48 states, it would stretch from Florida to Los Angeles.

Willow Ptarmigan
Forget-Me-Not

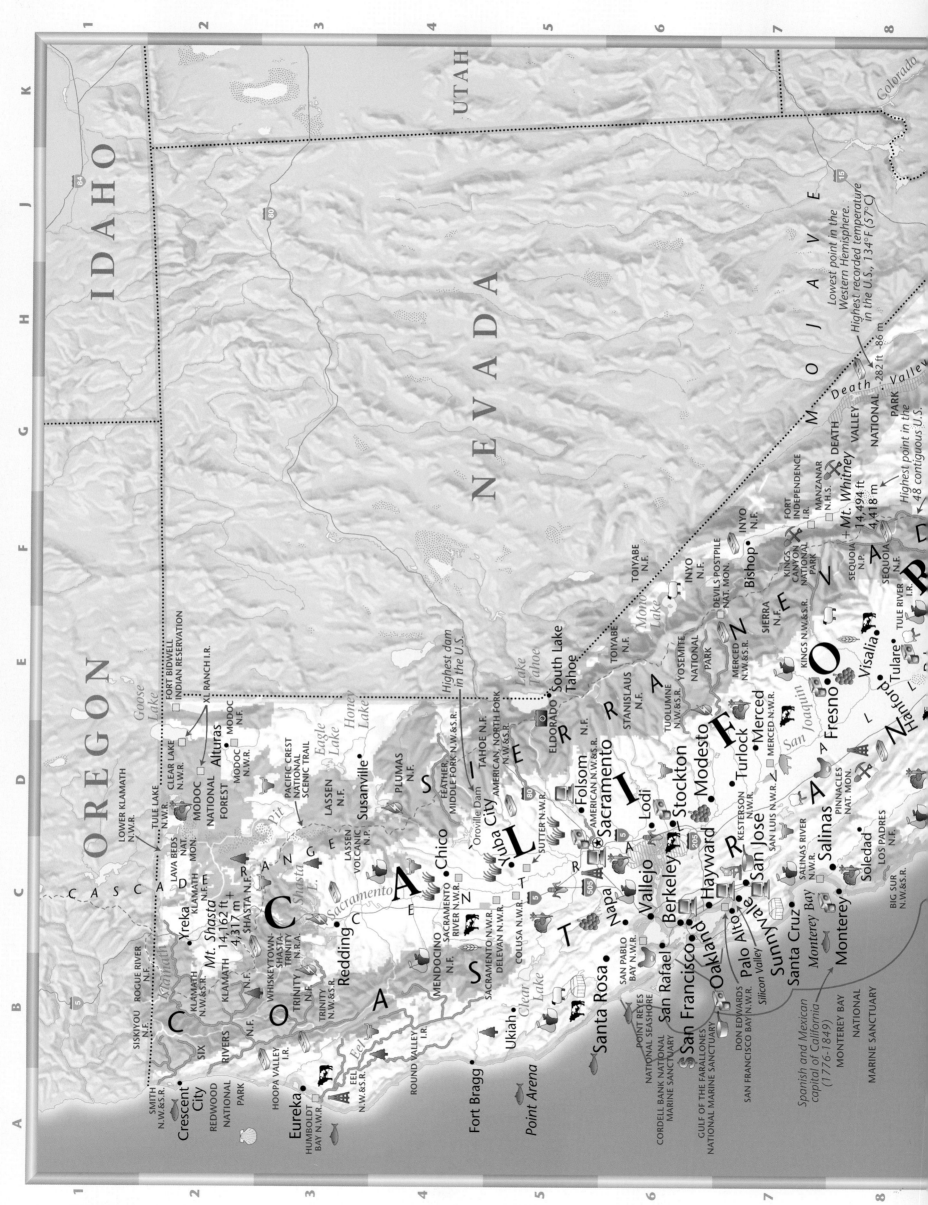

IDAHO

OREGON

NEVADA

UTAH

CALIFORNIA

M O J A V E

Lowest point in the
Western Hemisphere.
Highest recorded temperature
in the U.S., 134°F (57°C)

282 ft –86 m

Death Valley

DEATH VALLEY NATIONAL PARK

MANZANAR N.H.S.

FORT INDEPENDENCE I.R.

Highest point in the
48 contiguous U.S.

SEQUOIA + Mt. Whitney
14,494 ft
4,418 m

SEQUOIA N.F.

INYO N.F.

Bishop

DEVILS POSTPILE NAT. MON.

SIERRA N.F.

KINGS CANYON NATIONAL PARK

KINGS N.W.&S.R.

TULE RIVER I.R.

Visalia

Tulare

Haford

Fresno

MERCED N.W.&S.R.

San Joaquin

Merced

Turlock

Modesto

Stockton

Lodi

Sacramento

Folsom

ELDORADO N.F.

AMERICAN, NORTH FORK N.W.&S.R.

TAHOE N.F.

FEATHER, MIDDLE FORK N.W.&S.R.

South Lake Tahoe

Lake Tahoe

Mono Lake

TOIYABE N.F.

TOIYABE N.F.

STANISLAUS N.F.

TUOLUMNE N.W.&S.R.

YOSEMITE NATIONAL PARK

MERCED N.W.&S.R.

Highest dam
in the U.S.

Eagle Lake

Honey Lake

PLUMAS N.F.

LASSEN N.F.

Susanville

LASSEN VOLCANIC N.P.

PACIFIC CREST NATIONAL SCENIC TRAIL

Oroville Dam

Yuba City

Chico

R A N G E

MODOC N.F.

MODOC N.W.R.

Alturas

XL RANCH I.R.

FORT BIDWELL INDIAN RESERVATION

Goose Lake

CLEAR LAKE N.W.R.

TULE LAKE N.W.R.

MODOC NATIONAL FOREST

LAVA BEDS NAT. MON.

LOWER KLAMATH N.W.R.

KLAMATH N.F.

Yreka

Mt. Shasta 14,162 ft +
4,317 m

Shasta L.

SHASTA N.F.

WHISKEYTOWN-SHASTA-TRINITY N.R.A.

TRINITY N.F.

Redding

SACRAMENTO RIVER N.W.R.

SACRAMENTO N.W.R.

DELEVAN N.W.R.

COLUSA N.W.R.

Sacramento

C A S C A D E

SISKIYOU N.F.

ROGUE RIVER N.F.

SIX RIVERS N.F.

Klamath

KLAMATH N.W.&S.R.

TRINITY N.F.

HOOPA VALLEY I.R.

Crescent City

REDWOOD NATIONAL PARK

SMITH N.W.&S.R.

Eureka

HUMBOLDT BAY N.W.R.

ROUND VALLEY I.R.

Eel

EEL N.W.&S.R.

Fort Bragg

Point Arena

Ukiah

MENDOCINO N.F.

Clear Lake

Santa Rosa

POINT REYES NATIONAL SEASHORE

Napa

Vallejo

SAN PABLO BAY N.W.R.

San Rafael

San Francisco

GULF OF THE FARALLONES NATIONAL MARINE SANCTUARY

CORDELL BANK NATIONAL MARINE SANCTUARY

DON EDWARDS SAN FRANCISCO BAY N.W.R.

Oakland

Berkeley

Hayward

Palo Alto

Sunnyvale

Silicon Valley

San Jose

Santa Cruz

Monterey Bay

Monterey

MONTEREY BAY NATIONAL MARINE SANCTUARY

Spanish and Mexican
capital of California
(1776-1849)

Salinas

SALINAS RIVER N.W.R.

Soledad

PINNACLES NAT. MON.

SAN LUIS N.W.R.

KESTERSON N.W.R.

LOS PADRES N.F.

BIG SUR N.W.&S.R.

C O A S T

S I E R R A N E V A D A

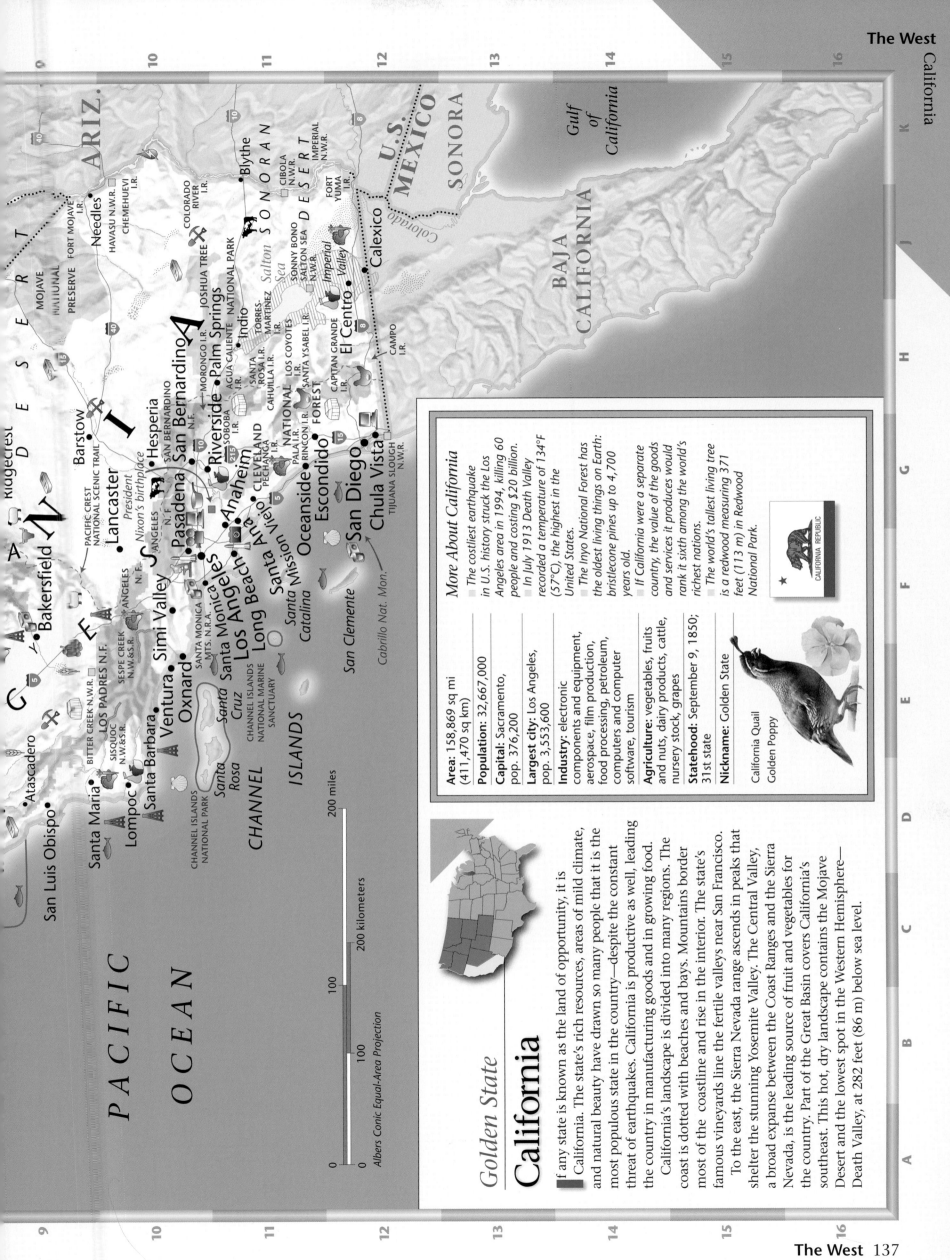

Golden State

California

If any state is known as the land of opportunity, it is California. The state's rich resources, areas of mild climate, and natural beauty have drawn so many people that it is the most populous state in the country—despite the constant threat of earthquakes. California is productive as well, leading the country in manufacturing goods and in growing food.

California's landscape is divided into many regions. The coast is dotted with beaches and bays. Mountains border most of the coastline and rise in the interior. The state's famous vineyards line the fertile valleys near San Francisco. To the east, the Sierra Nevada range ascends in peaks that shelter the stunning Yosemite Valley. The Central Valley, a broad expanse between the Coast Ranges and the Sierra Nevada, is the leading source of fruit and vegetables for the country. Part of the Great Basin covers California's southeast. This hot, dry landscape contains the Mojave Desert and the lowest spot in the Western Hemisphere—Death Valley, at 282 feet (86 m) below sea level.

Area: 158,869 sq mi (411,470 sq km)

Population: 32,667,000

Capital: Sacramento, pop. 376,200

Largest city: Los Angeles, pop. 3,553,600

Industry: electronic components and equipment, aerospace, film production, food processing, petroleum, computers and computer software, tourism

Agriculture: vegetables, fruits and nuts, dairy products, cattle, nursery stock, grapes

Statehood: September 9, 1850; 31st state

Nickname: Golden State

California Quail
Golden Poppy

More About California

- The costliest earthquake in U.S. history struck the Los Angeles area in 1994, killing 60 people and costing $20 billion.
- In July 1913 Death Valley recorded a temperature of 134°F (57°C), the highest in the United States.
- The Inyo National Forest has the oldest living things on Earth: bristlecone pines up to 4,700 years old.
- If California were a separate country, the value of the goods and services it produces would rank it sixth among the world's richest nations.
- The world's tallest living tree is a redwood measuring 371 feet (113 m) in Redwood National Park.

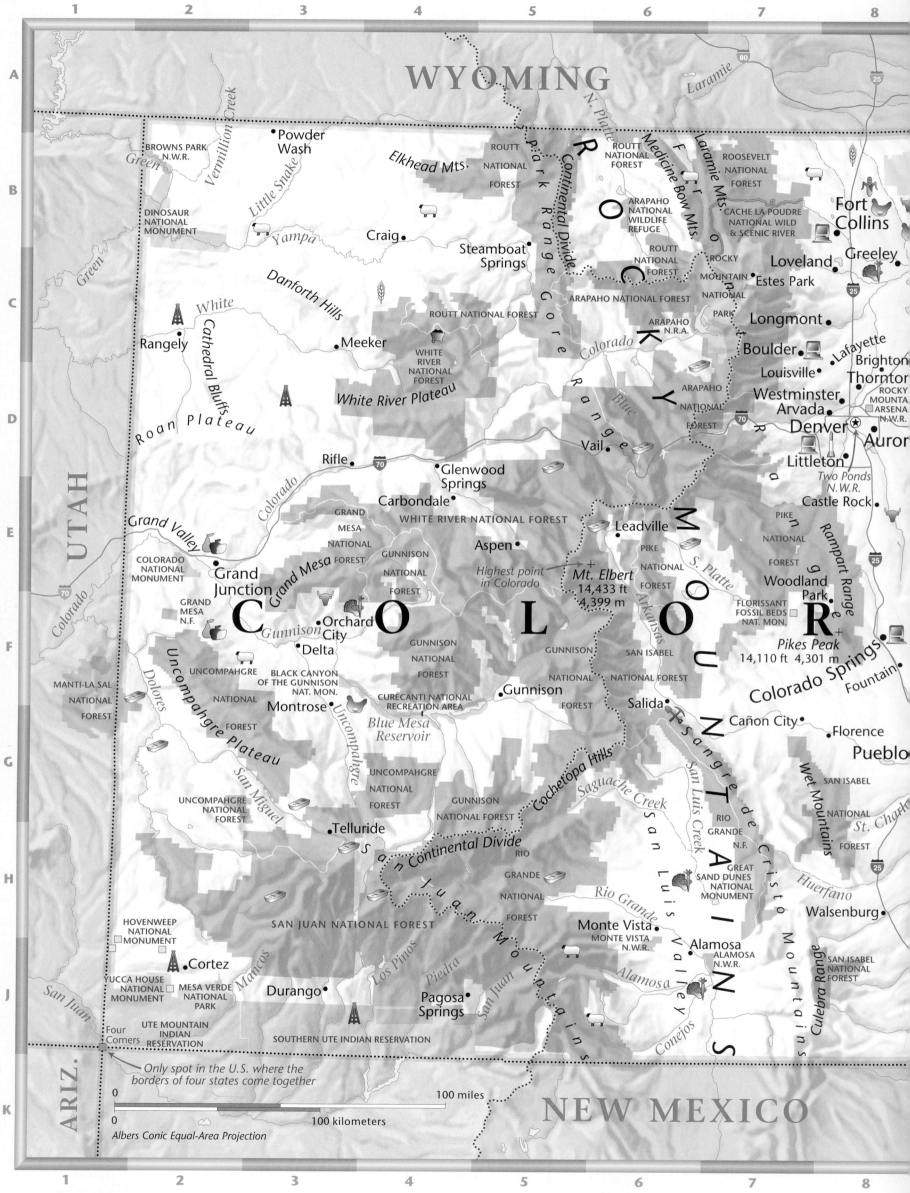

WYOMING

ROCKY
MOUNTAINS

COLORADO

UTAH

ARIZ.

NEW MEXICO

Powder Wash
BROWNS PARK N.W.R.
Green
Vermillion Creek
Little Snake
Elkhead Mts.
ROUTT NATIONAL FOREST
Park Range
Continental Divide
N. Platte
Laramie
Medicine Bow Mts.
Laramie Mts.
ROUTT NATIONAL FOREST
ROOSEVELT NATIONAL FOREST
CACHE LA POUDRE NATIONAL WILD & SCENIC RIVER
ARAPAHO NATIONAL WILDLIFE REFUGE
Fort Collins
Greeley
DINOSAUR NATIONAL MONUMENT
Yampa
Craig
Steamboat Springs
ROUTT NATIONAL FOREST
ARAPAHO NATIONAL FOREST
Loveland
Estes Park
ROCKY MOUNTAIN NATIONAL PARK
Green
White
Cathedral Bluffs
Danforth Hills
WHITE RIVER NATIONAL FOREST
ARAPAHO N.R.A.
Colorado
ARAPAHO NATIONAL FOREST
Longmont
Boulder
Lafayette
Brighton
Thornton
Westminster
Louisville
Rangely
Meeker
WHITE RIVER NATIONAL FOREST
White River Plateau
Blue
Roan Plateau
Rifle
Glenwood Springs
Carbondale
Vail
ROCKY MOUNTA ARSENAL N.W.R.
Arvada
Denver
Aurora
Colorado
Grand Valley
COLORADO NATIONAL MONUMENT
Grand Junction
Grand Mesa
GRAND MESA NATIONAL FOREST
WHITE RIVER NATIONAL FOREST
Leadville
PIKE NATIONAL FOREST
Littleton
Two Ponds N.W.R.
Castle Rock
Aspen
GUNNISON NATIONAL FOREST
Highest point in Colorado
Mt. Elbert 14,433 ft 4,399 m
PIKE NATIONAL FOREST
S. Platte
Rampart Range
Woodland Park
GRAND MESA N.F.
MANTI-LA SAL NATIONAL FOREST
Dolores
Orchard City
Delta
Gunnison
UNCOMPAHGRE NATIONAL FOREST
BLACK CANYON OF THE GUNNISON NAT. MON.
GUNNISON NATIONAL FOREST
SAN ISABEL NATIONAL FOREST
Akansas
FLORISSANT FOSSIL BEDS NAT. MON.
Pikes Peak 14,110 ft 4,301 m
Colorado Springs
Fountain
Uncompahgre Plateau
Montrose
CURECANTI NATIONAL RECREATION AREA
Blue Mesa Reservoir
Gunnison
GUNNISON NATIONAL FOREST
Salida
Cañon City
Florence
Pueblo
San Miguel
UNCOMPAHGRE NATIONAL FOREST
UNCOMPAHGRE NATIONAL FOREST
Cochetopa Hills
Saguache Creek
Sangre de Cristo Mountains
Wet Mountains
SAN ISABEL NATIONAL FOREST
St. Charl
Telluride
GUNNISON NATIONAL FOREST
Continental Divide
RIO GRANDE N.F.
San Luis Creek
RIO GRANDE NATIONAL FOREST
GREAT SAND DUNES NATIONAL MONUMENT
Huerfano
San Juan Mountains
Rio Grande
Walsenburg
HOVENWEEP NATIONAL MONUMENT
SAN JUAN NATIONAL FOREST
Los Pinos
Piedra
Monte Vista
MONTE VISTA N.W.R.
Alamosa
ALAMOSA N.W.R.
San Luis Valley
Culebra Range
SAN ISABEL NATIONAL FOREST
Cortez
YUCCA HOUSE NATIONAL MONUMENT
MESA VERDE NATIONAL PARK
Mancos
Durango
Pagosa Springs
San Juan
Alamosa
Conejos
San Juan
Four Corners
UTE MOUNTAIN INDIAN RESERVATION
SOUTHERN UTE INDIAN RESERVATION

Only spot in the U.S. where the borders of four states come together

100 miles

0

0   100 kilometers

Albers Conic Equal-Area Projection

Centennial State

Colorado

If you want to feel taller, head for Colorado. Colorado's elevation averages 6,800 feet (2,073 m) above sea level, higher than any other state. Colorado, in the heart of the Rocky Mountains, has more than 50 peaks over 14,000 feet (4,267 m). The mountains have extensive deposits of valuable minerals, including gold, silver, lead, iron, and molybdenum, used for strengthening steel. The mountains also bring skiers to resorts such as Vail, Aspen, and Telluride.

The mineral wealth of the Rockies, much of it washed into streams as placer deposits, established Denver as Colorado's most important city. Located at the foot of the Rockies' Front Range, Denver is one of a line of cities where about 80 percent of Colorado's population lives.

To the east lie high, dry plains. Oil and natural gas are found here, and farmers raise livestock and grow wheat, corn, and hay on irrigated land. West of the Rockies the landscapes change to plateaus, valleys, and flat-topped mesas.

Area: 104,100 sq mi (269,618 sq km)	
Population: 3,971,000	
Capital: Denver, pop. 497,800	

Largest city: Denver, pop. 497,800

Industry: real estate, state and local government, durable goods, communications, health and other services, nondurable goods, transportation

Agriculture: cattle, corn, wheat, dairy products, hay

Statehood: August 1, 1876; 38th state

Nickname: Centennial State

More about Colorado

■ Colorado's name comes from a Spanish word meaning "colored red." It was first given to the river that runs through red stone cliffs.

■ The tallest sand dunes in North America, some 700 feet (213 m) high, are in Great Sand Dunes National Monument at the foot of the Sangre de Cristo Mountains.

■ Mesa Verde National Park contains more than 4,000 homes of the ancient Pueblo people, ranging from pit houses to cliff pueblos.

■ North America's largest silver nugget, weighing 1,840 pounds (835 kg), was found near Aspen in 1894.

■ A tiny letter D on your coin means it was made in the Denver mint.

Lark Bunting
Columbine

Map labels

NEBRASKA

Hereford
PAWNEE NATIONAL GRASSLAND
Crow Creek
North Sterling Reservoir
Sterling
Frenchman Creek
Holyoke
South Platte
Brush
Akron
Yuma
Fort Morgan
Last Chance
Arikaree
South Fork Republican
Kiowa
Limon
Big Sandy Creek
Burlington
Punkin Center
Cheyenne Wells
Rush Creek
Great Plains Reservoirs
Lake Meredith
Ordway
BENT'S OLD FORT N.H.S.
John Martin Reservoir
Arkansas
Lamar
Rocky Ford
La Junta
Las Animas
Apishapa
COMANCHE NATIONAL GRASSLAND
Purgatoire
Chacuaco Canyon
Smith Canyon
Two Butte Creek
Bear Creek
Springfield
Sand Arroyo
North Fork
COMANCHE NATIONAL GRASSLAND
Cimarron
Trinidad
Mesa de Maya
OKLAHOMA
KANSAS

HIGH PLAINS
COLORADO

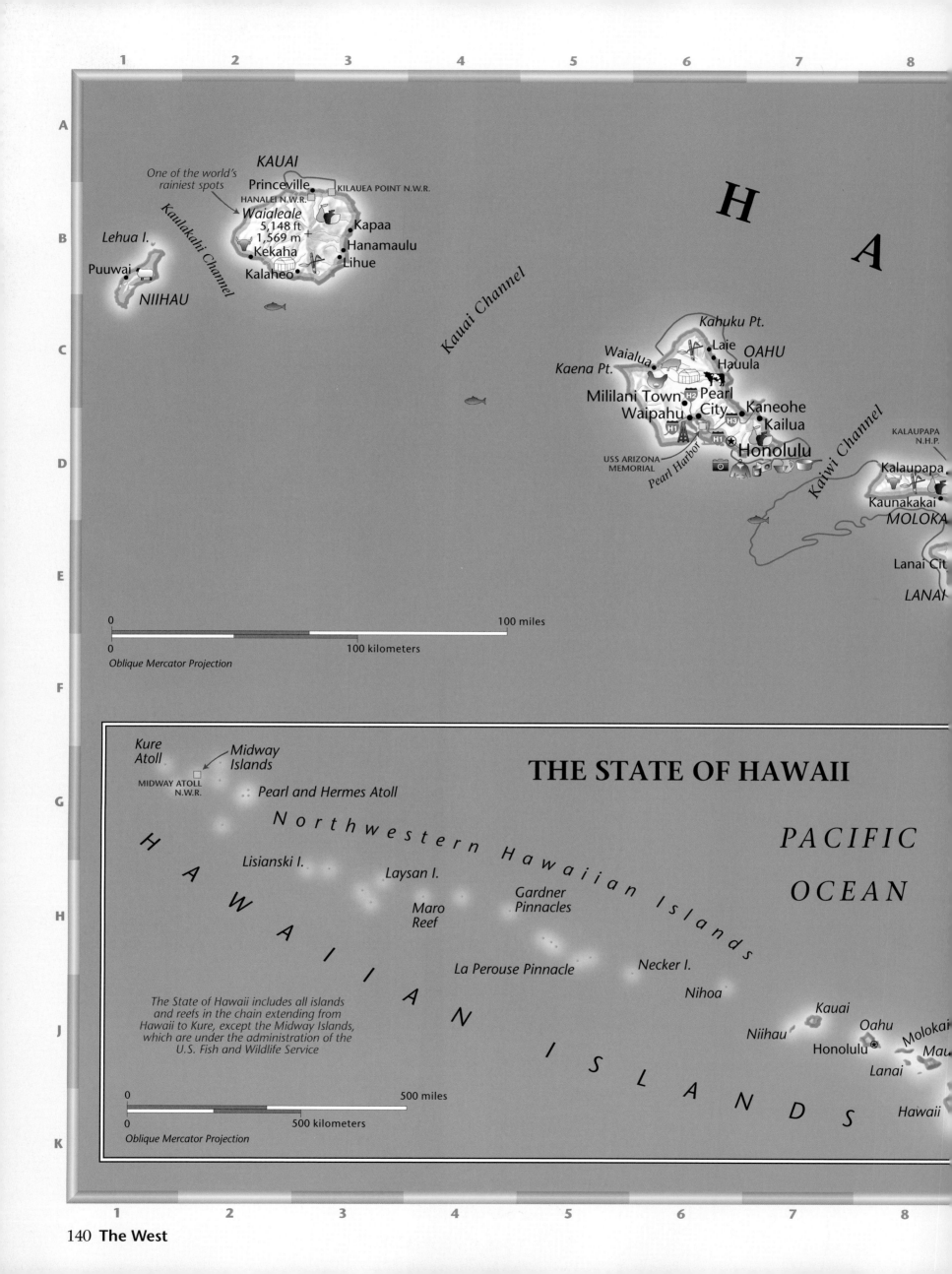

KAUAI

One of the world's rainiest spots

Princeville
KILAUEA POINT N.W.R.
HANALEI N.W.R.
Waialeale
5,148 ft
1,569 m
Kekaha
Kalaheo
Kapaa
Hanamaulu
Lihue

Kaulakahi Channel

Lehua I.
Puuwai
NIIHAU

Kauai Channel

Kahuku Pt.
Waialua
Laie
OAHU
Kaena Pt.
Hauula
Mililani Town
Pearl
City
Waipahu
Kaneohe
Kailua
USS ARIZONA
MEMORIAL
Honolulu
Pearl Harbor

Kaiwi Channel

KALAUPAPA
N.H.P.
Kalaupapa
Kaunakakai
MOLOKA

Lanai Cit
LANAI

0   100 miles

0   100 kilometers

Oblique Mercator Projection

H A

Kure
Atoll
*Midway
Islands*
MIDWAY ATOLL
N.W.R.
Pearl and Hermes Atoll

N o r t h w e s t e r n   H a w a i i a n   I s l a n d s

THE STATE OF HAWAII

PACIFIC

OCEAN

Lisianski I.

Laysan I.

*Maro
Reef*

*Gardner
Pinnacles*

La Perouse Pinnacle

Necker I.

Nihoa

*H
A
W
A
I
I
A
N*

Kauai
Niihau
Oahu
Molokai
Honolulu
Maui
Lanai
Hawaii

*I
S
L
A
N
D
S*

The State of Hawaii includes all islands
and reefs in the chain extending from
Hawaii to Kure, except the Midway Islands,
which are under the administration of the
U.S. Fish and Wildlife Service

0   500 miles

0   500 kilometers

Oblique Mercator Projection

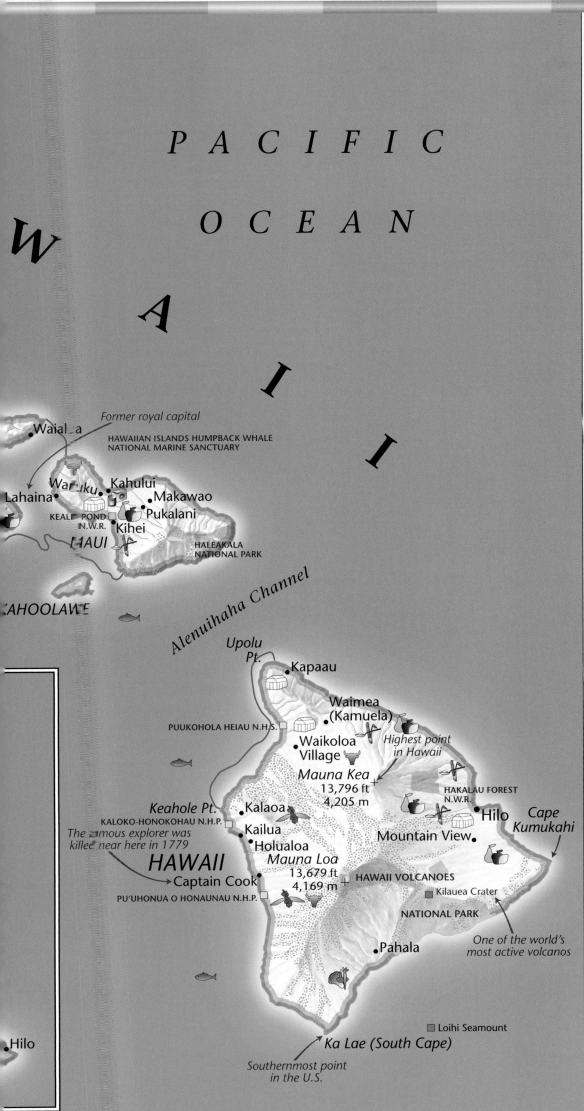

P A C I F I C

O C E A N

H A W A I I

Former royal capital

Waial.a

HAWAIIAN ISLANDS HUMPBACK WHALE
NATIONAL MARINE SANCTUARY

Wai.ku. Kahului

Lahaina
Makawao
KEAL. POND
N.W.R. Pukalani
Kihei
MAUI
HALEAKALA
NATIONAL PARK

KAHOOLAWE

Alenuihaha Channel

Upolu Pt.

Kapaau

Waimea
(Kamuela)

PUUKOHOLA HEIAU N.H.S.

Waikoloa
Village

Highest point in Hawaii

Mauna Kea
13,796 ft
4,205 m

HAKALAU FOREST
N.W.R.

Keahole Pt. Kalaoa

KALOKO-HONOKOHAU N.H.P. Hilo

The famous explorer was killed near here in 1779 Kailua

Holualoa
Mauna Loa
13,679 ft
4,169 m

Cape Kumukahi

Mountain View

HAWAII

Captain Cook

PU'UHONUA O HONAUNAU N.H.P.

HAWAII VOLCANOES

Kilauea Crater

NATIONAL PARK

One of the world's most active volcanos

Pahala

Loihi Seamount

Ka Lae (South Cape)

Southernmost point in the U.S.

Hilo

Aloha State

Hawaii

Located in the Pacific Ocean more than 2,400 miles (3,862 km) from the U.S. mainland, the southernmost state is a chain of 132 volcanic islands extending more than 1,500 miles (2,400 km). Most are small islands that total only three square miles (7.8 sq km). The eight main islands at the eastern end form most of Hawaii's territory.

People came to Hawaii about 1,500 years ago in double-hulled canoes from other Polynesian islands. In the late 19th century, European and American planters established pineapple and sugarcane plantations, bringing in workers from many Asian countries. As a result, Hawaii is one of the country's most ethnically diverse states.

Most residents live on Oahu, site of Honolulu, which lures many of the state's six million annual visitors. Hawaii, the Big Island, has more than half the state's land. Lanai is known for pineapples and tourism. Among the other islands, Molokai has jagged sea cliffs, Kauai is noted for beautiful gardens, and Maui for spectacular beaches.

Area: 6,459 sq mi
(16,729 sq km)

Population:
1,193,000

Capital: Honolulu, pop. 423,500

Largest city: Honolulu, pop. 423,500

Industry: tourism, trade, finance, food processing, petroleum refining, stone, clay, and glass products

Agriculture: sugarcane, pineapples, nursery stock, tropical fruit, livestock, macadamia nuts

Statehood: August 21, 1959; 50th state

Nickname: Aloha State

More about Hawaii

■ *Today, less than one percent of Hawaii's population is descended from the original Polynesian settlers.*
■ *There are only 12 letters in the Hawaiian alphabet—a,e,h,i,k,l,m,n,o,p,u, and w.*
■ *Many of Hawaii's plant and animal species, such as the Hawaiian goose, or nene, are unique to the islands—and endangered.*
■ *A new island is rising at the eastern end of the Hawaiian chain as the Pacific Plate carrying the islands slides over a hot spot. The Loihi Seamount is about 3,000 feet (914 m) below the ocean's surface and growing.*

Hawaiian Goose
(Nene)

Hibiscus

Gem State

Idaho

Idaho has some of the wildest terrain in the country. Jagged ranges of the Rocky Mountains carve up much of the state's central section. Hells Canyon, cut by the Snake River, is the deepest gorge in the United States at 7,900 feet (2,408 m).

The mountains reach into Idaho's panhandle, rich with evergreen forests and beautiful lakes. Lumbering and recreation—such as skiing, fishing, and river running—are major industries here. The panhandle also contains much mineral wealth, including gold and silver.

The Snake River Plain rims the mountains to the south. Here ancient lava flows contribute to the region's fertile soil, where the state's famous potatoes grow on irrigated fields. Boise is the home of the Basque Culture Center. Idaho's first Basque settlers were sheepherders from Europe's Pyrenees Mountains. Some still ranch, while others work in business and other professions. Idaho's southeast is part of the arid Great Basin region. Many people here are Mormons with close ties to neighboring Utah.

Area: 83,574 sq mi (216,456 sq km)

Population: 1,229,000

Capital: Boise, pop. 152,740

Largest city: Boise, pop. 152,740

Industry: electronics and computer equipment, tourism, food processing, forest products, mining, chemicals

Agriculture: potatoes, dairy products, cattle, wheat, alfalfa hay, sugar beets, barley, trout

Statehood: July 3, 1890; 43rd state

Nickname: Gem State

More about Idaho

- Idaho is known as the Gem State for the gemstones and precious metals found in the mountains north of the Snake River.
- The lava-formed landscape at Craters of the Moon National Monument is so much like the moon that Apollo astronauts trained there in the 1960s.
- The Salmon River is called the River of No Return because in times past its strong currents could not be navigated.
- About three-quarters of Idaho's people live within 30 miles (50 km) of the Snake River.
- Idaho was made from leftover territory of some of its neighbors after they became states.

Mountain Bluebird

Syringa (Mock Orange)

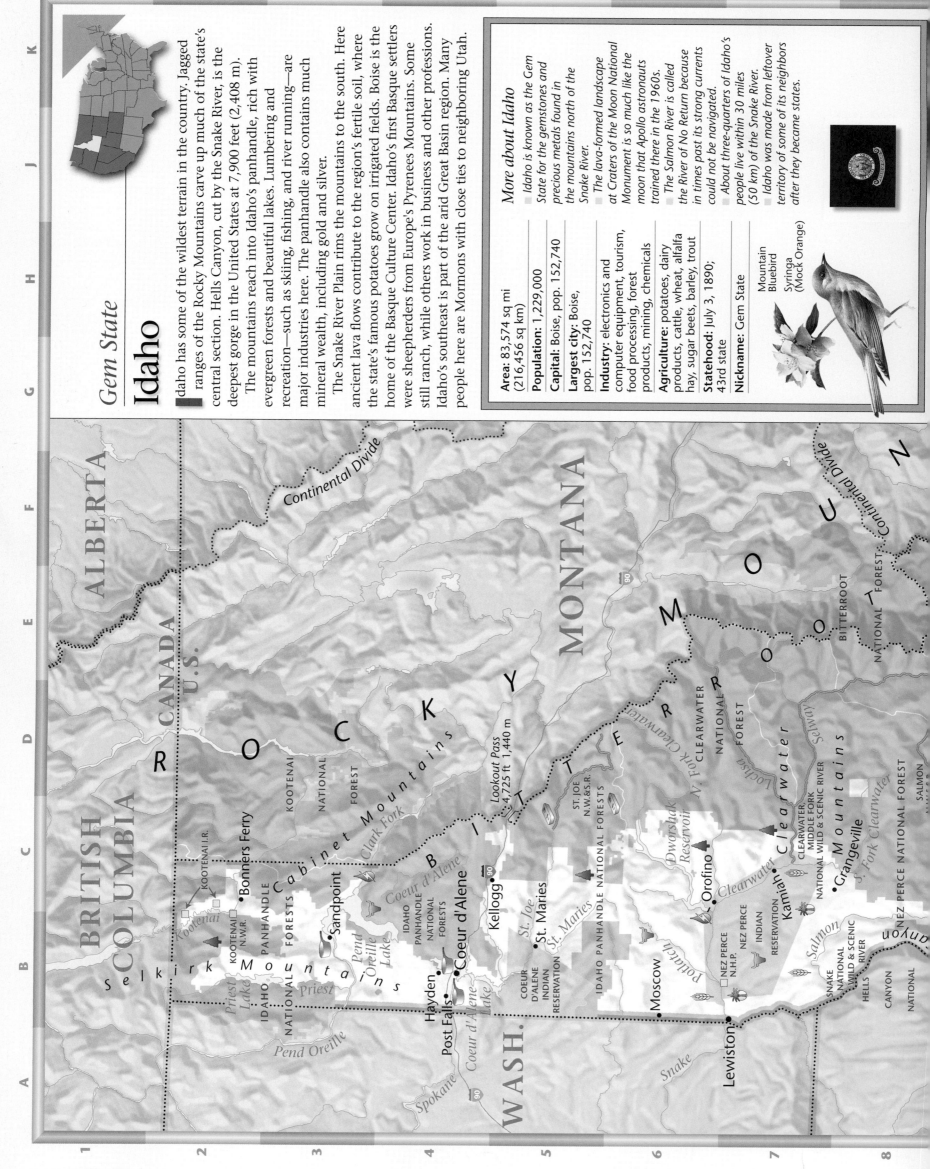

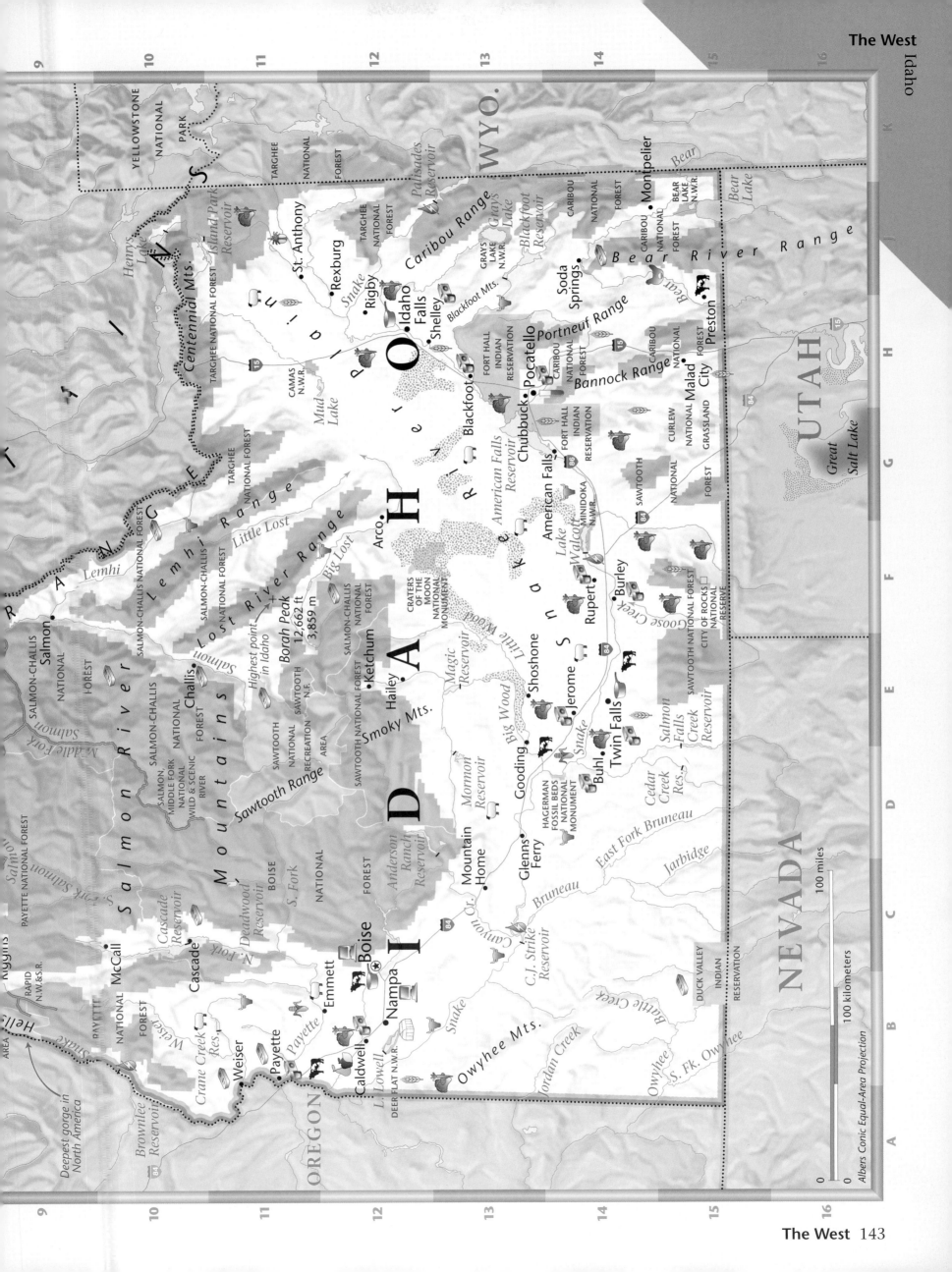

9 10 11 12 13 14 15 16

K

YELLOWSTONE NATIONAL PARK

WYO.

J

TARGHEE NATIONAL FOREST

Bear

Montpelier

Bear Lake

CARIBOU NATIONAL FOREST

Bear River Range

Bear Lake N.W.R.

BEAR LAKE N.W.R.

TARGHEE NATIONAL FOREST

Henrys Lake

Centennial Mts.

Island Park Reservoir

CENTENNIAL Mts.

TARGHEE NATIONAL FOREST

St. Anthony

Rexburg

Snake

Rigby

Idaho Falls

Shelley

Blackfoot Mts.

GRAYS LAKE N.W.R.

Grays Lake

Blackfoot Reservoir

Soda Springs

Portneuf Range

CARIBOU NATIONAL FOREST

CARIBOU NATIONAL FOREST

Preston

UTAH

I D A H O

CAMAS N.W.R.

Mud Lake

Blackfoot

FORT HALL INDIAN RESERVATION

Chubbuck

Pocatello

CARIBOU NATIONAL FOREST

Bannock Range

Malad City

CURLEW NATIONAL GRASSLAND

Great Salt Lake

Snake

American Falls Reservoir

Lemhi

Lemhi Range

Little Lost

Big Lost

Lost River Range

Arco

Borah Peak 12,662 ft 3,859 m

Highest point in Idaho

CRATERS OF THE MOON NATIONAL MONUMENT

American Falls

FORT HALL INDIAN RESERVATION

MINIDOKA N.W.R.

Lake Walcott

SAWTOOTH NATIONAL FOREST

Salmon River

N. Middle Fork Salmon

SALMON-CHALLIS NATIONAL FOREST

Salmon

SALMON-CHALLIS NATIONAL FOREST

Salmon

Challis

SALMON-CHALLIS NATIONAL FOREST

Ketchum

Hailey

Smoky Mts.

SAWTOOTH N.F.

SAWTOOTH NATIONAL FOREST

SAWTOOTH NATIONAL RECREATION AREA

Sawtooth Range

Snake River

Magic Reservoir

Little Wood

Big Wood

Shoshone

Jerome

Rupert

Burley

Goose Creek

SAWTOOTH NATIONAL FOREST

Salmon Falls Creek Reservoir

CITY OF ROCKS NATIONAL RESERVE

NEVADA

SALMON, MIDDLE FORK NATIONAL WILD & SCENIC RIVER

Mountains

S. Fork Salmon

PAYETTE NATIONAL FOREST

McCall

Cascade Reservoir

Deadwood Reservoir

BOISE NATIONAL FOREST

N. Fork

S. Fork

BOISE NATIONAL FOREST

Anderson Ranch Reservoir

Mountain Home

Gooding

Twin Falls

Buhl

HAGERMAN FOSSIL BEDS NATIONAL MONUMENT

Glenns Ferry

Snake

Cedar Creek Res.

East Fork Bruneau

Jarbidge

Cascade

Emmett

Boise

Nampa

Caldwell

Payette

Weiser

Weiser

Crane Creek Res.

PAYETTE NATIONAL FOREST

Hells Canyon N.W. & S.R.

RAPID N.W.&S.R.

Deepest gorge in North America

Snake

Brownlee Reservoir

L. Lowell

DEER FLAT N.W.R.

Payette

OREGON

Canyon Cr.

Bruneau

C.J. Strike Reservoir

Owyhee Mts.

Jordan Creek

Battle Creek

DUCK VALLEY INDIAN RESERVATION

Owyhee

S. Fk. Owyhee

100 miles

100 kilometers

Albers Conic Equal-Area Projection

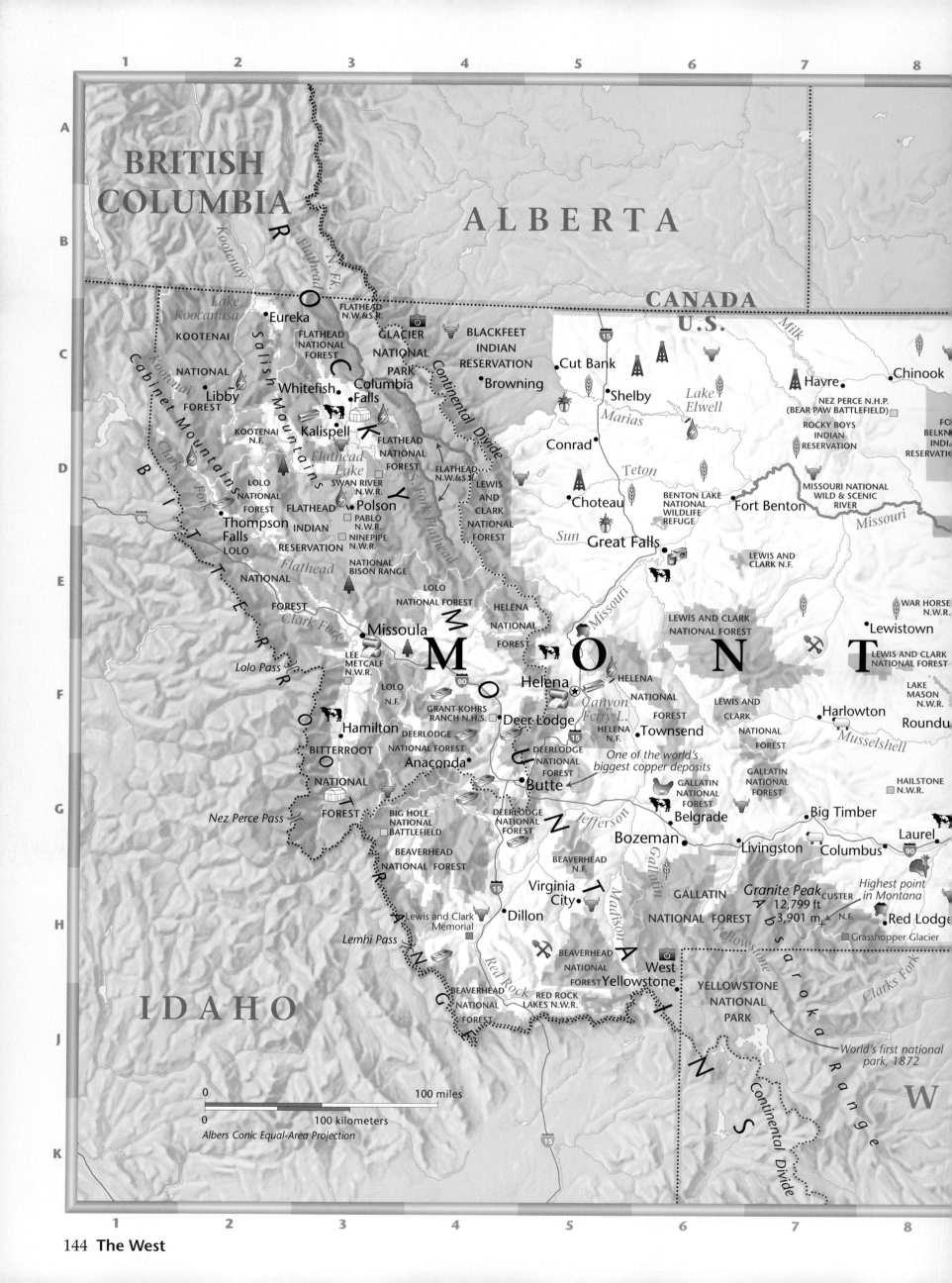

BRITISH COLUMBIA

ALBERTA

CANADA
U.S.

Kootenay

Lake Koocanusa

•Eureka

KOOTENAI

NATIONAL

•Libby

FOREST

Cabinet Mountains

Kootenai
N.F.

Salish Mountains

Clark Fork

R   O   C   K   Y

Flathead
N. Fk.

FLATHEAD
N.W.&S.R.

FLATHEAD
NATIONAL
FOREST

GLACIER
NATIONAL
PARK

Whitefish   Columbia
Falls

Kalispell

Flathead
Lake

LOLO
NATIONAL
FOREST

FLATHEAD
INDIAN
RESERVATION

SWAN RIVER
N.W.R.

•Polson

☐ PABLO
N.W.R.

☐ NINEPIPE
N.W.R.

Thompson
Falls

LOLO
NATIONAL
FOREST

Flathead

NATIONAL
BISON RANGE

Clark Fork

Continental Divide

S. Fork Flathead

FLATHEAD
N.W.&S.R.

LEWIS
AND
CLARK
NATIONAL
FOREST

BLACKFEET
INDIAN
RESERVATION

•Browning

•Cut Bank

•Shelby

Marias

Lake
Elwell

Milk

Havre

•Chinook

NEZ PERCE N.H.P.
(BEAR PAW BATTLEFIELD)

ROCKY BOYS
INDIAN
RESERVATION

FO
BELKN
INDIA
RESERVATI

•Conrad

Teton

•Choteau

Sun

BENTON LAKE
NATIONAL
WILDLIFE
REFUGE

Missouri

Fort Benton

MISSOURI NATIONAL
WILD & SCENIC
RIVER

•Great Falls

LEWIS AND
CLARK N.F.

Missoula

LEE
METCALF
N.W.R.

Lolo Pass

LOLO
N.F.

M O N T

HELENA
NATIONAL
FOREST

Missouri

LEWIS AND CLARK
NATIONAL FOREST

•Lewistown

LEWIS AND CLARK
NATIONAL FOREST

WAR HORSE
N.W.R.

LAKE
MASON
N.W.R.

Hamilton

BITTERROOT

NATIONAL

FOREST

Nez Perce Pass

GRANT-KOHRS
RANCH N.H.S.

DEERLODGE
NATIONAL FOREST

Anaconda

BIG HOLE
NATIONAL
BATTLEFIELD

BEAVERHEAD

NATIONAL FOREST

Lemhi Pass

Deer Lodge

DEERLODGE
NATIONAL
FOREST

Butte

HELENA
N.F.

Helena
★

Canyon
Ferry L.

One of the world's
biggest copper deposits

DEERLODGE
NATIONAL
FOREST

HELENA
NATIONAL
FOREST

Townsend

LEWIS AND
CLARK

NATIONAL

FOREST

Harlowton

Roundu

Musselshell

GALLATIN
NATIONAL
FOREST

HAILSTONE
☐ N.W.R.

Jefferson

GALLATIN
NATIONAL
FOREST

Belgrade

Bozeman

Gallatin

Madison

Virginia
City

Dillon

Red Rock

Lewis and Clark
Memorial

BEAVERHEAD
NATIONAL
FOREST

Livingston

Columbus

Big Timber

GALLATIN

NATIONAL FOREST

Granite Peak
12,799 ft
3,901 m

Laurel

Highest point
in Montana

CUSTER
N.F.

•Red Lodge

Grasshopper Glacier

IDAHO

R   A   N   G   E

BEAVERHEAD
NATIONAL
FOREST

RED ROCK
LAKES N.W.R.

West
Yellowstone

YELLOWSTONE
NATIONAL
PARK

World's first national
park, 1872

Absaroka Range

Clarks Fork

Yellowstone

Continental Divide

W

0   100 miles

0   100 kilometers

Albers Conic Equal-Area Projection

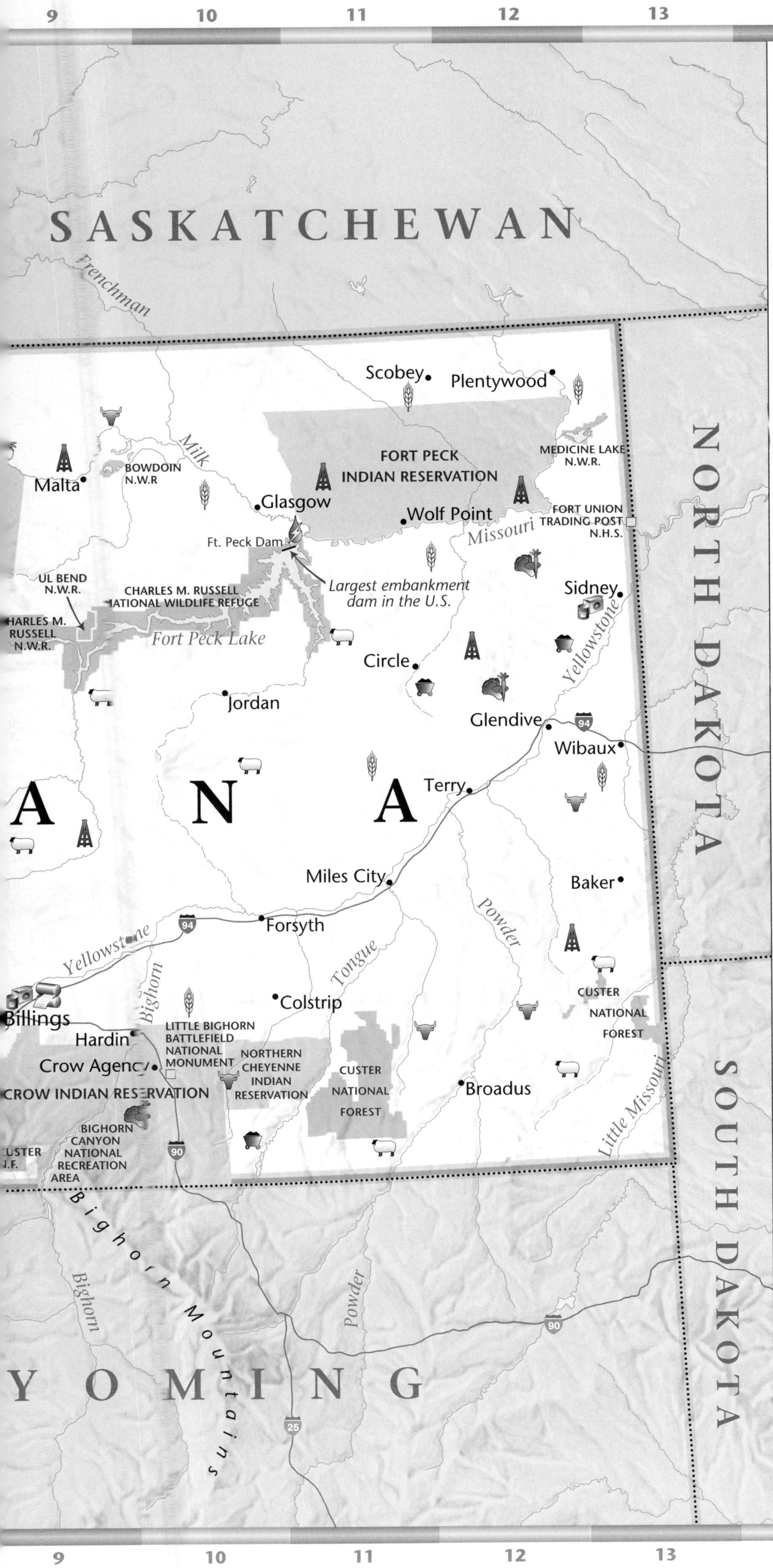

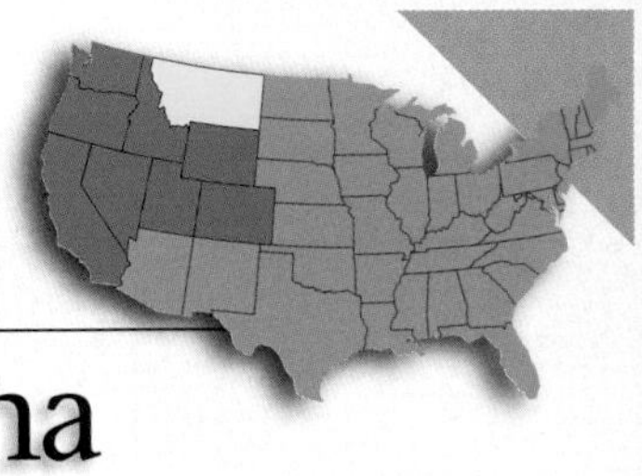

Map labels and geographic features:

SASKATCHEWAN

Frenchman

Malta

BOWDOIN N.W.R

Milk

Scobey

Plentywood

FORT PECK INDIAN RESERVATION

MEDICINE LAKE N.W.R.

Glasgow

Wolf Point

Missouri

FORT UNION TRADING POST N.H.S.

Ft. Peck Dam

UL BEND N.W.R.

CHARLES M. RUSSELL NATIONAL WILDLIFE REFUGE

Largest embankment dam in the U.S.

Sidney

HARLES M. RUSSELL N.W.R.

Fort Peck Lake

Circle

Jordan

Yellowstone

Glendive

94

Wibaux

NORTH DAKOTA

A

N

A

Terry

Powder

Miles City

Baker

Tongue

94

Forsyth

Yellowstone

Bighorn

Colstrip

CUSTER NATIONAL FOREST

Billings

Hardin

LITTLE BIGHORN BATTLEFIELD NATIONAL MONUMENT

NORTHERN CHEYENNE INDIAN RESERVATION

CUSTER NATIONAL FOREST

Crow Agency

CROW INDIAN RESERVATION

Broadus

Little Missouri

USTER I.F.

BIGHORN CANYON NATIONAL RECREATION AREA

90

SOUTH DAKOTA

Bighorn Mountains

Bighorn

Powder

90

25

WYOMING

Treasure State

Montana

Montana gets its name from the Spanish word for mountains. More than 50 ranges of the Rocky Mountains rise in the western half of the state. Some peaks are so rugged that they have never been climbed. Vast stands of evergreens—fir, pine, cedar, and spruce—cover lower mountain slopes. Loggers cut them to provide timber for Montana's valuable forest products industry.

Montana's mountains are laced with gold, silver, and other minerals. Erosion often deposits these minerals in streams and rivers, forming placer deposits. Placers sparked the rush that brought gold-seekers to Montana in the mid-1800s, and mining is still an important part of the economy.

The eastern three-fifths of the state is shortgrass prairie, part of the country's Great Plains. Mighty rivers, such as the Missouri and Yellowstone, wind across the plains. This region supports most of Montana's agriculture, with wheat being the most important crop. People there raise livestock, especially beef cattle, on enormous ranches.

MONTANA

Area: 147,046 sq mi (380,849 sq km)

Population: 880,000

Capital: Helena, pop. 28,000

Largest city: Billings, pop. 91,195

Industry: forest products, food processing, mining, construction, tourism

Agriculture: wheat, cattle, barley, hay, sugar beets, dairy products

Statehood: November 8, 1889; 41st state

Nickname: Treasure State

More about Montana

■ *Montana is second only to Texas in the number of acres devoted to agriculture.*
■ *Montana has more gem sapphires than any other state.*
■ *Grasshopper Glacier contains swarms of grasshoppers that became trapped in the ice and can still be seen.*
■ *In the snowy winter of 1997, the Montana Department of Transportation plowed 3,791,341 miles (6,101,405 km) of highway—equivalent to almost eight round trips to the Moon.*
■ *More than 35,000 waterfowl and shorebirds nest at Benton Lake National Wildlife Refuge each year.*
■ *In 1863 Virginia City, then known as Alder Gulch, had the richest deposits of gold ever found in the United States.*

Western Meadowlark
Bitterroot

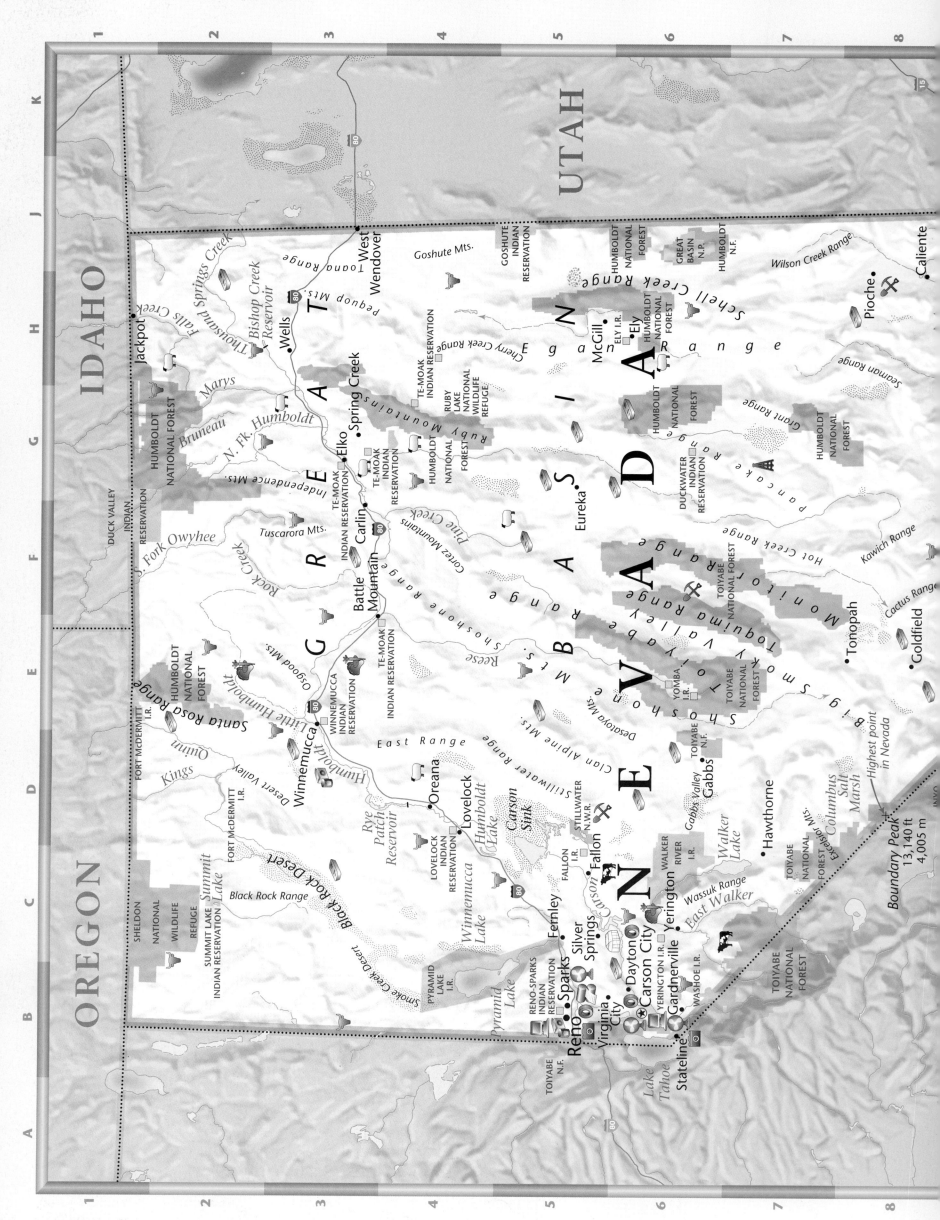

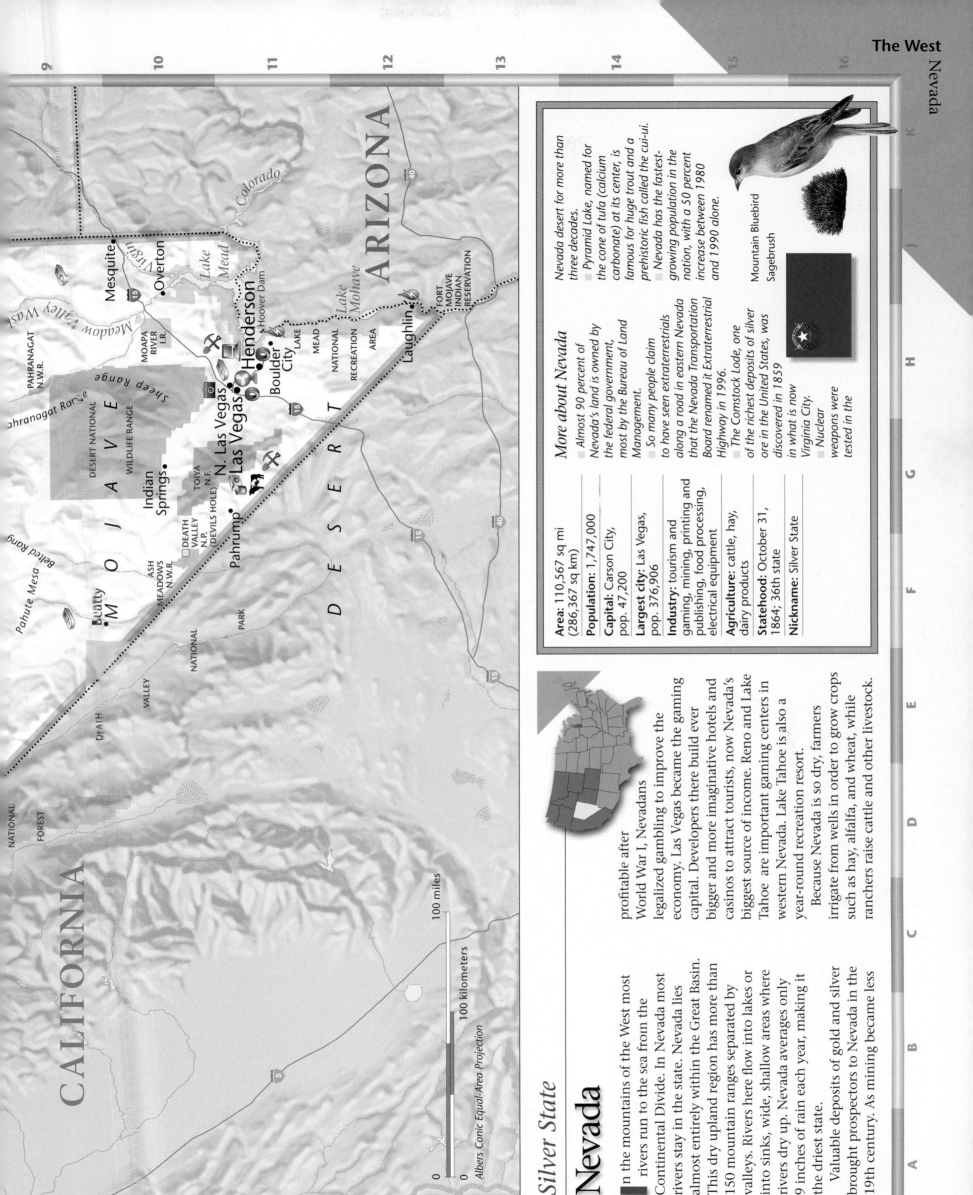

Silver State

Nevada

In the mountains of the West most rivers run to the sea from the Continental Divide. In Nevada most rivers stay in the state. Nevada lies almost entirely within the Great Basin. This dry upland region has more than 150 mountain ranges separated by valleys. Rivers here flow into lakes or into sinks, wide, shallow areas where rivers dry up. Nevada averages only 9 inches of rain each year, making it the driest state.

Valuable deposits of gold and silver brought prospectors to Nevada in the 19th century. As mining became less

profitable after World War I, Nevadans legalized gambling to improve the economy. Las Vegas became the gaming capital. Developers there build ever bigger and more imaginative hotels and casinos to attract tourists, now Nevada's biggest source of income. Reno and Lake Tahoe are important gaming centers in western Nevada. Lake Tahoe is also a year-round recreation resort.

Because Nevada is so dry, farmers irrigate from wells in order to grow crops such as hay, alfalfa, and wheat, while ranchers raise cattle and other livestock.

Area: 110,567 sq mi (286,367 sq km)

Population: 1,747,000

Capital: Carson City, pop. 47,200

Largest city: Las Vegas, pop. 376,906

Industry: tourism and gaming, mining, printing and publishing, food processing, electrical equipment

Agriculture: cattle, hay, dairy products

Statehood: October 31, 1864; 36th state

Nickname: Silver State

More about Nevada

■ Almost 90 percent of Nevada's land is owned by the federal government, most by the Bureau of Land Management.

■ So many people claim to have seen extraterrestrials along a road in eastern Nevada that the Nevada Transportation Board renamed it Extraterrestrial Highway in 1996.

■ The Comstock Lode, one of the richest deposits of silver ore in the United States, was discovered in 1859 in what is now Virginia City.

■ Nuclear weapons were tested in the Nevada desert for more than three decades.

■ Pyramid Lake, named for the cone of tufa (calcium carbonate) at its center, is famous for huge trout and a prehistoric fish called the cui-ui.

■ Nevada has the fastest-growing population in the nation, with a 50 percent increase between 1980 and 1990 alone.

Mountain Bluebird

Sagebrush

100 miles

100 kilometers

Albers Conic Equal-Area Projection

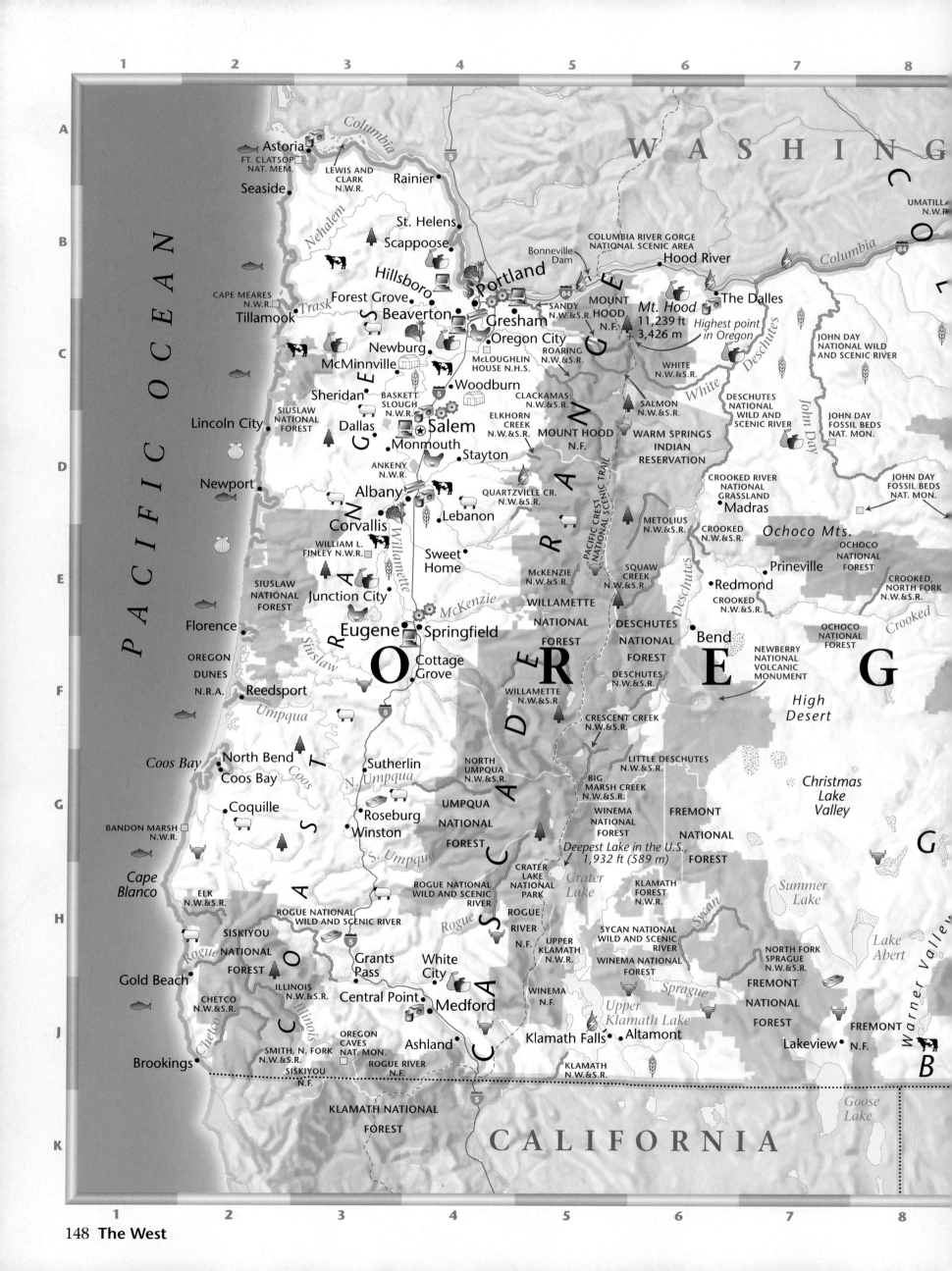

Map labels

Grid reference letters (left margin): A B C D E F G H J K

Grid reference numbers (top and bottom): 1 2 3 4 5 6 7 8

PACIFIC OCEAN

WASHINGTON

CALIFORNIA

OREGON

COAST RANGE

CASCADE RANGE

Columbia

Astoria
FT. CLATSOP NAT. MEM.
Seaside
Rainier
LEWIS AND CLARK N.W.R.
St. Helens
Scappoose
Hillsboro
Forest Grove
Portland
Beaverton
Gresham
Oregon City
CAPE MEARES N.W.R.
Tillamook
Trask
Nehalem
Newburg
McMinnville
Sheridan
Woodburn
BASKETT SLOUGH N.W.R.
McLOUGHLIN HOUSE N.H.S.
ROARING N.W.&S.R.
Bonneville Dam
COLUMBIA RIVER GORGE NATIONAL SCENIC AREA
Hood River
The Dalles
MOUNT HOOD N.F.
Mt. Hood 11,239 ft 3,426 m Highest point in Oregon
WHITE N.W.&S.R.
White
Deschutes
JOHN DAY NATIONAL WILD AND SCENIC RIVER
Lincoln City
SIUSLAW NATIONAL FOREST
Dallas
Salem
Monmouth
Stayton
ANKENY N.W.R.
CLACKAMAS N.W.&S.R.
ELKHORN CREEK N.W.&S.R.
SALMON N.W.&S.R.
MOUNT HOOD N.F.
WARM SPRINGS INDIAN RESERVATION
JOHN DAY FOSSIL BEDS NAT. MON.
JOHN DAY FOSSIL BEDS NAT. MON.
John Day
Newport
Albany
Lebanon
QUARTZVILLE CR. N.W.&S.R.
CROOKED RIVER NATIONAL GRASSLAND
Madras
METOLIUS N.W.&S.R.
Ochoco Mts.
Corvallis
Willamette
WILLIAM L. FINLEY N.W.R.
Sweet Home
McKENZIE N.W.&S.R.
SQUAW CREEK N.W.&S.R.
CROOKED N.W.&S.R.
Prineville
OCHOCO NATIONAL FOREST
CROOKED, NORTH FORK N.W.&S.R.
Crooked
SIUSLAW NATIONAL FOREST
Junction City
PACIFIC CREST NATIONAL SCENIC TRAIL
McKenzie
Deschutes
Redmond
OCHOCO NATIONAL FOREST
Florence
Eugene
Springfield
WILLAMETTE NATIONAL FOREST
DESCHUTES NATIONAL FOREST
Bend
NEWBERRY NATIONAL VOLCANIC MONUMENT
OREGON DUNES N.R.A.
Cottage Grove
Siuslaw
WILLAMETTE N.W.&S.R.
DESCHUTES N.W.&S.R.
High Desert
Reedsport
Umpqua
CRESCENT CREEK N.W.&S.R.
LITTLE DESCHUTES N.W.&S.R.
Coos Bay
North Bend
Coos Bay
Sutherlin
N. Umpqua
NORTH UMPQUA N.W.&S.R.
BIG MARSH CREEK N.W.&S.R.
Christmas Lake Valley
Coos
Coquille
Roseburg
Winston
UMPQUA NATIONAL FOREST
WINEMA NATIONAL FOREST
FREMONT NATIONAL FOREST
BANDON MARSH N.W.R.
S. Umpqua
Summer Lake
Cape Blanco
ELK N.W.&S.R.
Deepest Lake in the U.S., 1,932 ft (589 m)
Crater Lake
CRATER LAKE NATIONAL PARK
KLAMATH FOREST N.W.R.
Lake Abert
SISKIYOU NATIONAL FOREST
ROGUE NATIONAL WILD AND SCENIC RIVER
Rogue
ROGUE RIVER N.F.
Sycan
SYCAN NATIONAL WILD AND SCENIC RIVER
Gold Beach
Rogue
ROGUE NATIONAL WILD AND SCENIC RIVER
Grants Pass
White City
UPPER KLAMATH N.W.R.
WINEMA NATIONAL FOREST
NORTH FORK SPRAGUE N.W.&S.R.
Sprague
FREMONT NATIONAL FOREST
Warner Valley
ILLINOIS N.W.&S.R.
CHETCO N.W.&S.R.
Central Point
Medford
WINEMA N.F.
Upper Klamath Lake
Gold Beach
Illinois
Chetco
SMITH, N. FORK N.W.&S.R.
OREGON CAVES NAT. MON.
ROGUE RIVER N.F.
Ashland
Klamath Falls
Altamont
Lakeview
N.F.
Brookings
SISKIYOU N.F.
KLAMATH N.W.&S.R.
KLAMATH NATIONAL FOREST
Goose Lake

Beaver State

Oregon

Oregon was the end of the line for pioneers who traveled the Oregon Trail in the mid-1800s. The destination for most of them was the Willamette Valley, along the Willamette River in the western part of the state. There they found land so fertile that, as the saying went, you could poke a broomstick in the ground and it would grow.

Today, more than half of Oregon's people live in the valley. Many still farm, growing pears and other fruits and vegetables. Portland arose where the Willamette meets the Columbia River. An industrial center, Portland processes wood from the state's forests, produces computers and other electronics, and distributes Japanese cars.

Oregon's coast is rocky and edged with low mountains. It has a wet, mild climate. East of the Willamette Valley rise the Cascades, a volcanic range. Farther east the climate is drier and colder. Irrigated wheat and ryegrass grow on the rugged Columbia Plateau, built up of layers of lava. Southward, cattle ranches sprawl in the semiarid Great Basin.

STATE OF OREGON 1859

Area: 97,132 sq mi (251,571 sq km)

Population: 3,282,000

Capital: Salem, pop. 122,600

Largest city: Portland, pop. 480,824

Industry: real estate, retail and wholesale trade, electronic equipment, health services, construction, forest products, business services

Agriculture: nursery stock, hay, cattle, grass seed, wheat, dairy products, potatoes

Statehood: February 14, 1859; 33rd state

Nickname: Beaver State

More about Oregon

■ Oregon produces about one-third of the country's softwood lumber and plywood.

■ More than 90 percent of Oregon's energy needs are met by hydroelectric power, mostly from dams on the Columbia River.

■ Local legends say that Sasquatch, an apelike creature also known as Bigfoot, roams in Oregon's Coast Ranges.

■ Crater Lake, in the Cascade Range, was formed when a volcano called Mount Mazama erupted and blew its top about 7,000 years ago.

■ Hundreds of sea lions find shelter in sea caves near Florence.

■ Explorers Lewis and Clark ended their long journey in 1805 at the mouth of the Columbia River.

Western Meadowlark
Oregon Grape

Map labels

TON
Lake Wallula
82
Milton-Freewater
COLD SPRINGS N.W.R.
Hermiston
WENAHA N.W.&S.R.
UMATILLA NATIONAL FOREST
UMATILLA INDIAN RESERVATION
Pendleton
McKAY CREEK N.W.R.
Heppner
UMATILLA NATIONAL FOREST
COLUMBIA
GRANDE RONDE N.W.&S.R.
Grande Ronde
Mountains
JOSEPH CREEK N.W.&S.R.
WALLOWA N.W.&S.R.
WALLOWA-WHITMAN NATIONAL FOREST
Wallowa
Snake
SNAKE NATIONAL WILD AND SCENIC RIVER
HELLS CANYON NATIONAL RECREATION AREA
IMNAHA N.W.&S.R.
Enterprise
LOSTINE N.W.&S.R.
La Grande
84
MINAM N.W.&S.R.
WALLOWA-WHITMAN NATIONAL FOREST
WALLOWA- WHITMAN NATIONAL FOREST
N. POWDER N.W.&S.R.
Powder
EAGLE CREEK N.W.&S.R.
JOHN DAY, NORTH FORK NATIONAL FOREST
POWDER N.W.&S.R.
Baker City
Brownlee Res.
Blue Mountains
John Day
MALHEUR NATIONAL FOREST
JOHN DAY, SOUTH FORK NATIONAL WILD AND SCENIC RIVER
MALHEUR, NORTH FORK N.W.&S.R.
Snake
MALHEUR N.W.&S.R.
MALHEUR NATIONAL FOREST
OREGON
N. Fk. Malheur
Ontario
IDAHO
OCHOCO NATIONAL FOREST
Malheur
Malheur
PLATEAU
Burns
Malheur
Owyhee
84
Harney Basin
Lake Owyhee
Harney Lake
Malheur Lake
MALHEUR N.W.R.
Snake
OWYHEE NATIONAL WILD AND SCENIC RIVER
Steens Mountain
GREAT
DONNER UND BLITZEN NATIONAL WILD AND SCENIC RIVER
Owyhee
HART MOUNTAIN NATIONAL ANTELOPE REFUGE
OWYHEE, NORTH FORK N.W.&S.R.
WEST LITTLE OWYHEE NATIONAL WILD AND SCENIC RIVER
BASIN
FORT McDERMITT I.R.
NEVADA

0 100 miles
0 100 kilometers
Albers Conic Equal-Area Projection

IDAHO

WYOMING

NEV.

COLO.

UTAH

GREAT BASIN

Raft River Mts.
SAWTOOTH N.F.
Spring Bay
Promontory
GOLDEN SPIKE N.H.S. (PROMONTORY)
First transcontinental railroad system completed in 1869

Great Salt Lake

Newfoundland Evaporation Basin

Great Salt Lake Desert

Wendover

Tremonton
Wellsville
Brigham City
North Ogden
Ogden
Layton
Clearfield
Farmington
Centerville
Bountiful
Salt Lake City
Murray
W. Jordan
Riverton
Sandy
Grantsville
Tooele
WASATCH-CACHE NATIONAL FOREST
SKULL VALLEY I.R.

Smithfield
Logan
Providence
WASATCH-CACHE NATIONAL FOREST
BEAR RIVER MIGRATORY BIRD REFUGE

Bear Lake

FLAMING GORGE NATIONAL RECREATIONAL AREA
Flaming Gorge Reservoir
Green

Green

DINOSAUR NATIONAL MONUMENT

White

Bitter Creek

East Tavaputs Plateau

Willow Creek

Hill Creek

Vernal
OURAY N.W.R.
UINTAH AND OURAY INDIAN RESERVATION

Uinta Mountains
Kings Peak 13,528 ft 4,123 m
Highest point in Utah
WASATCH-CACHE NATIONAL FOREST
ASHLEY NATIONAL FOREST

Roosevelt
UINTAH AND OURAY INDIAN RESERVATION
ASHLEY NATIONAL FOREST

Desolation Canyon
Roan Cliffs
Nine Mile Creek
Price

Helper
Price

Castle Dale
San Rafael

Green River
ARCHES NATIONAL PARK

Heber City
TIMPANOGOS CAVE NAT. MON.
UINTA NATIONAL FOREST
Orem
Springville
Provo
Utah Lake
Pleasant Grove
Lehi
Spanish Fork
Payson
Nephi
UINTA NATIONAL FOREST

Mount Pleasant
Moroni
Ephraim
Manti
MANTI-LA SAL NATIONAL FOREST

Delta
Sevier
Sevier Desert
Sevier Lake

Fillmore
Richfield
FISHLAKE NATIONAL FOREST

Confusion Range
GOSHUTE INDIAN RESERVATION
FISH SPRINGS N.W.R.

Beehive State

Utah

Utah has three main land regions: mountains, basins and ranges, and plateaus. The Wasatch and Uinta, ranges of the Rockies form an L in the northeast. To the west is a dry region of wide basins and low ranges. Salt Lake City is there, as is the Great Salt Lake, the remnant of an ancient lake almost the size of Lake Michigan.

Irrigation supports agriculture in the valley at the foot of the Wasatch Range. The Colorado Plateau, which includes Zion, Bryce, and other national parks, covers the rest of the state. This region is also where the mining of oil, natural gas, and uranium take place.

Utah's name comes from the Ute tribe, one of four groups that white explorers met when they reached the area in the 1700s. The state was settled in the mid-1800s by Mormons—members of the Church of Jesus Christ of Latter-day Saints. Mormons now make up almost three-fourths of the state's residents. They developed the state and have built many profitable businesses. Today, the federal government owns about two-thirds of Utah's land, providing jobs for many residents.

Area: 84,904 sq mi (219,902 sq km)

Population: 2,100,000

Capital: Salt Lake City, pop. 172,600

Largest city: Salt Lake City, pop. 172,600

Industry: government, manufacturing, real estate, construction, health services, business services, banking

Agriculture: cattle, dairy products, hay, poultry and eggs

Statehood: January 4, 1896; 45th state

Nickname: Beehive State

More about Utah

- The Great Salt Lake is the largest natural lake west of the Mississippi. The lake, which has a high level of evaporation, is about eight times saltier than the ocean.

- Moab, in the southeastern part of the state, is a center for outdoor sports, such as mountain biking and rock climbing.

- Utah has five national parks and seven national monuments.

- Bonneville Salt Flats International Speedway, in the Great Salt Lake Desert, is the site of races where drivers try to break land speed records.

The state's nickname comes from a beehive symbol that stands for the constant industry and activity of its Mormon residents.

Most of Utah's population lives at the foot of the Wasatch Range in a line of cities that stretches from Ogden to Provo.

California Gull
Sego Lily

N. MEX.
ARIZONA
COLORADO PLATEAU
NAVAJO INDIAN RESERVATION

Four Corners
Only spot in the U.S. where the borders of four states come together

Moab
Blanding
HOVENWEEP NAT. MON.
Monument Valley
RAINBOW BRIDGE NAT. MON.
NATURAL BRIDGES NAT. MON.
San Juan
GLEN CANYON NATIONAL RECREATION AREA
Lake Powell
Escalante
Halls Creek
Bullfrog Creek
Henry Mts.
Dirty Devil
Fremont
Colorado
Green
CANYONLANDS NATIONAL PARK
MANTI-LA SAL NATIONAL FOREST
CAPITOL REEF NATIONAL PARK
GRAND STAIRCASE-ESCALANTE NATIONAL MONUMENT
DIXIE NATIONAL FOREST
Paria
Kanab
Kanab Creek
Virgin
Sevier
Otter Creek Reservoir
Panguitch
BRYCE CANYON NATIONAL PARK
DIXIE NATIONAL FOREST
Little Salt Lake
Beaver
Milford
FISHLAKE NATIONAL FOREST
Piute Res.
CEDAR BREAKS NAT. MON.
Cedar City
ZION NATIONAL PARK
Hurricane
St. George
Santa Clara
DIXIE NATIONAL FOREST
Wah Wah Mts.

0   100 miles
0   100 kilometers
Albers Conic Equal-Area Projection

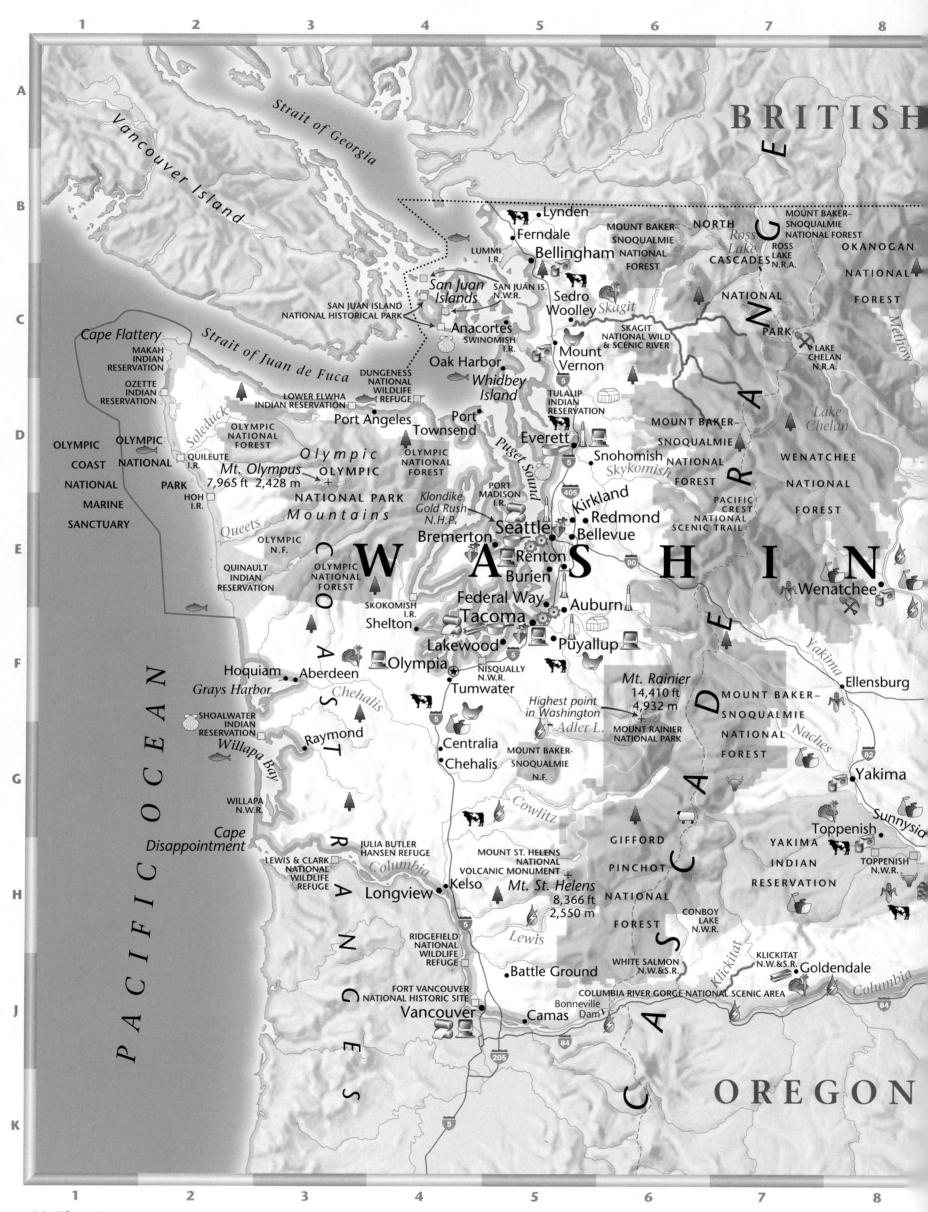

Strait of Georgia

Vancouver Island

B R I T I S H

Cape Flattery

Strait of Juan de Fuca

MAKAH
INDIAN
RESERVATION

OZETTE
INDIAN
RESERVATION

OLYMPIC
COAST
NATIONAL
MARINE
SANCTUARY

QUILEUTE
I.R.

HOH
I.R.

OLYMPIC
NATIONAL
PARK

Mt. Olympus
7,965 ft 2,428 m

Soleduck

OLYMPIC
NATIONAL
FOREST

Olympic

OLYMPIC

NATIONAL PARK

Mountains

Queets

OLYMPIC N.F.

QUINAULT
INDIAN
RESERVATION

OLYMPIC
NATIONAL
FOREST

Port Angeles

LOWER ELWHA
INDIAN RESERVATION

DUNGENESS
NATIONAL
WILDLIFE
REFUGE

Port
Townsend

OLYMPIC
NATIONAL
FOREST

Lynden
Ferndale
Bellingham

LUMMI
I.R.

San Juan
Islands

SAN JUAN IS.
N.W.R.

SAN JUAN ISLAND
NATIONAL HISTORICAL PARK

Anacortes

SWINOMISH
I.R.

Oak Harbor

Whidbey
Island

Sedro
Woolley

Mount
Vernon

Skagit

SKAGIT
NATIONAL WILD
& SCENIC RIVER

MOUNT BAKER–
SNOQUALMIE
NATIONAL
FOREST

NORTH

CASCADES

NATIONAL

PARK

Ross
Lake

ROSS
LAKE
N.R.A.

MOUNT BAKER–
SNOQUALMIE
NATIONAL FOREST

OKANOGAN

NATIONAL

FOREST

Lake Chelan
N.R.A.

Methow

TULALIP
INDIAN
RESERVATION

Everett

Snohomish

Skykomish

MOUNT BAKER–
SNOQUALMIE
NATIONAL
FOREST

Lake
Chelan

WENATCHEE

NATIONAL

FOREST

PORT
MADISON
I.R.

Klondike
Gold Rush
N.H.P.

Kirkland

Redmond

PACIFIC
CREST
NATIONAL
SCENIC TRAIL

W A S H I N

C
O
A
S
T

Seattle

Bremerton

Renton

Burien

Bellevue

Puget Sound

Federal Way

SKOKOMISH
I.R.

Shelton

Tacoma

Lakewood

Auburn

Puyallup

Wenatchee

Olympia

Hoquiam
Aberdeen

Grays Harbor

SHOALWATER
INDIAN
RESERVATION

Willapa Bay

Raymond

WILLAPA
N.W.R.

R A N G E S

Chehalis

Tumwater

NISQUALLY
N.W.R.

Centralia

Chehalis

MOUNT BAKER–
SNOQUALMIE
N.F.

Mt. Rainier
14,410 ft
4,932 m

Highest point
in Washington

Adler L.

MOUNT RAINIER
NATIONAL PARK

Yakima

Ellensburg

MOUNT BAKER–
SNOQUALMIE

NATIONAL

FOREST

Naches

Yakima

C A S C A D E

Cowlitz

Cape
Disappointment

JULIA BUTLER
HANSEN REFUGE

LEWIS & CLARK
NATIONAL
WILDLIFE
REFUGE

Columbia

Longview

Kelso

MOUNT ST. HELENS
NATIONAL
VOLCANIC MONUMENT

Mt. St. Helens
8,366 ft
2,550 m

GIFFORD

PINCHOT

NATIONAL

FOREST

Lewis

CONBOY
LAKE
N.W.R.

Toppenish

YAKIMA

INDIAN

RESERVATION

TOPPENISH
N.W.R.

Sunnysia

RIDGEFIELD
NATIONAL
WILDLIFE
REFUGE

Battle Ground

FORT VANCOUVER
NATIONAL HISTORIC SITE

Vancouver

Camas

Bonneville
Dam

WHITE SALMON
N.W.&S.R.

Klickitat

COLUMBIA RIVER GORGE NATIONAL SCENIC AREA

KLICKITAT
N.W.&S.R.

Goldendale

Columbia

O R E G O N

PACIFIC OCEAN

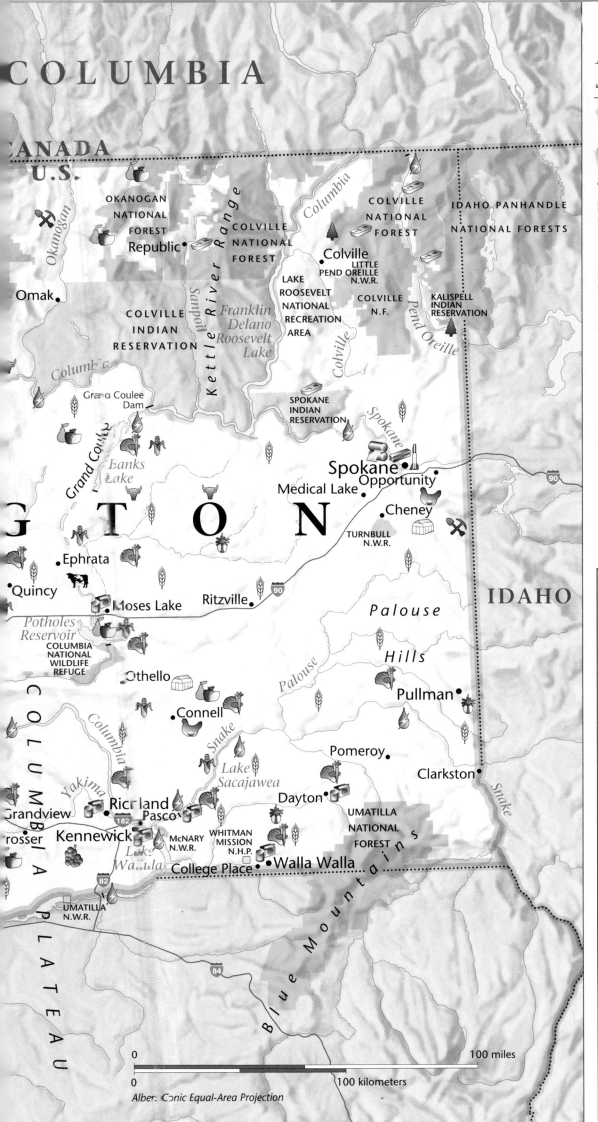

*Evergreen
State*

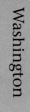

Washington

Washington has some of the wettest—
and driest—weather in the nation.
The volcanic Cascade Range separates wet
from dry in the state. Along the coast the
temperate rain forests of the Olympic
Peninsula receive more than 200 inches
(508 cm) of rain a year. Rain also soaks
Seattle and the whole Puget Sound area.
Nevertheless, this is where more than half
the population lives. People here work in
shipping and transportation, food processing,
computer software, and many other fields.

Wet western slopes support stands of
Douglas fir and other timber trees. At the
southern end of the Cascades rises Mount
St. Helens, a volcano that erupted with a huge
blast in 1980, killing 57 people and causing
billions of dollars in property damage.

To the east, blocked from moist winds by
the Cascades, the dry Columbia Plateau is
nourished by the Columbia and other rivers
that generate hydroelectric power and supply
water for irrigation. Wheat, hops, apples, and
other fruits thrive in eastern Washington.

Area: 70,637 sq mi (182,949 sq km)	
Population: 5,689,000	
Capital: Olympia, pop. 39,000	

Largest city: Seattle, pop. 524,700

Industry: aerospace, tourism, food processing,
forest products, paper products, industrial
machinery, printing and publishing, metals

Agriculture: seafood, apples, dairy products,
wheat, cattle, potatoes, hay

Statehood: November 11, 1889; 42nd state

Nickname: Evergreen State

More about Washington

■ *The Grand Coulee Dam, on the Columbia
River near Spokane, is the biggest producer
of hydroelectric power in North America.*

■ *The icy crags of Mount Rainier were used
in training the first U.S. team to climb Mount
Everest successfully.*

■ *The greatest snowfall in North America was
recorded at Rainier Paradise Ranger Station from
July 1971 to June 1972. A total of 1,122 inches,
or almost 95 feet (29 m), of snow fell during
that period.*

■ *Washington is the leading
producer of apples in the
United States.*

■ *Seattle is named
for Chief Sealth, a
Duwamish Indian.*

American Goldfinch
Coast Rhododendron

The Territories

Across Two Seas

Ranging from rocks inhabited only by seabirds to a land of almost four million people, the 13 U.S. territories in the Caribbean Sea and the Pacific Ocean include thousands of islands. Listed below are the five largest in size and population, beginning with Puerto Rico.

Caribbean Territories

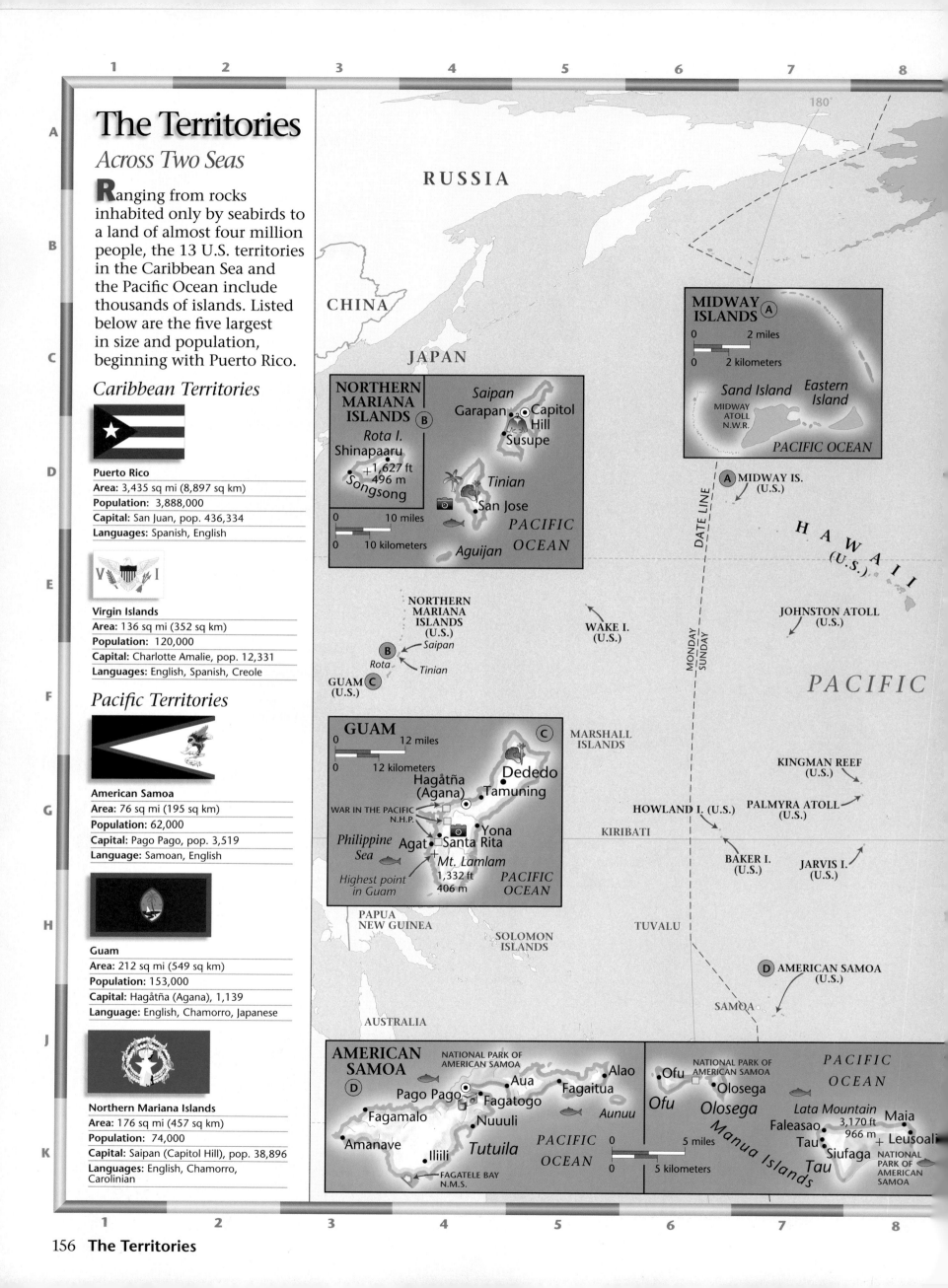

Puerto Rico

Area: 3,435 sq mi (8,897 sq km)

Population: 3,888,000

Capital: San Juan, pop. 436,334

Languages: Spanish, English

Virgin Islands

Area: 136 sq mi (352 sq km)

Population: 120,000

Capital: Charlotte Amalie, pop. 12,331

Languages: English, Spanish, Creole

Pacific Territories

American Samoa

Area: 76 sq mi (195 sq km)

Population: 62,000

Capital: Pago Pago, pop. 3,519

Language: Samoan, English

Guam

Area: 212 sq mi (549 sq km)

Population: 153,000

Capital: Hagåtña (Agana), 1,139

Language: English, Chamorro, Japanese

Northern Mariana Islands

Area: 176 sq mi (457 sq km)

Population: 74,000

Capital: Saipan (Capitol Hill), pop. 38,896

Languages: English, Chamorro, Carolinian

RUSSIA

CHINA

JAPAN

MIDWAY ISLANDS Ⓐ

0 — 2 miles

0 — 2 kilometers

Sand Island — Eastern Island

MIDWAY ATOLL N.W.R.

PACIFIC OCEAN

NORTHERN MARIANA ISLANDS Ⓑ

Saipan
Garapan — Capitol Hill
Susupe

Rota I.
Shinapaaru

+1,627 ft 496 m

Songsong

Tinian
San Jose

0 — 10 miles

0 — 10 kilometers

Aguijan

PACIFIC OCEAN

NORTHERN MARIANA ISLANDS (U.S.)
Saipan

Rota Ⓑ — Tinian

GUAM Ⓒ (U.S.)

GUAM Ⓒ

0 — 12 miles

0 — 12 kilometers

Dededo

Hagåtña (Agana) — Tamuning

WAR IN THE PACIFIC N.H.P.

Philippine Sea

Agat — Yona
Santa Rita

Mt. Lamlam
1,332 ft 406 m

Highest point in Guam

PACIFIC OCEAN

PAPUA NEW GUINEA

SOLOMON ISLANDS

AUSTRALIA

180°

DATE LINE

MONDAY SUNDAY

Ⓐ MIDWAY IS. (U.S.)

H A W A I I (U.S.)

JOHNSTON ATOLL (U.S.)

WAKE I. (U.S.)

MARSHALL ISLANDS

PACIFIC

KINGMAN REEF (U.S.)

HOWLAND I. (U.S.)

PALMYRA ATOLL (U.S.)

KIRIBATI

BAKER I. (U.S.)

JARVIS I. (U.S.)

TUVALU

Ⓓ AMERICAN SAMOA (U.S.)

SAMOA

AMERICAN SAMOA Ⓓ

NATIONAL PARK OF AMERICAN SAMOA

Alao
Aua
Fagaitua
Pago Pago
Fagatogo
Fagamalo
Nuuuli
Aunuu
Amanave
Iliili
Tutuila
FAGATELE BAY N.M.S.

PACIFIC OCEAN

NATIONAL PARK OF AMERICAN SAMOA

Ofu
Olosega

Ofu
Olosega

Manua Islands

Lata Mountain
Faleasao
3,170 ft 966 m
Tau
Siufaga
Tau

Maia
Leusoali

NATIONAL PARK OF AMERICAN SAMOA

PACIFIC OCEAN

0 — 5 miles

0 — 5 kilometers

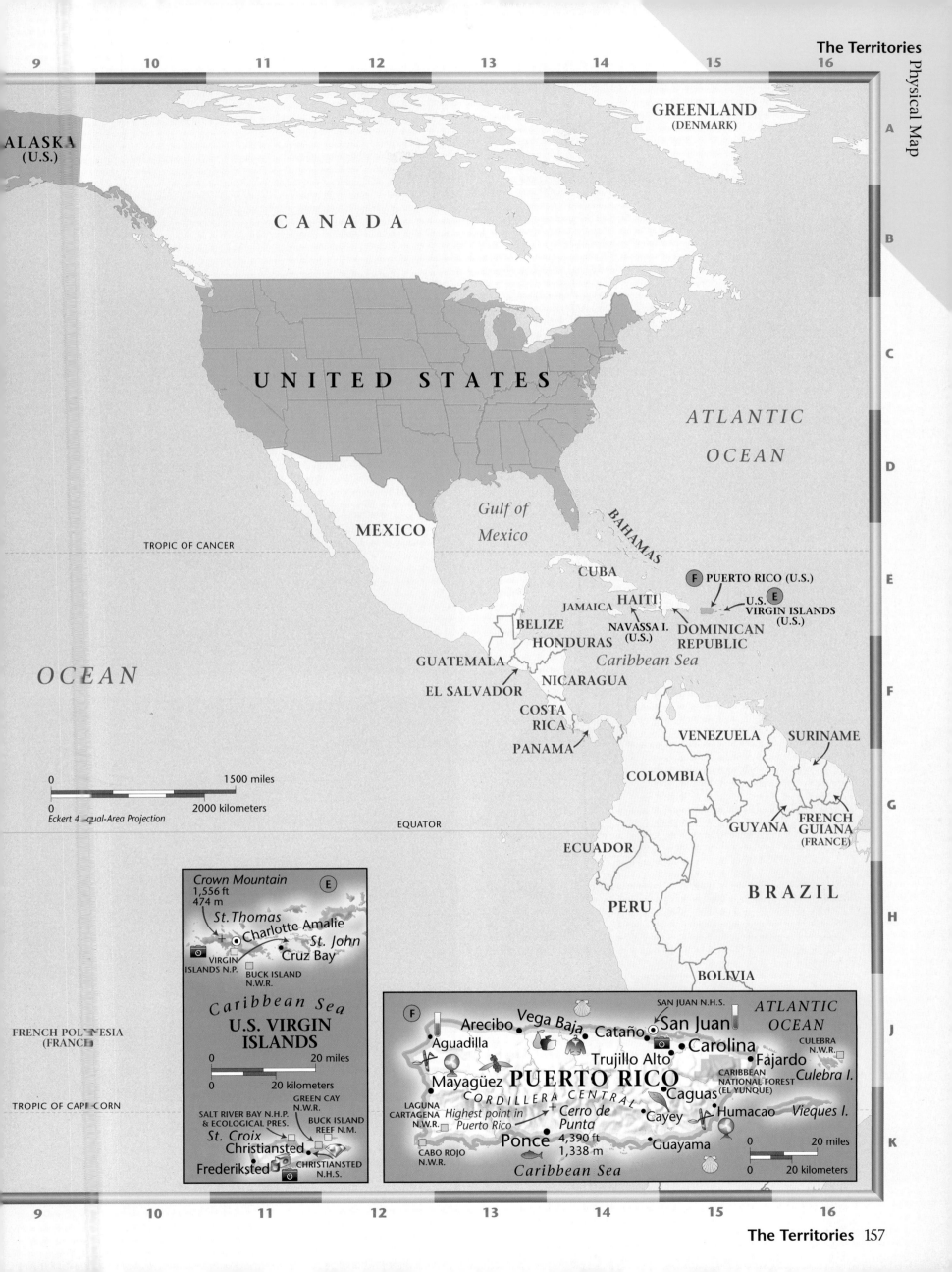

ALASKA
(U.S.)

GREENLAND
(DENMARK)

CANADA

UNITED STATES

ATLANTIC

OCEAN

Gulf of
Mexico

MEXICO

TROPIC OF CANCER

BAHAMAS

CUBA

F PUERTO RICO (U.S.)

HAITI

JAMAICA

U.S.
E VIRGIN ISLANDS
(U.S.)

NAVASSA I.
(U.S.)

DOMINICAN
REPUBLIC

BELIZE

HONDURAS

Caribbean Sea

OCEAN

GUATEMALA

NICARAGUA

EL SALVADOR

COSTA
RICA

VENEZUELA

SURINAME

PANAMA

COLOMBIA

GUYANA

FRENCH
GUIANA
(FRANCE)

0   1500 miles

0   2000 kilometers

Eckert 4 Equal-Area Projection

EQUATOR

ECUADOR

BRAZIL

PERU

BOLIVIA

Crown Mountain
1,556 ft
474 m   E

St. Thomas

Charlotte Amalie

St. John

VIRGIN
ISLANDS N.P.

Cruz Bay

BUCK ISLAND
N.W.R.

FRENCH POLYNESIA
(FRANCE)

Caribbean Sea
U.S. VIRGIN
ISLANDS

0   20 miles

0   20 kilometers

TROPIC OF CAPRICORN

GREEN CAY
N.W.R.

SALT RIVER BAY N.H.P.
& ECOLOGICAL PRES.

BUCK ISLAND
REEF N.M.

St. Croix

Christiansted

Frederiksted

CHRISTIANSTED
N.H.S.

SAN JUAN N.H.S.

ATLANTIC
OCEAN

F

Arecibo   Vega Baja   Cataño   San Juan

Aguadilla

Carolina

CULEBRA
N.W.R.

Trujillo Alto

Fajardo

Mayagüez   PUERTO RICO

CORDILLERA CENTRAL

CARIBBEAN
NATIONAL FOREST
(EL YUNQUE)

Culebra I.

Caguas

LAGUNA
CARTAGENA
N.W.R.

Highest point in
Puerto Rico

Cerro de
Punta

Cayey

Humacao

Vieques I.

Ponce

4,390 ft
1,338 m

Guayama

0   20 miles

0   20 kilometers

CABO ROJO
N.W.R.

Caribbean Sea

9   10   11   12   13   14   15   16

The Territories
Islands in the Family

More than 2,300 islands and islets, scattered across the Pacific Ocean and the Caribbean Sea, make up the 13 territories of the United States. These islands are not states, but they are associated with the U.S. in various ways. The five largest inhabited island territories have their own governments but receive economic and military help from the United States. Residents of these territories—except American Samoa—are U.S. citizens.

Puerto Rico is the largest territory. Three times citizens of this Caribbean island have voted on—and rejected—the idea of becoming the 51st state, in part because keeping their commonwealth status means they do not have to pay federal income taxes. The Caribbean also includes the U.S. Virgin Islands, acquired from Denmark in 1917 for strategic reasons.

Some Pacific territories were battle sites in World War II. The U.S. military still owns much of Guam. American Samoa and the Northern Marianas keep much of their traditional Polynesian culture.

▼ **A POLYNESIAN BOY** *shows off a sea turtle, flippered inhabitant of the South Pacific. Polynesians settled American Samoa.*

▶ **TURQUOISE WATERS** *ring the Midway Islands. Midway and eight other territories are administered by various departments of the U.S. government.*

▲ **LUSH BROMELIADS** *and other tropical plants thrive in the El Yunque rain forest in Puerto Rico. All U.S. territories except the Midway Islands lie in the tropical zone.*

▶ **A DIVER** *checks out life on a coral reef in the intense blue waters of the Caribbean. Excellent diving and snorkeling lure many tourists to territories in the Caribbean and Pacific.*

▲ **AN ABANDONED** *sugar mill is one of many that dot the countryside throughout the Caribbean. Cultivation and processing of sugarcane was once the area's main source of income.*

▼ **TWINKLING LIGHTS** *of a cruise ship sparkle in the harbor at Charlotte Amalie, the capital of the U.S. Virgin Islands. Tourism brings in about 70 percent of the territory's income.*

▶ **PALM-FRINGED** *beaches, such as these around Trunk Bay on St. John in the Virgin Islands, offer vacationers a year-round haven in many territories.*

▼ **SMILING FACES** *of Virgin Islands children reflect the varied African and European backgrounds of Caribbean peoples.*

Facts & Figures

Top States

Listed below are major farm products, fish, and minerals and the states that currently lead in their production. Following each list is a ranking of the top states in each category.

Farm Products

Cattle and calves: Texas, Nebraska, Kansas, Colorado
Dairy products: California, Wisconsin, New York, Pennsylvania
Soybeans: Iowa, Illinois, Minnesota, Indiana
Corn for grain: Iowa, Illinois, Nebraska, Minnesota
Hogs and pigs: Iowa, North Carolina, Minnesota, Illinois
Broiler chickens: Arkansas, Georgia, Alabama, North Carolina
Wheat: Kansas, North Dakota, Montana, Washington
Cotton: Texas, California, Mississippi, Georgia
Eggs: Georgia, Ohio, California, Pennsylvania
Hay: Texas, California, South Dakota, Nebraska
Tobacco: North Carolina, Kentucky, Tennessee, South Carolina
Turkeys: North Carolina, Minnesota, Missouri, Virginia
Oranges: Florida, California, Texas, Arizona
Potatoes: Idaho, Washington, Wisconsin, Colorado
Grapes: California, Washington, New York, Oregon
Tomatoes: Florida, California, Virginia, Tennessee
Rice: Arkansas, California, Louisiana, Texas

Top Ten in Farm Products
1. California
2. Texas
3. Iowa
4. Nebraska
5. Kansas
6. Illinois
7. Minnesota
8. North Carolina
9. Florida
10. Wisconsin

Fish

Shrimp: Texas, Louisiana, Florida, Alabama
Crabs: Alaska, North Carolina, Maryland, Louisiana
Lobsters: Maine, Massachusetts, New York, Florida
Salmon: Alaska, Washington, California, Oregon
Pollock: Alaska

Top Five in Fisheries
1. Alaska
2. Texas
3. Louisiana
4. Maine
5. Florida

Minerals

Crude oil: Alaska, Texas, California, Louisiana
Natural gas: Texas, Louisiana, Oklahoma, New Mexico
Coal: Wyoming, West Virginia, Kentucky, Pennsylvania
Crushed stone: Pennsylvania, Texas, Ohio, Florida
Copper: Arizona, Utah, New Mexico, Nevada
Cement: California, Texas, Pennsylvania, Missouri
Construction sand and gravel: California, Texas, Ohio, Michigan
Gold: Nevada, California, Arizona, Montana
Iron ore: Minnesota, Michigan
Clay: Georgia, North Carolina, Wyoming, Ohio
Phosphate rock: Florida, North Carolina, Idaho, Utah
Lime: Ohio, Alabama, Pennsylvania, Texas
Salt: Louisiana, Texas, New York, Kansas
Sulfur: Louisiana, Texas

Top Ten in Minerals
1. Texas
2. Louisiana
3. Oklahoma
4. New Mexico
5. Alaska
6. California
7. Wyoming
8. West Virginia
9. Kentucky
10. Pennsylvania

Extremes

World's Rainiest Spot
Waialeale (mountain), Hawaii: average annual rainfall 460 in (1,168 cm)

World's Strongest Surface Wind
231 mph (372 kmph), Mount Washington, New Hampshire, April 12, 1934

World's Oldest Living Tree
Methuselah bristlecone pine, California; about 4,700 years old

World's Tallest Living Tree
The "Mendocino Tree," a coast redwood at Montgomery State Reserve in California, 367.5 ft (112 m) high

World's Largest Gorge
Grand Canyon, Arizona; 290 mi (466 km) long, 600 ft to 18 mi (183 m to 29 km) wide, 1 miles (1.6 km) deep

Highest Temperature in U.S.
134°F (56.6°C), Death Valley, California, July 10, 1913

Lowest Temperature in U.S.
Minus 80°F (-62.2°C) at Prospect Creek, Alaska, January 23, 1971

Highest Point in U.S.
Mount McKinley (Denali), Alaska; 20,323 feet (6,194 m)

Lowest Point in U.S.
Death Valley, California; 282 feet (86 m) below sea level

Longest River System in U.S.
Mississippi-Missouri; 3,708 mi (5,971 km) long

Largest U.S. Metropolitan Areas
A metropolitan area is a city and its surrounding suburban areas.

1. New York, pop. 19,938,492
2. Los Angeles, pop. 15,495,155
3. Chicago, pop. 8,599,774
4. Washington, D.C., pop. 7,164,519
5. San Francisco, pop. 6,605,428
6. Philadelphia, pop. 5,973,463
7. Boston, pop. 5,563,475
8. Detroit, pop. 5,284,171
9. Dallas, pop. 4,574,561
10. Houston, pop. 4,253,428

Glossary

bog a poorly drained area, often a kettle hole, with wet, spongy ground; usually found in cool, northern climates

bromeliad one of a family of tropical plants that grows in trees and gets nutrients from the air rather than soil

butte a high, steep-sided rock formation created by the erosion of a mesa

canal an artificial waterway that is used by ships or to carry water for irrigation

city in the U.S., usually a populated place of at least 2,500 people who work in jobs requiring various skills

continental divide an elevated area that separates rivers flowing toward opposite sides of a continent; in the U.S. this divide follows the crest of the Rocky Mountains

copra dried coconut meat from which oil is extracted to make a variety of products, including soap, candles, and cosmetics; an important export of Pacific islands

delta lowland formed by silt, sand, and gravel deposited by a river at its mouth

elevation distance above sea level, usually measured in feet or meters

fork in a river, the place where two streams come together

glacier a large, slow-moving mass of ice

gorge a deep, narrow valley with very steep sides that is usually shorter and narrower than a canyon

ice age a very long period of cold climate when glaciers often cover large areas of land; with initial capital letters, the term refers to the most recent, or Pleistocene, ice age

intermittent lake a body of water whose surface area varies with the amount of precipitation or runoff

intermittent river a stream that flows only part of the time, usually after heavy rain or snowmelt

kettle hole a glacier-created depression that contains groundwater or rainwater

lava molten rock from Earth's interior that flows out on the surface through a deep crack or during volcanic activity

mesa an eroded plateau, broader than it is high, that is found in arid or semiarid regions

metropolitan area a city and its surrounding suburbs or communities

nursery stock young plants, including fruits, vegetables, shrubs, and trees, raised in a greenhouse or nursery

plain a large area of relatively flat land that is often covered with grasses

plateau a relatively flat area, larger than a mesa, that rises above the surrounding landscape

population density the number of people living on each square mile or kilometer of a specific land area (calculated by dividing population by land area)

Richter scale a means of ranking the power of an earthquake; the higher the number, the stronger the quake

scale on a map, a means of explaining the relationship between distances on the map and actual distances on the Earth's surface

swamp wetlands where trees are the dominant vegetation

territory land that is under the jurisdiction of a country but that is not a state or a province

tropical zone the area bounded by the Tropic of Cancer and the Tropic of Capricorn where it is usually warm year-round

wetland land that is either covered with or saturated by water; includes swamps, marshes, and bogs

Abbreviations

(See also page 6)

Br.	Branch
Cr.	Creek
°C	degrees Celsius
E.	East
°F	degrees Fahrenheit
Fk.	Fork
ft	feet
Ft.	Fort
I(s).	Island(s)
km	kilometers
L.	Lake
m	meters
mi	miles
Mt(s).	Mountain(s) or Mount(s)
Nat.	National
N.	North
Pk.	Peak
Pres.	Preserve
Pt.	Point
R.	River
Sprs.	Springs
sq km	square kilometers
sq mi	square miles
St(e).	Saint(e)
Str(s).	Strait(s)
W.	West

Two-Letter State Abbreviations

Alabama	AL
Alaska	AK
Arizona	AZ
Arkansas	AR
California	CA
Colorado	CO
Connecticut	CT
Delaware	DE
Florida	FL
Georgia	GA
Hawaii	HI
Idaho	ID
Illinois	IL
Indiana	IN
Iowa	IA
Kansas	KS
Kentucky	KY
Louisiana	LA
Maine	ME
Maryland	MD
Massachusetts	MA
Michigan	MI
Minnesota	MN
Mississippi	MS
Missouri	MO
Montana	MT
Nebraska	NE
Nevada	NV
New Hampshire	NH
New Jersey	NJ
New Mexico	NM
New York	NY
North Carolina	NC
North Dakota	ND
Ohio	OH
Oklahoma	OK
Oregon	OR
Pennsylvania	PA
Rhode Island	RI
South Carolina	SC
South Dakota	SD
Tennessee	TN
Texas	TX
Utah	UT
Vermont	VT
Virginia	VA
Washington	WA
West Virginia	WV
Wisconsin	WI
Wyoming	WY

Web sites

For the 50 states:

For each of the 50 states the address is the same except for inserting the state's standard, two-letter postal abbreviation (listed above) into the Web address. For example, Alabama's address is **http://www.state.al.us**

For D.C. and the Territories:

Washington, D.C.: **http://dcpages.ari.net**
American Samoa: **www.samoanet.com**
Guam: **www.gov.gu/index.html**
Northern Marianas: **www.saipan.com/gov**
Puerto Rico: **www.prstar.net**
U.S. Virgin Islands: **www.gov.vi**

Index

Map references are in boldface (**50**) type. Letters and numbers following in lightface (D12) locate the place-names using the map grid. Illustrations appear in italic (*140*); type and text references are in lightface. The key to state abbreviations is on page 161.

A

Abbeville, AL **61** J9
Abbeville, LA **70** H6
Abbeville, SC **76** D3
Aberdeen, MD **39** B12
Aberdeen, MS **72** H4
Aberdeen, SD **111** C10
Aberdeen, WA **152** F3
Abert, Lake, OR **148** H8
Abilene, KS 97, **97** D9
Abilene, TX **126** E7
Abingdon, VA **80** J4
Absaroka Range (mountains) **144** H7, **154** A3
Absecon, NJ **45** G13
Acadia N.P., ME 37, **37** G10
Ada, OK **125** F12
Adak Island, AK **135** K10
Adak Naval Station, AK **135** K10
Adams, MA **40** B3
Adamsville, RI **50** J8
Adel, GA **67** E10
Adirondack Mountains, NY *26–27*, **28** E7, **46** C8, 47
Adirondack Park, NY 47, **47** D9
Adler Lake, WA **152** G5
Admiralty Island Nat. Mon., AK **135** H12
Adrian, MI **99** H12
Afognak Island, AK **134** H7
Afton, WY **154** F2
Agat, Guam **156** G4
Agate Fossil Beds Nat. Mon., NE **104** D2
Agattu Island, AK **134** J7
Agawam, MA **40** E5
Agua Fria (river), AZ **120** E8
Aguadilla, Puerto Rico **157** J13
Aguijan (island), Northern Mariana Islands **156** E4
Ahoskie, NC **75** B13
Aiken, SC **76** F5
Ainsworth, NE **104** D7
Aitkin, MN **100** E6
Ajo, AZ **121** D10
Akron, CO **139** C11
Akron, OH **108** H4, 109
Alabama (river), AL **56** F7, **60** F8
Alabama (state) **56** E7, **60–61**
Alabaster, AL **60** E5
Alagnak Wild River, AK **134** G5
Alamogordo, NM **123** F9
Alamosa (river), CO **138** J6
Alamosa, CO **138** J6
Alao, American Samoa **156** J5
Alapaha (river), GA **67** F10
Alaska (state) *132–133*,**134–135**, **157** A9
Alaska Highway **135** F10
Alaska Peninsula, AK **134** J4
Alaska Range, AK **134** F7
Alatna Wild River, AK **134** C7
Albany, GA **67** D9
Albany, KY **69** J10
Albany, NY 47, **47** F10
Albany, OR **148** D3
Albemarle Sound, NC **57** C12, **75** C14
Albemarle, NC **74** D8
Albert Lea, MN **101** E11
Albertville, AL **60** G3
Albion, MI **99** G11
Albion, NE **105** E9
Albuquerque, NM **122** E5, 123
Alburg, VT **52** B1
Alenuihaha Channel, HI **141** F10
Aleutian Islands, AK **134** J1, 135, J7
Alexander Archipelago, AK **135** H11
Alexander City, AL **60** G6
Alexandria, IN **92** G5
Alexandria, LA **70** E5
Alexandria, MN **100** C7
Alexandria, SD **111** G11
Alexandria, VA **81** D13
Algoma, WI **112** J7
Algona, IA **94** C6
Alibates Flint Quarries Nat. Mon., TX **126** B6
Alice, TX **126** J8
Aliceville, AL **60** C6
Aliquippa, PA **48** F1
Allagash (river), ME **29** B11, **36** E3
Allagash Lake, ME **36** D4
Allagash Wilderness Waterway **36** D4
Allagash, ME **36** E2
Allatoona Lake, GA **66** C4
Allegheny (river), PA **28** G4, **46** H1, **48** F3
Allegheny Mountains **28** J4, **38** E1, **48** J4, **57** C9, **80** H5, **82** K4
Allegheny N.F., PA **48** C4
Allegheny N.W.&S.R., PA **48** C3
Allegheny Reservoir, PA **48** B4
Allendale, SC **76** G6
Allenton, RI **50** E8
Allentown, PA **49** F12
Alliance, NE **104** D3
Alliance, OH **108** J5
Alligator (river), NC **75** D15
Alma, MI **99** G9
Alma, NE **104** H7
Alpena, MI **98** J7
Alpine, TX **126** F4
Altamaha (river), GA **67** G9
Altamont, OR **148** J5
Altavista, VA **81** H9
Alton Bay, NH **43** H12
Alton, IL **91** D9
Altoona, PA **48** F5
Altoona, WI **112** C7
Alturas, CA **136** D2
Altus, Lake, OK **124** F7
Altus, OK **124** F7
Alva, OK **125** B9
Amana Colonies, IA **95** F10
Amanave, American Samoa **156** K3
Amarillo, TX **126** B5
Amchitka Island, AK **134** K8
American Falls Reservoir, ID **143** G13
American Falls, ID **143** G14
American N.W.&S.R., CA **136** D5
American Samoa **156** J7, 158
American, North Fork N.W.&S.R., CA **136** D5
Americus, GA **66** C8
Ames, IA **94** E7
Amesbury, MA **41** A12
Amherst, MA **40** D5
Amherst, NY **46** E2
Amistad Reservoir, TX **117** G9, **126** G6
Amite, LA **71** F9
Amlia Island, AK **135** K11
Ammonoosuc (river), NH **42** G7
Amory, MS **72** H4
Amsterdam, NY **47** E9
Anaconda, MT **144** G4
Anacortes, WA **152** C5
Anadarko, OK **125** E9
Anaheim, CA **137** G11
Anamosa, IA **95** E11
Anchorage, AK **134** F7, 135
Andalusia, AL **61** F10
Anderson Ranch Res., ID **143** D12
Anderson, IN **92** G6
Anderson, SC **76** C3
Andreafsky N.W.&S.R., AK **134** E4
Andreanof Islands, AK **135** K9
Andrews, TX **126** E5
Androscoggin (river), **37** B10, **42** H5
Angeles N. F., CA **137** F10
Angelina N.F., TX **127** F11
Angola, IN **92** H1
Aniak, AK **134** F5
Aniakchak Nat. Mon. & Preserve, AK **134** H5
Aniakchak Wild River, AK **134** J5
Ankeny, IA **94** F7
Ann Arbor, MI **99** H11
Anna, IL **91** F12
Anna, Lake, VA **81** F12
Annapolis, MD 38, **39** E11
Anniston, AL **60** G4
Ansonia, CT **32** G5
Anthony, KS **96** H7
Anthony, NM **123** E11
Anthony, RI **50** E6
Antigo, WI **112** G6
Antlers, OK **125** G14
Antrim, NH **43** E14
Apache N.F., AZ **122** A7
Apache N.F., NM **122** A7
Apache-Sitgreaves N.F., AZ **120** G6, J7
Apalachicola (river), FL **64** B6
Apalachicola N.F., FL **64** B6
Apishapa (river), CO **139** H9
Apostle Islands, WI **112** E2
Appalachian Mountains 9, **28–29** H5, **29**, **36** A9, **38** F3, **42** A10, **46** J6, **48** J5, **53** A11, **56–57** E8, *58*, **60** F4, **66** A3, 68, **69** K12, **74** E1, **79** G9, **80** J4, **82** K7
Appalachian N.S.T. **32** C3, **36** D7, 37, **38** E5, **40** E2, **42** J4, **44** H2, **47** E11, **48–49** F9, **53** D10, **66** E1, 67, **74** B5, **79** E13, **80** K4, **83** F11
Appalachian Plateau **28** H3
Apple (river), WI **112** A6
Appleton, WI **112** H8
Appomattox (river), VA **81** G11
Appomattox Court House N.H.P., VA **81** G10
Appomattox, VA 80, **81** H10
Arapaho N.F., CO **138** C5, D6
Arbuckle Mountains, OK **125** G11
Arcadia, FL **65** F11
Archbald, PA **49** C12
Arches N.P., UT **150** J8
Arco, ID **143** G12
Ardmore, OK **125** G11
Arecibo, Puerto Rico **157** J13
Arikaree (river), CO **139** D11
Arizona (state) **116** C2, **120–121**
Arkabutla Lake , MS **72** E2
Arkadelphia, AR **62** G5
Arkansas 62–63
Arkansas (river) **56** D3, **62** D3, 63, **86** H4, **96** F1, **117** B12, **125** A11, **131** G11, **138** F6
Arkansas (state) **56** D4, **62–63**
Arkansas City, KS **97** H9
Arlington Heights, IL **90** H2
Arlington, TX **127** D9
Arlington, VT *30*, **53** B14
Arlington, VA **81** D13
Armour, SD **111** H10
Armstrong, Louis 71
Aroostook (river), ME **36** F4
Arroyo del Macho (river), NM **122** F8
Artesia, NM **123** H9
Arvada, CO **138** D8
Arvon, Mount, MI **98** C4
Asbury Park, NJ **44** K8
Ash Lawn-Highland, VA **81** F10
Ashaway, RI **51** B10
Ashdown, AR **62** H3
Asheboro, NC **75** D9
Asheville, NC 74, **74** D4
Ashland, KY **69** E15
Ashland, ME **36** G3
Ashland, NE **105** F11
Ashland, NH **43** F10
Ashland, OH **108** F5
Ashland, OR **148** J4
Ashland, VA **81** G12
Ashland, WI **112** D3
Ashley N.F., UT **150** H4, F6
Ashley, ND **107** J9
Ashtabula, Lake, ND **107** F11
Ashtabula, OH **108** J2
Ashton, RI **50** F2
Ashuelot (river), NH **43** C15
Ashwaubenon, WI **112** H8
Aspen, CO **138** E5, 139
Assateague Island National Seashore, MD **39** H16, **81** F16
Assateague Island, MD **39** J16
Assawoman Canal, DE **35** H15
Assawompset Pond, MA **41** G12
Astoria, OR **148** A3
Atascadero, CA **137** D9
Atchafalaya (river), LA **70** G7
Atchafalaya Bay, LA *54–55*, **56** G5, **70** J7
Atchison, KS **97** C12
Athens, AL **60** E1
Athens, GA **66** E4
Athens, OH **109** G9
Athens, TN **79** D11
Athol, MA **40** B6
Atka Island, AK **135** K11
Atkinson, NE **104** D8
Atkinson, NH **43** H15
Atlanta, GA *59*, **66** C5, 67
Atlantic City Expressway, NJ **45** F11
Atlantic City, NJ 44, **45** H13
Atlantic, IA **94** G4
Atmore, AL **61** D11
Atoka, OK **125** G13
Attleboro, MA **41** F10
Attu (island), AK 135
Attu Island, AK **134** J6
Atwood Lake, OH **108** H6
Au Sable (river), MI **98** G7
Au Sable N.W.&S.R., MI **98** H7
Aua, American Samoa **156** J5
Aubrey Cliffs, AZ **120** D4
Auburn, AL **60** H7
Auburn, IN **92** H2
Auburn, ME **37** C11
Auburn, MA **40** E8
Auburn, NE **105** G12
Auburn, NY **46** E6
Auburn, WA **152** E5
Audubon Lake, ND **106** E6
Audubon Pkwy., KY **68** F5
Auglaize (river), OH **108** B4
Augusta, GA **66** G5
Augusta, KS **97** G9
Augusta, ME 37, **37** D10
Aunuu (island), American Samoa **156** K5
Aurora, CO **138** D8
Aurora, IL **90** G3
Aurora, MO **102** H5
Aurora, NE **105** F9
Austin, MN **101** F11
Austin, RI **50** C7
Austin, TX **126** F8, 127
Austintown, OH **108** J4
Automobile factory *89*
Ava, MO **102** H6
Avery Island, LA **70** H6, 71
Aziscohos Lake, ME **36** A8
Aztec Ruins Nat. Mon., NM **122** C2
Aztec, NM **122** C2

B

B. Everett Jordan Lake, NC **75** D10
Backbone Mountain, MD **38** C1
Bad (river), SD **110** F6
Bad Axe, MI **99** J9
Badlands (mountains), ND **106** G2
Badlands (plateau), ND **86** B2
Badlands N.P., SD **110** G4
Badlands, SD 111
Bainbridge, GA **67** C11
Baker (river), NH **43** E9
Baker City, OR **149** D11
Baker Island, United States **156** G6
Baker, MT **145** F13
Bakersfield, CA **137** F9
Bald Knob, AR **62** D8
Baldwyn, MS **72** H2
Baltic, CT **33** E11
Baltimore, MD 38, **39** C11
Bamberg, SC **76** F7
Bandelier Nat. Mon., NM **122** E4
Bangor, ME **37** F9
Bangor, PA **49** E12
Banks Lake, WA **153** E10
Bannock Range (mountains), ID **143** H14
Bantam Lake, CT **32** D4
Bar Harbor, ME **37** G10
Baraboo, WI 113, **113** F10
Baranof Island, AK **135** H12
Barataria Bay, LA **71** J10
Barberton, OH **108** H5
Bardstown, KY **69** F9
Barkhamsted Reservoir, CT **32** B6
Barkley, Lake, KY **56** C7, **68** J4, **78** B5
Barnegat Bay, NJ **45** J10
Barnstable, MA **41** G15
Barnwell, SC **76** F6
Barre, VT **52** E6
Barren (river), KY **68** H7
Barren River Lake, KY **68** J8
Barrington, RI **50** G5
Barrow, AK **134** A6, 135
Barstow, CA **137** G9
Bartlesville, OK **125** B13
Bartlett, TN **78** E2
Barton, VT **52** G3
Bastrop, LA **70** B6
Batavia, NY **46** E3
Batesburg-Leesville, SC **76** E5
Batesville, AR **62** C8
Batesville, MS **72** E3
Bath, ME **37** D11
Bath, NY **46** F5
Baton Rouge, LA **70** G8, 71
Battenkill River *30*, **53** A13
Battle Creek, ID **143** B15
Battle Creek, MI **99** G11
Battle Ground, WA **152** J5
Battle Mountain, NV **146** F3
Baudette, MN **100** D3
Baxter Springs, KS **97** H13
Baxter State Park **36** E5
Bay City, MI **99** H9
Bay City, TX **127** G10
Bay Minette, AL **61** C11
Bay of Fundy **29** D13
Bay Saint Louis, MS **73** F12
Bayard, NM **123** C9
Bayonet Point, FL **65** E9
Bayonne, NJ **44** J5
Bayou Bartholomew (river), AR **62** G7
Bayou Bartholomew (river), LA **70** B6
Bayou D'Arbonne (river), LA **70** B5
Bayou La Batre, AL **61** B12
Bayou Lafourche (river), LA **71** J9
Bayou Macon (river), LA **70** C7
Bayou Teche (river), LA **70** G6
Baytown, TX **127** G10
Beach Haven, NJ **45** J12
Beach, ND **106** G1
Beacon, NY **47** H10
Bear (river), ID **143** H15
Bear (river), WY **154** G1
Bear Creek N.W.&S.R., MI **98** F8
Bear Creek, AL **60** C3
Bear Creek, CO **139** J11
Bear Creek, KS **96** G1
Bear Lake, ID **130** E8
Bear Lake, UT **143** J15, **150** F2
Bear River Migratory Bird Refuge, UT **150** D2
Bear River Range (mountains) **143** J14
Bear, DE **34** C3
Bearcamp (river), NH **43** G10
Beardstown, IL **90** D6
Bears *13*
Beatrice, NE **105** G11
Beatty, NV **147** F10
Beaufort Sea **134** A7
Beaufort, SC **76** J7
Beaumont, TX 127, **127** F11
Beaver (river), OK **124** B5
Beaver (river), PA **48** D1
Beaver Creek N.W.&S.R., AK **134** D8
Beaver Creek, KS **96** C2
Beaver Creek, ND **106** H8
Beaver Dam, WI **113** G10
Beaver Falls, PA **48** E1
Beaver Island, MI **98** F6
Beaver Lake, AR **62** B3
Beaver, OK **124** B5
Beaver, UT **151** D9
Beaverhead N.F., MT **144**
Beaverton, OR **148** C4
Becharof Lake, AK **134** H5
Beckley, WV **82** J5
Bedford, IN **93** E9
Bedford, PA **48** H5
Bedford, VA **81** H9
Beebe, AR **62** E7
Beech Grove, IN **92** F7
Beeville, TX **126** H8
Bel Air, MD **39** B12
Belcourt, ND **106** C8
Belding, MI **99** G10
Belen, NM **122** E6
Belfast, ME **37** E10
Belgrade, MT **144** G6
Bella Vista, AR **62** A2
Bellaire, OH **108** J7
Belle Fourche (river), SD **110** E2
Belle Fourche (river), WY **155** D10
Belle Fourche, SD **110** E2
Belle Glade, FL **65** G12
Bellefontaine, OH **108** C6
Bellefonte, DE **34** E2
Belleville, IL **91** D10
Belleville, KS **96** C8
Bellevue, NE **105** F12
Bellevue, OH **108** E4
Bellevue, WA **152** E5
Bellingham, MA **41** E9
Bellingham, WA **152** B5
Bellows Falls, VT **53** E13
Belmar, NJ **44** K8
Beloit, KS **96** C7
Beloit, WI **113** G12
Belpre, OH **109** H9
Belted Range (mountains), NV **147** F9
Belton, MO **102** D4
Belton, SC **76** C3
Belton, TX **127** F9
Belvidere, IL **90** F2
Bemidji, MN **100** D5
Bench Lake, WA *128–129*
Bend, OR **148** E6
Bennettsville, SC **77** C10
Bennington, VT **53** B15
Benson, AZ **121** H11
Benson, MN **100** C8
Benton Harbor, MI **99** E12
Benton Lake National Wildlife Refuge, MT 145
Benton, AR **62** F6
Benton, IL **91** F11
Bentonville, AR **62** A3
Berea, KY **69** G11
Beresford, SD **111** H13
Bering Land Bridge Nat. Preserve, AK **134** C4
Bering Sea **134** G1
Bering Strait **134** D3
Berkeley Heights, NJ **44** H5
Berkeley, CA **136** C6
Berkeley, VA **81** H13
Berlin Lake, OH **108** J5
Berlin, MD **39** H16
Berlin, NH **42** H6

National Geographic Society

John M. Fahey, Jr.
President and Chief Executive Officer

Gilbert M. Grosvenor
Chairman of the Board

Nina D. Hoffman
Senior Vice President

William R. Gray
Vice President and Director of the Book Division

Staff for this book

Nancy Laties Feresten
Director of Children's Publishing

Suzanne Patrick Fonda
Project Editor

Marianne R. Koszorus
Art Director

Carl Mehler
Director of Maps

Dorrit Green
Designer

Patricia Daniels
Editor

Marilyn Mofford Gibbons
Illustrations Editor

Thomas L. Gray
Joseph F. Ochlak
Map Editors

Thomas L. Gray
Mapping Specialists, Ltd.
Joseph F. Ochlak
Map Research

John S. Ballay
James Huckenpahler
Mapping Specialists, Ltd.
Michelle H. Picard
Gregory Ugiansky
Martin S. Walz
Map Production

Tibor G. Tóth
Map Relief

Stuart Armstrong
Map Illustration

Catherine Herbert Howell
Judith E. Rinard
Writers

Mary Collins
Kristin Edmonds
Jocelyn G. Lindsay
Ann Perry
Marcia Pires-Harwood
Jo Tunstall
Text Research

Jennifer Emmett
Associate Editor

Janet Dustin
Illustrations Assistant

R. Gary Colbert
Production Director

Lewis R. Bassford
Production Manager

Connie D. Binder
Mapping Specialists, Ltd.
Indexing

Mark Caraluzzi
*Director of Direct Marketing
and Business Development*

Ellen Teguis
Marketing Director, Trade Books

Ruth Chamblee
Marketing Manager

Lawrence M. Porges
Marketing Coordinator

Vincent P. Ryan
Manufacturing Manager

Consultants

Overall Consultant
Martha Sharma
*National Cathedral School
Washington, D.C.*

Regional Consultants
Northeast
Sari Bennett
*Department of Geography
University of Maryland
Baltimore, Maryland*

Southeast
Joseph T. Manzo
*Department of Geography
Concord College
Athens, West Virginia*

Midwest
Mark H. Bockenhauer
*Department of Geography
St. Norbert College
De Pere, Wisconsin*

Southwest
Sarah Witham Bednarz
*Department of Geography
Texas A&M University
College Station, Texas*

West
Clifford B. Craig
*Department of Geography
and Earth Resources
Utah State University
Logan, Utah*

The world's largest nonprofit scientific and educational organization, the National Geographic Society was founded in 1888 "for the increase and diffusion of geographic knowledge." Since then it has supported scientific exploration and spread information to its more than nine million members worldwide.

The National Geographic Society educates and inspires millions every day through magazines, books, television programs, videos, maps and atlases, research grants, the National Geography Bee, teacher workshops, and innovative classroom materials.

The Society is supported through membership dues and income from the sale of its educational products. Members receive NATIONAL GEOGRAPHIC magazine—the Society's official journal—discounts on Society products, and other benefits.

For more information about the National Geographic Society and its educational programs and publications, please call 1-800-NGS-LINE (647-5463) or write to the following address:

National Geographic Society
1145 17th Street N.W.
Washington, D.C. 20036-4688 U.S.A.

Visit the Society's Web site: **www.nationalgeographic.com**

Illustrations Credits

Abbreviations for terms appearing below: (t)-top; (b)-bottom; (l)-left; (r)-right; (c)-center; NGS-National Geographic Staff

Photographs are from Tony Stone Images, except where noted with an asterisk (*).

Art for state flowers and state birds by Robert E. Hynes

Locator globes pages 8 and 16 created by Theophilus Britt Griswold

Cover art digitally created by Slim Films

Back Cover (tr)*Jeff Vanuga; (cl)*courtesy Melvin L. Prueitt, Los Alamos National Laboratory; (cr) Bob Thomason; (bl) Grandadam; (br) Brian Stablyk

2 (l) Cosmo Condina; (r) Zandria Muench; 2–3 Eurimage, Space Imaging Landsat Tm30m 1991–93; 2–3 (c)Andy Sacks; 3 (l) Chad Ehlers; (r) H. Richard Johnston; 4 (l) *Howard G. Castleberry; (r) Andy Sacks; 4–5 Paul Stover; 5 (l) Paul Damien; (c) Paul Grebliunas; (r) Chris Noble; 8–9 Slim Films

The Physical United States
10 (t) Charles Doswell III; (cl) Robert Cremins; (bl) *Chris Stewart/Black Star; (br) *Ravi Miro Fry; 11 (bl) NASA/GSFC: GOES-8 Imager, 9/12/96; (c) *courtesy Melvin L. Prueitt, Los Alamos National Laboratory; (r) Robert Yager; 12 (tl) Ken Biggs; (bl) Paul Chesley; (br) Tony Tickle; 12–13 Liz Hymans; 13 (t) Stephen Frink; (br) Barbara Gibson; 14 (t) *Jeff Vanuga; (bl) *Anthony Chen; (br) *Joel Sartore; 15 (bl) *Fred Bavendam; (cl) *Joel Sartore; 15 (br) *Alan D. St. John

The Political United States
16–17 Slim Films; 18 Robert Cremins; 20 (t) Slim Films; (b) Slim Films, based on compilations provided by the Population Reference Bureau; 23 Slim Films, based on data provided by ENO Transportation Foundation; 24 (tl) Will & Deni McIntyre; (bl) George Chan; (br) Greg Pease; 24–25 Marilyn Mofford; 25 Tony Stone Images

The Northeast
26–7 Cosmo Condina; 27 Jim Pickerell; 30 (tl) Jake Rais; (tr) *James L. Stanfield NGS; (b) Dennis O'Clair; 30–31 Jake Rais; 31 (tl) Thomas Cooke; (tr) George Lepp; (c) *Howard G. Castleberry; (bl) *Pete Souza; (br) *George Grall

The Southeast
54–55 Zandria Muench; 55 World Perspective; 58 (tl) Tom Raymond; (tr) Richard Howard; (bl) Owen Franken; (br) Bruce Hands; 58–59 Scott Goldsmith; 59 (t) Randy Wells; (c) Andy Sacks; (b) Bob Thomason

The Midwest
84–85 Andy Sacks; 85 Andy Sacks; 88 (t) *Phil Schermeister; (bl) Zane Williams; (br) Alan Klehr; 88–89 Paul Damien; 89 (t) Sara Gray; (cl) Gary Vestal; (cr) Mark Joseph; (b) Randy Wells

The Southwest
114–115 Chad Ehlers; 115 Tim Davis; 118 (t) David Hiser; (bl) Brian Stablyk; (br) Paul Grebliunas; 118–119 Robert Frerck; 119 (t) Gary Vestal; (c) Keith Wood; (bl) Chuck Pefley; (br) Mark Wagner

The West
128–129 H. Richard Johnston; 129 Chad Ehlers; 132 (tl) Natalie Fobes; (bl) Reg Watson; (r) Zigy Kalunzy; 132–133 Chris Noble; 133 (t) Glen Allison; (c) John Lawrence; (bl) Andy Sacks; (br) Bob Torrez

The Territories
158 (l) Grandadam; (r) Tom Bean; 158–9 *David Doubilet; 159 (tl) Randy Wells; (tr) Aldo Brando; (c) Donald Nausbaum; (bl) Cosmo Condina; (br) Cosmo Condina

Library of Congress Cataloging-in-Publication Data

National Geographic United States atlas for young explorers /
  photographs by Tony Stone Images.
    p.   cm.
  Includes index.
  Summary: Maps, photographs, illustrations, and text
present information about the regions and states of the
United States.
  ISBN 0-7922-7115-7
  1. Children's atlases.   [1. United States–Maps. 2. Atlases.]
  I. Title. II. Title: United States atlas for young explorers
G1200 .N355 1999   <G&M>
912—dc21

99-34653
CIP
MAPS

Published by the National Geographic Society
All rights reserved. Reproduction of the whole or any part of the contents without written permission from the publisher is prohibited.

Printed in Spain by Cayfosa
Copyright © 1999 National Geographic Society

Acknowledgments

We are grateful for the assistance of John Agnone, Peggy Candore, Alexander L. Cohn, Anne Marie Houppert, Sandra Leonard, and Lyle Rosbotham of the National Geographic Book Division.